Praise for *The Art of Spiritual Care across Religious Difference*

"Jill Snodgrass has woven together an indispensable analysis of spirituality and religious difference for a variety of audiences, including pastoral counselors, spiritually integrative psychotherapists, chaplains, pastors, and lay leaders. Snodgrass and the assembled authors reflexively navigate the shifting religious landscape to privilege praxis, identify systemic concerns, and offer spiritually rich practices of care. This text is timely and a must-read!"

—**Rev. Joshua T. Morris**, PhD, BCC, assistant professor of practical theology, Union Presbyterian Seminary

"In a world marked by increasing diversity and religious pluralism, *The Art of Spiritual Care across Religious Difference* is a remarkable and timely addition to the literature on pastoral care. In this insightful and thought-provoking book, the authors not only describe the intricacies of offering spiritual care but do so with a deep appreciation for the rich tapestry of religious beliefs that exist in our society today."

—**Trina A. Armstrong**, associate professor of pastoral theology and marriage and family therapy, Louisville Seminary

"*The Art of Spiritual Care across Religious Difference* is a compilation of writings on spiritual care within a pluralistic society that looks beyond interfaith or interreligious dialogue, code-switching, and other ways to connect across religious lines. The authors give insight into how to live out faith traditions' call for human relationships, caregiving, and community despite religious differences."

—**Tahara Akmal**, chaplain, ACPE-certified educator, and founder of Hayat CPE and Spiritual Care Services

THE ART OF SPIRITUAL CARE ACROSS RELIGIOUS DIFFERENCE

THE ART OF SPIRITUAL CARE ACROSS RELIGIOUS DIFFERENCE

REVISED EDITION

EDITOR

Jill L. Snodgrass

Fortress Press
Minneapolis

THE ART OF SPIRITUAL CARE ACROSS RELIGIOUS DIFFERENCE
Revised Edition

For Chapter 1, "Religious Location and Counseling: Engaging Diversity and Difference in Views of Religion" by Kathleen J. Greider is republished with permission of Springer Publishing Company, Inc., from *Understanding Pastoral Counseling*, Elizabeth A. Maynard and Jill L. Snodgrass, editors, 2015. Permission conveyed through Copyright Clearance Center, Inc.

For Chapter 2, "The Practice of Relational-Ethical Pastoral Care: An Intercultural Approach" by Carrie Doehring was originally published in *"After You!": Dialogical Ethics and the Pastoral Counselling Process* (pp. 159–81), Axel Liégeois, Roger Burggraeve, Marina Riemslagh, and Jozef Corveleyn, editors, 2013, Uitgeverij Peeters, Leuven, Belgium. Permission to reprint with minor revisions was granted by Paul Peeters of Uitgeverij Peeters.

For Chapter 5, Qur'an translation is by Nazila Isgandarova.

Library of Congress Control Number: 2023945652 (print)

Cover design: Marti Naughton
Cover illustration: Photograph of Isla Mujeres by Kathleen Greider and "Fantastic springtime landscape" in watercolor by Pobytov/Getty Images

Print ISBN: 978-1-5064-9943-7
eBook ISBN: 978-1-5064-9944-4

CONTENTS

INTRODUCTION

JILL L. SNODGRASS

EVERY INDIVIDUAL OCCUPIES a unique religious location. In the art of spiritual care, understanding and proficiently navigating religious difference is vital. Far too often spiritual care professionals, grounded in their knowledge of a religious tradition, assume an understanding of the care receiver's beliefs and fail to explore the uniqueness of their religious location. Providing competent care necessitates understanding a care receiver's religious location and the ways it intersects with their race, gender, sexual orientation, age, ability, immigration status, language, employment, and other identities and locations. Consider the ways religious difference arises in the following three vignettes.

Nadia was exhausted. As a chaplain at a level-one trauma center, she had spent the last five hours with the large, extended family of a fifteen-month-old boy who had drowned in the neighbor's pool. The end of her shift was near, but she had been referred to a patient on the telemetry unit. Nadia was relieved when she saw the patient's last name was Akhtar. After quickly establishing their shared Islamic faith, Nadia listened to the patient's fears about the impact of her newly-diagnosed heart condition on her teenage children. She affirmed that Allah's will (mashi'at) cannot be fully known, but is always right, just, good, and fair. Allah is all-powerful (Al-'Aziz), and Nadia encouraged the patient to surrender to Allah and trust in His goodness. As Nadia walked to the parking garage, she reflected on the visit and wondered if perhaps she should have asked the patient more about her own theology. Was affirming the foundation of their shared Islamic faith enough? Had she missed an opportunity to understand the patient's unique religious location and possible religious differences between them?

Rev. Moore loved the new member gatherings at Woodstock United Church (WUC). Formed in 1967 through the union of two small congregations, WUC remained affiliated with both the Alliance of Baptists and the United Church of Christ. When Rev. Moore met the Chang family, she learned that they had recently immigrated to the United States from Guangzhou, China, where they'd been part of a thriving house church. Rev. Moore was curious about how the liturgy and worship at WUC differed from what the Chang family was used to in China, and she was delighted when Mrs. Chang recounted all the similarities. Rev. Moore shared how some WUC members still identify more with either the church's Baptist or UCC roots, but that it was an inclusive church where difference was celebrated. Later that evening, Rev. Moore reflected on how she knew very little about Christianity in China. She had never considered what it meant that the Chang family belonged to a house church. But Mrs. Chang said they prayed the Lord's Prayer and the Nicene Creed, so surely their theological beliefs were the same. Afterall, their shared belief in Jesus as Lord and Savior has nothing to do with the culture and politics of China, right?

As a small liberal arts institution, the Chaplain's Office at Kennett College was dedicated to facilitating students' spiritual exploration and meaningful religious commitment. Ten years ago, the Office initiated a Dharmic Life program to meet the spiritual needs of Buddhist, Hindu, Jain, and Sikh students. Students from other faith backgrounds, including atheist, agnostic, and unaffiliated students, began attending the weekly Buddhist meditations. Eli, the office's interim associate director, was happy about the increased participation, but he wondered why the students from theistic traditions, many of whom were highly committed, did not attend the meditation and prayer services in their own tradition. Rather than considering the possibility of religious multiplicity–that a student may identify, for example, as Buddhist and Jewish–Eli assumed there was a problem with the office's programming. Following the Buddhist meditation session on Thursday night, Eli pulled a few students aside and asked if they had ever attended Rabbi Artson's Amidah meditation service. They said they had and thanked Eli as they headed to the Campus Center for dinner. Eli found himself questioning the students' commitment to Jewish life. Could they worship the God of Israel and venerate the Buddha? Eli considered if he should ask the students about this. He decided it was probably not worth mentioning as Buddhism could be a trendy spiritual exploration among college students.

These vignettes illustrate some of the myriad ways religious difference impacts the art of spiritual care. Nadia, Rev. Moore, and Eli are all attentive listeners with good communication skills. They are compassionate and easily build rapport with others. They are knowledgeable about their own faiths and others', yet they each missed the opportunity to navigate religious difference and offer more competent care. The art of spiritual care across religious difference can be challenging, yet it is not novel. Religious difference has always existed. However, there are factors that make navigating religious difference unique in today's context.

The Shifting Religious Landscape

The religious landscape continues to diversify in the United States and worldwide. Religious participation and the importance of religion are declining among Americans.[1] Nineteen percent of Americans report following "the teachings or practices of more than one religion," reflecting an increase in religious hybridity.[2] And the population of religiously unaffiliated has grown significantly in the United States. According to the Pew Research Center, roughly three in ten adults in the United States are now religiously unaffiliated.[3]

The move away from religion is also occurring globally. From 2007 to 2019, religious participation and belief declined in 43 of 49 countries that comprise 60 percent of the world's population.[4] The generation gap in religious

---

1   Jeffrey M. Jones, *U.S. Church Membership Falls Below Majority for First Time*, Gallup, March 29, 2021, https://news.gallup.com/poll/341963/church-membership-falls-below-majority-first-time.aspx; PRRI, *Religion and Congregations in a Time of Social and Political Uppheaval*, PRRI, May 16, 2023, https://www.prri.org/research/religion-and-congregations-in-a-time-of-social-and-political-upheaval/; David Roach, "Church Attendance Dropped Among Young People, Singles, and Liberals," *Christianity Today*, January 9, 2023, https://www.christianitytoday.com/news/2023/january/pandemic-church-attendance-drop-aei-survey-young-people-eva.html.

2   PRRI, *Religion and Congregations*, 4.

3   Gregory A. Smith, "About Three-in-Ten U.S. Adults Are Now Religiously Unaffiliated," *Pew Research Center*, December 14, 2021, https://www.pewresearch.org/religion/2021/12/14/about-three-in-ten-u-s-adults-are-now-religiously-unaffiliated/; PRRI, *Religion and Congregations*, 4.

4   Ronald F. Inglehart, "Giving Up on God: The Global Decline of Religion," *Foreign Affairs*, August 11, 2020, https://www.foreignaffairs.com/articles/world/2020-08-11/religion-giving-god?check_logged_in=1&utm_medium=promo_email&utm_source=lo_flows&utm_campaign=registered_user_welcome&utm_term=email_1&utm_content=20230605.

participation is widening globally as well. In a survey of 26 countries, Ipsos research center found that "in countries where religious practice is high, older adults tend to engage in it more than the young."[5]

If we delimited our inquiry to these statistics and demographics, we might think that the future of religious beliefs and practices is short-lived, maybe even doomed. But these trends do not illustrate a complete picture of spirituality and religiosity. While traditional religious life in places like churches, synagogues, or mosques may be on the decline, new practices and means of being in spiritual relationships and community are emerging. "Signs of life are popping up elsewhere: in conversations with chaplains, in communities started online that end up forming in-person bonds as well, in social-justice groups rooted in shared faith."[6]

Research in the psychology of religion demonstrates that people throughout the world sanctify, or imbue sacred significance, upon myriad domains of life beyond religion, including relationships, work, nature, and the arts.[7] Encountering the sacred in these domains can result in greater life satisfaction and an increased ability to cope with life's stressors. A meta-analysis of sixty-three peer-reviewed studies published between 1999 and 2019 indicated that sanctifying close interpersonal relationships was correlated with greater positive psychosocial adjustment and less maladaptive adjustment, supporting the view that ordinary dimensions of life can be spiritually sacred and contribute positively to personal well-being.[8] Religious and spiritual life may not look the same as it did fifty or one hundred years ago, in the United States and worldwide, but humans are still orienting themselves to the sacred and the spiritual.

---

5   Ipsos, *Global Religion 2023: Religious Beliefs Across the World*, May 2023, 2, https://www.ipsos.com/sites/default/files/ct/news/documents/2023-05/Ipsos%20Global%20Advisor%20-%20Religion%202023%20Report%20-%2026%20countries.pdf.

6   Wendy Cadge and Elan Babchuck, "American Religion Is Not Dead Yet," *The Atlantic*, January 16, 2023, https://www.theatlantic.com/politics/archive/2023/01/us-religious-affiliation-rates-declining/672729/.

7   Annette Mahoney et al., "Sanctification of Diverse Aspects of Life and Psychosocial Functioning: A Meta-Analysis of Studies from 1999 to 2019," *Psychology of Religion and Spirituality* 14, no. 4 (2022): 585–98, https://doi.org/10.1037/rel0000354.

8   Mahoney et al., "Sanctification of Diverse Aspects."

Navigating Religious Difference

Changes in the religious landscape in the United States and worldwide necessitate new theories and practices in the ancient art of spiritual care. Proficiently navigating religious difference is more imperative than ever as we embrace the reality that no two individuals' religious and spiritual experiences are the same. In considering religious difference, most often we think about the divergence between two religious traditions. Yet variations between two adherents of the same religious tradition are equally significant. With increasing religious hybridity, navigating religious multiplicity between people and within the same person also presents opportunities and challenges. This reality is unmistakable when considered through the theoretical lens of intersectionality. Intersectionality, as posited by critical race expert Kimberlé Crenshaw, provides a framework for analyzing the impact of intersecting identities, such as the way that Black women are multiply oppressed by the compounding subordination of racism and sexism.[9] All individuals' social locations and identities intersect, at times resulting in multiple marginalizations, multiple privileges, or both. Individuals' myriad, intersecting identities include the religious locations they occupy. The term *religious location* was initially coined by pastoral theologian Kathleen J. Greider, who argues in Chapter 1 that *"whether or not we are religious, all persons inhabit a particular location relative to religion."*[10]

Consider, for example, the unique civil religion that pervades US culture and the way that context impacts the beliefs and practices of religious traditions in the United States. More than fifty years ago, sociologist Robert Bellah argued that the United States operates with a civil religion, "a collection of beliefs, symbols, and rituals with respect to sacred things and institutionalized in a collectivity."[11] Even then, Bellah observed

---

9   Kimberlé Crenshaw, "Demarginalizing the Intersection of Race and Sex: A Black Feminist Critique of Antidiscrimination Doctrine, Feminist Theory and Antiracist Politics," *University of Chicago Legal Forum* 140 (1989): 139–67, https://chicagounbound.uchicago.edu/cgi/viewcontent.cgi?article=1052&context=uclf.

10   Kathleen J. Greider, "Religious Location and Counseling: Engaging Difference and Diversity in Views of Religion," in *Understanding Pastoral Counseling*, ed. Elizabeth A. Maynard and Jill L. Snodgrass (New York: Springer, 2015), 235.

11   Robert N. Bellah, "Civil Religion in America," *Daedalus* 96, no. 1 (1967): 8, https://www.jstor.org/stable/20027022.

the way an ideological fusion of "God, country, and flag" was used to "attack non-conformist and liberal ideas and groups of all kinds."[12] The beliefs, symbols, and rituals of US civil religion impact how Christianity along with Judaism, Islam, Buddhism, Hinduism, and every spiritual and religious tradition are practiced in the United States. When viewed through the lens of intersectionality, this context contributes to the ways Catholicism in the United States is markedly distinct from Catholicism in neighboring Mexico or in the Philippines, and how the Catholicism of a sixth-generation Irish American immigrant differs from that of a first-generation Salvadoran immigrant. Religiopolitical cultures throughout the world impact individuals' religious locations. In Chapter 6, Duane R. Bidwell and Daniel S. Schipani attend to how religious difference manifests among individuals acculturated in the quasi-religious, political ideologies of totalitarian contexts such as Vietnam and Cuba and those acculturated in democratic contexts.

The shifting religious landscape necessitates a theoretical understanding of religious location and proficiency in the art of navigating religious difference. Far too often spiritual care professionals, grounded in their knowledge of a religious tradition, assume an understanding of the care receiver's beliefs and fail to explore the uniqueness of their religious location. Spiritual care professionals today need to honor religious difference by providing competent care that privileges others' religious locations and the ways they intersect with their race, gender, sexual orientation, age, ability, immigration status, language, employment, and other identities and locations. Competent spiritual care is grounded not only in honoring others' religious locations, but also in navigating the religious difference resulting from caregivers' and receivers' religious locations. Far too often spiritual caregivers fail to think reflexively about how their own religious locations influence the relational dynamic. Spiritual care professionals need to practice self-reflexivity and attend to the relational dynamics engendered in the dance between their own and others' locations.

Sociologists of religion Wendy Cadge and Emily Sigalow conducted a study with twenty interfaith chaplains to understand how chaplains navigate

---

12   Bellah, "Civil Religion," 14.

religious difference.[13] Using ethnographic methods, the researchers determined that chaplains predominantly use two strategies, neutralizing and code-switching, in navigating religious difference. Chaplains neutralized religious differences with patients and patients' friends and family by emphasizing commonalities and the spiritual or human universals. Chaplains also engaged in code-switching to adopt the language and practices of care receivers—for example, a Jewish chaplain utilizing rosary beads when praying with a Catholic patient.

Yet neutralizing differences is not necessarily a way of acknowledging, honoring, or engaging them. Rather, it can function like a gloss, ignoring the grooves and etches carved by differences to create a smooth, surface-level encounter. Code-switching can be a means of honoring religious difference, yet Cadge and Sigalow stated clearly that chaplains are not always taught how to code-switch and many reported learning from patients on the job.[14] Chaplains also are not instructed how to acknowledge differences between their own and a patient's religious locations or how to practice the self-reflexivity necessary to analyze power and other differentials. Cadge and Sigalow acknowledged the limitations of neutralizing and code-switching for navigating religious difference and encouraged further research.

The Art of Spiritual Care across Religious Difference advances the fields of pastoral and practical theology as well as spiritual care and counseling by developing a robust, interreligious theory of religious difference grounded in insights from Christianity, Buddhism, Confucianism, and Islam. Given the need to navigate religious difference in a variety of contexts, including hospitals, prisons, places of worship, community mental health centers, and off campus ministry offices, the book attends to diverse settings as well as cultural environs. The thirteen chapters in this book explicate how students, educators, practitioners, supervisors, and scholars can identify, name, and engage religious differences that arise between and among spiritual care professionals and care seekers in various practices of spiritual care and in diverse cultural contexts.

---

13   Wendy Cadge and Emily Sigalow, "Negotiating Religious Differences: The Strategies of Interfaith Chaplains in Healthcare," *Journal for the Scientific Study of Religion* 52, no. 1 (2013): 150, https://doi-org.proxy-ln.researchport.umd.edu/10.1111/jssr.12008.

14   Cadge and Sigalow, "Negotiating Religious Differences," 156.

An Overview of the Book

Part 1 examines religious difference from a theoretical perspective informed by practice. Greider writes Chapter 1, which serves as the ground in which subsequent chapters are rooted. Greider defines religious location and examines forms and degrees of religious difference. She utilizes case illustrations and posits practices that promote ethical and compassionate relationships amid religious difference.

In Chapter 2, Carrie Doehring utilizes the relational ethics of Emmanuel Levinas to develop a theory of intercultural care. Doehring demonstrates how caregivers can radically open themselves up to the care seeker as *other* in a way that respects the care seeker's *religious world-making*, a concept in many ways analogous to religious location. Doehring outlines a process of spiritual integration and theological reflexivity that prepares spiritual care professionals to avoid imposing their own beliefs and values and to honor the alterity of the care seeker. She offers a theoretical description of how the caregiver's and the care seeker's religious world-making interact and illustrates this using a contemporary Canadian-French film.

Insook Lee, in Chapter 3, posits a Confucian-based model for engaging religious pluralism. Grounded in a Confucian understanding of ego, Lee suggests that spiritual care professionals paradoxically need the ego and need to overcome the ego. She develops the *Wheel*, a model evidencing how the ego, via a spiritual journey, can be transformed in a way that enables spiritual care professionals to look beyond their own egos toward valuing religious difference. Lee utilizes the case of a former student to demonstrate how the Wheel can be used as a tool for self-reflection and a map for guiding ego formation that can result in greater acceptance of religious difference.

In the next chapter, Victor Gabriel theorizes a Tibetan Buddhist understanding of religious location with implications for interfaith chaplaincy. This work is vitally important given the dominance of Christian perspectives in chaplaincy today. Gabriel utilizes Buddhist philosophies and hermeneutics to define religious location in a way that honors the two truths of Buddhism: all phenomena both reveal and conceal truth. Therefore, religious locations are never static but fluid, and they can both bare and obscure the path to ultimate truth. Gabriel draws upon the *Guhyagarbha* Tantra to further develop his theory and delineate three ways this theory influences interfaith chaplaincy.

According to Nazila Isgandarova, author of Chapter 5, little attention is given in the literature to how care seekers respond to spiritual care professionals' religious locations. As a Muslim mental health professional, Isgandarova illustrates how Islamophobia and political bias can cause care seekers to claim "cultural dominance and religious privilege."[15] Isgandarova draws upon the writings of the great Andalusian Sufi Muḥyi al-Din Ibn al-ʿArabi (d. 1240) to show how spiritual care professionals, particularly Muslim counselors, can practice what Ibn ʿArabi called the "religion of love." The religion of love is a Muslim universalist theology that Isgandarova uses as a call for Muslim counselors to embrace religious difference and accept those differences as the client's universal truth.

Part 2 marks a shift from theory to practice and offers insights for navigating religious difference in particular cultural contexts. In Chapter 6, Bidwell and Schipani utilize their experiences in Vietnam and Cuba, respectively, to posit implications for interreligious care in totalitarian contexts. Given that 37 percent of the world's population resides in totalitarian contexts, Bidwell and Schipani demonstrate the importance of attending to both religious and ideological differences between and among caregivers and care seekers.[16] The authors describe the Vietnamese and Cuban contexts and show how political ideologies function like quasi-religious beliefs that influence care seekers' religious locations. The chapter concludes by suggesting competencies that teachers and practitioners formed in and by democratic contexts can develop to navigate religious difference in authoritarian-totalitarian societies.

In the next chapter, the context shifts to Belgium, a country of increasing religious diversity engendered, in part, by a growing number of Muslim refugees. Dominiek Lootens utilizes the texts from two retreats led by Trappist monk Thomas Merton as a lens for viewing Catholic health care chaplaincy in Belgium. Catholic health care chaplains view and respond to

---

15   Nazila Isgandarova, "'I Follow the Religion of Love': Wisdom from Ibn ʿArabi for Engaging Religious Difference in Counseling," 116.

16   Michael J. Abramowitz, "Freedom in the World 2018: Democracy in Crisis," Freedom House, accessed June 29, 2023, https://freedomhouse.org/report/freedom-world /freedom-world-2018.

changes in the country's religious composition and health care practices in diverse ways. Some assert their professionalism and defend spiritual care as empirically-validated, and others argue that spiritual care has little to do with efficiency and patient outcomes. Lootens draws on Merton's wisdom to invite Catholic chaplains to a third response by realizing their vocation as interfaith chaplains. Lootens empowers Catholic chaplains to commit to becoming peacemakers, even while working within a high-tech, multifaith health care context.

In Chapter 8, Mazvita Machinga shows how indigenous African thought—a spirituality and cosmology grounded in relationality, community, and wholeness—influences the religious locations of the Shona people in Zimbabwe. Machinga describes the ontology, epistemology, and cosmology of indigenous African thought and develops a relational, transpersonal approach to counseling that acknowledges how this worldview influences clients' lived experiences. By utilizing three compelling case illustrations, Machinga demonstrates the importance of utilizing pastoral counseling interventions that reflect Ubuntu, the interdependence of all things.

The setting shifts again in Chapter 9 to the United States, where anti-Jewish discrimination is on the rise.[17] Such discrimination is perpetrated by organizations like the white nationalists and by neo-Nazi movements, but also by politically progressive individuals and organizations committed to the fight for equity and social justice. In this chapter, Rochelle Robins shows how anti-Jewish discrimination by politically progressive organizations and individuals most often results from a failure to recognize how Jews' intersectionality places them at the margins religiously, ethnically, and, for Jews of color, racially. Robins elucidates this experience by drawing on two case illustrations. Furthermore, she shows how anti-Jewish discrimination is prevalent in spiritual care training programs such as Clinical Pastoral Education (CPE). The chapter concludes by positing five competencies for eradicating anti-Jewish discrimination that spiritual care providers and educators are encouraged to develop.

---

17   ADL, "U.S. Antisemitic Incidents Hit Highest Level Ever Recorded, ADL Audit Finds," March 23, 2023, https://www.adl.org/resources/press-release/us-antisemitic -incidents-hit-highest-level-ever-recorded-adl-audit-finds.

In Chapter 10, Monica Sanford utilizes the findings from a qualitative research study with Buddhist chaplains along with her own experiences as a white Buddhist in the United States to highlight the internal and relational tensions encountered by Buddhist spiritual care professionals in a predominantly theistic society. Theists in the United States, even in spiritual care training programs like CPE, often fail to acknowledge the religious locations of Buddhist spiritual care professionals, causing Sanford and others to feel like "secret atheists." These dynamics negatively impact both training and interreligious caregiving. This chapter names and outlines the shape of this experience so that spiritual care providers and educators can find skillful ways to address it.

In the next chapter, Siroj Sorajjakool explains how early in his ministerial career he worked hard to promote health among Hmong people in northern Thailand but failed to see how their distinctive religious locations influenced their perspectives on sickness and healing. With the goal of better navigating the religious differences between Hmong patients and spiritual and health care professionals trained in Western medical models, Sorajjakool conducted a grounded theory study with ten Hmong participants to theorize a Hmong metaphysic of sickness and healing. The theory describes the role of shamans, the causes of sickness, and methods for diagnosis and healing. Rather than naïvely imposing Western, hegemonic conceptions of sickness and healing, Sorajjakool demonstrates how spiritual and health care professionals can navigate religious and other differences by acknowledging how the physical world and the spirit world impact the health of Hmong patients.

In Chapter 12, Pamela Ayo Yetunde offers a fascinating investigation into a relationship of intrareligious difference wherein she, a Black female Buddhist pastoral counselor, cared for "David," a white male Buddhist homicidal client. Yetunde narrates how she used both Buddhist and Christian sources of wisdom to reflect on the relationship and to guide her in navigating her own and David's intersecting and divergent social and religious locations. She explores how their social locations created power dynamics that may have contributed to David's failure to practice *Right Speech* when he stated, "I just want to kill you." Yetunde views David in many ways, including as "oppressor." By employing a Black womanist pastoral Buddhology,

Yetunde shows how pastoral counselors can engage in mindfulness to risk helping oppressors awaken from ignorance.

In the book's final chapter, Jennifer Yates and I examine how nonsexual spiritual abuse (NSA) perpetrated by Christians/Christianity in the United States impacts the religious locations of LGBTQ+ survivors. LGBTQ+ survivors of Christian oppression and persecution often fail to identify their experiences as abuse. Yates and I define NSA and complex trauma and utilize a case illustration to evidence the complex relational and therapeutic dynamics this experience can engender between client and counselor. The chapter presents three competencies for relational-ethical counseling with LGBTQ+ survivors of NSA.

An Invitation

The insights and practices put forth in *The Art of Spiritual Care across Religious Difference* provide readers with innovative approaches to theorizing and attending to religious difference. The contributing authors are scholars and spiritual care professionals committed to understanding how intersectionality and attention to religious location informs our ways of being, understanding, and intervening.[18] The contributing authors recognize that self-reflexivity is a critical component of navigating religious difference if we are to avoid imposing our own beliefs and values and to honor the alterity of those we care for. The reader is invited to consider the implications of the book's wisdom not only toward the practice of spiritual care but also toward the practice of compassionate global citizenship. Although religious difference is not novel, the effects of globalization compel us to honor religious difference as part of a larger effort toward increased respect for and valuing of diversity throughout the world.

Bibliography

Abramowitz, Michael J. "Freedom in the World 2018: Democracy in Crisis." Freedom House. Accessed June 29, 2023. https://freedomhouse.org /report/freedom-world/freedom-world-2018.

---

18   Sharon E. Cheston, "A New Paradigm for Teaching Counseling Theory and Practice," *Counselor Education and Supervision* 39, no. 4 (June 2000): 254–69, https://doi.org /10.1002/j.1556-6978.2000.tb01236.x.

ADL. "U.S. Antisemitic Incidents Hit Highest Level Ever Recorded, ADL Audit Finds." March 23, 2023. https://www.adl.org/resources/press-release/us-antisemitic-incidents-hit-highest-level-ever-recorded-adl-audit-finds.

Bellah, Robert. N. "Civil Religion in America." *Daedalus* 96, no. 1 (1967): 1–21. Accessed June 29, 2023. https://www.jstor.org/stable/20027022.

Cadge, Wendy, and Elan Babchuck. "American Religion is Not Dead Yet." *The Atlantic,* January 16, 2023. https://www.theatlantic.com/politics/archive/2023/01/us-religious-affiliation-rates-declining/672729/.

Cadge, Wendy, and Emily Sigalow. "Negotiating Religious Differences: The Strategies of Interfaith Chaplains in Healthcare." *Journal for the Scientific Study of Religion* 52, no. 1 (2013): 146–58. https://doi-org.proxy-ln.researchport.umd.edu/10.1111/jssr.12008.

Cheston, Sharon E. "A New Paradigm for Teaching Counseling Theory and Practice." *Counselor Education and Supervision* 39, no. 4 (June 2000): 254–69. https://doi.org/10.1002/j.1556-6978.2000.tb01236.x.

Crenshaw, Kimberlé. "Demarginalizing the Intersection of Race and Sex: A Black Feminist Critique of Antidiscrimination Doctrine, Feminist Theory and Antiracist Politics." *University of Chicago Legal Forum* 140 (1989): 139–67. https://chicagounbound.uchicago.edu/cgi/viewcontent.cgi?article=1052&context=uclf.

Greider, Kathleen J. "Religious Location and Counseling: Engaging Difference and Diversity in Views of Religion." In *Understanding Pastoral Counseling,* edited by Elizabeth A. Maynard and Jill L. Snodgrass, 235–56. New York: Springer, 2015.

Inglehart, Ronald. F. "Giving Up on God: The Global Decline of Religion." *Foreign Affairs.* August 11, 2020. https://www.foreignaffairs.com/articles/world/2020-08-11/religion-giving-god?check_logged_in=1&utm_medium=promo_email&utm_source=lo_flows&utm_campaign=registered_user_welcome&utm_term=email_1&utm_content=20230605.

Ipsos. *Global Religion 2023: Religious Beliefs Across the World.* May 2023. https://www.ipsos.com/sites/default/files/ct/news/documents/2023-05/Ipsos%20Global%20Advisor%20-%20Religion%202023%20Report%20-%2026%20countries.pdf.

Jones, Jeffrey M. *U.S. Church Membership Falls Below Majority for First Time.* Gallup. March 29, 2021. https://news.gallup.com/poll/341963/church-membership-falls-below-majority-first-time.aspx.

Mahoney, Annette, Serena Wong, Julie M. Pomerleau, and Kenneth I. Pargament. "Sanctification of Diverse Aspects of Life and Psychosocial Functioning: A Meta-Analysis of Studies from 1999 to 2019."

Psychology of Religion and Spirituality 14, no. 4 (2022): 585–98. https://doi.org/10.1037/rel0000354.

PRRI. *Religion and Congregations in a Time of Social and Political Uppheaval.* PRRI. May 16, 2023. https://www.prri.org/research/religion-and -congregations-in-a-time-of-social-and-political-upheaval/.

Roach, David. "Church Attendance Dropped Among Young People, Singles, and Liberals." *Christianity Today,* January 9, 2023. https://www .christianitytoday.com/news/2023/january/pandemic-church-attendance -drop-aei-survey-young-people-eva.html.

Smith, Gregory A. "About Three-in-Ten U.S. Adults Are Now Religiously Unaffiliated." *Pew Research Center.* December 14, 2021. https://www .pewresearch.org/religion/2021/12/14/about-three-in-ten-u-s-adults-are -now-religiously-unaffiliated/.

Part One

THEORIZING RELIGIOUS DIFFERENCE

❧ 1 ❧

RELIGIOUS LOCATION AND COUNSELING

Engaging Diversity and Difference in Views of Religion

KATHLEEN J. GREIDER

THIS CHAPTER EXPLORES religious differences between counselors and their clients. These differences exist whether or not counselors or clients are religious. The notion of "religious location," referenced in the chapter's title, calls our attention to the actuality that, *whether or not we are religious, all persons inhabit a particular location relative to religion.* Whether we call ourselves religious or not, are appreciative of religion or skeptical or ambivalent, we embody attitudes and positions toward religion that affect clinical work. Religious differences exist not simply because we have different religious beliefs or different beliefs about religion. Religious differences arise from the much more complex ground of our diverse religious locations. Religious location is akin to social location, our particular identities in social contexts, and personal location, the particularities of our individuality and our family and life history. Our religious location is but one aspect of—and also always dynamically interacting with—our complex cultural identity as a whole, which includes all aspects of our identity, such as personality, age, sexuality, economic status, gender, ethnicity and race, nationality, and first language.

The chapter begins by setting out the foundational concept of "language care," a part of which involves clarification of some terminology.[1] A second section explores religious location, including one aspect of religious location that can pose what is arguably the only insurmountable barrier

---

1 Leah Dawn Bueckert and Daniel S. Schipani, "Interfaith Spiritual Caregiving: The Case for Language Care," in *Spiritual Caregiving in the Hospital: Windows to Chaplaincy Ministry*, ed. Leah Dawn Bueckert and Daniel S. Schipani (Kitchener, ON: Pandora, in association with the Institute of Mennonite Studies, 2006), 245.

when the counselor and client occupy different religious locations. The chapter then reflects on forms and degrees of religious difference, challenges posed by religious differences in counseling, and the significance in counseling of the counselor's religious location. Therapeutic relationality is of concern throughout the chapter, but a brief concluding section examines a few practices especially valuable for nurturing therapeutic relationality given differences in clients' and counselors' religious locations. The spirit of these themes infers the chapter's thesis: religious particularity and differences between counselors and clients are ever present and, with appropriate attention, have the potential to contribute to more profound clinical relationships.

In addition to those readers for whom counseling and psychotherapy are their primary professional practices, this chapter also will have relevance for chaplains and congregation leaders. They often must provide counseling even if it is not their primary responsibility or specialization and, as the chapter argues, differences in religious location exist everywhere, even within congregations. Although I refer mostly to counselors and clients, I have formed these reflections also with supervisors and supervisees in mind, knowing that diversity in religious location also affects the relationship and process of supervision. Although the chapter may have relevance beyond the United States, the analysis addresses readers presumed to be located in the US context, where English language expression of certain Christian beliefs, practices, and values forms a dominant and majority culture.

Of course, my own religious location is inextricably related to the chapter's claims; throughout the chapter, I note some of its influences and those of other aspects of my personal and professional locations. Here I offer some grounding for those later reflections. I was born into and have lived all my life immersed in the diversity of beliefs and practices that are called Christian. My education in predominately white, liberal Protestant undergraduate and graduate schools preceded my ordination and entry into the vocation of caregiving and pastoral counseling. My earliest professional experiences were as a chaplain in a major urban medical center and as a pastoral counselor in a working-class city comprising mainly Portuguese immigrants. Later I worked as a mental health counselor in a state inpatient psychiatric facility, a pastoral counselor for the psychiatric unit in the Roman Catholic hospital, and a congregational pastor. I have an ongoing practice in psychotherapy and spiritual direction. However, most of my professional life has been spent as professor of practical theology, spiritual care, and spiritually integrative counseling in a so-called progressive graduate theological school characterized by significant religious, racial/ethnic, and national diversity. As a pastoral and practical theologian, I place care at the center of my concerns and practices, with attention especially to damage done by social and interpersonal violence. These commitments cause me to favor theological and social science theories and practices constructed for the sake of liberation and empowerment by persons in communities with histories of having been subjugated and traumatized. The school of psychotherapy that most foundationally informs me is relational-cultural theory, which is psychodynamic by heritage but primarily informed by the experiences of girls and women, feminist and womanist theory, and core values of authenticity, vulnerability, and mutuality.

Language Care

The power of language to disclose and obscure requires attention to semantics and the discussion of terminology used throughout the chapter. Indeed, I am persuaded by Bueckert and Schipani's discussion of "language care" that careful attention to language is arguably the most essential practice for effective counseling amid any kind of difference and a primary factor that makes it possible to engender meaningful care and counseling in relationships characterized by religious difference.[2] As they note, caring for persons through the language we use, as well as caring for language itself, especially by being attentive to the significance of the exact words used by our clients, goes a long way toward acknowledging and bridging the gaps frequently caused by religious difference. In fact, without painstaking attention to the meaning of the words spoken by client and counselor, we may think we understand each other when we do not. Instead, religiously significant gaps will undermine the therapeutic work.

For now, it is necessary to address two matters of foundational terminology. First, I favor definitions that point toward a close relationship between

---

2   Bueckert and Schipani, "Interfaith Spiritual Caregiving," 245.

"religion" and "spirituality." Definitions used by Worthington, Hook, Wade, Miller, and Sharp meet this criterion.[3] Spirituality can be described as "a person's search for the sacred" and religion as "a person's search for the sacred within an organized worldview of specified beliefs and values that are lived out within a community of faith."[4] I will refer primarily to religion and less frequently to spirituality precisely because religious difference tends to be more noticed and divisive than differences in spirituality. Nonetheless, most of our reflection will be relevant to counselors and clients whose religious locations are aligned more with spirituality than religion.

Second, I understand religion to be one aspect of culture and cultural diversity, not separable or fully distinguishable from other aspects of cultural diversity. Therefore, counseling amid religious difference is one dimension of intercultural (or multicultural) counseling. Intercultural competence is required for effective counseling amid religious difference, and competence amid religious difference is required for effective intercultural counseling. It is a gross simplification to discuss it, as for the most part I must do here, as if it were not affected by particularities, interconnectedness with, and power dynamics related to race and ethnicity, class, gender, nationality and first language, and other marginalized and dominating identities.

Religious Location(s) and One Insurmountable Barrier

As intercultural and multicultural counseling theories have been arguing for decades, all aspects of human particularity are at play in clinical work. Self-knowledge sufficient for clinical practice is not composed of declaring that we are or are not religious. Even if we are not religious—humanist, agnostic, spiritual, atheist—our attitudes and experiences relative to religion constitute a location, a position, that influences our clinical work. In part because religion is a dominant and often volatile aspect of human

---

3   Everett L. Worthington et al., "The Effects of a Therapist's Religion on the Marriage Therapist and Marriage Counseling," in *The Role of Religion in Marriage and Family Counseling*, ed. Jill D. Onedera, 17–34 (New York: Routledge, 2008).

4   Worthington et al., "The Effects of a Therapist's Religion," 17–18.

relations, our religious location merits the deep self-reflexivity we have learned to bring to our social and personal locations. Such reflection is the purpose of this chapter, especially the diverse, dynamic, and complex effects of religious location—our own and that of our clients—in clinical work.

Even among those of us who consider ourselves pastoral counselors, clinicians inhabit diverse religious locations. Some of us were born into religious families and communities, others of us into families or communities where religion was barely noticed. We may have grown to be antireligion, blasé, or positive toward religion. Surveys consistently report that counselors are less religious than the general public but also report that many of us consider ourselves spiritual, even if not religious.[5] We may be lifelong or occasional students of religion, had religious education only when we were children, or never had any education in religion. We may be leaders in religious communities, religious communities may have shunned us, or we lead from marginalized positions within religious communities. Among those of us who make our living doing work that concerns religion, some chose that work because of religion's positive potentials, others because of its dangers, most of us out of concern for religion's capacities both to harm and to help. We may belong to a tradition that is denied the status of a religion, such as indigenous "traditions" or something others call a "cult." Counselors and clients bring all these variations in religious location to counseling relationships.

Still, the situation is even more complex than these initial differentiations imply. Our particularities are not simple demographic markers. They are neither discrete categories nor static. They are alive, synergistically evolving. As with other aspects of identity, through our lifetimes, we inhabit more than one religious location. We become more, less, or differently religious. Our love of or neutrality toward religion is destabilized or destroyed by trauma done to us in the name of religion. We are religious but shaped by multiple religions, not only one, having been born into cultures and families where migration, immigration, and colonialism have created religious

---

5   Jill D. Onedera and Brian C. Greenwalt, "Introduction to Religion and Marriage and Family Counseling," in Ondera, *Role of Religion*, 3–13.

multiplicity. In these and many other ways, our relationship to religion is characterized by more than one experience, more than one location, sometimes more than one location in any given moment.

The diversity of our religious locations is demanding and perhaps daunting. Still, little evidence exists that diversity in religious location is inherently an obstacle to clinical work. Quite the opposite. A growing literature argues almost exclusively that with adequate education and clinical consultation, as well as the use of referral for specific religious counsel when needed, counselors and clients from diverse religious locations can work together effectively. Indeed, it is not uncommon to find in the literature documentation through clinical examples that difference in religious location is sometimes treasured by clients because they feel that they could not speak freely with someone from their own tradition.[6] This chapter presumes that under those specified conditions, counselors can work meaningfully with clients whose religious locations differ from the counselor's, with the following crucial caveat.

Counselors and clients do not have to agree about religion to do good clinical work together. Indeed, this chapter argues that significant religious difference *and disagreement* are at play in every clinical relationship, even if religion never surfaces as an explicit subject. However, therapeutic relationality amid religious difference and disagreement requires counselors to be open to the *possibility* that there is something of value in religious locations other than our own, even when we disagree vehemently. This is a challenge that is always demanding and becomes excruciating when a client conveys condemnation of our religious location(s) or other identities. It raises an intense question for contemplation: What values and practices will cultivate such openness, when we are impelled to judge, withdraw, strike back?

We each must find our own path to such openness and to practices that will help sustain us on that difficult path. I will offer here, though, a few words about my own religious locations relative to these demands, for

---

6   Julie Chijo Hanada, "'Listening to the Dharma': Integrating Buddhism into a Multifaith Health Care Environment," in *Buddhist Care for the Dying and Bereaved*, ed. Jonathan S. Watts and Yoshiharu Tomatsu, 249–69 (Boston: Wisdom, 2012); Froma Walsh, "Spiritual Diversity: Multifaith Perspectives in Family Therapy," *Family Process* 49, no. 3 (2010): 330–48, https://doi.org/10.1111/j.1545-5300.2010.01326.x.

the purposes of illustration. Decades of clinical teaching and practice have crafted in me a devotion to what I experience as the mysteriousness and ambiguities of life, which relativize my religious and clinical locations, as well as those of all others. Except for the enduring reality of this unfathomable quality of life, I have come to experience all other aspects of my worldview as partial, at best. Similarly, in my experience, both religion and the science of psychotherapy are partial; neither have proven adequate by themselves to prevent violence or cure woundedness. Thus, personally and professionally decentered, humility is required of me even and especially when I am required by professional codes of ethics to intervene in clients' behaviors or compelled by my ethics or morality to express some disagreement with a client. The practices of religion and spirituality I engage are to a large extent for the purposes of cultivating capacity for this openness and defusing any negativity I experience in relation to the religious locations of others.

But what if we find ourselves in a clinical relationship that exceeds our capacity to offer respectful openness to clients regarding their religious location? What if we find ourselves unable to shake our judgment, fear, voyeurism, or idealization toward a client's religiosity? First, to find ourselves unexpectedly in such a situation suggests that we failed to do a sufficiently thorough initial assessment of either the client's religious location and its interrelatedness with the clinical issues presented or our religious competence with respect to that client's religious particularity. We may need to revise how we do intake and history taking. Second, we need immediately to seek education and supervision to remedy our inadequate training relative to this client's religious location. Codes of ethics usually prohibit us from simply referring clients because we discover differences—religious or otherwise—between ourselves and clients.[7] Once we have made a commitment to care for a client, we are required to work diligently to develop competence in the area of religion to meet the client's needs. It is unethical for us precipitously to refer a client because we discover conflicts in deeply held values about, for example, gender roles, sexual practice, race relations, abortion, or military combat.

---

7   American Counseling Association, *ACA Code of Ethics*, accessed June 30, 2023, 8, http://www.counseling.org/resources/aca-code-of-ethics.pdf.

But, again, what if after our diligent effort to gain education and supervision, we still find ourselves unable to shake our judgment, fear, voyeurism, or idealization toward a client's religiosity? Counselors who cannot foster openness to the possibility of value in clients' religious locations need to refer. Counselors who dismiss, disallow, or otherwise disdain their clients' religious location need to refer. Our codes of ethics may not have adequately grappled with the reality that education and supervision often are insufficient to transform our most passionately held beliefs. Not unlike some of our clinical beliefs, some religious beliefs are nonnegotiable. Just as there are uncompromising disagreements among clinicians about clinical truths (the politics of symptomology and diagnostic criteria, for example), there are uncompromising disagreements among clinicians about what constitutes religious truth or truth about religion. Often referred to as attitudes of exclusivity, I respect that some persons hold those beliefs in good conscience. I am arguing here only that attitudes of exclusivity regarding differences in religious location pose an insurmountable barrier *in counseling* (not necessarily in other professional practices). How can therapeutic relationality be fostered if religious counselors regard a client's religious location as damning or if nonreligious counselors find clients' religious commitments nonsensical? As we will see, like precipitous referral, such personal beliefs also pose a serious ethical dilemma: They fail to meet the minimum criterion regarding religion in our codes of ethics, that of respect. Clients will readily detect when counselors have attitudes of superiority with regard to religion. They are likely to detect it even when we cloak our feelings of superiority in silence. It is intriguing that the old adage about polite conversation—avoid talking about religion and politics—seems strangely descriptive of counseling as well. Perhaps the widespread silence in counseling about religion (and politics) is our effort to mask our religious disagreements? But this is futile. As I argue later, our religious locations and differences are revealed, indirectly if not directly, when we and our clients delve into the profound issues of meaning and value that are at the heart of counseling.

Forms and Degrees of Religious Difference

As public attention is drawn to the necessity of dealing constructively with persons who differ from us religiously, emphasis is usually placed on similarities. We should and can treat with respect people whose religion differs from ours because, as this approach goes, religions share many common values. Or, if we encounter persons who are not religious, we can and should treat them with respect because, as humans, we are more alike than different. Focus on similarities is valuable and reassuring.

Focus on similarities is, however, insufficient by itself. The need to augment our awareness of similarity with attentiveness to religious difference is emphasized in this chapter for several reasons. Religious difference is highly prevalent, as I argued earlier. Furthermore, their religious particularity is usually important to clients, whether they are religious or not religious. Most somberly, inattentiveness to difference, along with misperception because of difference, fuels violence.[8] Finally, as has been widely argued in the health sciences, religion can and often does play a role in well-being, but this benefit is not generic. Rather, clients benefit not from religion in a generic way but from particular traditions, practices, and communities. Thus, attentiveness to religious difference is necessary to access religion's contributions to well-being.

The three vignettes that follow are merely suggestive of the three major forms of religious difference commonly encountered in counseling. I encourage you to pause as you read to try to identify situations in which you have experienced other examples of these three kinds of difference.

Interreligious (or Interfaith) Difference

The most widely recognized form is *interreligious* (or *interfaith*) difference: Clients and counselors may identify with different religions. But when we consider religious location and not only belief in religion, we can see that this difference also occurs when one values religion and the other does not.

Near the end of their fourth session, the therapeutic alliance is rocked by the emergence of religious difference. Jared and Dinah Butler have come to counseling with their two teenagers, Elijah and Tamara, because their once peaceable family life has become

---

8   Stephen Prothero, *God Is Not One: The Eight Rival Religions That Run the World—And Why Their Differences Matter* (New York: HarperCollins, 2010).

a battleground where parents and children are regularly fighting over values, behaviors, and their choice of friends. The family has participated for years in a Christian church where African American families like themselves try to instill the values and teach the behaviors that, among other purposes, equip them to resist racism nonviolently and with dignity. Thus, Elijah's recent declaration that he does not believe in God and feels like a hypocrite when he attends church has fueled the family conflict.

Also African American, their counselor, Aliyah, has cautiously assisted them in previous sessions to reflect on the role Christian values play in their conflicts and not only in the closeness that seems under threat. Now, as their fourth session draws to a close, Aliyah asks to reschedule their appointment for next week because of a religious holiday. This surprises Jared and Dinah—"What holiday is next week?" they ask Aliyah. "It is Eid-al-Fitr," she replies, "when Muslims celebrate the end of Ramadan." By the look on their faces, Aliyah can see that Jared and Dinah are stunned.

"You are Muslim?" they ask. "Not Christian? Why didn't you tell us?" As Aliyah tries in the few remaining minutes to figure out why her Muslim identity seems to be troubling the parents, the kids enthusiastically say to their parents, "That's great! You have been talking all the time about how great Aliyah is, and now you'll see that there is nothing wrong with our being friends with the Muslims at school!" But Aliyah knows the rocky history between African American Christians and African American Muslims. And since her conversion several years ago, she has been struggling to manage her skepticism toward clients and colleagues who are not religious, as Elijah now describes himself. She knows the gaps now uncovered will not be easily bridged.

Intrareligious (or Intrafaith) Difference

Clients and counselors may differ significantly even when they are located within the same tradition. The relative lack of attention to this form—*intra*religious or *intra*faith difference—is problematic because this form may be more challenging than interreligious difference. When clients and counselors know a tradition from the inside and are committed to it, the differences can be more recognizable, troubling, and divisive.

This vignette represents a composite of my own experience as a Christian counseling Christians. A similar dynamic could occur between counselors and clients who are both non-religious or both identify with a religion other than Christianity.

> *In our first session, Luisa speaks of the divorce that has left her struggling financially as a single mother. Her beliefs about divorce and the behavior that precipitated it—inculcated by Mexican cultural values, her family, and the pastor and ethos of her Pentecostal Christian megachurch—leave her feeling shame, she says, and sometimes suicidal. "Are you a Christian?" she asks me. "It's really important to me that my counselor is a Christian."*
>
> *I was born into a mainline Christian denomination in a theologically conservative and evangelically oriented community. Now, after years of life experience and of education in "progressive" theologies, I name myself a follower of Jesus. I know my understanding of Christianity is considerably "left of center" among Christians, many of whom would not consider me a Christian. I scramble to find words to respond to this complex question and the even more complex relational and contextual situation it references as we strive to find common ground.*

Differences Due to Religious Multiplicity

Historically and globally, engaging in more than one religious tradition is not uncommon. Recently, this way of being religious is becoming more public and widely practiced in the United States. This third form of religious difference stems from what is often called *religious multiplicity*. The next vignette illustrates only one of the many ways this religious location is embodied.[9]

> *A student is preparing his application for his first position as a mental health practitioner, hoping to work as a counselor at*

---

9 Kathleen J. Greider, "Religiously Plural Persons: Multiplicity and Care of Souls," in *Pastoralpsychologie und Religionspsychologie im Dialog [Pastoral Psychology and Psychology of Religion in Dialogue]*, ed. Isabelle Noth, Christoph Morgenthaler, and Kathleen J. Greider, 119–35 (Stuttgart: Kohlhammer, 2011).

the local Jewish Family Services Center. This job matters very much to Joshua, not only because it will be his first job after graduation but also because he has always wanted to work for a Jewish organization. Joshua experiences his religious identity, beliefs, and practices as inextricably related with his view of and commitment to the work of counseling. But he is struggling to write the application and is already preoccupied with the interview, wondering what they will ask him about his Jewish identity. Joshua treasures the Jewish culture that his parents taught to him and his siblings and that remains the foundation of their family life. Both his parents are rabbis in the conservative branch of Judaism, so he also knows well the religious history and practices of his Jewish heritage. Still, Joshua is not an observant Jew, religiously speaking, and is, in fact, atheist. He has joined the ranks of the many Jews who find in Buddhism the worldview, values, and practices that now serve as his spiritual foundation. He has studied Buddhism extensively with respected teachers. Over time, he feels that he has finally found himself, come home to himself, spiritually—he is a Jewish Buddhist and a Buddhist Jew. But how can he explain his multiplicity of religious identities to the interviewers? Will they be assessing whether he is an adequate representative of Judaism? Is he? Will they understand and embrace his complex religious identity? His family is still struggling to understand and accept it.

Degrees of Difference

Inherent in these forms is a spectrum of degrees of difference, ranging from comfortable or even intriguing variation within and between religious locations to extreme differences that give rise to anger or a sense of threat. As with the tendency to emphasize similarity, we may be tempted to focus on relatively manageable differences. Also, as in the three vignettes just presented, the actual or feared degree of difference may, with care and competence, be initially challenging but navigable. This makes all the more noteworthy a case study published by Aten in which religious difference constituted "opposing worldviews" that threatened to derail Aten from his clinical obligations.[10] In this refreshingly honest examination of his clinical work with "Bill," Aten details the clash between his own religious beliefs and Bill's affiliation with Odinism. Never having encountered an Odinist, Aten asks Bill to tell him more about it.

> CLIENT: My religion is an ancient Northern Scandinavian
> religion, it is a pagan religion. It is a white Aryan religion.
> And it is the guiding philosophy behind lots of white
> supremacy groups. I consider myself a Nazi. . . .
> THERAPIST: (Silence).[11]

Aten wryly sketches how he worked with his thoughts, feelings, and behaviors in the aftermath of Bill's religious self-explanation, eventually finding a religious location from which to cultivate empathy for and be of some help to Bill. From this disorienting experience in interreligious counseling, Aten gleaned guidelines for clinicians working with religious differences, some of which we consider in the final section of the chapter. For now, it is sufficient to note that this case illustrates how serious degrees of difference in religious location, if unattended, might derail a clinical relationship.

Challenges Related to Differences in Religious Location

Within the forms and degrees of religious difference are embedded additional complications especially crucial in counseling: exacerbated power dynamics, the remoteness of foundational meanings and values, and inadequacies in education and supervised clinical training.

Exacerbated Power Dynamics Due to Religious Difference

Difference in religious location exacerbates what Bueckert and Schipani aptly call the "inherent asymmetry" of professional relationships of care

---

10   Jamie D. Aten, "Addressing Religious Differences in Therapy: A Case Study from Behind Bars," *Journal of Psychology and Christianity* 30, no. 1 (2011): 81.

11   Aten, "Addressing Religious Differences," 82.

and counseling.[12] Certainly, the extent to which clients and counselors are conscious of these dynamics varies considerably. To engage these complications effectively, it is first necessary to develop our consciousness that *counselors and clients meet not merely as persons but as groups.* To analyze the complex meta-environment in which persons meet also as groups, Grefe deftly employs social psychology, social identity theory, intergroup theory, and theory and practice in interreligious dialogue and interfaith spiritual care.[13] Although Grefe is addressing a broader context than ours, her analysis helps us see how, as in all aspects of our living, clients and counselors embody and enact not only our individuality but also the culture and history of the groups to which we belong. Multicultural counseling theory has made clear that intercultural competence requires us to look beyond the influence of the family groups to which we and clients belong. More sophisticated is the capacity to take into account how membership in other collectivities is affecting counseling relationships. Clients, counselors, and the clinical work itself evidence the history and current realities of all the broader cultures to which we and clients belong: less emphasized, historically significant cultures of age, ability, and education, as well as the more widely recognized cultures and histories related to gender and sexuality, race and ethnicity, language and national origin, and so forth. Obviously, the culture and history of the groups associated with our religious locations are similarly at play.

Second, embedded in all these dimensions of our group belongingness are *power differentials between groups.* These power differentials are rarely benign. To the contrary, the history of intergroup contact is a record of oppression and suffering. What have come to be referred to handily as the "isms" constitute a painful legacy of pervasive misunderstanding, fear, stereotyping, and prejudice, which has festered into contemporary and impervious patterns of domination by the more powerful of the less powerful, enforced by subjugation and, too often, genocide. Because it concerns nothing less than ultimate meanings and values, religious location is arguably

---

12   Bueckert and Schipani, "Interfaith Spiritual Caregiving," 251.

13   Dagmar Grefe, *Encounters for Change: Interreligious Cooperation in the Care of Individuals and Communities* (Eugene, OR: Wipf & Stock, 2011).

one of the most potentially inflammatory power dynamics in intergroup contact. When meeting in counseling, counselors and/or clients may well see in each other someone who represents this excruciating legacy: Blacks may see descendants of white slave owners, Jews may see Christian inheritors of a long tradition of anti-Semitism, women may see men heedless of misogyny's history, and impoverished Third World people may see oblivious First World consumers.

This analysis may seem to be overly focused on the underside of religious difference. Such a perception, however, may well be evidence of the function of *religious privilege.* The notion of privilege—special advantages, rights, or immunity granted to a specific group of people—has become a crucial aspect of understanding dynamics within systems of domination and oppression. In contrast to emphasis on intentional acts of oppression and the disadvantages of belonging to oppressed groups, the concept of privilege calls our attention to advantages that accrue to being members of dominant groups. As McIntosh described it in her now oft-cited reflections on white privilege and male privilege, "Privilege is like an invisible weightless knapsack of special provisions, assurances, tools, maps, guides, codebooks, passports, visas, clothes, compass, emergency gear, and blank checks."[14] The privilege we enjoy is obvious to those who do not benefit from it but difficult for us to see because we are so immersed in and reliant on it. Also, we are socialized not to see it, lest conscience cause us to disturb the very social order that privileges our people.

As noted earlier, the privilege associated with our dominance also enables us to distance ourselves, if we choose, from the struggle and suffering endured by those our group dominates. If we choose it, this lack of awareness deforms us not only with regard to our ignorance in the present time but also with regard to history. We can think that the legacy of dominance and subjugation is not as bad as it seems to over-powered groups. We can easily overestimate the degree to which we and our groups foster just and fair relationality.

---

14   Peggy McIntosh, *White Privilege and Male Privilege: A Personal Account of Coming to See Correspondences Through Work in Women's Studies* (working paper 189, Wellesley Center for Research on Women, 1988), 1–2.

The concept is now being extended to privilege in the realm of religious difference. It is noteworthy that it was a colleague in counseling, Schlosser, who offered one of the early examinations of religious privilege.[15] Schlosser notes that he came to an awareness of religious privilege as he engaged in the process of identifying the invisible advantages he enjoys as a Caucasian male. Illustrating the complexity of power dynamics that we have been exploring, he notes that his privileges "led to the neglect and denial" of a dimension of his experience in which he experiences oppression—his "identification as a member of a minority religious group" in the United States, that is, a religious group other than Christianity.[16] In the United States, Christians are dominant insofar as we far outnumber persons affiliated with other religious groups. Our dominance accrues much more, however, from the fact that Christians far outnumber persons of other religious locations in positions invested with sociopolitical and economic power. Not all Christians enjoy the same level of privilege: The Christian majority discriminates against and marginalizes some of its own—for example, the Metropolitan Community Church, Latter-day Saints (Mormons), Seventh Day Adventists, and Jehovah's Witnesses. Also, as with whites and males, our dominance does not prevent Christians from claiming and sometimes experiencing disadvantage. At a meta-level, however, Christians in the United States enjoy religious dominance and privilege.

Thus, it is significant when Schlosser describes speaking of Christian privilege as "breaking a sacred taboo."[17] Similarly significant is the argument by two other colleagues that "religious bigotry" is "the neglected 'ism' in multicultural psychology and therapy."[18] In both cases, the exacerbation of power dynamics due to religious difference is being referenced. We can also

---

15   Lewis Z. Schlosser, "Christian Privilege: Breaking a Sacred Taboo," *Journal of Multicultural Counseling and Development* 31, no. 1 (2003): 44–51, https://doi.org/10.1002/j.2161-1912.2003.tb00530.x.

16   Schlosser, "Christian Privilege," 46.

17   Schlosser, "Christian Privilege," 44.

18   Charles Negy and Christopher J. Ferguson, "Religious Bigotry: The Neglected 'ism' in Multicultural Psychology and Therapy," in *Cross-cultural Psychotherapy: Toward a Critical Understanding of Diverse Clients*, ed. Charles Negy (Reno, NV: Bent Tree Press, 2004), 61.

see this exacerbation in the preceding vignettes. The cultural dominance and privilege associated with being Christian, as well as religious bigotry, are the meta-environment in which Jared and Dinah presume Aliyah is Christian, assume that it was her responsibility to correct their presumption, and for undisclosed reasons seem troubled that Muslims are becoming important persons relative to their family life. The power invested in Aliyah because of her professional role is undermined by her membership in a minority religious group toward which bigotry is often expressed. Yet it is Elijah whose religious location may be most religiously disadvantaged in this counseling situation, given the global bias and discrimination against atheists.[19]

Religious bigotry and privilege exist within communities, as exemplified by the acrimony between so-called conservative and liberal Christians, and the fledgling connection between Luisa and her pastoral counselor is now tested by that culture war. As a Jew and a person of multiple religious identities, Joshua is a member of two minority religious groups. But also, knowing the devastation wreaked upon the Jewish community by genocide and other costs of anti-Semitism, he understands that Jewish interviewers might well resent his religious choices, feeling they contribute to the diminishment of Judaism.

Remoteness of Meanings and Values Rooted in Religious Location

Religious location is often equated with conscious cognitions and observable practices. For example, we are clear that we believe in God or that we think religious belief is superstition. We participate in religious rituals as members of a religious community, or we do not. These easily accessible beliefs and concrete behaviors are, indeed, typically part of our religious location. This can give the mistaken impression that religious location is easily accessible, even obvious.

However, religious location is also associated with deep structures of meaning and value, sometimes referred to as our worldview or philosophy of

---

19   United States Commission on International Religious Freedom, *Annual Report of the U.S. Commission on International Religious Freedom*, April 2013, https://www.uscirf.gov /sites/default/files/resources/2013%20USCIRF%20Annual%20Report%20(2).pdf.

life. These structures are characterized by remoteness. They are remote relative to consciousness, visibility, and malleability. As we experience regularly, it is not always possible to say what our thoughts and feelings are with regard to profound matters. It is often the case that we behave in ways that conflict with the values we state most insistently. Our worldviews are so resistant to change that often only dramatic experiences like trauma or ecstasy can substantially transform them.

The influence of these profound meanings and values is ubiquitous, and few mental health professionals argue any longer that counseling is value free. What is not so widely acknowledged, however, is that the *meanings and values at the heart of counseling often have their roots in the religious location of both clients and counselors.* Negy and Ferguson put it bluntly: "Although psychology generally purports to be divorced from religious values, judgments about 'deviant' and 'optimal' behavior often are based on Western cultural values, which themselves are partially derived from a broader Judeo–Christian culture."[20]

When global and cultural variation is respected (not merely tolerated or assessed according to the judgments of our groups or personal choices), we are more able to recognize that religious location affects many, maybe all, of the issues of meaning and value that arise in counseling. The religious valence that inheres in these issues will vary in its characteristics: according to religious location, of course, but also from negative to positive, unconscious to conscious, determinative to disregarded, deeply considered or embraced with little thought, and historically obscure or prominent in current media. However, the religious valence is there. In the vignettes just presented, deep differences in meaning and value that have their roots in religious location will be most obvious in whatever clinical judgments Aliyah makes about parenting and, as Luisa's pastoral counselor, I make about divorce. But consider questions that suggest other religiously influenced clinical issues: Do human beings tend toward goodness or toward offense? In what situations might guilt and shame be warranted? Why is granting forgiveness given more attention than earning forgiveness? What is a family? When my obligations to myself and to others appear to conflict, which should I favor? Why do we

---

20   Negy and Ferguson, "Religious Bigotry," 67.

try to influence each other's health-related choices—diet, exercise, disease prevention, use of substances? What makes variation in gender, sexual identity, sexual expression, and sexual fidelity so incendiary? Why does nonconformity among humans cause problems? Given the vulnerability of children and the documented extent of neglect and abuse, why do we treat parenthood as an inalienable right? Why do we judge each other's choices related to how we choose to die—attitudes toward dying, resuscitation, euthanasia, suicide, treatment of the body after death?

Perhaps most significant in counseling is how our religious location affects our most deeply held positions on issues of ultimacy and authority. What constitutes a life well lived? What matters most? How do we live with brokenness and losses that are irreparable? What distinguishes honor over dishonor? As the popular slogan asks, why do we kill people who kill people to show that killing people is wrong? Why is military combat valorized and suicide stigmatized? If love and compassion are obviously good, why are they so often absent? When we disagree about what matters most, who decides? When religion and science diverge, or when my religious location diverges from my counselor's, or vice versa, whose authority prevails, and why?

This variation and this uncertainty inhere in the remoteness of our meanings and values, calling for our sustained personal and professional reflection and study. Otherwise, as with religious privilege, the close relationship between religion and the meanings and values at issue in counseling will continue to go without our notice. Without mindfulness and responsible behavior regarding how our attitudes toward religion are intertwined with what we deem to be healthy and good, we are at risk of practicing religious bigotry. This is the case whether we are religious, not religious, or against religion.[21] Of course, counselors' responsibility in these dynamics is greater than that of clients. "Arguably, the most insidious form of religious bigotry occurring in therapy is when therapists naïvely believe that their guidance is based on clinical judgment when such judgment really reflects therapists' own personal ideology."[22]

---

21   Negy and Ferguson, "Religious Bigotry."

22   Negy and Ferguson, "Religious Bigotry," 69.

Professional Competence and Ethics Challenged by Differences in Religious Location

Standards of professional competence and codes of ethics across the mental health professions now usually include at least a mention of religion. Most commonly, it is stated that clinicians are expected to *respect* clients' religious identity and practices. Some go a step further to state the need for *competence* with regard to clients' religion and/or to caution clinicians from practicing outside the scope of their training with regard to religion. But what constitutes respect and competence with regard to religion? The few codes that do specify competencies make clear that developing such competence requires extensive education and supervised clinical practice, far beyond that which is provided by most degree programs in mental health disciplines. The following extracts are illustrative.

In the statement of its ethical principles and code of conduct, the American Psychological Association includes religion in a lengthy enumeration of factors that psychologists are said to be "aware of," "respect," and "consider": "Psychologists are aware of and respect cultural, individual, and role differences, including those based on age, gender, gender identity, race, ethnicity, culture, national origin, religion, sexual orientation, disability, language, and socioeconomic status, and consider these factors when working with members of such groups."[23] Also, psychologists are described as aware and respectful of these factors in sections addressing "Human Relations," specifically Section 3.01 on Unfair Discrimination and Section 3.10 on Other Harassment.[24] These expectations set a high bar. Appropriately, then, the APA includes religion in Section 2.01, which addresses boundaries of competence. Part (b) states that "where scientific or professional knowledge in the discipline of psychology establishes that an understanding of factors associated with age, gender, gender identity, race, ethnicity, culture, national origin, religion, sexual orientation, disability, language, or socioeconomic status is essential for effective implementation of their services or research, psychologists have or obtain the training, experience, consultation,

---

23   American Psychological Association, *Ethical Principles of Psychologists and Code of Conduct*, accessed June 30, 2023, 4, http://www.apa.org/ethics/code/principles.pdf.

24   American Psychological Association, *Ethical Principles*, 5–6.

or supervision necessary to ensure the competence of their services, or they make appropriate referrals, except as provided in Standard 2.02, Providing Services in Emergencies."[25]

In what clinical situation would these factors *not* be essential for effective practice? Multicultural theory and practice has firmly established that all of the aforementioned dimensions of culture are significant and influential in therapeutic work and research. Thus, all psychologists who do not already have education and training necessary to ensure the competence of their work regarding religious location are obliged to seek it. Alternatively, the APA code of ethics requires that they seek consultation or supervision with, or refer their clients to, colleagues with such competence. The American Association of Pastoral Counselors (AAPC)[26] exists to provide credentialing of, and continuing education and collaboration for, the development of exactly such competence. That the first words of the AAPC code of ethics go beyond the simple signifier "religion" is modest evidence of such a mission: "As members of the American Association of Pastoral Counselors, we are respectful of the various theologies, traditions, and values of our faith communities and committed to the dignity and worth of each individual."[27] Similarly, Principle III, addressing client relationships, notes that competence in this arena of living goes beyond "religion" and places obligations on the clinicians regarding their own religious location. "We show sensitive regard for the moral, social, and religious values and beliefs of clients and communities. We avoid imposing our beliefs on others, although we may express them when appropriate in the pastoral counseling process."[28]

Interestingly, the American Counseling Association (ACA) links its code of ethics to fourteen competencies that go a long way toward making clear the substantial education and supervised practice necessary to develop clinical competency regarding religion. A division of the ACA, the Association

---

25   American Psychological Association, *Ethical Principles*, 5.

26   AAPC consolidated with ACPE in 2019. References to resources available through AAPC are now available via ACPE.

27   American Association of Pastoral Counselors, *Code of Ethics*, April 28, 1994, 1, https://presbyteryofli.com/wp-content/uploads/2016/01/American-Assoc.-of-Pastoral -Counselors-Code-of-Ethics.pdf.

28   American Association of Pastoral Counselors, *Code of Ethics*, 3.

for Spiritual, Ethical, and Religious Values in Counseling (ASERVIC), has developed a document entitled *Competencies for Addressing Spiritual and Religious Values in Counseling.*[29] ASERVIC articulates competencies in six categories:

Culture and Worldview: knowledge sufficient to compare and contrast spirituality and religion and knowledge of core beliefs of major traditions in spirituality, religion, agnosticism, and atheism; recognition of the interplay between clients' worldview and functioning and their beliefs regarding religion and spirituality

Counselor Self-Awareness: active development of awareness of one's own position relative to religion; continuous evaluation of its effects on the counselor's clinical work and clients; awareness of, and development of resources to offset, the limitations of one's knowledge regarding religion and spirituality

Human and Spiritual Development: knowledge of models of development and capacity for appropriate clinical use

Communication: acceptance and sensitivity regarding clients' communications regarding religion and/or spirituality; use of concepts consonant with clients' communications; capacity to recognize religious and/or spiritual themes in client communications, assess their therapeutic relevance, and address them appropriately

Assessment: during intake and assessment, seeking information from clients or other sources to understand clients' religious and/or spiritual perspective

Diagnosis and Treatment: recognition of the role of religion and/or spirituality in clients' well-being, problems, and symptoms; goal setting consistent with clients' spiritual and/or religious perspective; ability to modify therapeutic technique and use spiritual and/or religious practices when appropriate and acceptable to clients' viewpoints; ability to use theory and research therapeutically that

---

29   Association for Spiritual, Ethical, and Religious Values in Counseling, *Competencies for Addressing Spiritual and Religious Issues in Counseling,* accessed June 30, 2023, https://aservic.org/spiritual-and-religious-competencies/.

supports inclusion of clients' religious and/or spiritual beliefs and practices.[30]

Development of the competencies identified by ASERVIC can result only from substantial formal education about religious difference, disciplined and ongoing self-reflexivity regarding religious location, and clinical practice under the guidance of teachers and supervisors who possess these competencies. Again, a high bar is set.

Our codes of ethics and standards for competency put us in a bind. *It is unethical to ignore religion, and it is unethical to attend to religion incompetently.* Our ethics require us to seek to understand and build competence regarding religious difference. But the curricula and credentialing of mental health fields outside of pastoral counseling rarely and inadequately address religious location, so how many clinicians actually have these competencies? Does this gap between high expectations, a dearth of clinicians who actually meet those expectations, and the widespread influence of religious location and difference in counseling mean that many clinicians are working outside their scope of practice? Technically, the only ethical pathway out of this conundrum is consultation with and referral to colleagues with the kind of competencies identified here, such as pastoral counselors. But our vignettes point toward a more complex reality: Aliyah, Joshua, and I (and many other counselors) find that religiously tinged issues and religious difference are so prevalent and so intricately interwoven with other clinical issues and our own religious locations that we could benefit from seeking consultation on a daily basis! The very ubiquity of religious location and difference means that although referral and consultation are sometimes essential, we need also to be learning "in place," working every day toward developing these competencies. The remainder of the chapter delves into two aspects of such learning: self-reflexivity regarding our own religious location and clinical practices that directly address the gap between our competencies and clients' needs regarding religion. The effectiveness of combining these two emphases can be understood as akin to the synergy of self-differentiation

---

30   Association for Spiritual, Ethical, and Religious Values in Counseling, *Competencies for Addressing.*

and connection argued by family systems theory to be the fundamentals of effective relationality.

Self-Differentiation: The Significance of the Counselor's Religious Location

As we have seen, the religious location of the counselor matters in the clinical process. Like all aspects of our identities, whether we understand ourselves to be religious, spiritual but not religious, agnostic, humanist, atheist, utterly disinterested, or in some other position relative to religion, these locations influence the clinical process. There are sometimes good clinical reasons to try to imaginatively "bracket" our religious location, to minimize certain effects of it. These skills notwithstanding, we cannot fully neutralize our religious location(s). More to the point, as counselors, we should be well practiced in self-reflexivity—disciplined, accountable practices to decrease our unconsciousness and increase in depth our understanding of our life narrative, sense of self, participation in relationships, and social–historical location. Extending self-reflexivity to how our religious location is affecting our clinical work should be possible for all of us, even without specialized training regarding religion. Toward that end, we will reflect here on three mutually reinforcing areas of self-reflexivity that are akin to those identified in the category of Counselor Self-Awareness in the ASERVIC competencies:[31]

- Self-reflexivity regarding our own religious location
- Self-reflexivity regarding the effect of our religious location on clients and clinical situations
- Self-reflexivity regarding our limitations and offsetting them

Self-Reflexivity Regarding Our Own Religious Location

We begin by acknowledging that, as with other dimensions of our identity and self-awareness, our identity, awareness, and self-differentiation regarding religion are fluid. Our personal and group relatedness to religion and spirituality is, hopefully, not stagnant. Thus, the need for this aspect of

---

31   Association for Spiritual, Ethical, and Religious Values in Counseling, *Competencies for Addressing*.

self-reflexivity is ongoing. It is important to note here that although self-reflexivity does often lead to change, change is not a requirement of self-reflexivity. Out of respect for religious freedom, it is crucial not to expect that we (or others) will be changed in our religious location by self-reflexivity, although that may happen. Rather, the expectation here is the awareness of and, as needed, the capacity to articulate our positions relative to religion. As noted in the vignettes, Aliyah, Joshua, and I all face situations in which our readiness to speak explicitly about our religious location is needed.

Much of our self-reflexivity about religiosity will happen in our most personal contemplation. Religion is one of the tender and controversial matters that may seem to require the relative safety of one's private musings. Yet clinicians know that solitary reflection by itself is insufficient for clinical responsibility. Given denial, projection, and other forms of unconsciousness and defense, fullness of self-reflection regarding our religious location depends on augmentation through relationships of accountability. The expectation that counselors will seek both psychotherapy and supervision for themselves testifies to our professional acknowledgment that we need the perspective of others to reduce the risk of harm to clients. Similarly, we will also seek *relational* self-reflexivity for accountability as we consider our religious location. We therefore discuss our religious location and its clinical significance with our therapists, supervisors, and consultants. For counselors with a religious orientation, a commonly stated expectation in our codes of ethics is that we maintain relationships of support and accountability with our religious communities.[32] Another excellent, religiously relational resource for our self-reflexivity is the tradition of spiritual direction, a form of spiritual guidance developed in numerous religious and spiritual traditions.

Three domains of self-understanding and the interplay between them are important. Perhaps most obviously, we seek to comprehend the *personal and familial domains* of our religious location. We seek understanding of our personal life philosophy or worldview and consciousness of the particular beliefs that comprise them. Of course, this entails increasing realization of our beliefs about religion, whether we are religious, spiritual, agnostic, atheist, or actively antireligion. But our worldview entails far more, as indicated

---

32   American Association of Pastoral Counselors, *Code of Ethics*.

by the illustrative questions included previously in this chapter, in our reflection on the remoteness of foundational meanings and values. What are your responses to those questions and others like them?

Self-reflexivity in this domain includes attention to the familial aspects of our religious location. What might appear at first glance to be only our personal beliefs are revealed, when we trace the religious aspects of our genealogy, to be weighted with family history and ancestry. Of special value in this aspect of self-reflexivity is the spiritual genogram, because it nuances relative to religion a tool already widely embraced in clinical practice.[33] Developing our own genograms with attention to the influence of religion and spirituality in our family history and discussing them in therapy and/or in supervision and consultation groups will substantially advance our cognizance of our religious location. Hodge describes two other tools—spiritual histories and spiritual life maps—that are designed for use with clients but can easily be adapted for counselors' use to trace the personal and familial domain of our religious location.[34] But any practices that we might suggest to clients as they engage in self-reflexivity relative to their religious location are available to us to use as we work with ourselves, such as retreats, journaling, meditation, prayer, and artistic expression.

We need also to practice self-reflexivity with regard to a second domain of religious location: *the historical, sociopolitical, economic, and global terrain in which we are religiously located.* We investigate the role played by people of our religious location in the long record of interactions between groups inhabiting different religious locations. Especially, when and with whom were people of our religious location agents of violence and injustice or targets? We chart the gains and losses of sociopolitical and economic power and privilege of people in religious locations similar to ours. Just as important, now that migration globalizes almost all of our interactions, is how we are located relative to the history and the contemporary situation of religion

---

33   Marsha Wiggins Frame, "The Spiritual Genogram in Family Therapy," *Journal of Marital & Family Therapy* 26, no. 2 (2000): 211–16, https://doi.org/10.1111/j.1752-0606.2000.tb00290.x.

34   David R. Hodge, *Spiritual Assessment: Handbook for Helping Professionals* (Palos Heights, IL: North American Association of Christians in Social Work, 2003).

around the globe. The clinical tools of spiritual ecomaps and ecograms can be modified to help us chart these aspects of our own religious location.[35]

A third domain of our religious location crucial for self-reflexive work *is our appraisal of religious plurality:* How do you understand the relationship between the many religious and spiritual traditions, with their sometimes conflicting truth claims? Self-reflexivity in this domain is difficult to practice without the benefit of education in theological and religious studies. However, most major traditions offer books and articles that explore this question and can be used for independent reading. Knitter's *Introducing Theologies of Religions* differentiates diverse Christian attitudes toward religious plurality and painstakingly charts the strengths and limits of each for navigating a religiously diverse world.[36] It may serve as a prototype for persons of other traditions. Self-reflexive study of books like it will help us avoid the kind of cheap religious tolerance most clients will quickly detect and find alienating.

As noted earlier, if our religious location includes attitudes of religious superiority or exclusivistic beliefs, those likely pose an insurmountable barrier for clinical work related to religious location. But neither is it sufficient to claim religious tolerance blithely. Rather, long consideration is needed to identify how we tend to adjudicate religious differences and conflicts. As mentioned earlier, mystery is at the heart of my theology, and that core value results in large measure from decades of self-reflexivity about religious plurality. But there are countless alternatives, such as some represented by a metaphor widely used in interreligious dialogue: Are we all climbing the same mountain by different paths? Are we climbing different mountains? Are we all on a path but not all climbing mountains?

It is common that pastoral counselors write statements of belief, sometimes called a credo. These are written as part of our process of ordination, AAPC certification, and/or academic work. Such statements depend in large measure on years of self-reflexivity about our religious location. Of course, they reflect the fruits of our self-reflexivity only at the time of writing and

---

35   Hodge, *Spiritual Assessment.*

36   Paul F. Knitter, *Introducing Theologies of Religions* (Maryknoll, NY: Orbis Books, 2008).

not later developments. Examples of such statements can be found in Grefe and Greider.[37]

Self-Reflexivity Regarding Effects of Our Religious Location on Clients and Clinical Situations

Self-differentiation requires self-reflexivity regarding our relationships. Clinical relationality continuously interweaves our particular religious location with the diverse religious locations of our clients, also with the religious valence of the issues discussed in counseling. Most foundationally, we can detect the relational effects of religious location in our *countertransference*. When Aten discusses his reaction to his white supremacist Odinist client, one of the first questions he poses to himself is, "Why was I having such a strong reaction?"[38] This is an excellent question for all of us!

The following observations illustrate the use of self-reflexivity about my religious location to establish a reliable baseline that helps me identify when my religiously related countertransference is likely fueling my strong reactions in clinical situations: I know Christianity better than any other religious or spiritual location, intellectually and experientially. Therefore, clinically, when relating to Christians, I perceive similarity and difference at very nuanced levels and frequently have strong cognitive and emotional reactions that I am sure are not hidden. With Christians who appear to share my location within Christianity, these countertransferential reactions are usually positive, unless I discover that I misperceived, and then my countertransference quickly cools or turns negative. Negative projections may seem the more problematic aspect of countertransference, causing us to withdraw or become antagonistic. However, even if the countertransference remains positive, it can negatively affect my clinical work. I might, for example, run roughshod over the ambivalence a client, supervisee, or other colleague feels toward his or her religious location.

At a deeper level than mere difference and similarity is the psychospiritual and relational valence associated for me with doctrinal disagreement

---

37　　　Grefe, *Encounters for Change*; Kathleen J. Greider, "Do Justice, Love Kindness, Walk Humbly: A Christian Perspective on Spiritual Care," in *Multifaith Views in Spiritual Care*, ed. Daniel S. Schipani, 85–108 (Kitchener, ON: Pandora, 2013).

38　　　Aten, "Addressing Religious Differences."

about matters such as atonement, sin and salvation, and mission and evangelization. These are important intellectual differences but for me are also laden with experiential memory of painful judgments and exclusion. In the vignette, Luisa's question—"Are you a Christian?"—set off in me a chain reaction of countertransferential remembering that accounted for my having to scramble as I tried to decide how best to respond. By comparison, because I know other religious and spiritual traditions only as an outsider and only at the most superficial levels (if at all), it is relatively easy to show respect for other traditions or to stay composed even when confronted by aspects of other traditions that trouble me. Of course, my religiously related countertransference is made more complex by the transference of others, especially when it is related to their religious location.

The self-reflexivity we carry out concerning our own religious location pays off in another invaluable way as we examine differentials in power and privilege in clinical work. Again, offering my own self-reflexivity as an example, in all clinical situations but especially with clients whose religious location has been assailed by Christians, I strive to be mindful of and responsive to questions like these: How is the cultural dominance of Christianity affecting my clients and clinical work? Is the history of Christians being agents or targets of violence pertinent to this particular client's personal or ancestral religious location? What religious privilege do I have in the clinical relationship, whether because of my close relationship to Christianity or perhaps because of my extensive education in theological and religious studies?

Finally, self-reflexivity about our religious location alerts us to how our religious location(s)—especially our personal beliefs—inform our clinical judgment and the positions we take in clinical work. Worthington et al. offer an illustrative example.[39] They argue that marriage counselors who value "conscientiousness-based virtues" and those who value "warmth-based virtues" will "push" clients in different ways, probably unaware of their values-based bias:[40] "In most marital therapy, the therapist gives little conscious

---

39   Worthington et al., "The Effects of a Therapist's Religion."

40   Everett L. Worthington and Jack W. Berry, "Virtues, Vices, and Character Education," in *Judeo-Christian Perspectives on Psychology: Human Nature, Motivation, and Change,* ed. William R. Miller and Harold D. Delaney, 145–64 (Washington, DC: American Psychological Association, 2005).

attention to the virtues he or she most strongly advocates. Nevertheless, therapists' personal sense of virtue will often shape some of their therapeutic behaviors. Therapists who are oriented toward the conscientiousness-based virtues will likely push couples toward demonstrating truth, responsibility, honesty, and self-control. Therapists who are oriented toward warmth-based virtues will push their clients to manifest forgiveness, compassion, mercy, and sympathy."[41] We may be able to trace the effects of our religious location "backward": What can you learn about your religious location from the values toward which you tend to "push" clients and supervisees?

Self-Reflexivity Regarding Our Limitations and Offsetting Them

Self-reflexivity about our religious location and its effects on clients and clinical work will inevitably confirm that most of us need remedial education if we are to avoid working outside the scope of our practice. It is fortunate that some form of such education can now be accessed online from anywhere in the world. Those of us who want to specialize in working with religion and spirituality can take advantage of degree programs offered by theological schools, whether in pastoral or spiritually integrative counseling or other areas relevant to clinical practice. Certificate programs and ongoing programs of continuing education offer fewer intensive alternatives. Face-to-face (in person or video) supervised clinical education is essential. More immediately, when we have clients in religious locations unfamiliar to us, we treat this like any other clinical issue we encounter that is new to us: We immediately research it, whether through reliable internet or other resources, and/or through consultation.

Also, as with other areas outside our scope of practice, networks of professional collaboration and referral are essential. The clinically certified members of the AAPC comprise a referral and consultation network of clinicians who have expertise relative to religious location; they can be located through the Referral Directory on the AAPC website and through other online directories of clinicians. We also seek consultants from academic settings—for example, faculty at educational institutions that offer accredited

---

41   Worthington et al., "The Effects of a Therapist's Religion," 20.

degree programs in pastoral counseling. We have a supervisor or peer consultation group with whom we work explicitly on self-reflexivity about religious location, as described earlier in this section of the chapter.

Therapeutic Relationality: Connection Amid Religious Difference

Clinical relationship is served by all of the reflections in this chapter. Still, here we will reflect on a few practices that help us address religious location and difference precisely because they do not rely on extensive knowledge about religion. First, meeting constructively amid religious difference encourages more *power sharing*, which may also help offset the negative effects of religious privilege and/or bigotry. For example, it is entirely appropriate to ask clients about their religious location(s), stating explicitly our desire to know about their tradition from their point of view. Aten calls this a "teach me" approach.[42] Although never to be used in lieu of our own research, this is a "perspective shift" during which counselors make themselves students of their clients' religious knowledge and experience.[43] The humility involved in sharing power and in risking a perspective shift may also help relativize our religious privilege and reduce the risk of our religious bigotry. In his case study, Aten describes that, after a period of self-reflexivity, although still repelled by Bill's religious location, he was able to approach his client with questions posed with genuine concern and interest. Aten wisely asked, "How did you come to believe what you believe? Are there significant events in your life that have shaped your religious beliefs? How does your faith impact your life?"[44] Only then did Bill reveal that he had embraced Odinism after being imprisoned as a teen and experiencing physical assault in prison. Bill aligned himself with Odinism because it was the religious location of the dominant white supremacist culture in the prison, which Bill hoped would protect him. This perspective shift did not change Aten's disagreement with Bill, but it seems to have created in Aten some empathic understanding that allowed the clinical work to go forward. The counselor's willingness to yield

---

42   Aten, "Addressing Religious Differences."

43   Aten, "Addressing Religious Differences," 83.

44   Aten, "Addressing Religious Differences," 83.

power by learning from the client seems to have had connective, therapeutic power.

Sharing power is also a valuable practice with regard to assessment amid religious difference. The diversity of religious location as we have been exploring it dramatically relativizes our capacity for accurate clinical assessment. Our assessment of clients' religious location is ethical only insofar as we have adequate education and supervised clinical training in religion. This limitation is greatly offset, however, by the value of clients engaging in their own assessment of their religious location and its effects. Again, calling on clients' greater knowledge of their tradition and their desire to be reflective, we share power by making their assessment at least as important as any we might eventually be able to form. We might ask questions like these: How does your tradition describe well-being and its absence? Are there teachings in your tradition about [the clinical issue]? Are there differing interpretations of that teaching? How do others in your tradition approach [the clinical issue]? How do you assess the influence of your tradition in the ways you are experiencing [the clinical issue]? Sharing the power to assess is not abdication. Rather, our clinical aptitudes allow us to serve as consultants to clients as they seek to grow in understanding of how their religious location both serves and complicates the clinical issues they face.

A second practice that serves us well amid religious difference is that of *language care*, the concept of Bueckert and Schipani mentioned earlier, arguably the bedrock of care amid difference of any kind.[45] Care for language can deepen therapeutic relationality in at least two directions. We care *for* language. We have an interest in what clients say, in the exact words they choose. When clients say they "believe in God" or "don't believe in God," we express interest in their views of "God" and experience of "believing" and not believing. With Luisa, I bring to her use of the words *divorce* and *shame* the same level of attentiveness I bring to her use of the word *suicidal*, gently inquiring to understand more exactly her meanings and range of experiences, embedded in her choice of those specific words. We also care *through* language by trying to use words in common with clients whenever we can do so with integrity. This can be understood as a form of the multilingualism

---

45   Bueckert and Schipani, "Interfaith Spiritual Caregiving."

that deepens therapeutic connection between religiously different clients and counselors. If I strive to learn and speak the language of clients' religious location, although I will often not know what I am saying or may use the language wrongly, my effort will mean a great deal to clients and help our therapeutic relationality to mature.

Finally, therapeutic relationality is served well by allowing differences in our religious locations to *modify the kind of presence we offer* to clients. This practice is more ineffable and thus more difficult to articulate than power sharing and language care. However, arguably its most foundational element is an increased sense of what many religious traditions call *humility*—a modest, unpretentious, unassuming way of engaging. I am not referring to self-debasement, a mere caricature of humility. Mature humility is founded on comprehension of ourselves and our roles in accurate perspective, which serves as a moderating influence that tempers our presence. When we allow for the possibility that there is value in religious locations other than our own, something of value beyond the truth we perceive, our humanness in relating to clients is not equated with or limited to our being the expert. Counselors and clients meet as companions, all seekers relative to life's most perplexing dilemmas. Respect grows beyond mere tolerance or passive acceptance into a kind of *devotion to the integrity of clients' difference* from us. Our willingness to learn from our clients conveys explicitly that we honor them—their religious location and all aspects of their humanness, as we do our own.

Certainly, because we are providing a professional service, for which clients are likely paying a fee, the focus of the relationship remains on the needs of clients. Moreover, we have a *confident* humility with regard to clients' religious locations: We know our competencies and that they are valuable, but we also see them in perspective. Counselors remain ethically responsible guides on this path of seeking. But in clinical situations where religious difference is especially influential, clients sometimes guide, too. We feel just as responsible but not as big and imposing. Our presence is now comfortably relativized alongside clients' knowledge and responsibilities for their own therapeutic work. Both counselor and client have authority and competence.

Consciousness of the extent of religious diversity, the bounds of our expertise, the profound questions and unsolvable paradoxes of clinical work, the ambiguity and mystery of life—consciousness of all this *humanizes* our presence. More consciousness of our limits and thus of our vulnerability lends to our presence greater mutuality and authenticity. In this kind of therapeutic presence, our interactions with clients are tenderized. Counselor and client may feel and show their tears more readily. Both of us can speak more readily of our emotions, uncertainties, of seeking what we have not yet found. We are likely to talk more about transience, transcendence, mortality. In the midst of these acknowledgments, we and our clients may have a sense of awe, the sacred, even holiness.

Indeed, honoring religious difference and acknowledging mystery and inscrutability tend to cultivate in our presence *a quality of reverence,* most definitely a *reverent curiosity* offered to our clients. Reverent curiosity is an outward expression of our devotion to the integrity of clients' difference from us. Reverent curiosity is expressed in noninvasive but determined movement toward connection with clients, especially in areas of existential divergence. It is a gentle inquisitiveness that is brave and motivated enough to move toward our most profound differences with clients, precisely because mystery allows that something of spiritual value may be encountered other than where we are located, other than where we expect to find it. Reverent curiosity does not resolve our differences. It does, however, decenter those differences. It impels us to move especially toward those with whom we disagree vehemently, with a commitment to try to comprehend how another human could value something abhorrent to us. It is a spirit of reverence for the mystery of the difference, not necessarily the difference itself. It enables connection when we cannot afford to be divided by our differences.

This chapter has argued that particularities and differences in religious location are ever present between counselors and clients and, with appropriate attention, can increase the profundity of clinical relationships. The variety of insights and practices explored here suggest that whatever our positions relative to religion, those differences do not have to divide us but can be acknowledged and inquisitively engaged to open up new ways to connect with ourselves and with clients. Clients such as the Butler family and Luisa, professionals such as Joshua and his supervisors, counselors such as Aliyah, myself, and you—we embody different locations relative to religion precisely because we share but have not mastered the human condition.

We meet amid a common existential journey about which we often do not agree. Yet this brief, challenging human existence leaves all of us seekers to one degree or another. Our different religious locations, whatever they are, can serve us well, if we allow them to inform or perhaps even relativize our therapeutic theories and goals. What seems to be only disagreement about religion can turn out also to be agreement that all of us are searching. Our divergences can impel us to search together, for something *more*, perhaps something like wisdom.

Bibliography

American Association of Pastoral Counselors. *Code of Ethics*. April 28, 1994. https://presbyteryofli.com/wp-content/uploads/2016/01/American -Assoc.-of-Pastoral-Counselors-Code-of-Ethics.pdf.

American Counseling Association. *2014 ACA Code of Ethics*. Accessed June 30, 2023. http://www.counseling.org/resources/aca-code-of-ethics.pdf.

American Psychological Association. *Ethical Principles of Psychologists and Code of Conduct*. Accessed June 30, 2023. http://www.apa.org/ethics /code/principles.pdf.

Association for Spiritual, Ethical, and Religious Values in Counseling. *Competencies for Addressing Spiritual and Religious Issues in Counseling*. Accessed June 30, 2023. https://aservic.org/spiritual-and-religious -competencies/.

Aten, Jamie D. "Addressing Religious Differences in Therapy: A Case Study from Behind Bars." *Journal of Psychology and Christianity* 30, no. 1 (2011): 81–84.

Bueckert, Leah Dawn, and Daniel S. Schipani. "Interfaith Spiritual Caregiving: The Case for Language Care." In *Spiritual Caregiving in the Hospital: Windows to Chaplaincy Ministry*, edited by Leah Dawn Bueckert and Daniel S. Schipani, 245–63. Kitchener: Pandora, in association with the Institute of Mennonite Studies, 2006.

Frame, Marsha Wiggins. "The Spiritual Genogram in Family Therapy." *Journal of Marital & Family Therapy* 26, no. 2 (2000): 211–16. https://doi .org/10.1111/j.1752-0606.2000.tb00290.x.

Grefe, Dagmar. *Encounters for Change: Interreligious Cooperation in the Care of Individuals and Communities*. Eugene, OR: Wipf & Stock, 2011.

Greider, Kathleen J. "Do Justice, Love Kindness, Walk Humbly: A Christian Perspective on Spiritual Care." In *Multifaith Views in Spiritual Care*, edited by Daniel S. Schipani, 85–108. Kitchener, ON: Pandora, 2013.

———. "Religiously Plural Persons: Multiplicity and Care of Souls. In *Pastoralpsychologie und Religionspsychologie im Dialog* [*Pastoral Psychology and Psychology of Religion in Dialogue*], edited by Isabelle Noth, Christoph Morgenthaler, and Kathleen J. Greider, 119–35. Stuttgart: Kohlhammer, 2011.

Hanada, Julie Chijo. "'Listening to the Dharma': Integrating Buddhism into a Multifaith Health Care Environment." In *Buddhist Care for the Dying and Bereaved*, edited by Jonathan S. Watts and Yoshiharu Tomatsu, 249–69. Boston: Wisdom, 2012.

Hill, Peter C., and Todd W. Hall. "Relational Schemas in Processing One's Image of God and Self." *Journal of Psychology and Christianity* 21, no. 4 (2002): 365–73.

Hodge, David R. *Spiritual Assessment: Handbook for Helping Professionals.* Palos Heights, IL: North American Association of Christians in Social Work, 2003.

Knitter, Paul F. *Introducing Theologies of Religions.* Maryknoll, NY: Orbis Books, 2008.

McIntosh, Peggy. *White Privilege and Male Privilege: A Personal Account of Coming to See Correspondences Through Work in Women's Studies.* Working paper 189, Wellesley Center for Research on Women, 1988.

Negy, Charles, and Christopher J. Ferguson. "Religious Bigotry: The Neglected 'ism' in Multicultural Psychology and Therapy." In *Cross-cultural Psychotherapy: Toward a Critical Understanding of Diverse Clients*, edited by Charles Negy, 61–73. Reno, NV: Bent Tree Press, 2004.

Onedera, Jill D., ed. *The Role of Religion in Marriage and Family Counseling.* New York: Routledge, 2008.

Onedera, Jill D., and Brian C. Greenwalt. "Introduction to Religion and Marriage and Family Counseling." In Onedera, *Role of Religion*, 3–13.

Prothero, Stephen. *God is Not One: The Eight Rival Religions That Run the World—And Why Their Differences Matter.* New York: HarperCollins, 2010.

Schlosser, Lewis Z. "Christian Privilege: Breaking a Sacred Taboo." *Journal of Multicultural Counseling and Development* 31, no. 1 (2003): 44–51. https://doi.org/10.1002/j.2161-1912.2003.tb00530.x.

United States Commission on International Religious Freedom. *Annual Report of the U.S. Commission on International Religious Freedom.* April 2013. https://www.uscirf.gov/sites/default/files/resources/2013%20USCIRF%20Annual%20Report%20(2).pdf.

Walsh, Froma. "Spiritual Diversity: Multifaith Perspectives in Family Therapy." *Family Process* 49, no. 3 (2010): 330–48. https://doi.org/10.1111/j.1545-5300.2010.01326.x.

Worthington, Everett L., and Jack W. Berry. "Virtues, Vices, and Character Education." In *Judeo-Christian Perspectives on Psychology: Human Nature, Motivation, and Change*, edited by William R. Miller and Harold D. Delaney, 145–64. Washington, DC: American Psychological Association, 2005.

Worthington, Everett L., Joshua N. Hook, Nathaniel G. Wade, Andrea J. Miller, and Constance B. Sharp. "The Effects of a Therapist's Religion on the Marriage Therapist and Marriage Counseling." In Onedera, *Role of Religion* 17–34.

❦ 2 ❦

THE PRACTICE OF RELATIONAL-ETHICAL PASTORAL CARE

An Intercultural Approach

CARRIE DOEHRING

THE PURPOSE OF this chapter is to outline an intercultural approach to pastoral care based on the relational ethics of Emmanuel Levinas. I will describe this intercultural approach as a three-part process. First, spiritual care professionals must be able to use a comparative approach to religion that highlights what is different about each person's religious faith—the "strangeness of the Other, his irreducibility to the I, to my thoughts and possessions,"[1] such that "the absolutely foreign [aspects of those seeking care] can instruct us."[2] Second, spiritual care professionals must cultivate a critical self-awareness of who they are spiritually and theologically, so that they do not unwittingly impose their religious meaning-making and practices on those seeking care. Such self-reflexivity and other-awareness will decenter spiritual care professionals and reveal the care seeker as stranger and "other" in the *infini* (infinity), such that "the epiphany of the face as face opens up humanity."[3] When this remarkable relational space opens up, the third and culminating moment of intercultural care is possible. This is when spiritual care professionals and care seekers search for contextual provisional meanings and ways of experiencing holiness. As I elaborate this process, I will

---

1   Emmanuel Levinas, *Totality and Infinity: An Essay on Exteriority*, trans. Alphonso Lingis (Pittsburgh: Duquesne University Press, 1969), 43.

2   Emmanuel Levinas, *Otherwise Than Being or Beyond Essence*, trans. Alphonso Lingis (The Hague: Martinus Nijhoff, 1981), 207.

3   Emmanuel Levinas, "The Temptation of Temptation," trans. Annette Aronowicz, in *Nine Talmudic Readings*, ed. Emmanuel Levinas (Bloomington: Indiana University Press, 1990), 234.

highlight how the relational ethics of Emmanuel Levinas informs this intercultural approach to pastoral care.

Using a Phenomenological Comparative Approach that Respects Difference

Levinas's description of Western philosophy can be transposed upon Western theologies, to highlight how spiritual care professionals unwittingly impose religious meanings and interpretations on others: "Western philosophy has most often been an ontology: a reduction of the other to the same by interposition of a middle and neutral term that ensures comprehension of being."[4] Ontology is used as a way of "apprehending the individual (which alone exists) not in its individuality but in its generality."[5] The temptation of knowledge, described by Levinas as the temptation of temptation, "will no longer leave the other in its otherness but always include it in its whole . . . From this stems the inability to recognize the other person as other person, as outside all calculation, as neighbor, as first come."[6]

One of the ways in which spiritual care professionals and, more generally, members of religious communities have "reduced the other to the same" is in the theological or universalistic comparative approach they take to religions other than their own. Spiritual care professionals who simply use their theology to interpret the care seeker's narrative, practices, and meaning systems may believe in an exclusivist way that their meaning system is the only true meaning system. In an inclusivist theological approach that seemingly embraces the "truth" of all religious faiths, spiritual care professionals assume that all other meaning systems can be translated into their meaning system—for example, that everyone is an unconscious Christian whether they realize it or not.

When spiritual care professionals use this comparative approach covertly (without conscious awareness) they can easily end up submerging the other person's religious faith within their own. Paden noted, "Spiritual care-givers all tend naturally to reduce areas of [a care receiver's] life to certain

---

4   Levinas, *Totality and Infinity*, 43.

5   Levinas, *Totality and Infinity*, 44.

6   Levinas, "The Temptation of Temptation," 35.

uses that fit their own worldview."[7] Given the coercive and violent history of Christianity's participation in colonialism, spiritual care professionals need to be aware of the implicit comparative method underlying their practices of care, lest they colonize the religious or spiritual world of those who are not Christians. Levinas's experience of anti-Semitism made him acutely aware of the potential for violence when differences are not acknowledged. "According to Levinas, the core of racism consists not in the denial of, or failure to appreciate, similarities between people, but in the denial of, or better said, failure to appreciate and value, people's differences, or better still, the fundamental and irreducible otherness by which they fall outside of every genre and are thus 'unique.'"[8]

Levinas's use of the ethical imperative "Thou shalt not kill" continually reminds spiritual care professionals that failure to value difference can and has been part of insidious and horrifically overt webs of violence that desecrate that which is holy: the "other" that spiritual care professionals encounter when they recognize the differences between their religious faith and a care seeker's. "Caring for persons through the language we use, as well as caring for language itself, especially by being attentive to the significance of the exact words used by our clients, goes a long way toward acknowledging and bridging the gaps frequently caused by religious difference."[9]

In order to offer care that respects and does not erase the otherness of a care seeker's religious faith, spiritual care professionals need to pay attention to the differences between the unique religious, spiritual, and existential meaning systems and practices that each person constructs out of her or his various relational matrices. Practical theologian Elaine Graham called this a phenomenological approach to the ways each person practices their beliefs

---

7   William E. Paden, *Religious Worlds: The Comparative Study of Religion*, 2nd ed. (Boston: Beacon, 1994), 2.

8   Roger Burggraeve, "Violence and the Vulnerable Face of the Other: The Vision of Emmanuel Levinas on Moral Evil and Our Responsibility," *Journal of Social Philosophy* 30, no. 1 (1999): 29, https://doi.org/10.1111/0047-2786.t01-1-00003.

9   Kathleen J. Greider, "Religious Location and Counseling: Engaging Diversity and Difference in Views of Religion," in *Understanding Pastoral Counseling*, ed. Elizabeth A. Maynard and Jill L. Snodgrass (New York: Springer, 2015), 238.

and values in unique ways. Comparative theologians call this a particularist approach to religions in the world:

> *Thus, particularistic theologians state that the differences between the ethics of the religions are substantial and they question the value of global ethical declarations. Of course, one might say that all religions are for peace, love, hope, justice, human dignity and the protection of animals. However, these very formal notions and concepts come to mean very different things within each tradition. The stories, rituals and doctrines of each tradition give particular continence to each of these formal ethical terms, and at the level of the concrete religious and ethical praxis of the religious communities the differences are immense.*[10]

The term *religious world*, coined by William Paden in his comparative studies of religion, can be used to describe each person's religious faith as a habitat, "a system of language and practice that organizes the world in terms of what is deemed sacred."[11] From a relational perspective, we can understand each person's religious world as a syncretistic compilation of multiple religious and spiritual symbols, beliefs, and schema, all generated out of the web of relationships in which they are embedded. Bourdieu's concept of *habitus* as "embodied history, internalized as a second nature"[12] can be used to describe such religious practices. "Bourdieu is presenting a model of tradition and continuity by which the values of the past are encoded in social life yet continually evolve. . . . [Similarly] Christians [can be described] as participating in and reshaping a living faith through their contemporary practices of worship, care, and social concern."[13]

---

10   Marianne Moyaert, "Interreligious Dialogue and the Debate Between Universalism and Particularism: Searching for a Way Out of the Deadlock," *Studies in Interreligious Dialogue* 15, no. 1 (2005): 44, https://doi.org/10.2143/SID.15.1.583340.

11   William E. Paden, "Theaters of World-Making Behaviors: Panhuman Contexts for Comparative Religion," in *Comparing Religions: Possibilities and Perils?*, ed. Thomas Athanasius Idinopulos, Brian C. Wilson, and James Constantine Hanges (Boston: Brill, 2006), 10.

12   Pierre Bourdieu, *The Logic of Practice* (London: Routledge, 1992), 56.

13   Elaine Graham, Heather Walton, and Frances Ward, *Theological Reflection: Methods* (New York: SCM, 2005), 194.

Often the only way to identify what is in one's religious world is to dialogue with others (through reading and conversations) about one's practices. Here religion, spirituality, and theology are understood as performative knowledge rather than propositional knowledge, and praxis as the way in which communities and persons embody and enact their beliefs. The intercultural spiritual care process I describe follows Elaine Graham's inductive method of critical phenomenology.[14] This method begins with dialogue that identifies the concrete experiential theology that persons and communities enact in their practices. Intercultural spiritual care becomes an occasion for constructing a public critical account of the faith claims embedded in practices.

For those of us raised in individualistic Western cultures, we experience our religious world as a bounded set of beliefs, values, practices, and stories. When someone asks us to describe our spiritual journey, it is as if they have invited themselves into our spiritual or religious home. To us it feels as if there is a clear boundary demarking this highly personal religious world we have constructed over time. However, it is often the outsider who can see how much the various relational matrices in which we are embedded (our family of origin, formative relationships generated in life-giving, life-limiting, and life-threatening encounters, relationships within communities of faith, etc.) continually engage us in an ongoing process of world-making. As Paden noted, "To the inhabitant, the world is a singular experience and has an absoluteness; to the observer, it is an instance of common processes of construction and function."[15] What we identify as self-contained meaning systems are, in Paden's words, "Worlds [that] are the ever-changing precipitates of process of selection and transmission by which individuals chose imagined continuities from the past and versions of the past that applied to the present."[16] While the term *religious world* helps us visualize the uniqueness of each person's religious faith and spirituality, it doesn't help us appreciate how religious worlds are continually constructed and reconstructed within relational matrices, and not "within" a person's mind. For this reason,

---

14   Elaine Graham, *Transforming Practice: Pastoral Theology in an Age of Uncertainty* (New York: Mowbray, 1996).

15   Paden, "Theaters of World-Making Behaviors," 62.

16   Paden, "Theaters of World-Making Behaviors," 63.

I prefer a related, somewhat cumbersome term coined by Paden—*religious world-making*—to describe this ongoing process of putting into practice the religious and spiritual meanings and values formed out of these relational matrices.

A phenomenological approach to comparing the religious world-making of spiritual care professionals and care seekers utilizes various aspects of postmodern approaches to knowledge:

- a perspectival understanding of religious knowledge as socially constructed
- reflexivity that allows one to deliberate "on a given construction of the world from multiple, diverging standpoints"[17]
- an appreciation for the performative and constructive nature of theology

Spiritual care professionals may hesitate to use this comparative approach because of its postmodern orientation. Postmodern approaches to religious knowledge seem at first to open a deep fissure between first order religious expressions that imply universal faith claims (like confessions of faith, liturgies, prayers, and hymns) and second order languages that provide critical perspectives on religious sources of authority (like theological, historical, and biblical critical perspectives) used within their community of learning at graduate school. When spiritual care professionals experience the liberating possibilities of postmodern approaches to religious knowledge, then it can seem as though the same fissure separates them from communities of faith that most often use precritical first order religious language. This fissure or gap can be bridged, however, when they practice spiritual care using a relational ethic. Students can learn how to establish relationships in which they step into the precritical religious language used within the community of faith, appreciating the psychological, spiritual, and communal need to act as if this shared language points to transhistorical and universal religious truths.

It can be reassuring for spiritual care professionals to realize that in most contexts, people continually shift back and forth among what could be

---

17   Kenneth J. Gergen, *Therapeutic Realities: Collaboration, Oppression and Relational Flow* (Chagin Falls, OH: Taos Institute, 2006), 183.

called premodern, modern, and postmodern approaches to knowledge—for example, from precritical or premodern approaches to religious knowledge to modern approaches to scientific knowledge. Using the metaphor of trifocal lenses, I suggest that spiritual care professionals use the lens of premodern approaches to religious knowledge to assess whether people are yearning for an immediate sense of God's presence or a sense of holiness in a precritical way similar to how God was experienced in the premodern traditions of Christianity. Spiritual care professionals can help members of Muslim, Jewish, or Christian faith traditions use a modern lens when they are ready to turn to the Koran, the Hebrew Bible, or the New Testament for help in meaning making; they can be encouraged to think critically about how this source of authority can help them make sense of their lives. Modern psychological approaches to understanding how people use religion to cope with stress can also be helpful in using an evidence-based approach to spiritual care[18] that assesses when someone's religious world-making is correlated with stress-related spiritual and psychological growth or struggles.[19]

In the long-term process of helping people make sense of what is happening to them, spiritual care professionals can assess when people are ready to use a postmodern lens to appreciate the contextual and provisional nature of knowledge, including knowledge of God and that which is experienced as holy. This postmodern lens brings into view the importance of intrinsically meaningful religious and spiritual experiences that emerge from the particular cultural, communal, and family narratives of people.[20]

---

18   Carrie Doehring, "Military Moral Injury: An Evidence-Based and Intercultural Approach to Spiritual Care," *Pastoral Psychology* 68, no. 1 (2019): 15–30, https://doi.org/10.1007/s11089-018-0813-5.

19   Kenneth Pargament, *Spiritually Integrated Psychotherapy: Understanding and Addressing the Sacred* (New York: Guilford, 2007); Kenneth Pargament, Serena Wong, and Julie Exline, "Wholeness and Holiness: The Spiritual Dimension of Eudaimonics," in *The Handbook of Eudaimonic Well-being*, ed. Joar Vittersø, 379–94 (Cham, Switzerland: Springer International, 2016).

20   Carrie Doehring, *The Practice of Pastoral Care: A Postmodern Approach*, rev. ed. (Louisville, KY: Westminster John Knox, 2015); Carrie Doehring, "Searching for Wholeness Amidst Traumatic Grief: The Role of Spiritual Practices That Reveal Compassion in Embodied, Relational, and Transcendent Ways," *Pastoral Psychology* 68, no. 3 (2019): 241–59, https://doi.org/10.1007/s11089-018-0858-5.

Theological Reflexivity

In order to utilize an intercultural approach to understand the differences between their religious meaning-making and the meaning-making of others, spiritual care professionals need to have a critical awareness of who they are, culturally and theologically. They need to have resources, relationships, and communities of discourse and accountability that help them critically reflect upon the habitual qualities of their social location and religious world-making which will be unwittingly used as a lens to interpret the religious world-making of those seeking care. A religious and theological education and academic community provide them initially with relational ways of identifying and reflecting upon the spiritual and religious beliefs and practices embedded in their religious world-making since childhood, shaped by their experience of social privileges and disadvantages,[21] and the layers of meanings and practices that have accrued over a lifetime. "Our religious location is but one of—and also always dynamically interacting with—our complex cultural identity as a whole, which includes all aspects of our identity, such as personality, age, sexuality, economic status, gender, ethnicity and race, nationality, and first language."[22] Reflecting critically on the relational matrices that shape their religious world-making can help them identify how they may be using embedded theologies that potentially marginalize or dehumanize others or even themselves.

Their theological education and community of scholars and practitioners thus equip spiritual care professionals to pay attention to what is going on in their religious world-making by monitoring and evaluating theologically whether the religious symbols and practices that are activated under stress are truly life-giving for them in their current context. In order to provide spiritual care that does not violate the other, they have to develop this relational and communal capacity to understand and monitor what is going on in their religious world-making. Without such communal

---

21   Nancy J. Ramsay, "Resisting Asymmetries of Power: Intersectionality as a Resource for Practices of Care," *Journal of Pastoral Theology* 27, no. 2 (2017): 83–97, https://doi.org/10.1080/10649867.2017.1399784.

22   Greider, "Religious Location and Counseling," 236.

critical reflection, spiritual care professionals risk functioning in theologically naïve ways. Such naïveté is common now among health practitioners without any formal or informal theological education who practice at the intersection of health and spirituality, and who unwittingly impose their spiritual or religious world-making on others because they are not using second order language or participating in a community of theological accountability.[23]

Figure 2.1 visually depicts the process of spiritual integration and theological reflexivity. Spiritual care professionals need to be committed to their own process of spiritual integration. At the heart of integration are body-aware spiritual practices revealing compassion and benevolence in embodied, relational, and transcendent ways that help people search for meanings that are flexible, integrated, and complex enough to bear the weight of their suffering.[24] For example, meditative practices from Buddhist traditions help practitioners compassionately become aware of bodily stress and stress-related emotions, such as anxiety, shame, guilt, or anger. Contemplative practices from theistic traditions help practitioners experience God's compassionate presence in the midst of stress and stress-related emotions. Intentionally using such practices can increase awareness of how stress and related emotions generate a lived theology/orienting system of values, beliefs, and coping shaped by intersecting social systems that often reflect racist, classist, and sexist social systems.

Using spiritual practices to become more compassionately aware of stress opens up possibilities for more integrated and complex theologies of particular kinds of stress grounded in embodied and relational goodness.[25] Beliefs, for example, that we suffer because we are not smart enough or we don't work hard enough link experiences of suffering with

---

23   Carrie Doehring, "Theological Accountability: The Hallmark of Pastoral Counseling," *Sacred Spaces* 1, no. 1 (2009): 4–34.

24   Doehring, "Searching for Wholeness."

25   Carrie Doehring, "Resilience as the Relational Ability to Spiritually Integrate Moral Stress," *Pastoral Psychology* 64, no. 5 (2015): 635–49, https://doi.org/10.1007/s11089-015-0643-7; Carrie Doehring, "Systemically Exploring Student Debt: Methodological Challenges for Pastoral Theology," *Pastoral Psychology* 65, no. 5 (2016): 631–41, https://doi.org/10.1007/s11089-016-0696-2.

judgmental beliefs about aspects of our social identity such as gender, race, and class.

The box in the center represents an ongoing process of searching for meaning and putting into practice religious values and beliefs, using myself as an example. I have identified four primary relational matrices engaged in this process of religious worldmaking that arise out of ongoing "conversations" within these four matrices. The upper quadrants represent the relational matrices I have internalized from my formative years. The "conversations" I have, for example, within my family of origin are largely internal and unconscious. These conversations often put into practice an embedded theology[26] expressed in first order religious language statements about religious beliefs.[27]

The upper right-hand quadrant represents relationships formed when I first critically engaged my childhood religion and soon began theological studies in 1975. These relationships gave me initial ways to deliberate over this embedded theology through the second order religious languages of biblical critical and theological studies.

The lower quadrants represent ongoing matrices active in my life now. Participating in my community of faith (lower left hand quadrant)

---

26   *Embedded religion* is a term used to describe the implicit beliefs, values, and practices we live out in our everyday lives, as discussed in Howard W. Stone and James O. Duke, *How to Think Theologically*, 3rd ed. (Minneapolis: Fortress, 2013). They are so woven into our habitual ways of viewing the world and understanding peoples' lives that they are not even aware of them. The process of examining embedded beliefs engages people in the work of deliberative religion. They begin to examine critically which of their beliefs and practices are meaningful to them as adults.

27   Jennings used the terms *first, second, and third order religious language* to make distinctions among expressions of religious faith, critical reflections on religious faith, and reflections on methodology (for example, methods of relating different disciplinary perspectives to each other and to the practice of care), as discussed in Theodore W. Jennings, "Pastoral Theological Methodology," in *Dictionary of Pastoral Care and Counseling*, ed. Rodney J. Hunter, 862–64 (Nashville: Abingdon, 1990). Gergen made a similar distinction between first order morality ("the potential for all relations to generate moral goods. . . . generating first order commitment to the good") and second order morality ("a non-foundational ethic for sustaining the very possibility of co-creating the good") as cited in Kenneth J. Gergen, *Relational Being: Beyond Self and Community* (New York: Oxford University Press, 2002), 354.

provides a context for me to engage in religious worldmaking where I can experience a "second naïveté"[28] such that, for moments during communal worship, it is as if my religious world-making is wholly true for me. I can express my religious beliefs and experiences in first order language, realizing that such beliefs are true for me in the moment. The lower right-hand corner represents my ongoing communities of theological accountability, which include the ongoing reading and scholarly work I do in religious and theological studies. These relationships help me continually assess whether the religious and theological meanings constructed in my religious world-making and lived out in my practices are part of lifegiving, life-limiting, or violent relational webs.

Over the years I have tried to identify the ways in which the values, beliefs, and practices through which I connect with a sense of holiness are shaped by these relational matrices. For example, the "default" way I react to particular kinds of stress is with anxiety, guilt, and/or shame that generates a moralistic theology in which suffering is a consequence of my wrong doing. When I am able to use spiritual practices, I can be aware of this stress response and hold it in love.

---

28   Ricoeur distinguished primitive naïveté from second naïveté: "If we can no longer live the great symbols of the sacred in accordance with the original belief in them, we can, we modern men [and women], aim at a second naïveté in and through criticism. In short, it is by *reinterpreting* that we can *hear* again," as cited in Paul Ricoeur, *The Symbolism of Evil*, trans. Emerson Buchanan (New York: Harper & Row, 1967), 352. "I believe that [the holy] can still speak to me—no longer, of course, under the precritical form of immediate belief, but as the second immediacy aimed at by hermeneutics. This second naïveté aims to be the post critical equivalent of the precritical hierophany," as cited in Ricoeur, *The Symbolism of Evil*, 352. Ricoeur's notion of a second naïveté has been taken up by biblical critical scholars, even after Ricoeur himself abandoned this idea, as discussed in Patrick Vandermeersch, "The Failure of Second Naiveté: Some Landmarks in the History of French Psychology of Religion," in *Aspects in Contexts: Studies in the History of Psychology of Religion*, ed. Jacob A. Belzen, 235–79 (Atlanta: Rodopi, 2000). Zygmunt Bauman highlighted how "postmodernity can be seen as restoring to the world what modernity, presumptuously, had taken away from it; as a *re-enchantment* of the world that modernity tried hard to *disenchant*," as cited in Zygmunt Bauman, *Intimations of Postmodernity* (London: Routledge, 1992), x.

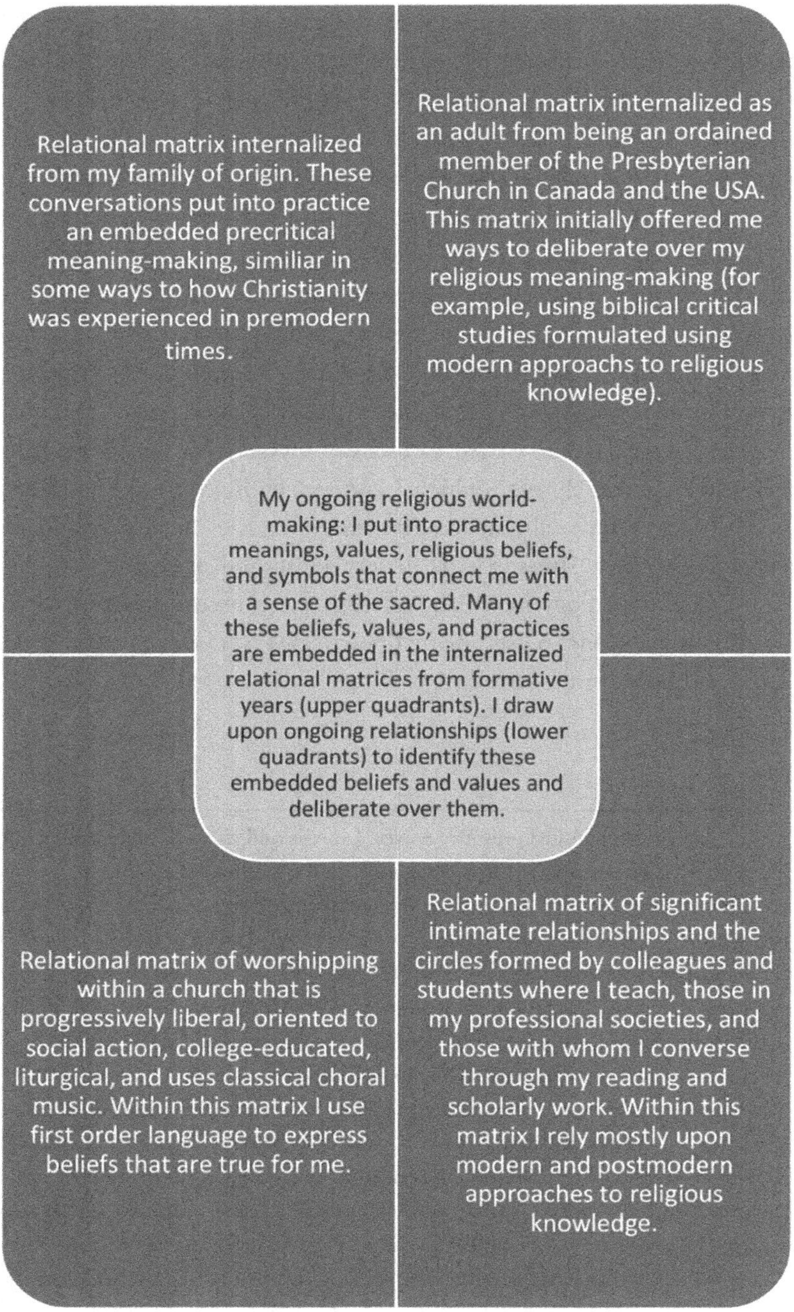

Relational matrix internalized from my family of origin. These conversations put into practice an embedded precritical meaning-making, similiar in some ways to how Christianity was experienced in premodern times.

Relational matrix internalized as an adult from being an ordained member of the Presbyterian Church in Canada and the USA. This matrix initially offered me ways to deliberate over my religious meaning-making (for example, using biblical critical studies formulated using modern approachs to religious knowledge).

My ongoing religious world-making: I put into practice meanings, values, religious beliefs, and symbols that connect me with a sense of the sacred. Many of these beliefs, values, and practices are embedded in the internalized relational matrices from formative years (upper quadrants). I draw upon ongoing relationships (lower quadrants) to identify these embedded beliefs and values and deliberate over them.

Relational matrix of worshipping within a church that is progressively liberal, oriented to social action, college-educated, liturgical, and uses classical choral music. Within this matrix I use first order language to express beliefs that are true for me.

Relational matrix of significant intimate relationships and the circles formed by colleagues and students where I teach, those in my professional societies, and those with whom I converse through my reading and scholarly work. Within this matrix I rely mostly upon modern and postmodern approaches to religious knowledge.

Figure 2.1 The Process of Spiritual Integration and Theological Reflexivity

Dwelling with the Other

Using a phenomenological comparative approach, spiritual care professionals will more likely experience the otherness of the religious world-making of those seeking care. Their self-awareness about the relational matrices in which their own religious world-making is embedded will help spiritual care professionals identify their usual horizons of meaning. These approaches to the care seeker's and their own religious world-making will help them transcend habitual ways of thinking about their own and the care seeker's religious world-making, so that these are not imposed on the pastoral care encounter in life-limiting or violent ways. Using these approaches and practices, spiritual care professionals are more likely to become immersed in the moment of immediacy that occurs before the presence of reflective and categorical "thought."[29] As Diedrich, Burggraeve, and Gastmans so eloquently noted, "It is in this moment that the other is, or can be, before me in and of herself. Levinas describes this moment as coming into contact with the *face of the other.* . . . The face is a living, naked presence. . . . This immediate moment of coming into contact with the face is a moment of transcendence, a kind of deliverance, if you will, from the ordinary structures of being."[30] In other words, spiritual care professionals will use these forms of reflective and categorical thought—a phenomenological comparative approach and theological self-awareness—in order to transcend the categories of thought that usually inhibit their experience of the care seeker's otherness. By not imposing their own religious world-making on others and by recognizing the otherness of the religious world-making of those seeking care, spiritual care professionals open themselves up to the alterity of the care seeker's religious world-making.

This opening up of oneself to the other arises from a radical recognition that this obligation to and responsibility for the other comes first. This is a relational way of understanding the very nature of what it means to be human, and the ways in which to be human is to be in these kinds of caring

---

29   W. W. Diedrich, Roger Burggraeve, and Chris Gastmans, "A Dialogue Between the Thoughts of Joan Tronto and Emmanuel Levinas," *Ethical Perspectives: Journal of the European Ethics Network* 13, no. 1 (2006): 42.

30   Diedrich, Burggraeve, and Gastmans, "A Dialogue Between the Thoughts," 42–43.

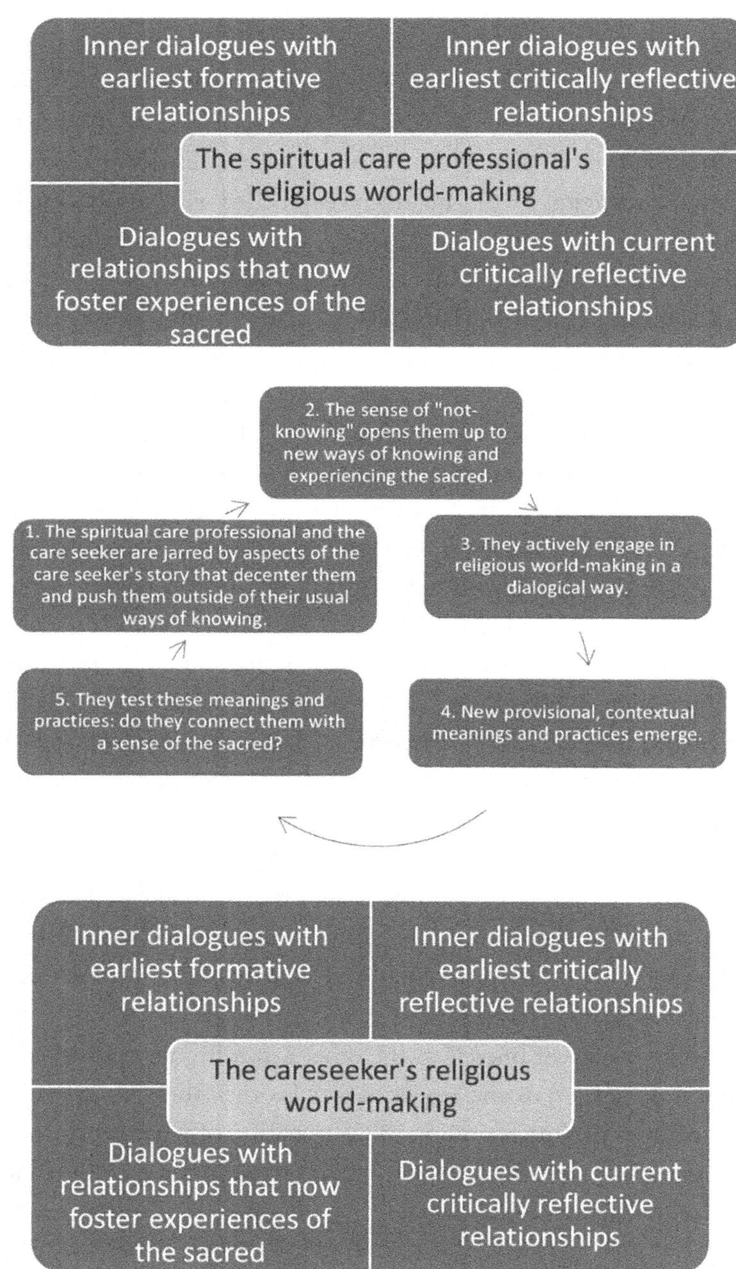

Figure 2.2 Interaction Between Spiritual Care Professional's and Care Seeker's Religious World-Making

relationships: "To say 'the self is for-the-other' does not mean that first there is a self and then this self becomes 'for-the-other,' but rather that insofar as the self is for-the-other it is itself. Its original way of being is moral."[31] This unconditional ethical responsibility is called goodness by Levinas; it is "neither naive or trivial, but rather the difficult struggle, never with obvious victory, to overcome racism and anti-Semitism, the most extreme forms of moral evil."[32] For spiritual care professionals, the moment when they surrender to their ethical responsibility for the other has theological meanings. "The other stands in a position over me because the other is that person who pulls me out of myself, which effects transcendence. The other stands above me as the only one who offers an alternative to dwelling within the labyrinthine circuits of my own interiority."[33]

Such transcendence allows spiritual care professionals to experience both the radical otherness of the one seeking care and the radical Otherness of whatever they name as transcendent: God or holiness. This transcendence and experience of alterity creates a relational space in which contextual provisional meanings and ways of experiencing holiness can be co-created, as represented in Figure 2.2. I have depicted the way the religious world-making processes of spiritual care professional and care seeker interact. I have described this interaction using an action-reflection-action method of theological reflection, paraphrasing the way pastoral theologian Loren Townsend described this method.[34]

In what follows, I will develop a brief case study that illustrates this intercultural approach to pastoral care, using the 2003 Québécois film *Les Invasions Barbares*, directed and written by Denys Arcand.[35]

---

31   Richard A. Cohen, "Maternal Psyche," in *Psychology for the Other: Levinas, Ethics, and the Practice of Psychology*, ed. Edwin E. Gantt and Richard N. Williams (Pittsburgh: Duquesne University Press, 2002), 42.

32   David A. Boileau, "Preface," in *The Wisdom of Love in the Service of Love: Emmanuel Levinas on Justice, Peace and Human Rights*, ed. Roger Burggraeve (Milwaukee: Marquette University Press, 2002), 18.

33   Diedrich, Burggraeve, and Gastmans, "A Dialogue Between the Thoughts," 50.

34   Loren Townsend, *Introduction to Pastoral Counseling* (Nashville: Abingdon, 2009), 140.

35   The film takes its title from a scene that replays news footage of the planes crashing into the twin towers on September 11, followed by footage from a commentary by

An Illustration

Les Invasions Barbares can be used to provide a lively case study of how a Roman Catholic chaplain in a *Montréal* hospital, Sister Constance Lazarre, offers pastoral care to Rémy, a terminally ill man in his fifties. In addition, a relationship that Rémy has with a young woman named Nathalie offers a form of what we could call existential care. These caregiving relationships provide relational opportunities for Rémy to engage in existential world-making that help him approach death.

Rémy was educated by the Jesuits in a pre-Vatican II era in Québec and then entered young adulthood during Québec's quiet revolution in the mid-1960s. This was a time when many young intellectuals, drawing upon the rigors of their Jesuit education, were catapulted from the kind of premodern religiosity that typified the Duplessis-era[36] in Québec into the beginnings of postmodern intellectualism. Rémy has been a history professor, and he and many of his circle of friends and colleagues have adopted a philosophically skeptical attitude to life. In one humorous scene, Rémy and his friends take turns chanting a list of ideologies they have fervently adopted:

> *We've been everything. . . . At first we were existentialists. We*
> *read Sartre and Camus. Then [reading] Fanon, we became*
> *anticolonialists. We read Marcuse and became Marxists. Marxists-*
> *Leninists. Trotskyites. Maoists. After Solzhenitsyn we changed. We*

Quebec historian Alain Lussier who says that the terrorists "struck at the heart of the Empire. In previous conflicts—Korea, Vietnam, the Gulf War—the Empire managed to keep the barbarians outside its gates, its borders. In that sense people may look back at 9/11, and I stress may, as the beginning of the great barbarian invasion." In the film, Remy also alludes to his cancer and approaching death as a kind of barbarian invasion. In his final moment of life, as he drifts into a heroin-induced coma clutching his son's hands, he murmurs, "The barbarians are coming."

36   Maurice Duplessis was Quebec's premier from 1936 to 1939 and 1944 to 1959, a period of Quebec's history now known as *La Grande Noirceur* ("The Great Darkness"), in part because of the Duplessis Orphans (*les Orphelins de Duplessis*)—several thousand orphaned children (often of unwed mothers) who were falsely certified as mentally ill by the provincial government in order to receive federal funds. Many of them were raised in psychiatric institutions.

> *were structuralists, situationists, feminists, deconstructionists. Is there an "ism" we haven't worshipped?*

Rémy describes himself as a sensual socialist, since he enjoyed and took advantage of the sexual revolution of the 1960s and 1970s by having sexual relationships with colleagues and students. As Arcand portrayed in the 1986 movie with this same cast of characters (*Le Déclin de l'Empire Américain*), Rémy enjoyed wine, women, and intellectual banter to excess.

The pastoral care conversations with Constance depicted in the movie illustrate the complex relationship they develop, which includes challenging, humorous, enraged, sorrowful, and intensely caring exchanges. The first two conversations the viewer sees have jarring qualities. The first occurs when the chaplain arrives bearing the sacrament of communion. She addresses Rémy by the wrong name and before she can offer communion, Rémy remonstrates, saying that he is not who she thinks he is. Constance apologizes. She complains that her computer list of Roman Catholic patients is often wrong and then she introduces herself to Rémy as Constance Lazare. He introduces the woman at his bedside as Louise, his wife. Constance offers a consoling word to Louise, saying that it must be hard having her husband in the hospital. Louise is quick to correct Constance's image of her as the distraught and devoted wife, saying that she threw Rémy out fifteen years ago. In the next breath she says she really doesn't care whether he is in the hospital or having sex with one of his co-ed students. Rémy retorts that his current sexual partner isn't one of his students; she is the student of a colleague. A heated argument erupts between them, with Louise using sexually explicit language to describe Rémy's sexual misconduct with his students. The chaplain looks surprised and quickly bids farewell, saying, "I best continue my rounds! Have a good day!" Rémy cheerily responds, "You, too Sister."

In this first encounter, Rémy and Louise vigorously jar various images the chaplain has of them. Rémy is not a terminally ill Catholic patient requesting the sacrament. Louise's suffering as Rémy's wife at this moment has less to do with his cancer and more to do with his sexual promiscuity with his students and colleagues. It is if they are saying, "Welcome to our worlds and the ways in which we are living with terminal cancer." It would be easy for this chaplain to conclude that this kind of welcome is a way for Rémy and Louise to close the door to further conversations.

As viewers we don't know what happens between this first conversation and the next one we see. We can only conclude that the chaplain has had enough conversations that she is now the one who challenges Rémy. In her opening salvo she declares that he is lucky to have such a caring son and that not many sons remain at their parents' bedsides. She asks Rémy about how he cared for his father when he was hospitalized at the end of his life. Did he visit? Rémy shrugs and protests that his father lived in Chicoutimi and he was in Montreal, about eighty miles away. The chaplain is quick to "remind" Rémy pointedly that his son has come from London, England, to care for him. With a steely look she asks whether coming from London and coming from Chicoutimi are the same thing, and whether he is becoming confused. Rémy looks chagrined. In this conversation it is the chaplain who jars Rémy's existential world in order to see if Rémy can break out of his negative stereotypes of his son as an Americanized capitalist and see him in a new light.

These two conversations suggest that Rémy and the chaplain are honest with each other by disclosing what is going on in their religious or existential world-making. In Rémy's existential world-making, he is living out a legacy of sexualizing relationships with students and experiencing the impact of this behavior on his wife and son. His ideologies, which lead him to dismiss his son as a capitalist, are blinding him to the quality of his son's caring. The disclosure of this kind of meaning-making going on in Rémy's world is jarring for the chaplain. She hangs in there with him, jarring him with her religious world-making, and the sense she makes of complex father-son relationships.

The third conversation we see occurs after Rémy has found out that his cancer is inoperable. His son wants to bring Rémy to a hospital in Baltimore where Rémy can receive the best possible care. Rémy refuses to go, shouting ideologies about socialized medicine and castigating his son's kind of caring. Later that night, Rémy is awake, looking frightened and alone. The next day, when Constance visits, Rémy does not talk about his fear of his approaching death. Instead, he delivers a lecture about evil. We pick up the conversation in the middle. Constance responds to something he has said about suffering, saying, "You say that because times [right now] are so terrible." Using his walker to hold himself upright as he moves jerkily from window to bed, Rémy declares,

Not especially terrible. Not at all. Contrary to belief, the twentieth century wasn't that bloody. It's agreed that wars caused 100 million deaths. Add 10 million for the Russian Gulags. How many were killed in the Chinese camps? We'll never know, but say 20 million. So [that's a total of] 130 or 135 million dead. Not all that impressive. In the sixteenth century, the Spanish and Portuguese managed without gas chambers or bombs to slaughter 150 million Indians in Latin America. With axes! That's a lot of work, Sister. Even if they had Church support, it was an achievement. So much so that the Dutch, English, French, and later Americans followed their lead and butchered another 50 million. [That's] 200 million dead in all! The greatest massacre took place right here. And [there is] not the tiniest Holocaust Museum. The history of mankind is a history of horrors!

By the end of this speech Rémy is stiff with rage and in the ensuing silence Sister Constance looks deeply troubled.

In this conversation, Rémy has invited Constance into his existential world-making as he draws upon relational matrices in his adult life as a historian in order to express his rage at suffering—not his own but the suffering of the colonized. Her presence as a member of a religious order connects Rémy with the childhood relational matrices formed in his Roman Catholic family and education. At this moment, his existential world-making is fueled by anger and vocalized as a kind of protest theodicy that questions suffering, puts God and the church on trial, and refuses to accept answers. His lament has a liturgical quality, if the rhetoric of the passionate college lecturer can be described as liturgy and Constance can be described as his congregation. She not only bears witness to his rage at the Church; her sadness and distress attest to the ways she, on behalf of the Church and God, accepts the horrors he describes as real. Her sorrow seems to encompass all of those who suffer, including Rémy.

The fourth conversation we view takes place several days later. Rémy's son has bribed the hospital administrator and union members to redecorate a vacant room and make it into a private suite where Rémy can receive hospice care. He has also contacted Rémy's old friends and invited them to visit.

In this scene, Sister Constance visits Rémy's suite for the first time and is astonished at the luxurious setting. She jokingly asks whether Rémy is "pals with the Premier [of the province of Québec] or a hockey star?" Rémy's wife says that his son is the one who takes care of him. The chaplain replies, "Yes, I know. And Dumbo won't even thank him." Rémy quickly defends himself, saying, "My son is an ambitious, puritanical capitalist. Whereas I was always a sensual socialist." At this point two women enter; they are Rémy's former lovers who were faculty colleagues with him. One of them delightedly exclaims, "Sensual isn't half of it, Sister! Lewd! Bestial! Debauched! Lascivious! Perverse!" After an exchange of kisses, Rémy declares, "You see, Sister? [I am surrounded by] my exquisite daughter-in-law, my heroic wife, and two most charming mistresses. I can die in peace." Rémy places his hands together as if in prayer, looks heavenward and smiles beatifically. Sister Constance pronounces her verdict: "You'll burn in the flames of hell." Rémy's rejoinder is swift: "And I won't be alone. [My wife and daughter-in-law] are safe. But given the depravity of these two [mistresses], they'll roast alongside me. Whereas you'll play the harp on a cloud for eternity, seated between John Paul the second and Mother Theresa." His wife rolls her eyes and says, "Excuse me, Sister, his malady has affected his brain." Rémy and his two former mistresses chant together a phrase from catechism they learned as children: "For the misfortunes of Poland are proof of God's existence."

In this exchange we see a humorous playing out of Rémy's existential world-making, in which Constance again is aligned with the church and with those who are "good": his wife and daughter-in-law. Rémy jokingly acknowledges his sexual transgressions, and he and his friends easily call to mind the first order language of childhood Catholic catechism. Rémy's humor and wit, which play a large part in his friendships, are much in evidence here, attesting to the ways that the chaplain is now included in the circle of family and friends. Beneath the humor are feelings and questions about death, judgment, and the afterlife. The parody of childhood beliefs, spontaneously sung in unison, reveals the ways in which they are, in face of Rémy's death, re-experiencing embedded childhood beliefs. Their jokes likely trigger some jarring questions for each of them—"What do I believe now? How in the world will I make sense of this death?"—especially when Rémy's sudden gasping contortions in response to stabbing pain disrupt the banter. The questions hang in the air as the existential and religious world-making continues. Rémy may be increasingly experiencing the limitations of seeking closeness through humor, intellect, and the sexualizing of relationships.

The second to last conversation we see between Rémy and Constance begins mid-stream, with Rémy sitting upright in bed, shouting, "[Pope] Pius the twelfth [was] sitting on his throne in his gilded Vatican, while Primo Levi was taken to Auschwitz. That's not sad! It's despicable! Hideous!" He slumps back, exhausted. The chaplain, looking tearful and distressed, says in a low voice, "If what you say is true and history is a series of abominable crimes then someone has to exist who can forgive us. That's my belief." Through clenched teeth, Rémy mutters, "I envy you." Once again, Rémy, outraged at his approaching death, finds expression in his protest theodicy. Constance tearfully acknowledges guilt, aligning herself with sinners and sharing a response from her religious world-making. They are each engaged in a kind of searching for ways of understanding and giving voice to Rémy's rage, pain, fear, and sorrow. The meanings they co-construct, to do with atrocities and forgiveness, are provisional and very much in process.

The last conversation that we see takes place as Rémy is being wheeled out of the hospital room on a stretcher. His son is there, packing up Rémy's belongings. Rémy is going with his entourage of family and friends to a house on Lake Memphremagog in the Eastern Townships of Québec, for his final days. This setting is significant in the film because it is here that Rémy re-experiences a sense of holiness through the beauty of these natural surroundings. His apprehension of this beauty allows him to be more fully present in the here and now as he approaches death. Constance comes into the room to say goodbye. Grasping his hand, she leans down and gently says, "Adieu." After gazing steadily at him, she whispers, "Embrace the mystery. Embrace the mystery and you'll be saved." They gaze at each other with great affection. Rémy kisses her hand and then is wheeled away. She turns to Rémy's son, puts her hand on his shoulder, and looks at him intently before saying, "Say you love him. Tell him. And touch him! Touch him!"

The scene discloses the tenderness and intimacy Rémy and Constance experience. Her calm sense of serenity as she says goodbye communicates a sense of peaceful acceptance of Rémy's approaching death. This time, she is the one who discloses her religious world-making while Rémy simply listens.

Her hope that Rémy will embrace the mystery seems like an alternative theodicy centered on the mystery of God, suffering, and death. We could interpret Sister Constance's counsel to embrace mystery as offering Rémy a way of subsuming his intellectual skepticism within a *via negativa* or negative theology that acknowledges the finitude of all of our human intellectual constructions. Her reference to being saved is jarring to viewers sensitized to comparative religious approaches that impose meanings: Is this reference to being saved an imposition of her Christian world-making on Rémy? He doesn't respond as if this is the case. He seems to accept the truth of this for her; perhaps he honors her searching and her provisional meanings in exchange for the times in which she has done this for him.

The spiritual care encounters between Constance and Rémy allow him to dialogue with the church and the God of his childhood Catholicism. These encounters can be juxtaposed with the kind of existential care encounters Rémy has with a young woman named Nathalie. The daughter of one of Rémy's former lovers, she is a heroin addict whom Rémy's son pays to provide his father with heroin, which is 800 percent more effective than morphine for dealing with pain. The first time they meet, Rémy asks Nathalie whether he remembers that he was "close" to her mother. Nathalie quickly identifies him as one of her mother's married lovers who never stayed until morning. Probably for the first time, Rémy sees what it must have been like for her as a child, saying, "From a child's perspective it must seem sordid. We called it sexual liberation." Prior to this conversation with Nathalie, Rémy might describe the ways he sexualized his relationships with women as a way of breaking free from his Roman Catholic upbringing. At an intellectual level, in humorous reminiscences with his friends, he appreciates the irony of how his Catholic teachings on the sinfulness of sexual desires actually fuelled his fantasies. Before this encounter with Nathalie, he is not able to acknowledge how his sexual liaisons threatened the relational fabric of his life. He has been unaware of how his lifestyle of embracing the "goodness" of the sexual revolution may have wounded his children and the children of his lovers.

When they meet to get high, Rémy talks about his approaching death more candidly than with anyone else. In one such conversation, Nathalie remarks that she will likely die of a heroin overdose. Rémy objects, saying she is young; there is still time to get help. He says he no longer has this kind of time, and he reminisces about how much he has loved life: "Wine, books, music. Women, above all, women. Their smell, their mouths, the feel of their skin." When Nathalie quizzes him on whether he still is able to enjoy all of these pleasures, and he admits he no longer can, she stuns him with her conclusion: "It's not the present you cling to; it's your past life. That life is already dead." Nathalie matter-of-factly recognizes that the passions which used to dominate Rémy's life and connect him with others, however superficially, have already been expended. She challenges him to live fully in the present moment; if Rémy can do this, he may find new ways to engage life, even as he approaches death.

In this exchange we see two people facing a harsh existential reckoning. The time has come for them to let go of the life-limiting ways in which they have grasped life. For Rémy, he has grasped life through his sexual and sensual desires. For Nathalie, she has grasped life by trying to re-experience the self-transcendence she experienced in her first drug-induced high, which she describes as riding the dragon. They both stand on the brink of death: will they choose life?

Rémy learns that he must face the existential questions that have tormented him without using the distractions of women, wine, food, and intellectual compatriots. Can he experience a communion or relational connection that goes beyond the kinds of sexual and intellectual intimacy of his past? Without these distractions and stripped of his self-identity as a sexual, sensual, witty, pugnacious rebel, he is forced to judge the worth of his life. In several conversations with his son and Nathalie, he agonizingly takes stock of his life using standards from his academic identity and laments that he has no living legacy—no aspect of himself, like books or students, that will survive him. In the brutal honesty of the relational space he and Nathalie have created, Rémy is highly agitated, searching for the purpose of his life and the meaning of his death. He finally acknowledges that he faces death, as he began, like a baby.

His conversations with Constance and Nathalie are both critical to Rémy's existential world-making as he faces death. The chaplain's presence prompts him to re-experience formative relationships in childhood and his embedded Catholicism, and he rages using critical conversations from young adulthood and years as a professor of history. With Nathalie, he reckons with the lifelimiting and destructive consequences of sexualized relationships with colleagues and students. With her he searches for a sense of transcendence, a way to be fully present as he faces death, without being able to sexualize, intellectualize, or distract himself with the pleasures of good food and wine. While his searching and questioning do not bring answers, they do bring Rémy to a resting place, where he can face death peacefully.

A significant feature of the pastoral and existential encounters with Constance and Nathalie is that he does not sexualize these relationships when he experiences moments of alterity (as he likely has in the past). Nathalie and Sister Constance remain in their roles as guardians of alterity. Sister Constance engages him with the Otherness he likely experienced at moments through his childhood religion, an otherness which became transposed onto the iconic images of women for whom he felt passionate sexual desire. Nathalie engages him in complex paradoxical ways first by releasing him from pain and introducing him to the physical transcendence of being high on heroin, and then through a brutal reckoning that helps him see beyond his usual horizons of what his life means. In his final moment of life, he tells Nathalie that she is his guardian angel. It is Nathalie, the most vulnerable person in Rémy's circle of family and friends, the one who is closest to death herself, who helps Rémy die. Instead of giving herself the overdose, she gives it to Rémy. She becomes his guardian angel as he crosses from life to death. He becomes her guardian angel as she crosses the line from dangerous overdoses to the relative safety of a methadone program and as she moves into his former home during her recovery.

This case study highlights how professional spiritual care is often one melodic thread in a polyphonic movement where jarring moments in various melodic threads amplify discordant harmonies that can finally break open horizons of meaning and reveal new ways for care seekers to reconnect with a sense of holiness.

> *Our being spreads out far beyond us and mingles with the beings of others. We live in other people's thoughts, in their plans, in their dreams. This is as if there were God. We have an infinite responsibility.*[37]

---

37   Iris Murdoch, *Nuns and Soldiers* (London: Penguin, 1980), 454.

Bibliography

Bauman, Zygmunt. *Intimations of Postmodernity.* London: Routledge, 1992.

Boileau, David A. "Preface." In *The Wisdom of Love in the Service of Love: Emmanuel Levinas on Justice, Peace and Human Rights,* edited by Roger Burggraeve, 17–19. Milwaukee: Marquette University Press, 2002.

Bourdieu, Pierre. *The Logic of Practice.* London: Routledge, 1992.

Burggraeve, Roger. "Violence and the Vulnerable Face of the Other: The Vision of Emmanuel Levinas on Moral Evil and Our Responsibility." *Journal of Social Philosophy* 30, no. 1 (1999): 29–45. https://doi.org/10.1111/0047-2786.t01-1-00003.

Cohen, Richard A. "Maternal Psyche." In *Psychology for the Other: Levinas, Ethics, and the Practice of Psychology,* edited by Edwin E. Gantt and Richard N. Williams, 32–64. Pittsburgh: Duquesne University Press, 2002.

Diedrich, W. W., Roger Burggraeve, and Chris Gastmans. "A Dialogue Between the Thoughts of Joan Tronto and Emmanuel Levinas." *Ethical Perspectives: Journal of the European Ethics Network* 13, no. 1 (2006): 33–61.

Doehring, Carrie. "Military Moral Injury: An Evidence-Based and Intercultural Approach to Spiritual Care." *Pastoral Psychology* 68, no. 1 (2019): 15–30. https://doi.org/10.1007/s11089-018-0813-5.

———. "Resilience as the Relational Ability to Spiritually Integrate Moral Stress." *Pastoral Psychology* 64, no. 5 (2015): 635–49. https://doi.org/10.1007/s11089-015-0643-7.

———. "Searching for Wholeness Amidst Traumatic Grief: The Role of Spiritual Practices that Reveal Compassion in Embodied, Relational, and Transcendent Ways." *Pastoral Psychology* 68, no. 3 (2019): 241–59. https://doi.org/10.1007/s11089-018-0858-5.

———. "Systemically Exploring Student Debt: Methodological Challenges for Pastoral Theology." *Pastoral Psychology* 65, no. 5 (2016): 631–41. https://doi.org/10.1007/s11089-016-0696-2.

———. "Theological Accountability: The Hallmark of Pastoral Counseling." *Sacred Spaces* 1, no. 1 (2009): 4–34.

———. *The Practice of Pastoral Care: A Postmodern Approach.* Rev. ed. Louisville: Westminster John Knox, 2015.

Gergen, Kenneth J. *Relational Being: Beyond Self and Community.* New York: Oxford University Press, 2002.

———. *Therapeutic Realities: Collaboration, Oppression and Relational Flow.* Chagin Falls, OH: Taos Institute, 2006.

Graham, Elaine. *Transforming Practice: Pastoral Theology in an Age of Uncertainty.* New York: Mowbray, 1996.

Graham, Elaine, Heather Walton, and Frances Ward. *Theological Reflection: Methods*. New York: SCM, 2005.

Greider, Kathleen J. "Religious Location and Counseling: Engaging Diversity and Difference in Views of Religion." In *Understanding Pastoral Counseling*, edited by Elizabeth A. Maynard and Jill L. Snodgrass, 235–256. New York: Springer, 2015.

Jennings, Theodore W. "Pastoral Theological Methodology." In *Dictionary of Pastoral Care and Counseling*, edited by Rodney J. Hunter, 862–64. Nashville: Abingdon, 1990.

Lartey, Emmanuel Y. *Pastoral Theology in an Intercultural World*. Cleveland: Pilgrim, 2006.

Levinas, Emmanuel. *Otherwise Than Being or Beyond Essence*. Translated by Alphonso Lingis. The Hague: Martinus Nijhoff, 1981.

———. "The Temptation of Temptation." Translated by Annette Aronowicz. In *Nine Talmudic Readings*, edited by Emmanuel Levinas, 30–50. Bloomington: Indiana University Press, 1990.

———. *Totality and Infinity: An Essay on Exteriority*. Translated by Alphonso Lingis. Pittsburgh: Duquesne University Press, 1969.

Moyaert, Marianne. "Interreligious Dialogue and the Debate Between Universalism and Particularism: Searching for a Way Out of the Deadlock." *Studies in Interreligious Dialogue* 15, no. 1 (2005): 36–51. https://doi.org/10.2143/SID.15.1.583340.

Murdoch, Iris. *Nuns and Soldiers*. London: Penguin, 1980.

Paden, William E. *Religious Worlds: The Comparative Study of Religion*. 2nd ed. Boston: Beacon, 1994.

———. "Theaters of World-Making Behaviors: Panhuman Contexts for Comparative Religion." In *Comparing Religions: Possibilities and Perils?*, edited by Thomas Athanasius Idinopulos, Brian C. Wilson, and James Constantine Hanges, 59–74. Boston: Brill, 2006.

Pargament, Kenneth. *Spiritually Integrated Psychotherapy: Understanding and Addressing the Sacred*. New York: Guilford, 2007.

Pargament, Kenneth, Serena Wong, and Julie Exline. "Wholeness and Holiness: The Spiritual Dimension of Eudaimonics." In *The Handbook of Eudaimonic Well-being*, edited by Joar Vittersø, 379–94. Cham, Switzerland: Springer International, 2016.

Ramsay, Nancy J. "Resisting Asymmetries of Power: Intersectionality as a Resource for Practices of Care." *Journal of Pastoral Theology* 27, no. 2 (2017): 83–97. https://doi.org/10.1080/10649867.2017.1399784.

Ricoeur, Paul. *The Symbolism of Evil*. Translated by Emerson Buchanan. New York: Harper & Row, 1967.

Stone, Howard W., and James O. Duke. *How to Think Theologically.* 3rd ed. Minneapolis: Fortress, 2013.

Townsend, Loren. *Introduction to Pastoral Counseling.* Nashville: Abingdon, 2009.

Vandermeersch, Patrick. "The Failure of Second Naiveté: Some Landmarks in the History of French Psychology of Religion." In *Aspects in Contexts: Studies in the History of Psychology of Religion,* edited by Jacob A. Belzen, 235–79. Atlanta: Rodopi, 2000.

ENGAGING IN RELIGIOUS PLURALISM

A Confucian-Based Model

INSOOK LEE

CONFLICTS RELATED TO religious differences are difficult to address.[1] One reason is that such conflicts usually lead to polarizing, cognitive debates where people argue in order to discriminate wrong from right, superior from inferior. Psychologically, such judgments and discriminations are driven by the individual's ego, which is inclined to compare, differentiate, and organize in order to make sense of phenomena in the world. Without such ego functions, an individual cannot live nor survive in a phenomenal world controlled by time and space. Despite the important role of the ego, I argue that using the ego alone to examine religious differences or competing doctrines is a seriously limited approach in our religiously pluralistic world.

Recognizing this limitation, Christian practical theologian Elizabeth Moore insisted that navigating religious differences should start with exploring and "sharing lived religious experiences and passion," rather than with a conceptual understanding rooted in dogmatic debates.[2] Moore, however, did not provide us with a rationale for why and how such an approach would work to eliminate, or reduce, the problems of religious pluralism. This chapter aims at providing both a theoretical and practical basis for understanding why and how a lived experiential approach makes navigating religious differences possible and easier. The ultimate purpose of this chapter is to outline recommendations for navigating religious differences, both intra- and

---

1   Simon J. A. Mason and Damiano A. Sguaitamatti, "Introduction and Overview: Religion in Conflict Transformation in a Nutshell," *Politorbis* 52, no. 2 (2011): 5–8.

2   Mary Elizabeth Moore, "Toward an Interreligious Practical Theology," YouTube video, 1:33:01, April 10, 2010, https://www.youtube.com/watch?v=8enGhBO1rKU.

interpersonally, that transcend dogmatic debates but do not deny distinctive doctrinal characteristics of each religion.

With this purpose in mind, I constructed a working model that describes the individual ego's spiritual journey toward accepting and embracing religious differences. The model is informed by my own multiple religious locations of Confucianism, Buddhism, and Christianity, but is primarily based on Confucian concepts.[3] Again, this effort is not to deny the different doctrines of each religion by only focusing on their similarities, as Kathleen Greider rightly opposed, but to understand and help prevent the violence and unnecessary power struggles that can occur when navigating religious differences.[4]

My Religious Location

Understanding the chapter's recommendations for the spiritual formation of the ego and for navigating religious differences requires that the reader understand something of my own religious location. I was born to Korean culture primarily represented by Confucianism and Buddhism. Those world-views have deeply shaped my consciousness, and the unconscious as well, even though I have never claimed myself as a believer in institutionalized Confucianism or Buddhism. When I was a teenager, I was baptized in the Catholic church under my mother's influence soon after the accidental death of my oldest brother, her oldest son. In my late twenties, I came to the United States to further my studies and attended a Presbyterian church organized for the Korean student community. I then converted to Presbyterianism, changed my major to theology, and was ordained in the PC(USA). In

---

3   In the Far East, multiple religions have long been mutually influenced by each other. Therefore, it is almost impossible to discuss Confucianism, Buddhism, or Taoism independently. Even though each of these religions is unique, they share many similar tenets or the same concepts with each other, but only in different forms. Christianity is a recently imported religion from the West that actively engages with the traditional religions and manifests uniquely given the cultural contexts.

4   Kathleen J. Greider, "Religious Location and Counseling: Engaging Diversity and Difference in Views of Religion," in *Understanding Pastoral Counseling*, ed. Elizabeth A. Maynard and Jill L. Snodgrass, 235–56 (New York: Springer, 2015).

retrospect, during those years between baptism and theological education, my Korean religiosity had lain suppressed.

I was completely soaked in Western Christianity, and it was only when I experienced a spiritual crisis in my late forties that I felt like I hit a dead end. I struggled to understand the exact reason. It was like I was disconnected or uprooted from something fundamental and essential to my being. Upon reflection, I realized my religious and spiritual identity was in peril. After much struggle, I was eventually reconnected with Korean religiosity. Since then, I have continuously explored the inner dynamics and the interplay between my newly acquired Christian spirituality and culturally innate Korean religious heritage.

Confucian "I" and Selfhood

Confucians believe in the existence of Principle, an invisible order which governs both the cosmos and the human mind. Cheng Yi, a Neo-Confucian scholar in the eleventh century, stated that "Principle is one but its manifestations are many."[5] Principle is also called Original Nature or True Nature because it exists *a priori* in the universe. What Original Nature imparts to humans is called nature. Therefore, Original Nature refers to the Heaven-endowed human nature that everyone possesses from birth.[6] As Original Nature exists *a priori*, humans cannot directly experience it because they experience reality only via the phenomenal concepts of time and space. Instead, humans know the existence of Original Nature, or Principle, through traces of it that are perceivable only by our mind and senses as phenomena. Confucians refer to those traces as the "Four Sprouts," the manifestations of Original Nature in the phenomenal world.

All particularities, including each individual ego, emerged from Original Nature. Ego is regarded as a particular individual, called "small I" (*so-ah*), because its function is to take care of an individual's self-interest and self-preservation. When the individual is hungry, for example, the ego is aware of the hunger and determines how to feed him or her. When one

---

5   Wing-Tsit Chan, *A Source Book in Chinese Philosophy* (Princeton: Princeton University Press, 1963), 499.

6   Young-chan Ro, "Spirituality, Spontaneity, and Moral Charisma in Korean Confucianism," *Journal of Korean Religions* 9, no. 2 (2018): 66, https://doi.org/10.1353/jkr.2018.0012.

perceives danger, the ego tries to find a way to protect the individual. In other words, ego is a psychological entity that functions in the phenomenal world for each individual and maintains the distinction between the individual and the rest of the world. As a result, there is a clear distinction between me and you, we and they, and we and the rest of the world. Without ego, an individual, or a group, cannot sustain its identity because this boundary will dissipate for that particularity. The boundary creates binary thinking which consequently dominates all relationships in the phenomenal world. Binary thinking is born, for example, between big and small, cold and warm, good and bad, love and hate, etc.

As described, ego is an inevitable and necessary part of an individual. However, the ego is innately oriented toward self-preservation and concomitant self-centeredness. In other words, the reference point is self. Each ego stands at its center and, from that reference point, interacts with others and the world. Because of this self-referenced inclination, Confucians both acknowledge the necessity of ego and, at the same time, are cautious, warning our ego is precarious. Ego likes and does only things that benefit it, and avoids whatever is not beneficial. The ego's self-centeredness can easily slip into solipsistic narcissism, which can cause harm to others and oneself. To prevent this potential downside of the ego, Confucians claim that there must be a countermeasure that keeps the ego in check while also permitting it to perform its own necessary functions. Original Nature thus monitors and guides the ego to stay within its proper boundary. The good news is that Original Nature is already available to everyone: it exists *a priori* even before all particularities, like egos, are born.

As mentioned, Original Nature, or Principle, cannot be directly perceived by an individual who lives in the phenomenal world because the phenomenal world is limited by time and space. Instead, individuals must access Principle through its traces manifested in the phenomenal world. Those traces are called *sa-dan*, translated as "Four Sprouts."[7] These four sprouts

---

7   The theory of Four Sprouts was originally developed by Mencius, who claimed that all humans have innate but incipient tendencies toward benevolence, righteousness, wisdom, and propriety. Employing an agricultural metaphor, he refers to these tendencies as "sprouts," as discussed in Mencius, *Mencius*, trans. D. C. Lau (New York: Penguin Books, 2005), 2A6.

represent the four prototypes that exist in Principle or Original Nature. Those include *In* (humaneness or benevolence), *Eui* (rightness), *Yeh* (propriety), and *Gee* (wisdom). These four metaphysical prototypes leave their traces in the phenomenal world in forms that we can perceive with our mind and senses: we perceive the existence of *In* (humanity) as a form of benevolence; *Eui* (rightness) as a form of justice; *Yeh* (propriety) as a form of courtesy; and *Gee* (wisdom) as a form of discernment between right and wrong. Confucians sometimes add one more, sincerity, to the four sprouts and refer to them as the "Five Actions."[8]

The law of Yin-Yang and Five Actions governs the whole universe, including the human mind. An example of yin-yang and the five actions is found in the seasons. In spring, yang energy is getting power while yin energy decreases. In summer, yang gets its most energy and yin remains in the background. In fall, yang begins to lose its power and concedes its throne to yin. In winter, yin energy prevails while yang is preparing for the upcoming spring. This order or pattern repeats with sincerity, the fifth component of the Principle. *In* (benevolence) is compared to spring because it is understood as the source of warm heart and compassion. *Yeh* (propriety) is compared to summer, as the culmination of love when our love is expressed outward to others in socially appropriate ways. *Eui* (righteousness) is like fall energy and represents the cold energy of when we have to judge and punish other's wrongdoing but, by doing so, we harvest the fruit of true love for everyone. *Gee* (wisdom) refers to the energies that are not yet expressed outward, like nature in the winter. Gee exists only as potential for love and justice when people use their wisdom to interact with the world. Thus, the principle of yin-yang and the five actions are applicable to all phenomena, whether the phenomena are visible (nature) or invisible (human mind).

Every individual is inscribed with these four (or five) prototypes, but some people manage to keep the four sprouts growing and others do not. Even if one fails to nourish the sprouts, we cannot delete these inscribed traces of Original Nature which make us human. From this existential

---

8   H. S. Yoon, [3분 인문학] 태극과 음양오행의 원리 _홍익학당.윤홍식,YouTube video, 5:46, September 18, 2017, https://www.youtube.com/watch?v=Y_txDasbiXw.

condition emerges the idea of self-cultivation. Without a life-long process of self-cultivation, those sprouts perish, and the individual cannot achieve full humanity.

This whole situation creates a paradox: ego is limited and precariously self-centered, but the ego is the only channel through which Original Nature, or Principle, manifests itself in the phenomenal world. In that sense, ego is both our friend and enemy. Confucians say in the *Book of Odes,* the power of the ego is precarious, and the influence of Principle is minimal and subtle.[9] This sentiment captures the Confucian understanding of the human condition. We need ego, but ego alone is dangerous. We need the guidance of Original Nature, but the power of Original Nature is too weak to guide the ego without proper awareness by the individual of its function. As such, individuals must start a spiritual journey to fully grow in their humanness, and ego, paradoxically, must be involved in this spiritual journey.

Ego's Spiritual Journey

Confucians claim that every individual is born with a differently conditioned ego. Because the phenomenal world works in a binary system, with love and hate, warm and cold, and good and bad, some have relatively "clear" ego and others have a "turbid" ego. How an individual can access the traces of Principle depends upon the quality of ego. If one's ego is clear, Principle can be seen more clearly to the individual who lives in the phenomenal world. If one's ego is turbid, the light of Principle is shadowed and blurred. A spiritual journey, for Confucians, is therefore to cultivate the ego for the traces of Principle to become more transparent in the phenomenal world. The aim is not to demolish the ego but to align it in accordance with Principle, or to be in a harmonious relationship with Principle. The model which I present offers a roadmap for the ego's spiritual journey whose goal is to cultivate an individual egocentric self in harmony with something larger than the ego.

What follows is a model for developing the ego toward spiritual maturity. This model employs a metaphorical Wheel from 0° to 360°

---

9   H. S. Yoon, [윤홍식의 인문학 강의] 조선 성리학 특강 - 5강, YouTube video, 59:20, October 19, 2015, https://www.youtube.com/watch?v=kIZkAdS0yBY.

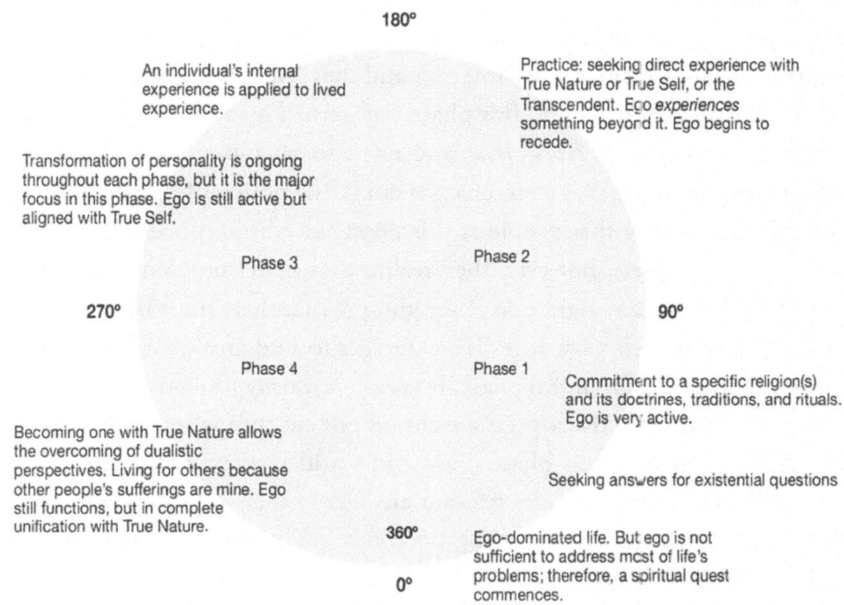

Figure 3.1 Ego's Religious/Spiritual Journey

(see Figure 3.1).[10] The Wheel in its entirety represents an inseparable, continuous process comprised of four distinguishable phases of the ego's development. In each phase, the ego has different needs, tasks, and characteristics in one's journey to spiritual growth. Often, the phases may overlap with each other, or go back and forth as necessary, but each phase depends on ego's different focus and need.

---

10   The inspiration for the Wheel metaphor came from a lecture I attended by Chong-An Sunim, a Hungarian Buddhist monk, who studied in the tradition of Korean Cho-gye Buddhism. He used a wheel as a way to explain a Buddhist journey to obtain nirvana and bodisatteva (a person who is able to reach nirvana but delays doing so out of compassion in order to save suffering beings). Another inspiration for the Wheel came from a Korean Confucian scholar, Yoon Hong Sik, who used the Western concept of ego to explain Confucian ethics and spirituality, but he utilized circles rather than a wheel to explain Confucianism. I combined these two ideas, Chong-An Sunim's and Yoon Hong Sik's, in order to develop a psychological and spiritual model of ego's journey toward spiritual growth.

The Wheel: From 0°–90°

At 0º, people have not yet embarked on their spiritual journey. They are wrapped up with their own self-interests and they live only by the ego's primitive and instinctual demand. This phase is governed by a specific rule, which Confucians call egoistic *Hori-pihae*, and refers to pursuing personal interests and avoiding anything that counteracts them.[11] The notion of "I" based on the ego's rule is so strong that people at this phase have little concern for others. As their lives progress, however, they realize that many problems cannot be solved only by the ego's rigid rule. They glimpse that there must be something else and begin to seek what it is. Their quest is to find answers for existential questions. One's search in this phase, however, is mostly limited to a cognitive level even though affective aspects are always present throughout the Wheel.

Many people in this phase often end up identifying with a particular religious tradition that provides relevant answers to their questions. What follows is the commitment to learning doctrines, traditions, and rituals of that particular religious system(s). The ego is the main agent in this phase of seeking and finding. At the 90º, the pinnacle of this phase, believers have managed to accumulate a significant amount of doctrinal knowledge and some can develop somewhat pious religious lifestyles through self-discipline. In other words, they become *religious* and adamantly defend their religious location against others.

Confucians claim that in this phase people get in touch with Original Nature embedded in themselves from birth. They glimpse the existence of something more than the ego in the universe and in themselves, which is Original Nature. In this initial phase, however, the force of Original Nature is minimal or precarious, and the influence of ego is predominant to a dangerous level. A characteristic of those in this phase is that they become attached to and strictly identify their spirituality with a particular doctrinal formula that they have chosen to embrace. Ego is most active in this stage, struggling between reality and the ideal of Original Nature. Similarly, in Buddhism, the spiritual journey of ego is carefully laid out.

In the Buddhist tradition of Korean Cho-gye lineage, beginners are not allowed to do intensive sitting meditation. Rather, they do initial work to build a foundation that enables Zen practice. During the first three years, therefore,

---

11   Yoon, [윤홍식의 인문학 강의] 조선 성리학 특강 - 5강.

they usually work in a kitchen or other working places while being allowed to attend regular public dharma teaching sessions and do a personal study of sutras between working hours. For them, working itself is a meditation, and they call it "working meditation." Psychologically, this is time to de-learn and retrain their ego's habitual patterns. Without this preparatory stage, Buddhists assert that meditators could go astray and be lost in a spiritual world, and their spiritual quest may turn into another attachment to ego's self-interest. Only after the initial years are they allowed to learn sutras more seriously, namely all day long. Meditation accompanies the study of sutras, but intensive meditation is not the major focus of their spiritual practice yet. They must wait until the next phase of a journey.

The Wheel: From 90°–180°

During this phase, individuals seek personal and direct *experience* of what they learned and understood in the previous phase. In seeking one's personal experience beyond cognitive understanding, one focuses on the inward betterment of self. Old thinking and behavioral patterns are loosened and new patterns begin to set in. At this stage, self-discipline and practice is required and ego is still a major agent. Personality change can occur. The irony is that ego's limit is now clearly recognized, and yet the major means to overcome this limit, in this phase, is through the ego's rigorous efforts and struggle. Ego must consciously deconstruct old patterns of thinking and acting which permeate every aspect of life. Subsequently, new habits have been acquired through the diligent self-discipline of inward contemplation/prayer/meditation and outward application of the practice. Owing to the ego's hard work, the presence of True Nature gets stronger and takes over the center of the individual's personality. At the end of this phase, therefore, a new sense of liberation from the binary thinking of ego begins to develop. As the ego's grip is loosened, the person now moves beyond dualistic dichotomy through the expansion of consciousness aligned with True Nature. They are more open to the ideology of other religions and less defensive of their own religious location.

The Wheel: From 180°–270°

This is the phase where the individual attempts to actualize what has been experienced. Actualization likely began in earlier phases and has always been in progress, but it is the major focus of this phase. This actualization first occurs in the individual's personal life. The feeling of euphoria is often accompanied as one is freed from the narrow world of ego. Ego, in its pursuit of personal desires and greed, has been noticeably weakened as it is getting attuned to Original Nature. Without much effort, ego can now peacefully coexist with Original Nature and even invites Original Nature to the center of the individual's life. As ego retreats to the periphery, its binary perception is significantly reduced. As a result, the individual acquires an expanded consciousness in which he or she can identify himself or herself with others in deeper compassion. As opposed to being defensive against other religions where ego is at center-stage, this stage finds individuals dynamically engaging with other religions as strongly as their own, even though all of their religious particularities remain intact. Original Nature, the unity of existence, becomes manifested in one's consciousness as a wholeness that is beyond the dimension of ego.

The Wheel: From 270°–360°

This phase is distinguished mostly by the shift of people's focus from personal freedom, as experienced in the previous phase, to concern for others. Ego seems to be well aligned with Principle. A rigid boundary between me and you disappears, not in a schizophrenic or fragmented way but in a unified, mystical way. From this holistic, nondualistic perception comes genuine compassion for others' sufferings because such suffering is felt as one's own. This state is described as mystical. Particular doctrines, which appeal to the cognitive dimension and the ego's differentiation, are transcended but without losing their religious identities and locations. In the phase of 270°–360°, ego still executes its own unique functions of self-preservation, but now in perfect harmony and alliance with True Nature. This state was described by Confucius in the second book of his *Analects* as the ability to "give my heart-and-mind free rein without overstepping the boundaries."[12] True Nature and personal desires are now the same. Those who reach this dimension are called saints in many religions.[13] In the next section, I use

---

12 Confucius, *The Analects of Confucius: A Philosophical Translation*, trans. Roger T. Ames and Henry Rosemont Jr. (New York: Ballantine Books, 1999), 77.

13 As long as we live as a particularity in the phenomenal world limited by time and space, we will never overcome the binary perception of the ego: we only become closer to the ideal status. That means that even saints are not completely free from their own personal needs and desires.

this model of the ego's spiritual journey as a Wheel to understand how Bria (pseudonym) navigated intra- and interpersonal religious differences.

Navigating Intra- and Interpersonal Religious Differences: The Case of Bria

I teach a small class composed of four Buddhists and seven Christians. Every class starts with a five-minute devotion led by a student(s). One day, Eva, a Christian student, read Psalm 23 and shared her personal reflection on it. After the devotion, a Buddhist student, Bria, said with an emotional tone, "I was deeply moved by your gentle reading of Psalm 23." She tearfully continued, "It would be a comfort to know that Someone is always there to be with you and for you. As a Buddhist, I don't have that feeling."

Several days after that class, I asked her for an interview about her religious location. She willingly agreed, and we talked for two hours in a relatively unstructured setting. Bria is a sixty-seven-year-old Caucasian woman who works as a manager at a dance company. Due to her father's job, she spent several years of her childhood in South Africa, later moving around the world every two years. Her parents were faithful Presbyterians. When she was twelve years old, a pastor at her parents' church touched her in a way that made her uncomfortable and, since then, she refused to return. In college, she participated in the street demonstrations against the Vietnam War and was involved in the feminist movement. She gained an interest in Asian arts and religions, particularly Hinduism and Buddhism. In particular, she liked Gandhi's ideology of nonviolent resistance. After college Bria was married and had one son. However, she lost him due to an accident while he was in college. This incident traumatized her and motivated her to go to a Buddhist seminary, where she was trained as a meditation instructor.

When asked what made her leave Christianity, she immediately said, "Violence, hypocrisy. . . . I need a space for myself. . . . I need freedom. . . . I don't want to be told by anyone what to do." She abhors "zealous Christians" who try to proselytize people. Furthermore, she cannot accept a male image of God, nor does she believe in miracles. What is "real" is important for her. She does not want to be deceived by anything that is not real. She also views Buddhism and Hinduism to be more in balance given the traditions' gendered images of gods.

When asked if she had found in Buddhism what she was not able to find in Christianity, she answered, "Yes, Buddhism has taught me a different way of thinking about life. . . . I feel like I am home. Buddhism works 100 percent for me." Particularly, Buddhism's pacifism attracted her. I then asked her about her tears in class as she listened to Psalm 23. She could not give me a clear answer. At the end of the interview, she mentioned, "I realize that my Christian memories have been all wiped out . . . repressed. I had good, beautiful memories. I've lost them . . . my Christian past. . . . I got my first Bible when I was a child. I was loved as a child. I was happy as a child. . . . There was a minister whom I loved."

In trying to find answers to her life problems, Bria was not able to find them in Christianity and converted to Buddhism. She, however, seems to be caught in the conflicts between the different doctrines of Buddhism and Christianity. Her priorities are to be free from the coercive power of violence and from patriarchal oppression. Bria believes she has solved her religious crisis, yet she was confused by her emotional and strong reaction to Psalm 23. She, on a conscious level, seems to be happy with Buddhism but, on the subconscious level, suffers from the doctrinal clash between the two religions. On the one hand, she views Christianity as soaked in patriarchy, while Buddhism gives her freedom. On the other hand, Christianity has taught her the necessity to depend on grace and a personal God, while Buddhism provides her with a sense of self-sufficiency. In her religious space, these two different doctrines exist as an internal conflict, without any sort of integration.

Using the Wheel as a model for the ego's spiritual journey, we see that Bria is clearly in the phase of 0°–90°, where her quest for answers to existential questions are in active process. Her ego is diligently searching for answers by comparing, analyzing, and criticizing each doctrinal component relevant to her quest. In this struggle, she, on a conscious level, has a need to protect her choice of religion and becomes extremely defensive and understandably critical towards the religion that seemingly failed her.

As long as Bria stays in this phase, however, it will be difficult, or impossible, for her to overcome the conundrum she is currently experiencing because, as discussed earlier in this chapter, ego's major functions are both necessarily and inevitably to protect an individual's self-interest and self-preservation. Rather, the answers to her existential questions can be found only in the realm beyond this egocentric dimension.

Therefore, Bria needs a spiritual turning point that can direct her to overcome ego's analytical realm. Bria must experience True Nature that exists outside the ego's realm. Though the ego, with its dualistic function, cannot enter the realms of True Nature, it can point toward it. Bria has rightly followed her ego's lead up to this point and is now arrested at its border.

In order for her to move beyond this border and experience True Nature, she must let go of the ego's dominance. This is the paradox of ego's functionality in one's spiritual journey. A paradox of the ego refers to the dilemma that the ego faces in the relationship with True Nature. Ego can only perceive things that exist in the phenomenal world, but True Nature exists outside the phenomenal world. Except through the ego, however, there is no way for humans to access True Nature. In short, ego is the only channel to access True Nature, but the ego is innately flawed in its access to it. Despite the ego's imperfection, therefore, humans must depend upon their egos, namely self-discipline, to get closer to True Nature. Confucians claim that how to live by this paradox is a daunting task for those who seek dynamic spiritual growth.

This paradox implies that, though the ego is limited, it has some innate openness or sensitivity toward True Nature. Otherwise, humans would be completely blind and unable to transcend reality, with no access to True Nature at all. Past the border of 90°, the ego begins to recede from its dominance but continues to function to survive in the phenomenal world, but now in compliance with True Nature.

Bria must go to the next phase, 90°–180°, in which her ego's dualistic perception will begin to be overcome but without losing the ego's integrating function. Many spiritual persons call this pursuit a mystical experience of something beyond the ego. With this spiritual experience, Bria can be liberated from a doctrinal conundrum without becoming fragmented in her spiritual and religious identity and location.

The negative effects of becoming cemented inside unwavering doctrinal beliefs (0°–90°) is that this learned method of intellectual evaluation often manifests itself in other areas of social behavior. Critical thinking skills may become stunted in similar patterns which value certainty or absolute knowledge. Exploration of alternative possibilities to already known beliefs becomes impossible for the individual. Radical defense of known beliefs even in the face of factual evidence feeds ego's need for self-protection and can lead to rage, violence, and the demonization of the other. An individual who cannot grow beyond this spiritual position no longer finds the same comfort in his or her faith. One's religious location is one of constant defense. We see this manifested in the current sociopolitical context of daily events. Many citizens refuse to alter their beliefs in light of known facts, which has led to a dangerous state of affairs where world leaders, both political and religious, have become emboldened by lies, dishonesty, and even murder and war.

If Bria understands this dynamic and understands her location on the Wheel, she could be less defensive of her current religious position against Christianity. At the same time, she may be able to move beyond an unrealistic idealization of Buddhism as if it satisfies "100 percent" of her needs. The Wheel could help alter her questions in relation to both Buddhism and Christianity. For example, instead of attacking Christian people as hypocrites, she may ask, "Which aspect of my Christian background deters my spiritual journey and keeps me rooted in place?" or "Which doctrinal teaching of Buddhism helps mend my spiritual wounds?" By engaging these questions, Bria can navigate her intrapersonal religious differences that, if left unexamined, will continue to thwart her ego's spiritual journey.

Thus, using the Wheel as a basis for navigating religious differences changes the nature of religious debate. It shifts the argument from religious primacy (whose religion is best/worst) to an explorative conversation with others. Conflicts become a series of explorative questions rather than combative propositions. Bria can better navigate her intrapersonal religious differences if she can locate herself, and others as well, in the Wheel. Instead of repeating the flaws of the other's viewpoint, she may be able to look inside her, and the other's, present journey. She may also ask similar questions to Christian classmates, including, "What doctrines do you find most comforting, revealing, and instructive for your everyday life?" Asking these types of questions to those with competing doctrinal beliefs and deeply listening to responses could help to uncover an individual's religious location and, therefore, trigger more compassionate retorts in each other's quest for spiritual growth.

Pastoral counselors can use this Wheel to facilitate similar conversations with clients from different religious backgrounds. Without creating unnecessary conflict, they can talk about specific doctrines and traditions of the client's religion. Both counselors and clients exchange conversations based on their active egos' exploration in search for spiritual growth, yet the Wheel forces them to move from a defensive and often combative position to that of a spiritual partner with the other, where the details of doctrine are transcended or embraced or even become irrelevant to one's personal growth in the faith.

Conclusion

I have examined how interreligious dialogue is theoretically and practically possible beyond the doctrinal debates, without ignoring or underestimating the essential dimension of cognitive, doctrinal engagement. For this purpose, I have created a "Wheel" which traces one's spiritual journey. The Wheel is primarily based on Confucian concepts of selfhood which can also be applied to many other religions, such as Buddhism and Christianity. To delineate each position on the Wheel, I have used the psychological concept of ego and its unique role in each different phase of the journey. By identifying our location on the Wheel and understanding each unique phase of the spiritual journey, we can avoid unnecessary conflicts and clashes that possibly lead to extreme self-defense and violence toward others who are in different positions.

Navigating religious differences is enhanced when people first work on their own faith inside of the religious circles they have chosen. In this phase, they should mature spiritually by reaching the dimension of at least 90° on the Wheel. A commitment to a particular religious system helps the individual reach that point because many mainstream religions have well-developed systems and traditions which have been accumulated and tested through many generations. However, at some point between 0° and 90°, they must also acknowledge that commitments to particular religious systems by themselves cannot propel the ego's spiritual journey. They must make a leap into the next dimensions of expanded and transformed consciousness and spirituality, which is represented as 90° and beyond on the Wheel. In that new dimension, they do not have to discard their sincere dedication to their chosen religions, but instead they must gain a new horizon that opens radically different perspectives. Only in this dimension of transformed ego are people capable of navigating religious differences in a way that results in a deeper level of shared humanity.

Bibliography

Chan, Wing-Tsit. *A Source Book in Chinese Philosophy*. Princeton: Princeton University Press, 1963.

Confucius. *The Analects of Confucius: A Philosophical Translation*. Translated by Roger T. Ames and Henry Rosemont Jr. New York: Ballantine Books, 1999.

Greider, Kathleen J. "Religious Location and Counseling: Engaging Diversity and Difference in Views of Religion." In *Understanding Pastoral Counseling*, edited by Elizabeth A. Maynard and Jill L. Snodgrass, 235–56. New York: Springer, 2015.

Mason, Simon J. A., and Damiano A. Sguaitamatti. "Introduction and Overview: Religion in Conflict Transformation in a Nutshell." *Politorbis* 52, no. 2 (2011): 5–8.

Mencius. *Mencius*. Translated by D. C. Lau. New York: Penguin Books, 2005.

Moore, Mary Elizabeth. "Toward an Interreligious Practical Theology." YouTube video, 1:33:01. April 10, 2010. https://www.youtube.com /watch?v=8enGhBO1rKU.

Ro, Young-chan. "Spirituality, Spontaneity, and Moral Charisma in Korean Confucianism." *Journal of Korean Religions* 9, no. 2 (2018): 55–82. https://doi.org/10.1353/jkr.2018.0012.

Yoon, H. S. [윤홍식의 인문학 강의] 조선 성리학 특강 - 5강. YouTube video, 59:20. October 19, 2015. https://www.youtube.com /watch?v=kIZkAdS0yBY.

———. [3분 인문학] 태극과 음양오행의 원리 _홍익학당. 윤홍식. YouTube video, 5:46. September 18, 2017. https://www .youtube.com/watch?v=Y_txDasbiXw.

❦ 4 ❦

IMPLICATIONS FOR INTERFAITH CHAPLAINCY FROM A TIBETAN BUDDHIST UNDERSTANDING OF RELIGIOUS LOCATION AND THE TWO TRUTHS

VICTOR GABRIEL

THIS CHAPTER PUTS forth an understanding of religious location that builds upon the work of Kathleen Greider,[1] and is reflective of Tibetan Buddhist thought, in order to suggest implications for interfaith chaplaincy practice. The implications for practice use as source text the *Guhyagarbha* Tantra (the Tibetan pronunciation is *gyü sangwé nyingpo*; the Tibetan transliteration, using the Wylie system, is *rgyud gsang ba'i snying po*) as the ultimate foundation.[2] In addition, the Tibetan hermeneutical device called ground, path, and fruition,[3] which is also used by the *Guhyagarbha* Tantra, is employed, with emphasis placed upon ground or ultimate truth.

Kathleen Greider has done excellent work in defining religious location with all its nuances.[4] Greider defined religious location as one aspect of our cultural identity that interacts dynamically with the other aspects of our identity like our personality, age, sexuality, economic status, gender,

---

1   Kathleen J. Greider, "Religious Location and Counseling: Engaging Diversity and Difference in Views of Religion," in *Understanding Pastoral Counseling*, ed. Elizabeth A. Maynard and Jill L. Snodgrass, 235–56 (New York: Springer, 2015)

2   Lama Chönam and Sangye Khandro, trans. *Guhyagarbha Tantra: Secret Essence Definitive Nature Just As It Is* (Boston: Snow Lion, 2011).

3   Judith L. Leif, Appendix 2 of "Working with Threefold Logic," in *The Profound Treasury of the Ocean of Dharma: The Path of Individual Liberation*, ed. Chögyam Trungpa, 549–50 (Boston: Shambhala, 2013).

4   Greider, "Religious Location and Counseling."

ethnicity, nationality, and first language. She put forward three therapeutic practices of power sharing, language care, and mature humility to promote therapeutic relationality amidst the caregiver's and care seeker's diverse religious locations. These three therapeutic practices make the field of chaplaincy inclusive and allow for interfaith/interreligious engagement with non-dominant and non-majority chaplains. This chapter, and the implications it offers to the field of chaplaincy, would not exist if not for the pioneering work of Greider and others.[5] Based upon my assumption that the majority of readers will be most familiar with Christian theological thinking, the chapter does not utilize the styles and turns of phrases common to Buddhist writings and speech. For example, within Tibetan Buddhism the use of non-affirming negations is considered the best articulation of ultimate truth, but this can be confusing for unfamiliar readers and is therefore avoided.

The Importance of Articulating a Tibetan Buddhist Understanding of Religious Location

I would like to begin by acknowledging how my own religious location and cultural identities influence my perspective on the importance of articulating a Tibetan Buddhist understanding of religious location. I grew up in Singapore and was born into a multiethnic and multireligious family.[6] My undergraduate and postgraduation education was in Australia, after which I then worked as a psychotherapist. After a second near-death experience, I was encouraged to pursue postgraduate studies in Tibetan Buddhism in the United States. I was ordained as a Tibetan Buddhist priest (*ngakpa*; *sngags pa*) and have worked in congregational, chaplaincy, and educational settings. In Singapore, Australia, and America I often occupied non-dominant and non-majority positions. These life experiences and my continual professional, religious, and chaplaincy formation lead me to acknowledge, like Greider, the importance of recognizing our diverse religious locations.[7]

---

5   Sheryl A. Kujawa-Holbrook, *God Beyond Borders: Interreligious Learning Among Faith Communities* (Eugene, OR: Pickwick, 2014).

6   My spiritual biography is one of five case studies in Duane Bidwell's book *When One Religion Isn't Enough: Lives of Spiritually Fluid People* (Boston: Beacon, 2018).

7   Greider, "Religious Location and Counseling."

Religious locations are distinct as they emerge from distinctive foundations. For a Christian, the ultimate foundation of one's religious location is grounded on God's saving grace. The covenantal relationship between God and the individual Christian, as expressed in the life of Christ, grounds the individual's religious location.[8] For a Buddhist, the ultimate foundation of one's religious location is established on the belief that there is no inherent essence or externally given essence, nor is there any independent, enduring, immutable identity. According to Buddhist thought, there is an interdependence and interconnection of all things that is expressed in the interconnective ebb and flow of multiple identities. This focus on interdependence, in turn, led Buddhist thinkers like Thich Nhat Hanh,[9] Ken Jones,[10] and Sulak Sivaraksa[11] to associate their own thinking with systems theories. Whether the ultimate foundations of Buddhist thought and Christian thought can be analogous or remain unreconcilable has been the source of much debate among Buddhists and Christians; Bidwell provided a summary of these issues.[12]

Positing a Tibetan Buddhist understanding of religious location with implications for chaplaincy is important given the dominance of the Christian perspective in chaplaincy today. Buddhist perspectives on the field of chaplaincy in North America are multivalent because Buddhist thinkers in the discipline engage with the dominant Christian culture through the lenses of postmodernism, postcolonialism, and post-patriarchy.[13] On one hand, Buddhist thinking in the field of chaplaincy needs to engage with

---

8   Bidwell provides an extended discussion on the difference between Christian and Buddhist religious locations, as discussed in Bidwell, *When One Religion Isn't Enough*.

9   Thich Nhat Hanh, *Interbeing* (Berkley: Parallax, 1987).

10   Ken Jones, *The New Social Face of Buddhism* (Somerville, MA: Wisdom, 2003).

11   Sulak Sivaraksa, *Seeds of Peace: A Buddhist Vision for Renewing Society* (Berkeley: Parallax, 1992); Sulak Sivaraksa, *Conflict, Culture and Change: Engaged Buddhism in a Globalizing World* (Somerville, MA: Wisdom, 2005).

12   Duane R. Bidwell, "Practicing the Religious Self: Buddhist-Christian Identity as Social Artifact," *Buddhist-Christian Studies* 28 (2008): 3–12, https://www.jstor.org/stable/30152924; Bidwell, *When One Religion Isn't Enough*.

13   Roger R. Jackson and John J. Makransky, eds., *Buddhist Theology: Critical Reflections by Contemporary Buddhist Scholars* (London: Routledge Curzon, 2000).

the dominant Christian culture to stay relevant to the needs of our communities; and on the other hand, Buddhist thinking in this field needs to continue to remain connected to the Buddhist tradition.[14] Thai Buddhist thinker Bhikkhu Buddhadasa challenged contemporary Buddhists to mine the extensive and fecund Buddhist tradition and history for contemporary solutions.[15] It is because of this challenge that this chapter returns to the *Guhyagarbha* Tantra as the source text and ultimate ground for putting a Tibetan Buddhist understanding of religious location into practice.

The articulation of a Tibetan Buddhist understanding of religious location is not only important for Buddhist thinkers engaged in the field of chaplaincy, but is germane to the dominant Christian culture of chaplaincy. When Buddhist thinkers speak to the field and thus invariably engage in interreligious dialogue, this allows Buddhist thinkers to contribute meaningfully to a theology of religious pluralism.[16] Perhaps this will prompt the dominant Christian culture to expand its thinking about God's revelation and salvation with regard to the diversity of religious traditions that have extensive history employing power sharing, language care, and mature humility in caregiving relationships.

A Tibetan Buddhist Understanding of Religious Location

The Diamond Sutra,[17] a traditional Buddhist writing, can be employed to modify Grieder's definition of religious location as follows:[18]

Those who set forth on the path of the Buddhist chaplain should give birth to this thought: However many beings there are, in whatever realms of

---

14   Cheryl A. Giles and Willa B. Miller, eds., *The Arts of Contemplative Care: Pioneering Voices in Buddhist Chaplaincy and Pastoral Work* (Boston: Wisdom, 2012).

15   Bhikkhu Buddhadasa, "Democratic Socialism," in *Me and Mine: Selected Essays of Bhikkhu Buddhadasa*, ed. Donald K. Swearer, 42–58 (Albany: State University of New York Press, 1989).

16   Paul F. Knitter, *Introducing Theologies of Religions* (Maryknoll, NY: Orbis Books, 2002).

17   Red Pine, *Diamond Sutra: The Perfection of Wisdom* (Washington, DC: Counterpoint, 2011).

18   Greider, "Religious Location and Counseling."

being that might exist, occupy a religious location. Religious locations are "neither discrete categories nor static. They are alive, synergistically evolving. As with other aspects of identity, through our lifetimes, we inhabit more than one religious location."[19] For some beings their "love of or neutrality toward religion is destabilized or destroyed by trauma done [to us] in the name of religion."[20] Other beings are "shaped by multiple religions . . . migration, immigration, [and] colonialism" that often result in religious multiplicity.[21] And though all beings occupy a religious location, there is not a single being or a single religious location to be found.

The ultimate truth in this definition is expressed by the final statement—the understanding that there is no static religious location and all religious locations are affected by other cultural identities; influences like migration, colonialism, and assimilation; and changes throughout a person's lifetime. This thinking allows Buddhist chaplains to engage both their own religious location and their care seeker's with curiosity and flexibility.

Two Truths

According to Greider,[22] language can both reveal and conceal. In the field of chaplaincy, it is this capacity of language that counsels the best of chaplains to be mindful of their terminology and semantics in their therapeutic conversations. Buddhist thinkers, while acknowledging this capacity of language, extend and apply this motif to all of reality. The Buddhist tradition acknowledged that Siddhārtha Gautama became a Buddha or "fully awakened one"[23] because he awakened to the two truths (*denpa nyi, bden pa gnyis*).[24] Siddhārtha Gautama awakened to both the conventional and the ultimate truth. Nāgārjuna, a Buddhist thinker from the second century, explained in his *Mūlamadhyamakakārikā* that

---

19   Greider, "Religious Location and Counseling," 237.

20   Greider, "Religious Location and Counseling," 238.

21   Greider, "Religious Location and Counseling," 238.

22   Greider, "Religious Location and Counseling."

23   The Tibetan word for Buddha is *sang gye* (*sangs rgyas*) and is a gloss on the Sanskrit "fully awakened one." *Sang* means to awaken while *gye* means "to blossom."

24   Reginald A. Ray, *Indestructible Truth: Living Spirituality of Tibetan Buddhism* (Boulder: Shambhala, 2002).

> *The Buddha's teaching of the Dharma*
> *Is based on two truths:*
> *A truth of worldly convention*
> *And an ultimate truth.*[25]

What exactly comprises the two truths has been the source of debate and sectarian polemics across Buddhist traditions and throughout Buddhist history.[26] However, all Buddhist traditions agree that the experience of reality, including language, both reveals and conceals the two truths. It must be remembered that this is a system of two truths, not one truth and one falsehood. Conventional truth is a *truth* that within the confines of its relevant context is true.

The two truths are analogous, in some ways, to the movement of revelation and concealment within Christian theology. David Tracy also observed the ability of language to reveal and conceal but went further to say that "what we mean in naming certain texts, events, images, rituals, symbols and persons 'classics' is that here we recognize nothing less than the disclosure of a reality we cannot but name truth."[27] Tracy's statement acknowledges that certain symbols have the power to reveal the truth, while from a Tibetan Buddhist lens, the Buddhist thinker would remark that *all* phenomena can reveal the truth. In this chapter, truth is analogous to the "experience of the ultimate truth" of reality (*nyams su myong ba*; *nyam su mong wa*).

Before proceeding further, it is important to clarify that the idea of the two truths means that there can be two truths regarding the religious location of any follower of Tibetan Buddhism or of any religious tradition.[28]

---

25   Nāgārjuna, *The Fundamental Wisdom of the Middle Way: Nāgārjuna's Mūlamadhyamakakārikā*, trans. Jay L. Garfield (New York: Oxford University Press, 1995), 68.

26   Yaroslav Komarovshi, *Tibetan Buddhism and Mystical Experience* (Oxford: Oxford University Press, 2015); Sonam Thakchoe, "The Theory of Two Truths in India," in *Stanford Encyclopedia of Philosophy*, ed. Edward N. Zalta, Summer 2022, https://plato.stanford.edu /entries/twotruths-india/#:~:text=The%20central%20thesis%20in%20the,mind%20to%20 which%20it%20corresponds.

27   David Tracy, *Analogical Imagination: Christian Theology and the Culture of Pluralism* (New York: Crossroad, 1981), 108.

28   Komarovshi, *Tibetan Buddhism*; Thakchoe, "The Theory of Two Truths."

A Tibetan Buddhist understanding of religious location is both conventional and conceptual as well as nonconventional and nonconceptual. An accurate understanding of the religious locations of both chaplains and care seekers needs to consider the many conventional cultural variables as well as the ultimate truth of both chaplains and care seekers.

Although all phenomena can reveal the truth, it does not follow that the truth can be effortlessly perceived. Buddhists prepare themselves through years of study, ethical development, meditation, and contemplation for the truth of ultimate reality to be effortlessly perceived. In the field of chaplaincy, study, ethical development, meditation, and contemplation become the conventional truth of Buddhist chaplain formation. These conventional practices in turn lead the Buddhist chaplain to perceive the nonconceptual direct experience of the ultimate truth of Buddhist chaplaincy. Bhāviveka (ca. 490–570) expressed the relationship between conventional training and ultimate truth in these words:

> *It is not appropriate for the learned ones to scale the building*
> *Of the true [meaning] without the ladder of true*
> *conventionalities.*[29]

This means that the Buddhist chaplain must train in the many conventional therapeutic methods and then use these conventional methods to perceive the ultimate truth for themselves and their care seekers.

Ground and Truth

This discussion on what is conventional truth and ultimate truth is expanded into the Tibetan hermeneutical device of ground, path, and fruition (*gzhi, lam, 'bras bu*; *zhi, lam, bre bu*).[30] In this system, the ground represents the foundational or primary aspect of a situation. The path represents its process or implementation. Finally, fruition represents its result or outcome. Within the Tibetan Buddhist tradition, there are several understandings of how the two truths integrate with the ground, path, and fruition. This chapter takes

---

29   Komarovshi, *Tibetan Buddhism*, 63.
30   Leif, "Working with Threefold Logic."

one of among many of these approaches. Here, the ground is considered the ultimate truth as foundation, the path is related to the conventional truth, and finally the fruition is related to the ultimate truth as result.

The system of ground, path, and fruition is also more commonly encountered as the Four Noble Truths (*pakpé denpa shyi; 'phags pa'i bden pa bzhi*). The First Noble Truth refers to the reality of suffering. The Second Noble Truth refers to the true causes of suffering. The First and Second Noble Truths are the ground. The Third Noble Truth refers to the reality that suffering can end. The Third Noble Truth is the fruition, that is, the ultimate truth. The Fourth Noble Truth refers to the way to end suffering and is related to the path.[31] In the field of Buddhist chaplaincy, the very necessity to get the work done means that many Buddhist chaplains devote considerable time and have made significant progress in articulating several paths, several ways to end suffering, in Buddhist chaplaincy.

Here the chapter expands the scope of the ground using the *Guhyagarbha* Tantra (GT). The GT, or the *Glorious Secret Essence Definitive Nature as It Is*, returns the attention to the ultimate truth of reality. The *Guhyagarbha* Tantra is also known as the "king of all tantras"; the "peak of all yanas";[32] the "source of all doctrinal schools"; the "universal explanation of all scriptures"; the "final intention, thought, and realization of all buddhas"; the "ultimate result of all yanas"; the "great passage of all the Victorious Ones of the three times"; and the "supreme highway of all yogis and yoginis." These eight additional titles point to the fact that this scripture is the source text for these eight topics within the Nyingma tradition of Tibetan Buddhism.

In its English translation, this scripture consists of forty-four pages divided into twenty-two chapters. The ritual/liturgical compliment of this scripture is the Hundred Peaceful and Wrathful Deities from which another scripture is associated—*The Great Liberation through Hearing in the Bardo,*

---

31   Monica Sanford related the Four Noble Truths to Richard Osmer's four tasks of practical theology in her doctoral dissertation entitled "The Practice of Dharma Reflection Among Buddhist Chaplains: A Qualitative Study Of 'Theological' Activity Among Non-theocentric Spiritual Caregivers," PhD diss. (Claremont School of Theology, 2018), 9–11. See also Richard Osmer, *Practical Theology: An Introduction* (Grand Rapids, MI: Eerdmans, 2008).

32   "Yanas" mean "vehicles" in Sanskrit and in turn refer to cycles of Buddhist teachings.

which is more commonly known in the West as the *Tibetan Book of the Dead.*
This scripture has been effectively used as a source text in Buddhist chaplaincy and hospice work as it balances contemporary needs while remaining rooted in the tradition.[33]

These twenty-two chapters focus on ten topics (*gyü kyi ngöpo chu; rgyud kyi dngos po bcu*), of which this chapter addresses only the first and last—view and mantra.[34] The main point of these ten topics is, through analogy of deities, their retinues, and celestial palaces, that the cause and the potential of becoming a Buddha is within us. Our entire reality (the conventional truth) is never separate from this divine nature (the ultimate truth). The appearance we see, the sounds we hear, and the awareness we connect to are pure from their beginning.

The second chapter of the GT expresses the two truths as follows:

> *From within the essence of the sugatas, [confusion occurs].*
> > *Through the karmic causes of each individual's concepts:*
> > *Countless forms and abundance of places, sufferings and so forth,*
> > *The self and the individualized fixation with the self all*
> *emanate.*
> > *Due to the conceptualization of fixating upon a self.*
> > *Like insisting upon tying knots in space,*
> > *No one has ever bound or released.*
> > *In order to reveal this primordial, spontaneously perfected*
> *doctrine of the Buddha,*
> > *Diverse manifestations emanate.*
> > *Thus, the Tathāgata himself intentionally bring forth the*
> *subject to the Tathāgata himself.[35]*

These verses explain that it is because there is fixation with the self and the conceptualization of a self that suffering occurs. However, all phenomena,

---

33   Margaret Coberly, *Sacred Passage: How to Provide Fearless, Compassionate Care for the Dying* (Boston: Shambhala, 2003); Francesca Fremantle, *Luminous Emptiness: Understanding the Tibetan Book of the Dead* (Boston: Shambhala, 2003).

34   The other eight topics are samadhi; action; mandala; empowerment; commitment; accomplishment; offerings; and enlightened activity.

35   Chönam and Khandro, *Guhyagarbha Tantra*, 41.

including the individual person, are primordially and spontaneously pure. The Buddhist path is likened to a Buddha reaching out to the Buddha themselves and by analogy is like untying knots made of air into air itself.

The fourth chapter of the GT expresses the two truths from a different perspective. Here the ultimate truth is expressed in the conventional truth:

> *Then all the* tathāgatas *express the aphorism in this way. Ah is empty and not empty, and the Middle Way as well has never been conceptualized. Everything is only labeled. All buddhas abide in this garland of syllables. Ah itself appears as diverse aspects; then there are forty-two [letters], such as ka and so forth.*[36]

The analogy in this passage points to a particular example: when the writer writes a letter "A" and it is seen by the reader, both the writer and reader see the letter "A" but know it is a sign for the sound "Ah."

In a therapeutic example, the chaplain can see the anger of a care seeker when told of the death of a loved one. But the anger is like the letter "A" as it refers to the connection that the care seeker wants to continue to hold on to with their loved one—the sound of "Ah." This analogy in the GT challenges the chaplain to look beyond the destructive behaviors of care seekers to see how they express their inner pure natures, their connection to their wholeness.[37] The fourth chapter of the GT also compels one to see how interreligious dialogue helps individuals and communities to express commitment to our various faith traditions while, at the same time, instead of looking into the truth claims of various religious traditions, we instead look at the varied ways other traditions articulate and demonstrate our connection to what we call truth.

Implications for Interfaith Chaplaincy

In addition to the implications posited above, a Tibetan Buddhist understanding of religious location and the two truths offers important wisdom

---

36   Chönam and Khandro, *Guhyagarbha Tantra*, 47.
37   This analogy expands Anton Boisen's concept of the living human document as discussed in Robert C. Dykstra, *Images of Pastoral Care* (St. Louis: Chalice Press, 2005).

for chaplaincy in interreligious contexts. First, a Tibetan Buddhist understanding of religious location is founded on the notion of a groundless ground. An individual's religious location is not related to an independent, enduring, immutable identity. Instead it is a seed with potential for change. In its most basic explanation, it is a reminder that we all are subject to change and we can use this change to become better versions of ourselves.

In addition, wisdom about the two truths derived from the GT demonstrates that the potential of becoming a Buddha is within us. This can be a helpful reminder to the Buddhist chaplain when the chaplain or the care seeker loses hope or doubts her/his capacity to change. The chaplain and care seeker can have firm faith that change does happen and it can be employed for progress. There are conventional Buddhist locations, but there is also an ultimate Buddhist location. In fact, the different Tibetan Buddhist locations are founded on this ultimate location. When this wisdom from the GT is applied to interreligious dialogue in chaplaincy, and when the conversations begin on a place of equality—when there is power sharing, language care, and mature humility—then the three practices enable the dialogue partners to enter into fuller intimacy with each other and to be open to change and transformation.[38]

Finally, Buddhist chaplains can hold in harmony the two truths when caring for individuals whose suffering seems intractable. For example, consider the care a chaplain offers to a care seeker struggling with alcohol or drug addiction. Conventionally the care seeker is a person struggling with strong impulses to engage in destructive behavior, and who occupies a particular religious location; yet at the same time, the care seeker is a buddha whose potential is momentarily concealed. The therapeutic intervention by the chaplain is a ministry of presence that does two things: accompanies the care seeker through the processes of conventional recovery but also holds for the care seeker the insight into the care seeker's ultimate nature until such time that the care seeker can live from this ultimate truth. The work of the Buddhist chaplain is then to hold in harmony their own two truths and the two truths of their care seekers.

---

38   Greider, "Religious Location and Counseling."

Conclusion

This chapter evidenced how a Tibetan Buddhist understanding of religious location and the two truths offers implications for Buddhist chaplaincy and interreligious dialogue. Through the hermeneutic of ground, path, and fruition, and insights from the GT as source text, important insights for how the two truths influence intra- and interreligious care are offered. The two truths propose a conventional and an ultimate truth that is relevant to therapeutic practice and in interreligious dialogue.

Bibliography

Bhikkhu Buddhadasa. "Democratic Socialism." In *Me and Mine: Selected Essays of Bhikkhu Buddhadasa,* edited by Donald K. Swearer, 42–58. Albany: State University of New York Press, 1989.

Bidwell, Duane R. "Practicing the Religious Self: Buddhist-Christian Identity as Social Artifact." *Buddhist-Christian Studies* 28 (2008): 3–12. https://www.jstor.org/stable/30152924.

———. *When One Religion Isn't Enough: Lives of Spiritually Fluid People.* Boston: Beacon, 2018.

Bueckert, Leah Dawn, and Daniel S. Schipani. "Interfaith Spiritual Caregiving: The Case for Language Care." In *Spiritual Caregiving in the Hospital: Windows to Chaplaincy Ministry,* edited by Leah Dawn Bueckert and Daniel S. Schipani, 245–63. Kitchener: Pandora, in association with the Institute of Mennonite Studies, 2006.

Chönam, Lama, and Sangye Khandro, trans. *Guhyagarbha Tantra: Secret Essence Definitive Nature Just As It Is.* Boston: Snow Lion, 2011.

Coberly, Margaret. *Sacred Passage: How to Provide Fearless, Compassionate Care for the Dying.* Boston: Shambhala, 2003.

Dykstra, Robert C. *Images of Pastoral Care.* St Louis: Chalice Press, 2005.

Fremantle, Francesca. *Luminous Emptiness: Understanding the Tibetan Book of the Dead.* Boston: Shambhala, 2003.

Giles, Cheryl A., and Willa B. Miller, eds. *The Arts of Contemplative Care: Pioneering Voices in Buddhist Chaplaincy and Pastoral Work.* Boston: Wisdom, 2012.

Greider, Kathleen J. "Religious Location and Counseling: Engaging Diversity and Difference in Views of Religion." In *Understanding Pastoral Counseling,* edited by Elizabeth A. Maynard and Jill L. Snodgrass, 235–56. New York: Springer, 2015.

Jones, Ken. *The New Social Face of Buddhism.* Somerville, MA: Wisdom, 2003.

Knitter, Paul F. *Introducing Theologies of Religions.* Maryknoll: Orbis Books, 2002.

Komarovshi, Yaroslav. *Tibetan Buddhism and Mystical Experience.* Oxford: Oxford University Press, 2015.

Kujawa-Holbrook, Sheryl A. *God Beyond Borders: Interreligious Learning Among Faith Communities.* Eugene, OR: Pickwick, 2014.

Leif, Judith L. Appendix 2 of "Working with Threefold Logic." In *The Profound Treasury of the Ocean of Dharma: The Path of Individual Liberation,* edited by Chögyam Trungpa, 549–50. Boston: Shambhala, 2013.

Jackson, Roger R., and John J. Makransky, eds. *Buddhist Theology: Critical Reflections by Contemporary Buddhist Scholars.* London: Routledge Curzon, 2000.

Nāgārjuna. *The Fundamental Wisdom of the Middle Way: Nāgārjuna's Mūlamadhyamakakārikā.* Translated by Jay L. Garfield. New York: Oxford University Press, 1995.

Osmer, Richard R. *Practical Theology: An Introduction.* Grand Rapids, MI: Eerdmans, 2008.

Pine, Red. *Diamond Sutra: The Perfection of Wisdom.* Washington: Counterpoint, 2011.

Ray, Reginald A. *Indestructible Truth: Living Spirituality of Tibetan Buddhism.* Boulder: Shambhala, 2002.

Sanford, Monica. "The Practice of Dharma Reflection Among Buddhist Chaplains: A Qualitative Study of 'Theological' Activity Among Non-theocentric Spiritual Caregivers." Ph.D. diss. Claremont School of Theology, 2018.

Sivaraksa, Sulak. *Conflict, Culture and Change: Engaged Buddhism in a Globalizing World.* Somerville, MA: Wisdom, 2005.

———. *Seeds of Peace: A Buddhist Vision for Renewing Society.* Berkeley: Parallax, 1992.

Thakchoe, Sonam. "The Theory of Two Truths in India." In *Stanford Encyclopedia of Philosophy,* edited by Edward N. Zalta. Summer 2022. https://plato.stanford.edu/entries/twotruths-india/#:~:text=The%20central%20thesis%20in%20the,mind%20to%20which%20it%20corresponds.

Thich Nhat Hanh. *Interbeing.* Berkley: Parallax, 1987.

Tracy, David. *Analogical Imagination: Christian Theology and the Culture of Pluralism.* New York: Crossroad, 1981.

❦ 5 ❧

"I FOLLOW THE RELIGION OF LOVE"

Wisdom from Ibn ʿArabi for Engaging Religious Difference in Counseling

NAZILA ISGANDAROVA

To God belong the east and the west. Wherever you turn, there is the face of God. God is all-encompassing, all-knowing.

—Qurʾan 2:115

MANY MENTAL HEALTH professionals recognize the importance of acknowledging clients' religious locations;[1] however, how clients respond and react to the counselor's religious location is rarely examined. In particular, Muslim counselors face specific challenges because Islam has been at the forefront of world news since 9/11. Muslim counselors are frequently judged by clients when their religious locations are assumed and not understood. Therefore, there are unique challenges and rewards faced by both Muslim counselors and their non-Muslim clients. For example, the following two cases reported by Haider Javed Warraich,[2] an MD working in Chapel Hill, North Carolina, illustrate how a patient and members of a care team reacted to this helping professional's Islamic identity.

---

1   Kathleen J. Greider, "Religious Location and Counseling: Engaging Diversity and Difference in Views of Religion," in *Understanding Pastoral Counseling*, ed. Elizabeth A. Maynard and Jill L. Snodgrass, 235–56 (New York: Springer, 2015).

2   Haider Javed Warraich, "Some People See Me as Muslim First and a Doctor Second. That's How Prejudice Works," *The Guardian*, February 13, 2015, https://www.theguardian.com/commentisfree/2015/feb/13/muslim-doctor-prejudice -chapel-hill.

Case One: "I am from Pakistan"

*A few days before Deah Barakat, Yusor Mohammed AbuSalha
and Razan Mohammad Abu-Salha were gunned down in their
apartment, I walked to the bedside of an elderly woman just
admitted to the cancer ward and, as I started taking her medical
history, I led with my tried and tested opening: "Sorry to see you
here, but it's nice to meet you."*

*Midway through her story of how she was admitted, she
stopped abruptly, looked me straight in the eye and asked: "Tell me
where you're from?"*

"I am from Pakistan," I said without hesitating.

*Her face immediately contorted, "Oh, Pakistan? A good
Pakistani usually blows things up." . . . She wasn't a bad person;
she was actually a wonderful human being who quickly realized
that she had said something wrong. She apologized as soon as the
words finished coming out of her mouth and, even as I tried to
change the subject by talking about her medical issues, I could tell
that she was still thinking about it.*[3]

Dr. Warraich reported that after treating this patient, she held his hand
and told him, "Doc, I trust you."[4] He noted, "What made that moment
special was that, in it, I was just her doctor—no one else."[5]

Case Two: "This is What Your People Are Doing"

*Though the stereotype is that doctors are accorded a certain amount
of dignity in American society, it's not always true for doctors who
happen to be Muslim; for many Americans, they remain Muslims
who just happen to be doctors. For instance, a Canadian-Muslim
medical student was making rounds with a surgical team at a
hospital in New York the day after a gunman killed a guard outside
the National War Memorial in Ottawa when, at 5:00 am, her*

---

3   Warraich, "Some People See Me as Muslim First."

4   Warraich, "Some People See Me as Muslim First."

5   Warraich, "Some People See Me as Muslim First."

*attending physician pulled her in front of a television, pointed to
the gunman and said, "Look, this is what your people are doing.
What a shame these people still follow what some idiot wrote in a
book 1500 years ago."*[6]

Case Three: "People Who Look Like You Make Me Uncomfortable"

In another incident, Dr. Jalal Baig,[7] a hematology/oncology fellow at the University of Illinois at Chicago, vividly described how some non-Muslim clients can be extremely uncomfortable with the presence of Muslim helping professionals in the room:

*So, as I went into a patient's room that day, I was saddled,
or burdened, with some of these thoughts. And when I went
to examine her I saw that she was completely engrossed in the
television. And she was distressed. Outraged. It was quite palpable.*

*As I examined her she started speaking, very upset. She looked
at me and said, "These foreign people only come here to kill and
ruin things." And then: "Donald Trump is right. America should
ban all Muslims from immigrating here."*

Naturally, I was shaken.

*Then she said, "I'm sorry, but your people and people who
look like you make me uncomfortable." She refused to let me take
care of her any further. Refused to let me provide any further
medical treatment.*[8]

Muslim counselors, spiritual caregivers, social workers, and other helping professionals are not immune to what both Dr. Warraich and Dr. Baig reported: they are also first seen as Muslim and then as the members of the

---

6   Warraich, "Some People See Me as Muslim First."

7   Jalal Baig, "I'm a Muslim Doctor. My Patient Refused Treatment Because of My Religion," *The World,* August 15, 2016, https://www.pri.org/stories/2016-08-15/im-muslim-doctor-my-patient-refused-treatment-because-my-religion.

8   Baig, "I'm a Muslim Doctor."

multidisciplinary team.[9] Dr. Warraich and Dr. Baig did not write about the process and content of their helping relationships. We do not know how they navigated the religious differences between their own and their patients' religious locations. However, their reflections adequately illustrate the frustration experienced by many helping professionals regarding patients' and clients' reactions to their religious backgrounds. Therefore, many Muslim health care professionals, including me, can relate to Dr. Baig's experience: "There's this voice in the back of your [client's] mind you keep hearing: 'Please don't be Muslim. Please don't be Muslim.'"[10]

In the above cases the religious locations of the patients were unknown; however, the cases described "power dynamics due to religious difference" that overcame the power of the doctors over patients in general.[11] More precisely, the patients in these cases claimed cultural dominance and the religious privilege and advantage associated with being non-Muslim. Although literature extensively discusses the religious bigotry and privileges that exist among counselors, it rarely addresses these issues among our clients. Therefore, less is known about how we, as Muslim helping professionals, process our grief and frustration when we are subject to situations like the ones which Warraich and Baig described.[12]

The case examples above also illustrate the specific barriers Muslim helping professionals face, such as Islamophobia, xenophobia, and political bias in general, in the delivery of service to non-Muslim clients. In light of these challenges, this chapter focuses on the religious locations of Muslim counselors and discusses the practice of relational-ethical spiritual care and counseling with non-Muslim clients. I will provide theological reflection, via the writings of the great Andalusian Sufi Muḥyi al-Din Ibn al-Arabi (d. 1240), that offers insights for practicing the religious values of love, mercy, and empathy in a way that enables counselors not only to become highly tolerant to religious differences but to accept those differences as the client's universal truth. I will also draw upon insights from counselor education and the social sciences to describe how Muslim spiritual caregivers

---

9   Warraich, "Some People See Me as Muslim First"; Baig, "I'm a Muslim Doctor."

10   Baig, "I'm a Muslim Doctor."

11   Greider, "Religious Location and Counseling," 244.

12   Warraich, "Some People See Me as Muslim First"; Baig, "I'm a Muslim Doctor."

and counselors can engage non-Muslim clients and address the unique challenges that may arise because of their own personal and religious locations. I argue that in order to deal with cultural issues effectively, clinical work needs to be grounded not only in theory but in the knowledge of clients' cultures in order to accurately evaluate clients' responses and varied behaviors.

Universalism and the Religion of Love

Since the nineteenth century, many scholars of religious studies have acknowledged "the idea of the fundamental unity of religions—or what may be reasonably termed liberal universalism."[13] The word "universalism" comes from the original Latin word *univer̄ses*, which means "altogether, all taken collectively, whole, entire."[14] In his seminal work on the great Andalusian Sufi Muḥyi al-Din Ibn al-Arabi, or more popularly referred to as Ibn 'Arabi and "the Greatest Master" (*al-shaykh al-akbar*), Gregory A. Lipton acknowledged conflicting perspectives on universalism that contribute to diverse, even divergent, interpretations of Ibn 'Arabi's work.[15] "Inclusivist and pluralistic perspectives" of universalism focus on "the essential unity of various religions as a *plurality* rather than on the universal nature of one particular tradition."[16] In contrast, universalism is also used to describe ideologies, including religions, whose adherents claim that their truth claims are valid for all people and all times.[17] Lipton's interpretation of Ibn 'Arabi's writings supports the second perspective on universalism. Lipton wrote, "Ibn 'Arabi's understanding of the religious Other is founded on a political metaphysics in which the Prophet Muhammad, and thus the religion of Islam, not only triumphs over but also *ultimately subsumes* all previous religions and their

---

13   Tomoko Masuzawa, *The Invention of World Religions: Or, How European Universalism Was Preserved in the Language of Pluralism* (Chicago: University of Chicago Press, 2005), 316.

14   Gregory A. Lipton, *Rethinking Ibn 'Arabi* (New York: Oxford University Press, 2018), 2.

15   Lipton, *Rethinking Ibn 'Arabi*.

16   Lipton, *Rethinking Ibn 'Arabi*, 3.

17   Marshall G. S. Hodgson, *The Venture of Islam: Conscience and History in a World Civilization*, vol. 1 (Chicago: University of Chicago Press, 1974).

laws."[18] In contrast, William Chittick,[19] Reynold A. Nicholson,[20] and others argue for a more inclusive, perennialist reading of Ibn 'Arabi wherein "every single path we take is not only created by but leads to God."[21] In my own understanding of Ibn 'Arabi's work, his appeal to universalism does not deny the particularities and differences of religious traditions nor is it supercessionist.

Ibn Al-'Arabi wrote the following in *The Interpreter of Desires* (*Tarjuman al-ashwaq*):

> *My heart has become capable of every form: it is a pasture for gazelles and a convent for Christian monks,*
> *And a temple for idols and the pilgrim's Ka'ba and the Tables of the Torah and the book of the Koran.*
> *I follow the Religion of Love: whatever way Love's camels take, that is my religion and my faith.*[22]

With this statement, Ibn 'Arabi argued that his religious location was influenced by the "the Religion of Love" via the heart "capable of every form."[23] Ibn 'Arabi issued a "call for universality" that can only be achieved "through the inner transformation of the individual's heart."[24] British Orientalist Nicholson translated and commented on *The Interpreter of Desires* (*Tarjumān al-ashwaq*) in 1911, and he was so much inspired by Ibn 'Arabi that he noted, "Love is the essence of all creeds: the true mystic welcomes it whatever guise it may assume."[25]

---

18   Lipton, *Rethinking Ibn 'Arabi*, 6.

19   William C. Chittick, *Imaginal Worlds: Ibn al-'Arabi and the Problem of Religious Diversity* (Albany: State University of New York Press, 1994).

20   Reynold A. Nicholson, *The Mystics of Islam* (Bloomington, IN: World Wisdom, 2002).

21   Lipton, *Rethinking Ibn 'Arabi*, 7.

22   Ibn Al-'Arabī, *The Tarjumán al-Ashwáq: A Collection of Mystical Odes*, trans. Reynold Alleyne Nicholson (1911, reis., London: Royal Asiatic Society, 1978), 67.

23   Lipton, *Rethinking Ibn 'Arabi*, 18.

24   Michael A. Sells, "Ibn 'Arabi's Garden among the Flames: A Reevaluation," *History of Religions* 23, no. 4 (1984): 287–88, http://www.jstor.org/stable/1062643.

25   Nicholson, *The Mystics of Islam*, 75.

By advocating for the religion of love that emphasizes "the divinity of beliefs" (*al-ilah fi al-i'tiqadat*), Ibn 'Arabi laid the foundation for a universalist metaphysics in the Islamic tradition that recognizes the correctness of all paths. This cannot be understood, however, from Euro-American presuppositions about what constitutes a religion. The dominant Euro-American perspective presents religion as "a set of beliefs to be confessed" which can be true or false.[26] Ibn 'Arabi did not maintain this perspective on religion. Rather, he coined the term *divinity of beliefs* as the "divine self-manifestation in the forms of beliefs" or similarly "the divine transmutation in form."[27] In the Islamic context, and according to Ibn 'Arabi, "religion (*al-din*) is equivalent to your obedience, and that which is from God, Most High, is the revealed law (*al-shar'*) to which you are obedient. So religion is obedience (*al-inqiyad*), and the Law (*al-namus*) is the revealed way (*al-shar'*) that God, Most High, has prescribed (*sha'a*)."[28] Within the traditional understanding of religion, one can take Ibn 'Arabi's concept of religion and obedience literally. However, the Sufi traditions of Islam and Ibn 'Arabi's writing evidence that religious obedience is not a choice. Rather, "it is the essences (*dhawat*) of human beings that determine whether they obey or transgress,"[29] and our essence is *of* God and *is* God.

Implications of the Religion of Love in Practice

Religious location based on the foundational principles of love, mercy, compassion, and universalism, as supported by the writings of Ibn 'Arabi, inspires Muslim counselors to address the pitfalls and dogmatic assertions of organized religious traditions. Doing so enables Muslim counselors to work with clients of various religious locations. Ibn 'Arabi believed that God created the first human in God's own image because of God's deep

---

26   William T. Cavanaugh, *The Myth of Religious Violence* (New York: Oxford University Press, 2009), 73.

27   Lipton, *Rethinking Ibn 'Arabi*, 27.

28   Ibn Al-'Arabi, *The Ringstones of Wisdom (Fusus.: al-hikam)*, trans. Caner K. Dagli (Chicago: Great Books of the Islamic World, 2004), 201.

29   Lipton, *Rethinking Ibn 'Arabi*, 32.

longing for intimacy.[30] The divine origin of all creation places love to humanity and empathy for all at the foundation of Muslim health care professionals' work. The religion of love enables Muslim counselors not only to become highly tolerant of religious differences but to accept them as the client's universal truth. In this regard, Ibn ʿArabi stated: "People have formed different beliefs about God, / And I *behold all* that they believe."[31] Ibn ʿArabi can also be an anchor for Muslim counselors even in difficult situations where we might be enraged with a client's offensive comments with regard to our religious location. According to Ibn ʿArabi, the "heart [is] capable of every form," meaning "capable of every 'belief" (*i ʿtiqad*)."[32] For Ibn ʿArabi, when "God lifts the veil from between Himself and His servant," Ibn ʿArabi claims, ". . . the servant sees Him in the *form of his belief (ṣurat mu ʿ taqadihi*)."[33] This implies an intimacy between God and the believer, the ability for all beliefs and understandings of God to be synonymously held in our hearts, and the capacity for counselors and clients to evolve in character and belief.

Ibn ʿArabi's call to work from an open heart and open mind is a call to recognize the real and universal truth. All of creation is ontologically contingent upon the "Truth" or simply "each belief is a specific reflection of God."[34] In this regard, Ibn ʿArabi noted, "Do not attach yourself," Ibn al-ʿArabi says, "to any particular creed exclusively, so that you disbelieve in all the rest; otherwise, you will lose much good, nay, you will fail to recognize the real truth of the matter. Let your soul be capable of *embracing all forms of belief*. God, the omnipresent and omnipotent, *is not limited by any one creed*."[35] This statement is encouraging in the way that it allows Muslim spiritual caregivers and counselors to agree with and embrace significant religious differences, and even disagreements, in their practice. In this regard, it is a

---

30   Saʾ diyya Shaikh, *Sufi Narratives of Intimacy: Ibn Arabī, Gender, and Sexuality* (Chapel Hill: University of North Carolina Press, 2012).

31   Abul Ela Affifi, *The Mystical Philosophy of Muḥyid Din-ibnul ʿArabī* (Cambridge, UK: Cambridge University Press, 1939), 151.

32   Lipton, *Rethinking Ibn ʿArabi*, 26.

33   Lipton, *Rethinking Ibn ʿArabi*, 27.

34   Lipton, *Rethinking Ibn ʿArabi*, 28.

35   Lipton, *Rethinking Ibn ʿArabi*, 28.

call "to be open to the possibility that there is something of value in religious locations other than our own, even when we disagree vehemently."[36]

Enacting Ibn 'Arabi's religion of love entails demonstrating unconditional love, positive regard, congruence, and empathy.[37] In this regard, Ibn 'Arabi's notion of love should be practiced on three levels: (1) love to human beings, (2) love to the universe, and (3) love to the human self. For Ibn 'Arabi these three dimensions of love are part of his concept of *wahdat al-wujud*, which refers to the unity of being. Since everything comes from God and God takes care of the creation, God unconditionally loves all the creation. In this respect, God does not discriminate against anyone, which is also supported by the famous Qur'anic verse that states, "He made beautiful all that He created" (Q. 32:7); "'He formed you, so He made your forms beautiful" (Q. 40:64). In this respect, Ibn 'Arabi offered an invitation to see and witness God and universal love in all people and all creation.

In reflecting on Ibn 'Arabi's legacy, it is evident that he did not ignore his religious location when he engaged with people from different religious locations: he still had a strong attachment to his Islamic faith, which was the foundation of his rich spirituality. However, according to Ibn 'Arabi, religion, faith, and spirituality are important aspects of our humanness and should not be overlooked. As mentioned before, such a position opposes the tendency in the academic field toward a superficial universalism, "false and partial pretenses at universalism" that "serve only to disguise and mask reality."[38] Ibn 'Arabi's universalist ethic of love compels Muslim counselors to embrace religious difference, not to overlook it.

Ethical Foundations for Counseling Clients with Different Religious Locations

When we face clients who question our religious locations and are suspicious of our services, Muslim counselors might ask themselves questions that reflect their clients' fears, doubts, and concerns: "How am I going to

---

36   Greider, "Religious Location and Counseling," 238.

37   Carl R. Rogers, *On Becoming a Person: A Therapist's View of Psychotherapy* (1961, reis., New York: Houghton Mifflin Company, 1995).

38   Alison Assiter, *Revisiting Universalism* (New York: Palgrave Macmillan, 2003), 3.

help this client? Will I be secure when I work with this client?" When clients show mistrust and lack of respect due to the counselor's religious location, how can the counselor enact care of self and care of other? Ibn 'Arabi's conception of the religion of love inspires a relational ethic for navigating differences between the counselor's and the client's religious locations. The wisdom of Ibn 'Arabi, combined with insights from the discipline of counselor education, results in four principles counselors can employ to ethically navigate religious difference.

First, counselors need to begin by self-reflexively examining their own religious locations, the "deep structures and values, sometimes referred to as our worldview or philosophy of life."[39] Since they are located deep in our subconscious mind, they are not easily accessible to our consciousness. When we are not aware of these remote structures of meaning and value, "we behave in ways that conflict with the values we state most insistently."[40]

Self-awareness as a skill is an evolving capacity within each care provider. This aspect of cross-cultural competence implies that counselors "need to become more aware of their cultural values, assumptions, and biases about human behaviour; the lessons they learned from their own upbringing and culture."[41] Counselors learn self-awareness as a skill in their training programs because they need to know themselves before they attempt to learn their clients. Reflexivity helps counselors become aware of their worldview and culture in order to overcome ethnocentrism and cultural encapsulation.[42]

Most counselor training programs foster personal reflection on gender, ethnicity, family background, and life experience. Few training programs lead counselors in reflecting on their religious locations, beliefs, values, and biases. Counselors should not ignore the importance of their religious locations in the therapeutic setting. As Seymour stated,

---

39   Greider, "Religious Location and Counseling," 244.

40   Greider, "Religious Location and Counseling," 244.

41   Derek Truscott and Kenneth H. Crook, *Ethics for the Practice of Psychology in Canada* (Edmonton: The University of Alberta Press, 2004), 119.

42   Elise Cole, "Navigating the Dialectic: Following Ethical Rules Versus Culturally Appropriate Practice," *The American Journal of Family Therapy* 36, no. 5 (2008): 425–36, https://doi.org/10.1080/01926180701804642.

*We must be aware of, admit to, and try to understand fully
the impact of personal values as we go about our day-to-day
business of marriage and family counselling. If we are indeed,
even occasionally selling our values in one form or another to our
clients, we should at least be aware of what it is we are selling, and
the consumer client should rightfully demand from us "truth in
packaging."* [43]

What helps counselors to identify the impact of their values in the counseling process is rigorously exploring their personal beliefs and values about therapy, families, and change along with the moral effects of those values on clients. This process involves critical evaluation and awareness of morality, integrity, and accountability. If counselors choose to act as moral consultants, then they choose to be in a collaborative endeavour in which they guide their clients in an exploration of the moral implications of their decisions.[44] However, the other option may also be acting from the perspective of moral relativism, which is influenced by social constructionism that considers power and privilege, culture, and the unique context of a person's life. Counselors who act from the moral relativism perspective tend to be aware of their accountability for the moral effects of their actions on the lives of their clients.

Second, in addition to self-awareness, counselors need to be aware of and informed about the client's religious location as well. The ethics of multifaith counseling require that when counselors work with clients who belong to different religious traditions, they have to acquire cultural knowledge or multicultural literacy of this client population. In this respect, Muslim counselors can be inspired by Ibn 'Arabi's "multifaith" experience and what he learned through his extensive journeys to different countries where he was exposed to and learned diverse cultures, languages, historical

---

43   Warren R. Seymour, "Values, Ethics, Legalities and the Family Therapist: III. Counselor/Therapist Values and Therapeutic Style," *Journal of Family Therapy Collections* 1 (1982): 43.

44   Thomas D. Carlson and Martin J. Erickson, "Re-capturing the Person *in* the Therapist: An Exploration of Personal Values, Commitments, and Beliefs," *Contemporary Family Therapy* 21, no. 1 (1999): 57–76, https://doi.org/10.1023/A:1021962604658.

experiences, values, spiritual and religious beliefs, and customs and life-styles. Such awareness of cultural practices can be of immense benefit to counselors in expanding our sense of cultural pliancy and knowledge of different communication styles, body language cues, use of interpersonal space, tone of voice, eye contact, and passivity/assertiveness patterns. All these assist counselors in understanding different ways of being and of communicating within cultures, and in developing and delivering culturally appropriate services for clients.

From this perspective, being culturally literate regarding the client's spirituality and religion may be considered as having a cultural knowledge in counseling. Even when the religious difference between counselor and client is overt and offensive, as was shown in the cases presented above, multiculturally competent Muslim counselors can effectively use spirituality to empower their clients. This is because the majority of clients adopt some identifiable form of expression for their spirituality; therefore, it is logical that Muslim counselors should attend to the spiritual belief systems of clients if they are to fully understand them.

Third, based on the counselor's own self-awareness and awareness of the client's religious location, the counselor can then listen for three kinds of religious differences:

> *(1) interreligious (or interfaith) difference, which occurs when the counselor and client share different religious locations or "when one values religion and the other does not";*
> *(2) intrareligious (intrafaith) difference, which occurs when clients and counselors "differ significantly even when they are located within the same tradition"; and*
> *(3) differences due to religious multiplicity, which occurs when the counselor or client "engages in more than one religious tradition."[45]*

Embracing Ibn 'Arabi's religion of love entails radical acceptance of religious difference, whether that difference is inter- or intrafaith, or due to religious multiplicity. Sadly, Muslims are portrayed in the mainstream

---

45   Greider, "Religious Location and Counseling," 241.

media as if their religious and cultural beliefs conflict with mainstream Western values. This has already caused "us" vs. "them" scenarios that divide society. Meanwhile, Muslim counselors should also be mindful of their own biases that foster uncertainty and lack of trust. Muslim counselors should acknowledge that respecting cultural behaviors and religious differences takes time and persistence while simultaneously honoring their own religious locations. Such an approach will allow Muslim counselors to avoid interpreting the client's "narratives, practices and meaning systems" in an exclusivist manner that suggests that the counselor's "meaning system is the only true meaning system."[46] Also, they will be encouraged to apply "an inclusivist theological approach that seemingly embraces the 'truth' of all religious faiths."[47]

Fourth, practicing the religion of love in counseling entails recognizing barriers to integrating spirituality in counseling and learning how to overcome those barriers. There are several barriers to addressing clients' spirituality and navigating religious difference in counseling, yet when counselors succumb to such barriers, clinical work is impoverished. One barrier is that the spiritual dimension is seen as esoteric and unobservable, and therefore subjectivity is inevitable.[48] Counselors may feel comfortable discussing explicit religious beliefs and behaviors, yet not know how to raise or engage the more esoteric aspects of clients' spiritual lives. A second barrier concerns fears about the imposition of a particular frame of reference on clients. Clinicians are obliged to provide a non-imposing, non-judgmental practice. Fear of imposing our own beliefs can sometimes result in ignoring the client's, especially if the counselor is viewed as the "religious other." For some counselors, "rather than attempting to monitor appropriately our spiritual expression in clinical work as we monitor other areas, many practitioners have simply discounted the need to explore the spiritual aspect of clients'

---

46   Carrie Doehring, "The Practice of Relational-Ethical Pastoral Care: An Intercultural Approach," in *"After You!" Dialogical Ethics and the Pastoral Counseling Process*, ed. Axel Liégeous, Roger Burggraeve, Marina Reimslagh, and Jozef Corveleyn (Leuven: Uitgeverij Peeters, 2013), 160.

47   Doehring, "The Practice of Relational-Ethical Pastoral Care," 160.

48   Allie C. Killpatrick and Thomas P. Holland, *Working with Families: An Integrative Model by Level of Need* (New York: Pearson, 2006).

lives."[49] Counselors can overcome these barriers by engaging in the following practices:

> *1) explain the relationship between religion and spirituality, including similarities and differences, 2) describe religious and spiritual beliefs and practices in a particular context, 3) engage in self-exploration of his/her religious and/or spiritual beliefs in order to increase sensitivity, understanding and acceptance of his/her belief system, 4) describe one's religious and/or spiritual belief system and explain various models of religious/spiritual development across the lifespan, 5) demonstrate sensitivity to and acceptance of a variety of religious and/or spiritual expressions in the client's spiritual expression, and demonstrate appropriate referral skills and general possible referral sources, 7) assess the relevance of the spiritual domains in the client's therapeutic issue, 8) be sensitive to and respectful of spiritual themes in the counselling process as befits each client's expressed preference, and 9) use a client's spiritual beliefs in the pursuit of the client's therapeutic goals as befits the client's expressed preference.[50]*

Conclusion

The descriptions of who is responsible for 9/11 and the publicity attached to Muslims do not always reflect the reality. However, discriminatory environments and public images make Muslims responsible for all tragedies in the world. Muslim counselors and other health care professionals are not immune to the consequences of this false public image of Muslims. This reality directly and indirectly affects Muslim counselors who work with non-Muslim clients. This chapter highlighted the importance of identifying and avoiding false assumptions concerning Muslim beliefs, values, and practices. However, it also highlighted that Muslim counselors need to be

---

49   Killpatrick and Holland, *Working with Families*, 63.

50   Mary Thomas Burke, "From the Chair," *The CACREP Connection* (Winter 1998/99): 2, https://www.cacrep.org/wp-content/uploads/2013/03/Winter-1998-1999.pdf.

acutely aware of religious issues and practices in counseling, which are sensitive. By presenting Ibn ʿArabi's religion of love and general ethical principles, the chapter identified a relational-ethical approach to counseling within the boundaries which religious beliefs set.

Bibliography

Affifi, Abul Ela. *The Mystical Philosophy of Muḥyid Dīn-ibnul ʿArabī*. Cambridge, UK: Cambridge University Press, 1939.

Assiter, Alison. *Revisiting Universalism*. New York: Palgrave Macmillan, 2003.

Baig, Jalal. "I'm a Muslim Doctor. My Patient Refused Treatment Because of My Religion." *The World,* August 15, 2016. https://www.pri.org /stories/2016-08-15/im-muslim-doctor-my-patient-refused-treatment -because-my-religion.

Burke, Mary Thomas. "From the Chair." *The CACREP Connection* (Winter 1998/99): 2. https://www.cacrep.org/wp-content/uploads/2013/03 /Winter-1998-1999.pdf.

Carlson, Thomas D., and Martin J. Erickson. "Re-capturing the Person *in* the Therapist: An Exploration of Personal Values, Commitments, and Beliefs." *Contemporary Family Therapy* 21, no. 1 (1999): 57–76. https://doi.org/10.1023/A:1021962604658.

Cavanaugh, William T. *The Myth of Religious Violence*. New York: Oxford University Press, 2009.

Chittick, William C. *Imaginal Worlds: Ibn al-ʿArabi and the Problem of Religious Diversity*. Albany: State University of New York Press, 1994.

Cole, Elise. "Navigating the Dialectic: Following Ethical Rules Versus Culturally Appropriate Practice." *The American Journal of Family Therapy* 36, no. 5 (2008): 425–36. https://doi.org/10.1080/01926180701804642.

Doehring, Carrie. "The Practice of Relational-Ethical Pastoral Care: An Intercultural Approach." In *"After You!" Dialogical Ethics and the Pastoral Counseling Process*, edited by Axel Liégeous, Roger Burggraeve, Marina Reimslagh, and Jozef Corveleyn, 159–81. Leuven: Uitgeverij Peeters, 2013.

Greider, Kathleen J. "Religious Location and Counseling: Engaging Diversity and Difference in Views of Religion." In *Understanding Pastoral Counseling*, edited by Elizabeth A. Maynard and Jill L. Snodgrass, 235–56. New York: Springer, 2015.

Hodgson, Marshall G. S. *The Venture of Islam: Conscience and History in a World Civilization*. Vol. 1. Chicago: University of Chicago Press, 1974.

Ibn Al-'Arabī. *The Ringstones of Wisdom (Fuṣūṣ.: al-ḥikam)*. Translated by Caner K. Dagli. Chicago: Great Books of the Islamic World, 2004.

———. *The Tarjumán al-Ashwáq: A Collection of Mystical Odes*. Translated by Reynold Alleyne Nicholson. London: Royal Asiatic Society, 1978. First published in 1911.

Killpatrick, Allie C., and Thomas P. Holland. *Working with Families: An Integrative Model by Level of Need*. New York: Pearson, 2006.

Lipton, Gregory A. *Rethinking Ibn 'Arabi*. New York: Oxford University Press, 2018.

Masuzawa, Tomoko. *The Invention of World Religions: Or, How European Universalism Was Preserved in the Language of Pluralism*. Chicago: University of Chicago Press, 2005.

Nicholson, Reynold A. *The Mystics of Islam*. Bloomington, IN: World Wisdom, 2002.

Rogers, Carl R. *On Becoming a Person: A Therapist's View of Psychotherapy*. New York: Houghton Mifflin Company, 1995. First published in 1961.

Sells, Michael A. "Ibn 'Arabi's Garden among the Flames: A Reevaluation." *History of Religions* 23, no. 4 (1984): 287–315. http://www.jstor.org/stable/1062643.

Seymour, Warren R. "Values, Ethics, Legalities and the Family Therapist: III. Counselor/Therapist Values and Therapeutic Style." *Journal of Family Therapy Collections* 1 (1982): 41–60.

Shaikh, Sa'diyya. *Sufi Narratives of Intimacy: Ibn Arabi, Gender, and Sexuality*. Chapel Hill: University of North Carolina Press, 2012.

Truscott, Derek, and Kenneth H. Crook. *Ethics for the Practice of Psychology in Canada*. Edmonton: The University of Alberta Press, 2004.

Warraich, Haider Javed. "Some People See Me as Muslim First and a Doctor Second. That's How Prejudice Works." *The Guardian*, February 13, 2015. https://www.theguardian.com/commentisfree/2015/feb/13/muslim -doctor-prejudice-chapel-hill.

Part Two

NAVIGATING RELIGIOUS DIFFERENCE
IN DIVERSE CONTEXTS

❧ **6** ☙

INTERRELIGIOUS CARE IN TOTALITARIAN CONTEXTS

Learnings from Cuba and Vietnam

DUANE R. BIDWELL AND DANIEL S. SCHIPANI

CULTURAL, POLITICAL, AND economic systems shape spiritual care in significant ways, as pastoral theologians increasingly recognize.[1] Thirty-seven percent of the world's population lives under authoritarian-totalitarian conditions; another 24 percent lives in partial freedom; and freedom worldwide has consistently declined since 2006.[2] Religion, in particular, faces "high" or "very high" government restrictions in 28 percent of nations around the world.[3] While most literature addressing the nexus of care and politics focuses on democratic societies in the Global North, even those contexts face challenges to their freedoms. In 2018, for example, the political rights and civil liberties of people living in the United States decreased at accelerating rates.[4]

---

1   Marlene Ferreras, *Identity and Eschatology among Latinas Working in Transnational Corporations in México*, PhD diss. (Claremont School of Theology, 2019); Cedric C. Johnson, *Race, Religion, and Resilience in the Neoliberal Age* (New York: Palgrave MacMillan, 2016); Ryan LaMothe, *Care of Soul, Care of Polis: Toward a Political Pastoral Theology* (Eugene, OR: Cascade, 2017); Josh T. Morris, *Narratives of Moral Injury and Reintegration: Toward a Critical, Liberative Practical Theology*, PhD diss. (Claremont School of Theology, 2019); Bruce Rogers-Vaughn, *Caring for Souls in a Neoliberal Age* (New York: Palgrave MacMillan, 2016).

2   Michael J. Abramowitz, "Freedom in the World 2018: Democracy in Crisis," Freedom House, accessed June 29, 2023, https://freedomhouse.org/report/freedom-world/freedom-world-2018.

3   Pew Research Center, *Global Uptick in Government Restrictions on Religion in 2016*, June 21, 2018, https://www.pewforum.org/2018/06/21/global-uptick-in-government-restrictions-on-religion-in-2016/.

4   Abramowitz, "Freedom in the World 2018."

These realities demand that scholars and practitioners identify, name, and engage not only religious but also ideological differences between and among caregivers and care seekers. This might be especially true in authoritarian-totalitarian societies, which provide a "comprehensive qualitative orientation"[5] that orders human desire, including religious desire, toward an ultimate horizon established by and supporting the state.[6] This orientation serves religious as well as political-economic purposes, and religion and spirituality in authoritarian-totalitarian societies unfold within this ideological field. This dynamic creates complex (or multiple) religious bonds among caregivers and care receivers;[7] makes all spiritual care implicitly interreligious; and requires religious leaders engaged in "caring across traditions" to account for a pervasive, quasi-religious ideal that carries real consequences for the practice of religion.[8] These spiritual care providers constantly navigate competing teleologies and truth claims among religious traditions while maintaining dialogue with a dominant ideology that also makes claims to truth and ultimacy.

Effective spiritual care in such settings requires both multi- and interreligious sensitivity and awareness of sociopolitical ideologies that function like religious systems. Yet most scholarship on spiritual care promotes the norms of representative democracies without accounting for authoritarian-totalitarian norms that influence religious life in a number of contemporary nations. Thus, this chapter asks two questions: What influences intercultural and interreligious collaboration in authoritarian-totalitarian settings? What competencies do teachers and practitioners formed by democratic

---

5   John J. Thatamanil, "Eucharist Upstairs, Yoga Downstairs: On Multiple Religious Participation," in *Many Yet One? Multiple Religious Belonging*, ed. Peniel Jesudason Rufus Rajkumar and Joseph Prabhakar Dayam (Geneva: World Council of Churches, 2016), 13–15.

6   John J. Thatamanil, "Does Multiple Religious Belonging Necessarily Mean Internal Conflict?" (plenary address, International Association for Spiritual Care, Union Theological Seminary, New York, NY, July 9, 2018).

7   Duane R. Bidwell, *When One Religion Isn't Enough: The Lives of Spiritually Fluid People* (Boston: Beacon, 2018).

8   Duane R. Bidwell, "Religious Diversity and Public Pastoral Theology: Is It Time for a Comparative Theological Paradigm?," *Journal of Pastoral Theology* 25, no. 3 (2015): 143, https://doi.org/10.1080/10649867.2015.1122427.

thought need to understand, participate in, and influence spiritual care in authoritarian-totalitarian settings? Drawing on our experiences living, teaching, and providing care in Cuba and Vietnam, we identify challenges and opportunities for care across (and among) religious traditions in each setting. Then we recommend practices for future collaborations in such settings and identify what we have learned about spiritual care from working in authoritarian-totalitarian societies.

We draw on our experiences as spiritual care providers and theological educators in countries governed by communist political systems. Daniel has taught pastoral and spiritual care to seminarians and chaplains in training in Matanzas, Cuba, since 2013, while Duane taught practical theology and Christian pastoral care in 2016 to seminarians in Hồ Chí Minh City (formerly Sài Gòn). Both contexts required us to navigate the forms and degrees of religious difference identified by Kathleen Greider: interreligious (differences among multiple religious traditions), intrareligious (differences among people who share a religion tradition), and religious multiplicity (differences created when people are shaped by more than one religious or spiritual tradition at the same time).[9] After describing Cuba and Vietnam as contexts for care, we identify influences on intercultural and interreligious collaboration in authoritarian-totalitarian societies, as well as competencies that teachers and practitioners formed by democratic thought can develop to better understand, participate in, and influence spiritual care in authoritarian-totalitarian societies.

Making Sense of Context

Both Cuba and Vietnam are governed by communist political systems, but those systems differ significantly. Cuba has had an authoritarian-totalitarian political system since 1959, strongly influenced by the former Soviet Union's Marxist-Leninist model. A new constitution was approved by a national referendum on February 24, 2019. It includes reference to new rights, such as equal rights for women; it paves the way to recognition of

---

9   Kathleen J. Greider, "Religious Location and Counseling: Engaging Diversity and Difference in Views of Religion," in *Understanding Pastoral Counseling*, ed. Elizabeth A. Maynard and Jill L. Snodgrass, 235–56 (New York: Springer, 2015).

same-sex marriages and the right to private property (subject to regulations). It categorically states in Article 3 (Daniel's translation from Spanish), "Socialism and the social and political revolutionary system established by this Constitution are irrevocable"; and, in Article 5, "The Communist Party of Cuba . . . guided by the teachings of [independence hero José] Martí, Fidel [Castro] and Marxism Leninism, organized vanguard of the Cuban nation . . . is the superior leading force of society and state."[10] Public political speech is restricted and private economic initiatives are highly regulated and controlled.

In contrast, Vietnam unified as a communist nation in 1975 after more than forty years of civil war, which was preceded by wars for independence from colonial powers. Philosophically and strategically, Vietnam's government and social system reflect more influence from Chinese than Soviet-Russian communism. In 1986, Vietnam shifted from a failed, centrally planned economy to a socialist-oriented market economy based on state-owned industry. This has allowed Vietnam to integrate into the global market economy. As a single-party state, Vietnam continues to control all dimensions of social and political life, including education and religion. It restricts free speech, the media, freedom to assemble, and freedom of association. Peaceable complaints, public demonstrations, and criticism of the regime regularly result in detention, trial, and imprisonment.

Religion in Contemporary Cuba

Cuba is officially a secular state with the explicit provision for the separation of church and state. In 1992, the constitution was amended by dropping the characterization of the state as atheistic. According to the constitution, the state recognizes, respects, and guarantees freedom of religion; different beliefs and religions enjoy the same considerations under the law; and discrimination based on religion is prohibited.

The government and the Communist Party, through the party's Office of Religious Affairs (ORA), supervise most aspects of religious life.

---

10   Juris Cuba, *Indice Proyecto de Constitución de la República de Cuba. Fundamentos Políticos. Principios Fundamentals de la Nación (28–65)*, accessed July 11, 2023, http:// juriscuba.com/legislacion-2/leyes/proyecto-constitucion-cuba-indice/fundamentos-politicos -principios-fundamentales-de-la-nacion/.

Nevertheless, it is the case that religious freedom has generally increased in the last decades. Most religious groups can conduct charitable and educational projects, such as operating before- and after- (public) school community service programs, assisting with care for the elderly, providing potable water in small towns, growing and selling fruits and vegetables at below-market prices, and establishing health clinics. Generally speaking, Cuban citizens can practice their faiths without fear of persecution or discrimination, and openly religious persons can become members of the Communist Party. However, some religious organizations and human rights groups denounce the government for continuing to threaten, detain, and use violence against outspoken people critical of the authorities and the political situation.

It is estimated that, for a total population of 11.2 million, religious affiliation in Cuba is as follows: 60–70 percent Roman Catholic and 5 percent Protestant (mainly Pentecostals, Baptists, Methodists, Seventh-day Adventists, Presbyterians, and Anglicans).[11] More than 15 percent of the population practices a folk religion, such as Santería, which integrates West African and Congo River Basin religious beliefs and rituals with Roman Catholicism.[12] That is the case especially, although not exclusively, among Cubans of African descent. The Virgen de la Caridad del Cobre, the Catholic patroness of Cuba and a symbol of Cuban culture, in Santería has been syncretized with the goddess Oshun.

Roman Catholicism, the largest religion in Cuba, has its origins in Spanish colonization. It remains the dominant faith. Pope John Paul II and Pope Benedict XVI visited Cuba in 1998 and 2011, respectively, and Pope Francis visited Cuba in September 2015. Prior to each papal visit, the Cuban government pardoned prisoners as a humanitarian gesture. The government's relaxation of restrictions on house churches in the 1990s has led to an explosion of Pentecostalism. However, Evangelical Protestant denominations, organized into the umbrella Cuban Council of Churches, remain more publicly active and powerful in terms of their relationship with the government.

---

11   United States Department of State, Bureau of Democracy, Human Rights and Labor, *Cuba 2017 International Religious Freedom Report*, accessed July 13, 2023, https://www.state.gov/wp-content/uploads/2019/01/Cuba-2.pdf.

12   United States Department of State, *Cuba 2017.*

Religion in Contemporary Vietnam

Vietnam officially protects freedom of religion and worship. Buddhism, Catholicism, Protestantism, Islam, and the indigenous religions Hòa Hảo and Cao Đài are officially recognized, while Taoism, Confucianism, and animism inform popular piety. The indigenous Đạu Mẫu ("mother goddess") spirituality became more visible after 2016, when the United Nations designated it an intangible cultural heritage. Nonetheless, Vietnam remains a predominately secular nation. About 73 percent of the population identifies as non-religious or as practitioners of animistic folk religion (including Đạu Mẫu); 12.2 percent as Buddhist (primarily Mahayana); 6.8 percent as Catholic; 6.8 percent as Cao Đài; 1.5 percent as Protestant; and 1.4 percent as Hòa Hảo.[13]

Religious practices perceived to threaten state authority are restricted or forbidden. A 2004 ordinance criminalizes religious activities that "abuse the right to freedom of belief and religion to undermine the country's peace, independence, and unity," and religious statements "against State laws or policies" are expressly forbidden.[14] Religious groups must be recognized and registered by the state, which also controls religious leadership and education. For example, Christian ordinations, pastoral appointments, and seminaries require state approval, and leadership of the Buddhist *sangha* is determined by the government. It is illegal to proselytize, and Western missionaries find it difficult to receive visas.

The quasi-religious nature of the state in Vietnam is enshrined in language. The highest honorific is reserved for Hồ Chí Minh, the founder of the Vietnamese Communist Party, but Christians use it also for Jesus—causing some people to resent the implication that a colonial deity could be equal to Hồ (and some Christians to resent the implication that Hồ is equal to God). In Vietnam, no authority, values, or ideal may supersede the state and its authority over religious practice and institutions. Some Christian leaders in Vietnam assert that Christian affirmations of an ultimate beyond the state—insistence on the sovereignty of God, the primacy of baptismal identity, and the coming kingdom (or commonwealth) of God—are viewed as

---

13　　World Atlas, *Major Religions in Vietnam*, accessed July 13, 2023, https://www.worldtlas.com/articles/religious-beliefs-in-vietnam.html.

14　　Thanh Xuan Nguyễn, *Religions in Việt Nam* (Hanoi: Thế Gió, 2012), 319.

autonomous thoughts and thus potentially seditious doctrines that undermine the state.

Protestant Christianity faces particular challenges. Catholicism, introduced to Vietnam in 1533, is perceived as a European faith, while Protestantism, introduced at the turn of the twentieth century, is perceived as a US American religion. Religious leaders in Vietnam say both that Protestants are perceived as pro-democracy and that there is a strong belief that Protestant congregations are funded, at least in part, by overseas Vietnamese opposed to the Communist regime.[15] Some of the most egregious human rights violations in contemporary Vietnam are reserved for ethnic minority Protestants, especially among those historically aligned with the South Vietnam and its US advisors during the civil war (i.e., the Hmong, Muong, and other tribal people in mountainous regions).

Daniel's Role in Cuba

I have been a yearly visiting professor at the Seminario Evangélico de Teología (SET), in Matanzas, since 2013. I have also lectured occasionally at the Institute for the Sciences of Religion in Havana. The SET was founded in 1946 as a collaborative project of the Anglican (Episcopal), Methodist, and Reformed Presbyterian churches.

The SET is a progressive theological school. It supported the Revolution that in 1959 overthrew the US-backed, corrupt, and oppressive national government. During the first decades of Fidel Castro's rule, some of its faculty developed a Cuban version of liberation theology while participating in national programs to increase production of food and raw materials. In recent years, the school as such is not politically involved in direct ways. Like other religious and non-religious organizations, it provides counsel to the government on matters related to public policy and ethics (e.g., issues related to sexuality, marriage and family, nonviolent conflict resolution, etc.). The SET also relates daily with its surrounding community by freely providing drinking water, produce, and food to numerous economically vulnerable neighbors.

15　　Open Doors International, *World Watch List 2022: Situation of Religious Freedom for Christians: Vietnam* (Santa Ana: Open Doors International, 2021).

The SET offers both undergraduate and graduate degree programs. I teach courses in pastoral and spiritual care for the Master's program and, for the last two years, I have been an advisor and workshop presenter for the school's newest program, namely, a Certificate in Chaplaincy. The Cuban government recently authorized the SET to train chaplains to serve in prisons and hospitals on a voluntary basis. This is a significant development as the very first initiative to design a chaplaincy program in Cuba.

Duane's Role in Vietnam

For a semester, I enrolled in the Vietnamese studies and language program of National University in Hanoi. As a volunteer, I taught two week-long, intensive courses—Introduction to Practical Theology and Introduction to Pastoral Care—with MDiv and DMin students at an unapproved seminary in Hồ Chí Minh City. The seminary, affiliated with a US Protestant denomination that has never sought state approval, prepares women and men for pastoral service throughout the country, especially in isolated rural areas and among ethnic minorities. The decision to remain unapproved as a church and seminary reflects a strategic choice: unapproved institutions cannot be regulated as effectively as "official" expressions of religion, and the school's affiliated pastors and seminary officials protect themselves, church members, and students by maintaining positive relationships with local authorities.

There are no Vietnamese-language textbooks on practical or pastoral theology, and students found it difficult to respond to my questions about indigenous theology and ministry. In Protestant Vietnam, Jesus speaks with a North American dialect—specifically, a nineteenth-century evangelical and conserving dialect shaped by the Christian and Missionary Alliance (CMA), a traditional Protestant denomination that first evangelized the region. To offer a contrasting voice, I wrote a progressive statement of faith in Vietnamese. Intended for use in worship, it is shaped by liberation theologies and the Presbyterian Church (USA)'s "Brief Statement of Faith." After using the statement in class for a week, a male student invited me to preach—in Vietnamese—at his rural congregation during Advent. His congregation, composed primarily of ethnic minorities, responded enthusiastically to the statement's liberative frame.

Teaching Care in Cuba

The students enrolled in the chaplaincy formation program—roughly 70 percent women and 30 percent men—already serve in caregiving ministry in their congregations, whether as pastors or lay ministers. The majority belong to Baptist, Pentecostal, and Presbyterian churches. The practice as well as the teaching of pastoral care in Cuba is conditioned by a number of contextually significant factors such as the following: political accommodation, economic vulnerability, migration, and Evangelical piety and conservative theology.

First, citizens' de-facto political accommodation within a sixty-year-old totalitarian system is a notable feature of social reality that must be taken into consideration. Currently, the government does not make available an accurate picture of people's political views at the national level; nevertheless, it is my observation that the majority of the population experiences daily life conformed to the multidimensional reality of the political situation. Most religiously self-identified people say that they have divided loyalties regarding the demands of both the state and their faith. The state ideology is enacted with a typically fundamentalist structure defined by dogmatism, sectarianism, and proselytism. Further, the state's totalitarian ideology necessitates authoritarian political leadership.

Economic vulnerability is another major factor to consider. Chronic systemic dysfunction determined by a centralized, state-controlled economy is exacerbated by the embargo imposed and maintained by the United States in open violation of international law. Frequent shortages of state-guaranteed food staples and raw material for infrastructure work, for instance, are common. The monetary experiment resulting in two sub-systems linked to "Cuban peso" and "Convertible peso" seems to contribute to growing inequality. Under those circumstances, it's understandable that there tends to develop a culture of mere coping connected with resignation and widespread corruption.

Directly related to those two variables briefly mentioned above, internal and external migration presents an additional challenge. Churches have had to develop strategies and programs focusing on both those wishing to leave the country as well as relatives, friends, and other members who choose to stay or cannot emigrate. The impact of Cuban emigration on the family is a particular concern.[16]

A fourth factor present is the increase of freedom for the practice of religion together with frequent visits by, and support from, diverse religious (mainly conservative Evangelical) groups. Various Pentecostal, Baptist, and self-defined "nondenominational" Christian groups continue to grow as a consequence of the government's increased tolerance of religious activities of various kinds. The practice of care within those groups and congregations tends to be, at best, effectively intrafaith and, at worst, a special means for "evangelization" understood as conversion.

Finally, it continues to be difficult for Cubans to receive textbooks for seminary use from the United States. I made available electronically my recently published books in Spanish on pastoral care[17] and Christian and pastoral counseling.[18] Those texts, which are published and distributed by the Association for Hispanic Theological Education in the United States, present an adaptable model of psycho-spiritual care.

Teaching Care in Saì Gòn

Students at the seminary in Hồ Chí Minh City come from across Vietnam for intensive courses to earn MDiv and DMin degrees toward ordination or advanced practice in their respective denominations. Most are dual-career, earning a living in agriculture or another sector while serving as volunteer pastors in rural areas. The students taught me that at least five dynamics shape pastoral care in Vietnam: religious multiplicity, trauma, migration, surveillance, and Christian oppression.

First, most families and individuals in Vietnam are religiously hybrid to some degree.[19] Christians, Buddhists, and Taoists share homes; people view

---

16   Patricia Arés Muzio, "La Emigración y Su Impacto en la Familia Cubana," *Didajé* 5 (2014): 16–29; Ana Celia Pereira Pintado, "Religiosidad y Migraciones en Cuba," *Didajé* 5 (2014): 40–45.

17   Daniel S. Schipani, *Manual de Psicología Pastoral: Fundamentos y Principios de Acompañamiento* (Orlando: AETH, 2017).

18   Daniel S. Schipani, *Camino de Sabiduría – Consejería: Cuidado Psicoespiritual* (Orlando: AETH, 2019).

19   Bidwell, *When One Religion Isn't Enough.*

religion in terms of function rather than belief, praying at different altars and visiting various places of worship according to need; and Confucian values prioritize family relationships—including relationships with longdead ancestors—over religious commitments. All care is interreligious, implicitly or explicitly; therefore, theologies that prohibit ancestor veneration—a central practice in Vietnamese culture, across religious traditions—or require Christians to reject their non-Christian family members contribute to personal, interpersonal, and existential suffering. The state's sociopolitical ideology adds to these complex religious bonds; people face implicit and explicit pressures to ensure that religion, spirituality, and doctrine support the interests of the state (just as Christians in the United States are implicitly and explicitly pressured to idolize capitalism). When I wrote in my "Vietnamese Statement of Faith," for example, that Jesus ate with political dissidents, one of my language teachers protested that God would not associate with people who threatened the state. If Jesus ate with political dissidents, my teacher argued, either Jesus could not be God (because God would not associate with "bad people") or I misunderstood how dangerous dissidents could be.

Second, intergenerational trauma remains a hallmark of Vietnamese life. The past forty years have been the longest period without war in hundreds of years, and the dead are everywhere.[20] Every family has experienced some degree of war-related death and dislocation, and those who survived the French and American wars suffered from famine and severe poverty from 1975 to 1985. As a child, my adopted son's grandfather watched US airmen shot by Vietnamese troops fall from the sky, and his family's village had no electricity until the mid-2000s, when roads finally connected it to the provincial capital.

Third, migration is a fact of life in contemporary Vietnam. Rural residents relocate to cities to find work; Northerners go south for the same reason. In the north, women live with extended family, raising children alone while their husbands live and work in the south. Migration dismantles traditional family and community structures that provide support, including care

---

20   Quan Barry, *She Weeps Each Time You're Born: A Novel* (New York: Pantheon Books, 2015).

for children and the elderly. Migrants are distant not only from immediate family but also from ancestors, who are tied to the land. Agrarian practices and rhythms that provide identity are impossible to maintain in cities. Urban areas lack infrastructure to appropriately house, feed, or care for migrants who have no local family support.

Fourth, all Vietnamese live under surveillance—state surveillance and self-surveillance. The state's network of authority extends to granular levels—down to a few streets in cities. Neighborhood party chairs report to local and district chairs; district chairs, to provincial chairs; provincial chairs, to national officials. Any behavior perceived as threatening to peace can be reported. Email, telephone conversations, text messages, and internet use are monitored; the state blocks texts and social media posts that contain certain words or information; and activists and bloggers are arrested for sedition. Neighborhood chalkboards carry information from the party. Twice daily, loudspeakers broadcast announcements and patriotic songs. When I preached at a local congregation, its pastor had to notify local police of my presence and purpose; when I leased an apartment, I had to be registered as a foreigner, and the apartment manager sought approval from neighborhood officials. Government "minders" monitor tourists and locals at historic and religious sites, especially Buddhist pagodas and other institutions associated with historic resistance to the state. If private conversation turns to religion, especially to Christianity, some people drop their voices to a whisper. Christians report more invasive surveillance than others.

Fifth, Christians, particularly Protestants, face oppression and discrimination, especially those who serve in the military, work as police, or hold government jobs. Laws place the Christian minority at a disadvantage, and local implementation of those laws can lead to persecution, especially in isolated rural areas. Churches are vandalized; assets of Christian communities and individuals are seized; pastors are jailed; and violent attacks occasionally occur among ethnic minority communities. Police disrupt and disband worship gatherings; officials favor non-Christians when distributing land and other benefits; and pastors spend a good deal of time running interference with local officials to protect the congregants. Christians remain acutely aware of the risk involved in attending worship, reading religious literature, and engaging in social outreach.

Interreligious Care and Collaboration in Authoritarian-Totalitarian Systems

Factors shaping interreligious care and collaboration in authoritarian-totalitarian systems include state ideology, mixed-faith families, risks of religious practice and identity, and the relationship of religious leaders to state authority. In such systems, spiritual care providers teach and represent their religion in constant dialogue with—and sometimes in contrast to—a dominant state ideology that makes broad public claims to truth and to ultimacy. In both Cuba and Vietnam, especially among younger generations, this means reckoning with the official and popular image of the state as an agent of peace, virtue, justice, and goodness. As such, people affirm that religious leaders and institutions should support and promote the state; religious behavior or beliefs contrary to state ideology are condemned as threats to peace and security. Culturally, a person's highest allegiance should be to the state, followed by family; religious commitments and practices should be personal, private, non-communal (outside of family), and secondary to concerns for the political and economic well-being of citizens and the state. In Cuba, this is the expectation of the government and is made explicit when conflicts arise; it is the case, for instance, in connection with public accountability and allocation of funds and other resources coming from overseas. Government officials make sure that the hegemony of the state is not undermined or even challenged in any way. In Vietnam, religions that condemn Confucian-Taoist ancestor veneration, as some forms of Christianity advocate, are particularly problematic, as they interrupt the ongoing care of ancestors seen as vital to the virtue and success of individuals, families, and the nation as a whole.

State-centered ideology means that spiritual care providers in authoritarian-totalitarian systems are always working across complex religious bonds, which Greider identified as a religious difference created by multiplicity.[21] For example, a person might be Christian and a member of the Communist Party, with the competing worldviews, commitments, and values implied by such dual belonging. For those who doubt that authoritarian-totalitarian ideology serves a religious function, note China's recent move

---

21   Greider, "Religious Location and Counseling."

to create a state version of the Christian Bible to provide a "correct under-standing of the text" that aligns more closely with Chinese socialist ideals.[22] In Cuba, conservative and fundamentalist Christian caregivers cannot rec-oncile their faith claims with those of the fundamentalist state ideology. As expected, major tension arises when those caregivers encounter highly ideo-logically committed staff in prisons and hospitals. In Vietnam, exclusivist Christian theology creates difficulties for those whose families follow the cultural norm of worshiping at Buddhist, Taoist, and Confucian temples, as well as praying to protective local deities found in most neighborhoods. In mapping people's "theological houses,"[23] caregivers must be particularly adept at recognizing and moving across religious lines—especially when interreligious difference and difference created by religious multiplicity lead to conflict in families, marital relationships, and congregations.

Religious identity and practice not only contribute to family and com-munity conflict but can also present social and political risks. In Vietnam, for example, Christian providers of spiritual care must be careful about approaching people in public and carefully frame their relationships to people, lest they "out" a member of the congregation, lead others to believe that someone is sympa-thetic to Protestant Christianity, or open a person to political, professional, or personal discrimination or retaliation. It can be difficult for a Christian woman, for example, to marry a non-Christian man or someone employed by the mili-tary, police, or government; being married to a Christian—or someone who has a Christian family member—serves as a barrier to professional advancement.

Finally, caregivers need the interreligious intelligence to establish posi-tive, supportive relationships with state authorities: local police officers, cadre members, military members, and others. In Cuba, the challenge of progressive Christian caregivers consists in maintaining ethical and theological integrity while closely working with the government in implementing certain public policies conducive to the common good. The work of the Cuban Council

---

22   Lily Kuo, "In China, They're Closing Churches, Jailing Pastors—and Even Rewriting Scripture," *The Guardian*, January 13, 2019, https://www.theguardian.com /world/2019/jan/13/china-christians-religious-persecution-translation-persecution -translation-bible.

23   Carrie Doehring, *The Practice of Pastoral Care: A Postmodern Approach*, rev. ed. (Louisville, KY: Westminster John Knox, 2015).

of Churches and the Martin Luther King Center (MLKC) in Havana is an exemplar in this regard, for instance, as they function as frequent consultants on issues of human rights, marriage and family, and the law. In Vietnam, establishing and maintaining relationships with authorities on behalf of parishioners can be one of a pastor's primary means of providing care. This is not advocacy, per se, but an instrumental relationality to protect and "run interference" with state power to ensure fair treatment, protect the right to worship, and communicate appropriate Confucian respect for authorities.

What We've Learned

Most scholarship on spiritual care promotes the norms of representative democracies without accounting for authoritarian-totalitarian norms. Christian liberation theologies perceived to threaten state control and state ultimacy are particularly problematic. In authoritarian-totalitarian contexts, these theologies must be carefully parsed to protect pastors and congregants. For example, in Cuba the MLKC and other progressive Christian congregations and organizations function with a peace-with-justice theological view that undergirds their work (e.g., distribution of medicines, HIV prevention programs, housing projects, etc.).

There are similarities between care in authoritarian systems and in racial-ethnic congregations in the United States. The norms and functions of care in authoritarian-totalitarian systems, as in some Black, Latinx, and Asian communities in North America and elsewhere, are communal, not individual; concerned with physical and economic safety, not individual growth; give social and spiritual authority to the care provider; and may value contextual wisdom more than the insights of psychology and other social sciences. Our experience thus invites care providers, scholars, and educators of pastoral theology to engage in serious critical reflection. We must reconsider and even challenge and correct prevailing normative frameworks in caregiving theory and practice, and our implicit (and sometimes explicit) connection with the neo-liberal ideology that sustains market capitalism.[24]

---

24   Rogers-Vaughn, *Caring for Souls;* Bruce Rogers-Vaughn, "Class Power and Human Suffering: Resisting the Idolatry of the Market in Pastoral Theology and Care," in *Pastoral Theology and Care: Critical Trajectories in Theory and Practice*, ed. Nancy J. Ramsay, 55–77 (Hoboken, NJ: John Wiley & Sons, 2018).

Finally, care providers in the United States can learn much about care in the midst of volatile ideological divides from religious leaders in authoritarian-totalitarian societies. For instance, the potential of religious leaders as facilitators of mediation between competing ideologies and claims is particularly intriguing. Parsing these lessons, however, is beyond the scope of this chapter.

Competencies for Collaboration

Carrie Doehring's recommendations for intercultural care—a comparative approach that highlights difference; critical self-awareness of religious location and meaning; and co-creation of provisional contextual meanings and ways of experiencing holiness—serve well in authoritarian-totalitarian contexts.[25] The same can be said regarding principles—i.e., dependable guides to practice—stemming from the fields of interfaith spiritual care and intercultural counseling.[26] In the case of the latter, two areas of consideration are competence for caregivers of marginalized groups, and political and social justice implications.[27] We have found that the heuristic import of those theories of care applies to contexts where the state's political ideology functions like a religious system; it does so by facilitating pedagogic communication in teaching care and therapeutic communication in actual caregiving practice. At the same time, it remains to be studied whether learnings from involvement in authoritarian-totalitarian contexts can in turn further illumine intercultural and interfaith dynamics as currently understood and engaged in the United States.

In addition, effective spiritual care in authoritarian-totalitarian settings requires multi- and interreligious sensitivity and awareness of sociopolitical

---

25   Carrie Doehring, "The Practice of Relational-Ethical Pastoral Care: An Intercultural Approach," in *"After You!" Dialogical Ethics and the Pastoral Counseling Process*, ed. Axel Liégeous, Roger Burggraeve, Marina Reimslagh, and Jozef Corveleyn, 159–81 (Leuven: Uitgeverij Peeters, 2013).

26   Daniel S. Schipani, "Pastoral and Spiritual Care in Multifaith Contexts," in *Teaching for a Multifaith World*, ed. Eleazar S. Fernandez, 124–46 (Eugene, OR: Pickwick, 2017).

27   Derald Wing Sue and David Sue, *Counseling the Culturally Diverse: Theory and Practice*, 7th ed. (Hoboken, NJ: John Wiley & Sons, 2016).

ideologies that function like religious systems. Teachers and care providers from Western democracies must identify and clarify the embedded democratic and liberative assumptions that inform their approaches to care, theological norms, and classroom management. Especially, caregivers from the United States and Europe must identify and "hold lightly" their own political ideologies to enter into the worldview and theological norms of people and congregations in authoritarian-totalitarian systems.

Reading contemporary fiction and memoirs written by people living in totalitarian systems can be one way of heightening awareness of one's own political ideologies and increasing understanding and empathy toward the experiences of students and care receivers. In Cuba and in Vietnam there are multiple artistic expressions of resistance to authoritarianism and the totalitarian state; they include creative work in the fields of literature, cinema, theater, and the visual arts that circulate in semi-clandestine fashion. We also find the following texts useful: Reinaldo Arenas's *Before Night Falls: A Memoir*,[28] Quan Barry's *She Weeps Each Time You're Born: A Novel*,[29] Viet Nguyễn's *The Sympathizer: A Novel*,[30] Bao Ninh's novel *The Sorrow of War*,[31] and Ludmila Ulitskaya's *The Big Green Tent: A Novel*.[32]

Suggestions for Teaching and Learning in Authoritarian-Totalitarian Contexts: Implications for Ongoing Collaboration

Our experience within totalitarian systems further illumines the understanding that pastors and other caregivers are embedded in their communities. Those ministering persons have more education than most in their contexts, and they are experts on what is useful, effective, and necessary in their contexts; therefore, they can correct, reform, and adapt what we bring from other contexts. We recognize the need to apprentice ourselves to their

---

28   Reinaldo Arenas, *Before Night Falls: A Memoir*, trans. Dolores M. Koch (New York: Viking Adult, 1993).

29   Barry, *She Weeps Each Time*.

30   Viet Thanh Nguyễn, *The Sympathizer: A Novel* (New York: Grove Press, 2015).

31   Bao Ninh, *The Sorrow of War* (New York: Vintage, 1994).

32   Lyudmila Ulitskaya, *The Big Green Tent: A Novel*, trans. Polly Gannon (New York: Farrar, Straus & Giroux, 2015).

practices rather than impose our norms. For example, we find that most pastors in these contexts adopt a posture of solidarity, advocacy for the "least of these"—but their understandings of "the least" are likely to be different from ours; we need to believe and trust their contextual exegesis and social-cultural analysis.

Pastors in authoritarian-totalitarian settings can, because of their education, religious authority, and perceived class location, become co-opted by the state to legitimize government power and policies. Yet, as recognized by Italian social theorist Antonio Gramsci,[33] clergy who emerge organically from the lower classes can align themselves with the oppressed instead of with the state, using their intellectual and religious power on behalf of the people they serve. "As educated professionals, clergy and other pastoral workers have considerable resources in terms of understanding and the ability to use and manipulate information. This can be of use to those who may have little access to tools for understanding and changing their own situations in the face of ideological and other forces ranged against them."[34] Introducing the Gramscian notion of the "organic intellectual," then, might be useful in helping pastors in authoritarian-totalitarian contexts to develop and use pastoral identity and authority in ways that communicate across religious and ideological lines.[35] Indeed, exploring how to develop hermeneutic and translation competencies is a necessary focus for further collaboration.

In addition, it can be useful to help students in totalitarian systems identify and articulate their theologies of care and their intersections and divergences from state ideology; this can mean bringing embedded values, assumptions, preferences, and biases into consciousness and making a choice about whether (and how) to embody them in interreligious settings. Finally, we can model our approach to care for those caught in dominant systems (e.g., police, military, government) and invite pastors and religious leaders to show us what is useful and what's not in our approaches developed

---

33   Antonio Gramsci, *Selections from the Prison Notebooks*, ed. and trans. Quintin Hoare and Geoffrey Nowell Smith (New York: International Publishers, 2014).

34   Stephen Pattison, *Pastoral Care and Liberation Theology* (Cambridge, UK: Cambridge University Press, 1997), 227.

35   Morris, *Narratives of Moral Injury.*

outside of authoritarian-totalitarian contexts. We thus again acknowledge that our modest contributions need to be viewed and experienced as a two-way street.

Conclusion

We remain committed to exploring the meaning and function of spiritual care in authoritarian-totalitarian contexts. Indeed, we find such work increasingly necessary in the current US political climate, an environment in which freedoms are increasingly at risk. At the same time, our experiences in Cuba and Vietnam raise our awareness of the ways that both our embedded political assumptions and the norms of neoliberal capitalism shape our ecclesiologies, eschatologies, theological anthropologies, and understandings of interreligious care. We are not immune to the influence of state ideologies and the ways they order religious desire toward particular ultimate horizons and understandings of human beings. Thus, the decolonization of our own practices and ideas remains a vital, primary challenge for teaching and practicing care in authoritarian-totalitarian contexts. Indeed, that is a challenge for our work in US contexts as well; offering excellent care requires decolonizing both practice and theory.[36] We are always at risk of subconsciously imposing our perspectives through spiritual care in the name of limited conceptualizations of "liberation," "freedom," "agency," and "self-determination." Self-reflexivity, humility, and a healthy dose of skepticism toward our own knowledge might be the most important competencies for interreligious education and care in totalitarian systems.

Bibliography

Abramowitz, Michael J. "Freedom in the World 2018: Democracy in Crisis." Freedom House. Accessed June 29, 2023. https://freedomhouse.org/report/freedom-world/freedom-world-2018.

Arenas, Reinaldo. *Before Night Falls: A Memoir.* Translated by Dolores M. Koch. New York: Viking Adult, 1993.

---

36   Emmanuel Y. A. Lartey, "Postcolonializing Pastoral Theology: Enhancing the Intercultural Paradigm," in Ramsay, *Pastoral Care and Theology*, 79–97.

Arés Muzio, Patricia. "La Emigración y Su Impacto en la Familia Cubana." *Didajé* 5 (2014): 16–29.

Barry, Quan. *She Weeps Each Time You're Born: A Novel.* New York: Pantheon Books, 2015.

Bidwell, Duane R. "Religious Diversity and Public Pastoral Theology: Is It Time for a Comparative Theological Paradigm?." *Journal of Pastoral Theology* 25, no. 3 (2015): 135–50. https://doi.org/10.1080/10649 867.2015.1122427.

———. *When One Religion Isn't Enough: The Lives of Spiritually Fluid People.* Boston: Beacon, 2018.

Doehring, Carrie. *The Practice of Pastoral Care: A Postmodern Approach.* Rev. ed. Louisville: Westminster John Knox, 2015.

———. "The Practice of Relational-Ethical Pastoral Care: An Intercultural Approach." In *"After You!" Dialogical Ethics and the Pastoral Counseling Process*, edited by Axel Liégeous, Roger Burggraeve, Marina Reimslagh, and Jozef Corveleyn, 159–81. Leuven: Uitgeverij Peeters, 2013.

Ferreras, Marlene. *Identity and Eschatology among Latinas Working in Transnational Corporations in México.* PhD diss., Claremont School of Theology, 2019.

Gramsci, Antonio. *Selections from the Prison Notebooks.* Edited and translated by Quintin Hoare and Geoffrey Nowell Smith. New York: International Publishers, 2014.

Greider, Kathleen J. "Religious Location and Counseling: Engaging Diversity and Difference in Views of Religion." In *Understanding Pastoral Counseling,* edited by Elizabeth A. Maynard and Jill L. Snodgrass, 235–56. New York: Springer, 2015.

Human Rights Watch. "Vietnam: End 'Evil Way' Persecution of Montagnard Christians." June 26, 2015. https://www.hrw.org/news/2015/06/26 /vietnam-end-evil-way-persecution-montagnard-christians.

Johnson, Cedric C. *Race, Religion, and Resilience in the Neoliberal Age.* New York: Palgrave MacMillan, 2016.

Juris Cuba. *Indice Proyecto de Constitución de la República de Cuba. Fundamentos Políticos. Principios Fundamentals de la Nación (28–65).* Accessed July 11, 2023. http://juriscuba.com/legislacion-2/leyes /proyecto-constitucion-cuba-indice/fundamentos-politicos-principios -fundamentales-de-la-nacion/.

Kuo, Lily. "In China, They're Closing Churches, Jailing Pastors—and Even Rewriting Scripture." *The Guardian,* January 13, 2019. https://www .theguardian.com/world/2019/jan/13/china-christians-religious -persecution-translation-persecution-translation-bible.

LaMothe, Ryan. *Care of Soul, Care of Polis: Toward a Political Pastoral Theology*. Eugene, OR: Cascade, 2017.

Lartey, Emmanuel Y. A. "Postcolonializing Pastoral Theology: Enhancing the Intercultural Paradigm." In Ramsay, *Pastoral Theology and Care*, 79–97.

Morris, Josh T. *Narratives of Moral Injury and Reintegration: Toward a Critical, Liberative Practical Theology*. PhD diss., Claremont School of Theology, 2019.

Nguyễn, Thanh Xuan. *Religions in Việt Nam*. Hanoi: Thế Giớ, 2012.

Nguyễn, Viet Thanh. *The Sympathizer: A Novel*. New York: Grove Press, 2015.

Ninh, Bao. *The Sorrow of War*. New York: Vintage, 1994.

Open Doors International. *World Watch List 2022: Situation of Religious Freedom for Christians: Vietnam*. Santa Ana: Open Doors International, 2021.

Pattison, Stephen. *Pastoral Care and Liberation Theology*. Cambridge, UK: Cambridge University Press, 1997.

Pereira Pintado, Ana Celia. "Religiosidad y Migraciones en Cuba." *Didajé* 5 (2014): 40–45.

Pew Research Center. *Global Uptick in Government Restrictions on Religion in 2016*. June 21, 2018. https://www.pewforum.org/2018/06/21/global-uptick-in-government-restrictions-on-religion-in-2016/.

Ramsay, Nancy J., ed. *Pastoral Theology and Care: Critical Trajectories in Theory and Practice*. Hoboken, NJ: John Wiley & Sons, 2018.

Rogers-Vaughn, Bruce. *Caring for Souls in a Neoliberal Age*. New York: Palgrave MacMillan, 2016.

———. "Class Power and Human Suffering: Resisting the Idolatry of the Market in Pastoral Theology and Care." In Ramsay, *Pastoral Theology and Care*, 55–77.

Schipani, Daniel S. *Camino de Sabiduría – Consejería: Cuidado Psicoespiritual*. Orlando: AETH, 2019.

———. *Manual de Psicología Pastoral: Fundamentos y Principios de Acompañamiento*. Orlando: AETH, 2017.

———. "Pastoral and Spiritual Care in Multifaith Contexts." In *Teaching for a Multifaith World*, edited by Eleazar S. Fernandez, 124–46. Eugene, OR: Pickwick, 2017.

Sue, Derald Wing, and David Sue. *Counseling the Culturally Diverse: Theory and Practice*. 7th ed. Hoboken, NJ: John Wiley & Sons, 2016.

Thatamanil, John J. "Does Multiple Religious Belonging Necessarily Mean Internal Conflict?" Plenary Address, International Association for

Spiritual Care, Union Theological Seminary, New York, NY, July 9, 2018.

———. "Eucharist Upstairs, Yoga Downstairs: On Multiple Religious Participation." In *Many yet One? Multiple Religious Belonging,* edited by Peniel Jesudason Rufus Rajkumar and Joseph Prabhakar Dayam, 5–26. Geneva: World Council of Churches, 2016.

Ulitskaya, Lyudmila. *The Big Green Tent: A Novel.* Translated by Polly Gannon. New York: Farrar, Straus & Giroux, 2015.

United States Department of State. Bureau of Democracy, Human Rights and Labor. *Cuba 2017 International Religious Freedom Report.* Accessed July 13, 2023. https://www.state.gov/wp-content/uploads/2019/01/Cuba-2.pdf.

World Atlas. *Major Religions in Vietnam.* Accessed July 13, 2023. https://www.worldtlas.com/articles/religious-beliefs-in-vietnam.html.

❦ 7 ❦

THOMAS MERTON AND THE VOCATION OF PEACEMAKING

Catholic Chaplaincy in a Multifaith Context

DOMINIEK LOOTENS

THOMAS MERTON (1915–1968) was a famous Trappist monk, spiritual writer, pacifist, poet, and social activist. He died fifty years ago on December 10, 1968. To commemorate his life and writings, I focus in this contribution on two of his retreats. My aim is to illustrate how relevant his work still is, especially for Catholic chaplains working in today's high-tech, multifaith health care context.

Thomas Merton: A Short Biography

Thomas Merton was born on January 31, 1915, in Prades, in the South of France. His parents were artists who met each other in Paris. Owen Merton, his father, came originally from New Zealand, and his mother, Ruth Jenkins, was a citizen of the United States. They both had Protestant roots. When Thomas Merton was six, his mother died of cancer. Ten years later, his father died because of a brain tumor. After a turbulent time as a student at Cambridge, in 1935 Merton started studying English literature at Colombia University. In 1939 he converted to Catholicism. After finishing his studies, he worked as a lecturer in English literature at St. Bonaventure University. In 1941 he entered the Trappist monastery of Gethsemani in Kentucky. Supported by his superiors, Merton published his autobiography in 1948, *The Seven Story Mountain*, which became an international bestseller.

From 1955 till 1965 Thomas Merton was master of novices in the abbey. In that period, he thought deeply about the role of education and about monastic reform. He also organized several ecumenical retreats. Thanks to his letters, the many visitors whom he received in the abbey, and the travels he undertook at the end of his life, Merton was very well aware of what was happening in the United States and around the world. The list of people with whom he was in contact is impressive and included Daniel Berrigan, Dom Helder Camara, Ernesto Cardenal, Dorothy Day, Katherine de Hueck Doherty, Erich Fromm, Thich Nhat Hanh, Abraham Joshua Heschel, the Dalai Lama, Jacques Maritain, Louis Massignon, Henry Miller, Czeslaw Milosz, Henri Nouwen, Victoria Ocampo, Boris Pasternak, Pope John XXIII, Pope Paul VI, Rosemary Radford Ruether, and Evelyn Waugh.

In 1965 Merton received permission to live as a hermit near the abbey. In 1968 he travelled to Asia and visited religious places in India, Sri Lanka, and Thailand. On December 10, 1968, Merton died in Bangkok after giving a lecture at a conference for superiors of religious orders. Today, Thomas Merton is best known as a spiritual author. People who are more familiar with his work know that in his later writings he devoted himself strongly to social themes: interfaith and intrareligious dialogue, poverty and social exclusion, peace and non-violence, literature and art, and ecology and technology.

In December 1967, during one of the retreats he gave for a group of contemplative prioresses,[1] Merton said the following about reading the Bible: "It's wonderful how you can take text after text, and the same text over and over again, and just apply them to different situations, how much light comes out of them in the new situation."[2] Merton of course never wrote any holy scripture himself. Nevertheless, in my experience, the key he offered to reading the Bible can also be applied to the texts that he wrote in the last decade of his life.

In this contribution I will focus on the edited texts of the two retreats Merton organized for the group of contemplative prioresses. These texts serve as a lens for viewing Catholic health care chaplaincy practice in Belgium and making a call for revised practice. The chapter starts with a short clarification

---

1   Merton organized two retreats for this group of prioresses, one in December 1967 and one in May 1968. The edited texts of both retreats can be found in *The Springs of Contemplation: A Retreat at the Abbey of Gethsemani* by Thomas Merton (New York: Farrar, Straus & Giroux, 1992). For a critical discussion of the editing of the original recordings of the retreats, see Patrick F. O'Connell, Review of *Thomas Merton on Contemplation* (Introduction by Fr. Anthony Ciorra + 5 Lectures: 4 CDs), *The Merton Annual* 26 (2013): 230–32, http://merton.org/ITMS/Annual/26/OConnellRevTapes220-232.pdf.

2   Merton, *The Springs of Contemplation*, 97.

of the Belgian context. I then present three common responses by Catholic chaplains to this changing context. Several fragments from Merton's text offer insights for viewing these three common responses and demonstrate the promising nature of the third response. These fragments invite Catholic chaplains to realize their vocation as interfaith chaplains and empowers them to commit to becoming peacemakers, even while working within a high-tech, multifaith health care context.

A Brief Look at the Belgian Context

The hot topic in European society today is the so-called refugee crisis. Liberal and conservative politicians alike stress that migrants have to behave as "normal" people; they have to accept the values associated with European history. One basic assumption is that Europe is ethically and politically more evolved than the Muslim world. In Europe, the "Muslim world is still often seen as a monolithic, unchanging, under-developed, violent, anti-democratic space as a direct result of the perceived characteristics of Islam."[3] Although some secular thinkers in Belgium admit that Muslims have the right to bring their religion to the public fore, they fear that they will use this right to undermine Western democratic values. According to Loobuyck, the enemy of the secular state is not religion, but (fundamentalist) religion and other ideologies in so far as they do not accept the fundamental rights and principles of liberal democracy.[4]

The percentage of Muslims in Belgian society is increasing, and this is something that health care professionals have to take into account. An estimated 55 percent of the Belgian population identifies as Christian and 38 percent as religiously unaffiliated.[5] Furthermore, 7.6 percent of the population identifies as Muslim and, in a medium migration scenario, this is

---

3   Jeffrey Haynes, "Constructions of European Identity in Relation to the Muslim 'Other' During the Age of Globalization," in *Perceptions of Islam in Europe: Culture, Identity, and the Muslim "Other,"* ed. Hakan Yilmaz and Çagla E. Aykaç (London: I. B. Tauris, 2012), 52.

4   Patrick Loobuyck, *De Seculiere Samenleving: Over Religie, Atheïsme en Democratie* [*The Secular Society: Religion, Atheism and Democracy*] (Antwerpen: Houtekiet, 2013), 242.

5   Pew Research Center, *Being Christian in Western Europe*, May 29, 2018, http://www.pewforum.org/2018/05/29/being-christian-in-western-europe/.

estimated to increase to 15.1 percent by 2050.[6] From a secular perspective, Loobuyck argued in an interview with Polis that health care professionals should learn how to deal with the diversity of religious traditions in a professional way.[7] According to Loobuyck, you need a professional attitude to deal with this diversity and with your own philosophy of life.[8]

If you look at the health care context in Belgium today, especially hospitals, you find much stress on medical innovation and managerial efficiency. These two developments go hand-in-hand. There is the belief that progress in the medical sciences will make health care less costly. All disciplines are pushed to take up their responsibility to become more evidence-based and efficient. In the above-referenced interview with Polis, Loobuyck stated that there reigns a systemic distrust which implies that the health care professional constantly has to prove herself, make dashes at the number of beds she has done and conversations had. On top of that, there is an inflation of evaluation procedures, which often are based on criteria that have little or nothing to do with the profession practiced.[9]

Developments in Catholic Chaplaincy in Belgium

Looking at the history of health care chaplaincy in Europe, we see that a lot has changed in the last few decades. Twenty years ago, I started to work in Belgium as a pastoral educator and supervisor in the Catholic Diocese of Antwerp. In those days the majority of chaplains were priests and people from religious orders. Now the vast majority of Catholic chaplains are lay people.

Working for Caritas Flanders as a white, male, Catholic layperson, I had the opportunity to write a dissertation on chaplaincy education.[10]

---

6   Pew Research Center, *Europe's Growing Muslim Population*, November 29, 2017, http://www.pewforum.org/2017/11/29/europes-growing-muslim-population/.

7   Harold Polis, "De Kleur van Zorg. Patrick Loobuyck Zoekt naar Hedendaagse Ethische Waarden [The Color of Care: Patrick Loobuyck Searches for Contemporary Ethical Values]," *Weliswaar* 126 (2015): 26–27, https://issuu.com/weliswaar/docs/weliswaar-nr.126.

8   Polis, "De Kleur van Zorg," 27.

9   Polis, "De Kleur van Zorg," 27.

10   Dominiek Lootens, *Die Kraft der Phantasie in Bildungsarbeit und Seelsorge: Lernen von Kierkegaard* (Freiburg: Lambertus, 2009).

My position as an educator and pastoral supervisor enabled me to build relationships with professionals, managers, and academics in Belgium and abroad. Through the years it became more and more clear to me that it is not so easy to be a Catholic chaplain in today's health care context. People who do this kind of work often feel marginalized.[11] Management and other disciplines ask why chaplains are still necessary in a secular context. Patients are not interested in talking about religion; they just want to get better. Chaplaincy is very costly, and chaplains are unable to present any reliable results.

Yet from a multifaith perspective, I am more aware than ever that Catholic chaplains in Belgium occupy a privileged position. Catholic chaplains are able to work in Catholic and public hospitals, while only a small number of Protestant chaplains and Humanist counselors work in public hospitals. Moreover, only a few Muslim chaplains work on a voluntarily basis, and mostly in public hospitals. The lack of state-paid Muslim chaplains in hospitals and prisons is viewed as further evidence of the inequitable treatment provided to the growing population of Belgian Muslims.[12]

Chaplains' Responses to the Changing Health Care Context

Catholic chaplains react differently to Belgium's changing health care context, yet many respond in one of the following three ways.[13] The first response is to assert themselves as real professionals. The second response entails concentrating exclusively on the unique characteristics of pastoral

---

11   Frances Norwood, "The Ambivalent Chaplain: Negotiating Structural and Ideological Difference on the Margins of Modern-Day Medicine," *Medical Anthropology* 25, no. 1 (2006): 1–29, https://doi.org/10.1080/01459740500488502.

12   Konrad Pędziwiatr, *The New Muslim Elites in European Cities: Religion and Active Social Citizenship Amongst Young Organized Muslims in Brussels and London* (Saarbrücken: VDM Verlag, 2010).

13   Catholic practical theology started to develop in Belgium in the 1990s, and little research has been done on health care chaplaincy. For discussion on this, see Annemie Dillen, Eveline Vanderheijden, and Anne Vandenhoeck, "'Wat Doe Jij hier Eigenlijk?' Resultaten van Empirisch Onderzoek naar de Tijdsbesteding van Vlaamse Ziekenhuispastores," *Collationes* 48 (2018): 163–90. The distinction I make here is based on my twenty years of experience as a pastoral supervisor and educator and on my work as editor of the chaplaincy journal *Pastorale Perspectieven*.

care. The third response is to commit themselves to interfaith chaplaincy, based on a contemplative perspective.

Chaplains who choose the first approach stress that patients have spiritual needs when they enter the hospital. Through screening it is possible to find out what these needs are. It has been empirically proven that patients cope better with their situation when spiritual care is provided.[14] Chaplains look to the medical discipline as an example and try to prove that their work is as professional and as efficient as that of their medical colleagues. The presupposition is that chaplains can play a relevant role during the whole health care process.

Not every chaplain chooses this approach. A second group stresses that chaplaincy is not about efficiency at all. Catholic chaplains should avoid imitating other disciplines. What they have to offer is unique. Pastoral care brings the human and the community dimension within the health care context. Other disciplines and management should do what they have to do. The task of chaplains, however, is to concentrate on authentic pastoral encounters in which patients and relatives can be themselves.

There is a third response which can be described as interfaith chaplaincy.[15] This approach is not yet well established but can be seen as a very promising third way. Catholic chaplains who choose this approach are convinced that they have to look critically at the dominant myths in society and health care. They are not social activists who want to change society and institutions from the outside. Rather, they want to change the structure and culture of the hospital from the inside. They realize that they risk minimizing the uniqueness of their identity and practice as Catholic chaplains if they try to imitate other disciplines or professionals. They also realize that within the hospital, when compared to professionals of other faith traditions, they still have a privileged position. However, they do not want to cling to this historical privilege anymore. That is why it is not

---

14   Harold G. Koenig, *Spirituality in Patient Care: Why, How, When, and What*, 3rd ed. (West Conshohocken, PA: Templeton, 2013).

15   Emmanuel Van Lierde, "'Verschil Scherp Stellen om Eigenheid te Bewaren': Jezuïet Vincent Ferrant over Interlevensbeschouwelijk Samenwerken in Ziekenhuizen," in *Ontsluitende Zorg: De Toekomst van het Pastorale Beroep*, ed. Dominiek Lootens, 60–67 (Antwerpen: Halewijn/UCSIA, 2011).

enough for them to concentrate on their counseling and liturgical work. They proactively create room for patients and chaplains who belong to other faith traditions. Interestingly, Catholic chaplains who choose this kind of approach stress that contemplation is a crucial starting point for their work.[16]

The writings and work of Thomas Merton offer us a lens to look closer at the three responses Catholic chaplains give to the changing, high-tech, multifaith health care landscape in Belgium today.

Thomas Merton as Organizer of Retreats

In November 1964 Merton organized an interfaith retreat for peacemakers. Members (lay and clerical) of Catholic, mainline Protestant, historic peace church, and Unitarian traditions participated. It was the time of the Cold War, the Vietnam War, and the peace and civil rights movements. The majority of the men who participated, as women were not included, were radical pacifists who wanted to change the system from the outside. As such they acted as social activists. Thomas Merton invited them to look with him at "the spiritual roots of protest."[17]

In December 1967 and May 1968 Merton organized two retreats for contemplative prioresses.[18] He invited them to reflect on their vocation from a prophetic perspective. His aim was not so much to convince them to become social activists. He wanted them to find out what it means to be prophetic as members of established contemplative institutions.

---

16   Vincent Ferrant, "Vier Weken voor een Ziekenhuispastor," in *God in Heel de Schepping: Jonge Jezuïeten over de Inspiratie van Ignatius van Loyola*, ed. Rob Faesen and Nicolas Standaert, 146–53 (Kapellen: DNB/Pelckmans, 1990).

17   Gordon Oyer, *Pursuing the Spiritual Roots of Protest: Merton, Berrigan, Yoder, and Muste at the Gethsemani Abbey Peacemaker Retreat* (Eugene, OR: Wipf & Stock, 2014); Dominiek Lootens, "Thomas Merton and the Spiritual Roots of Protest: Educational Reflections on the Peacemaker Retreat," *The Merton Seasonal* 42, no. 1 (2017): 12–16.

18   Bonnie Bowman Thurston, "'An Absolute Duty to Rebel' Thomas Merton, Religious Women and the Challenges of Vatican II," *The Merton Seasonal* 39, no. 2 (2014): 14–25; Bonnie Bowman Thurston, "'The Best Retreat I Ever Made': Merton and the Contemplative Prioresses," *Thomas Merton Annual* 14 (2000): 81–95.

Merton organized the two retreats for contemplative prioresses with the substantial support of the Sisters of Loretto.[19] In 1967 Merton made a recording for their Special General Chapter.[20] In the edited version of this recording, one can read how he reflected on the way individuals are pushed to conform to society:

> *Now let us remember that there is a whole dialectical relationship between the individual and society and that the individual has to be open to others; he has to be responsible and responsive to society; he has to accept the institution as just not a necessary evil, but as a real good in his life. All this we are remembering, but at the same time we also remember the fact that society tends to make things easy for itself by enforcing certain roles upon individuals and making them accept these roles and punishing them for not accepting these roles, and for demanding as a sacrifice of the personality that the person be untrue to himself in order to be true to society. Consequently, whether in secular or religious society, we are constantly finding ourselves in positions where people are rewarded for betraying themselves and betraying those whom they love, and this is praised as an act of sacrifice and homage to the supremacy of the organization.[21]*

In Belgium, Catholic chaplains are sent by the diocese. At the same time, they are employees of the hospital. This means that they are structurally positioned in a twofold way: within the Church and within the health care institution. I concur with Thurston that within his retreats for contemplative prioresses, Merton offered crucial insights that are "applicable

---

19   George A. Kilcourse, "Life through the Lens of Inner and Outer Freedom: An Interview with Jane Marie Richardson, SL," ed. Paul Stokell, *Thomas Merton Annual* 13 (2000): 127–43; Bonnie Bowman Thurston and Mary Swain, eds., *Hidden in the Same Mystery: Thomas Merton and Loretto* (Louisville, KY: Fons Vitae, 2010).

20   Thomas Merton, "Comments about the Religious Life Today: Transcript of a Recording Made by and Edited by Father Louis Merton for Special General Chapter Sister of Loretto, 1967," *The Merton Annual* 14 (2001): 14–32.

21   Merton, "Comments about the Religious Life Today," 17–18.

to everyone who is trying to live fully and authentically as a Christian."[22] Merton's insights can support Catholic chaplains in reflecting on their work from a contemplative and prophetic perspective. Furthermore, in doing so they are invited to respond to the health care context in Belgium by realizing their vocation as interfaith chaplains.

Thomas Merton's Invitation to Interfaith Chaplaincy

Thomas Merton's writings help to reveal the inadequacy of the first two responses made by Catholic chaplains to the changing health care context in Belgium: asserting themselves as real professionals and concentrating exclusively on the unique characteristics of pastoral care. For example, Merton wrote,

> *I'll go along with official people as long as I can, but many of the people I'm in tune with—like artists, philosophers, and scientists, are outside the Church. It seems to me that even the progressive voices, Christians among them, are still more or less just Great Society Liberals. They have an optimism that basically accepts the status-quo, and they are not all that different from those who are fearful. They offer some good insights and new images, but for the most part, they're happy, not alienated, and think our society is good and really going somewhere. What they say is useless. In reality, they see no alternative.*[23]

A Catholic chaplain who calls herself progressive likes to be related to all kinds of people. In her workplace she wants to build up good relations with management, medical doctors, and professionals in other disciplines. Although she sees herself as related to the Church, she stresses the importance of situating herself inside the high-tech, multifaith medical institution. She has interesting things to say about screening processes, diagnostics, efficiency, and empirical research. Merton's wisdom helps to clarify that the risk of her approach is that she becomes a cynic. She accepts that she has to

---

22   Thurston, "'The Best Retreat I Ever Made,'" 94.

23   Merton, *The Springs of Contemplation*, 71.

adapt herself to the status quo. For her there is no use in acting prophetically to change the culture and structure of the workplace in order to make it more human and just. "Some monks feel that it's enough to live a more or less authentic and somewhat updated life. That's not enough, there is no future in that. The mere fact of living an honest life that is also a little bit human may tide us over until we die. There's nothing wrong with it, but in our hearts we know that's not what we're called for. We have to be more than sincere people of prayer."[24]

Merton had a sincere respect for people who try to live an authentic life. A Catholic chaplain who stresses the uniqueness of pastoral care is an honest person who tries to do just that. She knows that not all the patients call themselves religious. She stresses that chaplaincy is not about proclaiming rules or dogmas, but about personal encounters. However, the wisdom from Merton's writings invites her to dig a little deeper and to look honestly into her heart. She risks feeling secure in her work, without taking into account what is really happening in today's society and health care context. He urges her to realize that she could do more than just concentrate on her counseling and liturgical work. Given the inadequacies of the first and second responses, Merton's work then invites the Catholic chaplain to explore the merits of true interfaith chaplaincy.

Acknowledging and Evaluating the Power of the Catholic Chaplain

Merton's writing encourages Catholic chaplains to acknowledge and evaluate their own power in relation to patients, other chaplains, and within the health care context. "For centuries the Church has been involved in worldly power. The Church is, in fact, a worldly power. The great problem of contemplative life, of religious life, of the priesthood and of everyone else, is that we have been corrupted by that power. We have been used by this structure to justify a power politics in the Church."[25] Merton was not afraid to say that he had a privileged position as a Catholic monk living in the United States. Catholic chaplains who feel marginalized today feel this way exactly because

---

24   Merton, *The Springs of Contemplation*, 68.
25   Merton, *The Springs of Contemplation*, 69.

they somehow want to keep the privilege they had until now. Chaplains have to take into account that they have power. Merton's own self-awareness invites them to do just that. The question is if using their power to keep their privilege is the most meaningful thing to do. Chaplains have to open their eyes to the fact that they have a responsibility to the people who do not have access to the same kind of power.

> *We do need praise. It's not good for us to fall on our face, and we have to take that into account. Basically, we have to deal with a mixture of motives, non-Christian motives, ego motives, pagan motives, superstitious motives. There are plenty of these in our racial and ethnic backgrounds. And we carry them with us. But as Christians, we constantly try to rise above these things. Our only real justification is the freedom of the children of God.*[26]

Acknowledging and Evaluating Society's Shortcomings

The wisdom evident in Merton's work invites Catholic chaplains to open themselves to what is going wrong in today's society. There is a one-sided focus on prestige. People need affirmation, of course, but not only based on the position they acquire in society, the amount of money they make, or the technological character of their job. Western society today can be characterized as xenophobic and racist, especially with regard to migrants and refugees with a Muslim background.[27] When we reflect on ourselves, we discover that the characteristics of this society are also in us. In order to open themselves to the world, chaplains are invited to take a critical look at their own mixed motives. That is how they can discover how much they are influenced by the myths which create exclusion and injustice in Western society. "We have a prophetic task. We have to rock the boat, but not like the hippies. Herbert Marcuse[28] claims that even when you rock the boat you

---

26   Merton, *The Springs of Contemplation*, 84.

27   Liz Fekete, *A Suitable Enemy: Racism, Migration and Islamophobia in Europe* (New York: Pluto, 2009).

28   Thomas Merton refers here to Herbert Marcuse in *One-Dimensional Man: Studies in the Ideology of Advanced Industrial Society* (Boston: Beacon, 1966).

are meeting the demands of a totalitarian society, which requires a certain amount of boat-rockers."[29]

Merton stressed that it is important for social activists to look critically at the work they do. In the end it is possible that their protest actions only strengthen the position of the political and institutional powerbrokers. Catholic chaplains are situated within the structures of the Church and the hospital. Based on a contemplative perspective, Merton's perspectives invite chaplains to become prophets within these contexts.

> *We are all sinners. God speaks and we do not listen. On the other hand, the mercy of God is constant. It cannot be overcome. God's promises are absolute. Being Christian doesn't mean "being on the right side." A Christian does not always know where justice lies, does not always see clearly. But the Christian is aware that, while in the human being there is falsity and infidelity, in the mercy of God there is always absolute fidelity. So we reject no one, but still try to dissociate ourselves from anything that is going to hurt other people. Every Christian has to stand up for the truth that God's mercy is without repentance. God never takes back mercy. We are in a world where many people are in despair. That is where God is really needed. Our Christian witness of mercy is not, after all, credible to a lot of people, because it is not very profound. That is why we have to bear witness to the word of God. The renewal of the whole Church hinges on it. And not just in ideological terms. We also have to dig in and really help those in trouble.*[30]

Acknowledging and Serving Those Most in Need

Chaplaincy today developed out of a dialogue between pastoral care and psychotherapy. Because of this, it risks becoming a service that reaches only middle-class people. Catholic chaplains have to ask themselves, "Where in the hospital are the people who are most in need?"[31] I interviewed a chaplain

---

29   Merton, *The Springs of Contemplation*, 69.

30   Merton, *The Springs of Contemplation*, 37.

31   Not only chaplains can be concerned about this question. For an intriguing account of nursery care for vulnerable people, based on Thomas Merton, see Elizabeth Mo-

who told me that in her work she focuses especially on people who are poor. She gave the example of lobbying for a migrant woman who had just lost her husband and did not have the necessary money to bring him back to his native country for the burial.[32]

> *Real charity is involved here. It's a choice between the union of charity with people who are alive and growing and a legalistic union with those who want to hold things back. . . . This is not something I'm just permitted to do, but something I should do. . . . If you are choosing for life, for a living entity, it's a better choice. If you are choosing for a dead, rigid thing, it's a worse choice. Even if a choice turns out to be imprudent, there's a build in safeguard because it's alive, it's warm, it's real. We have to choose life, always.*[33]

Acknowledging and Cooperating with the Religious "Other"

Merton suggested that people who are committed to contemplative living should support life-oriented activities of young people. While studying the life narratives of young Belgian Muslims, I discovered how they are engaged in voluntary work in prisons and hospitals.[34] Thus, I am invited to support them in their vocation as chaplains. Catholic chaplains can become bridgebuilders and introduce them to the hospital. Catholic chaplains can stop clinging to privilege and work proactively in cooperation with Muslims and other marginalized caregivers. "I'm deeply impregnated with Sufism. In Islam, one of the worst things that any human being can do is to say that

---

ran Fitzgerald, Judith G. Myers, and Paul Clark, "Nurses Need Not Be Guilty Bystanders: Caring for Vulnerable Immigrant Populations," *The Online Journal of Issues in Nursing* 22, no. 1 (2016): 1–11, https://doi.org/10.3912/OJIN.Vol22No01PPT43.

32   Dominiek Lootens, "Wanneer Men Samen Droomt, Begint een Nieuwe Werkelijkheid: Een Gesprek met Birgit Burbaum," *Pastorale Perspectieven* 152 (2011): 33–38, https://www.kuleuven.be/thomas/cms/docs/pastcralePerspectieven/pp152 _burbaum.pdf.

33   Merton, *The Springs of Contemplation*, 101.

34   Pędziwiatr, *The New Muslim Elites in European Cities*.

there is another besides the One, to act implicitly as if God needed a helper, as if God couldn't do what needs to be done."[35]

Out of his contemplative perspective, Merton developed a keen interest for other faith traditions, in this case Islam. He encouraged Christians to learn from other traditions. Listening closely to people from other faiths can remind us of our own blind spots. When Catholic chaplains avoid thinking critically about their privileged position within the hospital, they risk behaving like the "saviors" of patients and colleagues of other traditions. Honest discussion can help them to find out how to make their vocation as interfaith chaplains concrete in everyday praxis. "True unity is the work of love. It is the free union of beings that spontaneously seek to be one in the truth, preserving and elevating their separate selves by self-transcendence. False unity strives to assert itself by the denial of obstacles. True unity admits the presence of obstacles and of divisions in order to overcome both by humility and sacrifice."[36]

The fragment above comes from a text Thomas Merton wrote in 1962, which is also included in *The Springs of Contemplation*. In this text, he commemorated the shared history of the monks of the Abbey of Gethsemani and the Sisters of Loretto. To support patients and to cooperate with chaplains from other traditions is not always easy. Catholic chaplains are urged not to strive for false unity. Admitting the presence of obstacles and of divisions, as well as seeing oneself and the other honestly, is an integral part of the process.

Conclusion: The Catholic Chaplain as Peacemaker

During the first retreat, one of the prioresses asked Merton how his view on contemplative living related to his work for peace and non-violence. In his response he made clear that contemplatives can be peacemakers, even when they are positioned within an established institution.

*This is what we have to do: avoid lining up on the side of a
revolution as well as on the side of a counter-revolution. We need to*

---

35   Merton, *The Springs of Contemplation*, 196.

36   Merton, *The Springs of Contemplation*, 207.

line up on the side of the people. Wherever there is human presence,
we have to be present to it. And wherever there is a person, there
has to be personal communication. There Christ can work. Where
there is presence, there is God. A Christian is one who continues
to communicate across all the boundaries, a sign of hope for a
convergence back to a kind of unity.[37]

Catholic chaplains can learn from Merton that it is important and meaningful to stress the uniqueness of pastoral care: it is about presence and personal communication. But this is not enough. Looking from a contemplative and prophetic perspective, it is also necessary to communicate across boundaries. As such chaplains can offer pastoral care for migrants from different religious backgrounds.

One of the dominant boundaries in today's European society is the "clash of civilizations" myth in which migrants with a Muslim background are seen as essentially different from white people. Merton's contemplative and prophetic perspective provokes Catholic chaplains to question their privileged position. His work urges them to look at today's context and to involve themselves in the introduction of and the cooperation with chaplains of other faith traditions, especially Islam. As such Catholic chaplains in Belgium can become peacemakers within the high-tech hospital context and realize their vocation as interfaith chaplains.

Bibliography

Dillen, Annemie, Eveline Vanderheijden, and Anne Vandenhoeck. "'Wat Doe Jij hier Eigenlijk?' Resultaten van Empirisch Onderzoek naar de Tijdsbesteding van Vlaamse Ziekenhuispastores." *Collationes* 48 (2018): 163–90.

Fekete, Liz. *A Suitable Enemy: Racism, Migration and Islamophobia in Europe.* New York: Pluto, 2009.

Ferrant, Vincent. "Vier Weken voor een Ziekenhuispastor." In *God in Heel de Schepping: Jonge Jezuïeten over de Inspiratie van Ignatius van Loyola,* edited by Rob Faesen and Nicolas Standaert, 146–53. Kapellen: DNB/Pelckmans, 1990.

---

37   Merton, *The Springs of Contemplation*, 35.

Fitzgerald, Elizabeth Moran, Judith G. Myers, and Paul Clark. "Nurses Need Not Be Guilty Bystanders: Caring for Vulnerable Immigrant Populations." *The Online Journal of Issues in Nursing* 22, no. 1 (2016): 1–11. https://doi.org/10.3912/OJIN.Vol22No01PPT43.

Haynes, Jeffrey. "Constructions of European Identity in Relation to the Muslim 'Other' During the Age of Globalization." In *Perceptions of Islam in Europe: Culture, Identity, and the Muslim "Other,"* edited by Hakan Yilmaz and Çagla E. Aykaç, 49–69. London: I. B. Tauris, 2012.

Kilcourse, George A. "Life through the Lens of Inner and Outer Freedom: An Interview with Jane Marie Richardson, SL." Edited by Paul Stokell. *Thomas Merton Annual* 13 (2000): 127–43.

Koenig, Harold G. *Spirituality in Patient Care: Why, How, When, and What.* 3rd ed. West Conshohocken, PA: Templeton, 2013.

Loobuyck, Patrick. *De Seculiere Samenleving: Over Religie, Atheïsme en Democratie* [*The Secular Society: Religion, Atheism and Democracy*]. Antwerpen: Houtekiet, 2013.

Lootens, Dominiek. *Die Kraft der Phantasie in Bildungsarbeit und Seelsorge: Lernen von Kierkegaard.* Freiburg: Lambertus, 2009.

———. "Thomas Merton and the Spiritual Roots of Protest: Educational Reflections on the Peacemaker Retreat." *The Merton Seasonal* 42, no. 1 (2017): 12–16.

———. "Wanneer Men Samen Droomt, Begint een Nieuwe Werkelijkheid: Een Gesprek met Birgit Burbaum." *Pastorale Perspectieven* 152 (2011): 33–38. https://www.kuleuven.be/thomas/cms/docs/pastorale Perspectieven/pp152_burbaum.pdf.

Marcuse, Herbert. *One-Dimensional Man: Studies in the Ideology of Advanced Industrial Society.* Boston: Beacon, 1966.

Merton, Thomas. "Comments about the Religious Life Today: Transcript of a Recording Made by and Edited by Father Louis Merton for Special General Chapter Sister of Loretto, 1967." *The Merton Annual* 14 (2001): 14–32.

———. *The Springs of Contemplation: A Retreat at the Abbey of Gethsemani.* New York: Farrar, Straus & Giroux, 1992.

Norwood, Frances. "The Ambivalent Chaplain: Negotiating Structural and Ideological Difference on the Margins of Modern-Day Medicine." *Medical Anthropology* 25, no. 1 (2006): 1–29. https://doi .org/10.1080/01459740500488502.

O'Connell, Patrick F. Review of *Thomas Merton on Contemplation* (Introduction by Fr. Anthony Ciorra + 5 Lectures: 4 CDs); *Finding True*

Meaning and Beauty (4 Lectures: 2 CDs); *Thomas Merton's Great Sermons* (Introduction by Fr. Anthony Ciorra + 4 Lectures: 2 CDs); *Vatican II: The Sacred Liturgy and the Religious Life* (7 Lectures: 4 CDs); *Thomas Merton on Sufism* (Introduction by Fr. Anthony Ciorra + 13 Lectures: 7 CDs); *Ways of Prayer: A Desert Father's Wisdom* (Introduction by Fr. Anthony Ciorra + 13 Lectures: 7 CDs); *Thomas Merton on the 12 Degrees of Humility* (Introduction by Fr. Anthony Ciorra + 16 Lectures: 8 CDs); *Solitude and Togetherness* (Introduction by Fr. Anthony Ciorra + 11 Lectures: 11 CDs); *The Prophet's Freedom* (Introduction by Fr. Anthony Ciorra + 8 Lectures: 8 CDs), by Thomas Merton. *The Merton Annual* 26 (2013): 230–32. http://merton.org/ITMS/Annual/26/OConnellRevTapes220-232.pdf.

Oyer, Gordon. *Pursuing the Spiritual Roots of Protest: Merton, Berrigan, Yoder, and Muste at the Gethsemani Abbey Peacemaker Retreat.* Eugene, OR: Wipf & Stock, 2014.

Pędziwiatr, Konrad. *The New Muslim Elites in European Cities: Religion and Active Social Citizenship Amongst Young Organized Muslims in Brussels and London.* Saarbrücken: VDM Verlag, 2010.

Pew Research Center. *Being Christian in Western Europe.* May 29, 2018. http://www.pewforum.org/2018/05/29/being-christian-in-western-europe/.

———. *Europe's Growing Muslim Population.* November 29, 2017. http://www.pewforum.org/2017/11/29/europes-growing-muslim-population/.

Polis, Harold. "De Kleur van Zorg. Patrick Loobuyck Zoekt naar Hedendaagse Ethische Waarden [The Color of Care: Patrick Loobuyck Searches for Contemporary Ethical Values]." *Weliswaar* 126 (2015): 26–27. https://issuu.com/weliswaar/docs/weliswaar-nr.126.

Thurston, Bonnie Bowman. "'An Absolute Duty to Rebel': Thomas Merton, Religious Women and the Challenges of Vatican II." *The Merton Seasonal* 39, no. 2 (2014): 14–25.

———. "'The Best Retreat I Ever Made': Merton and the Contemplative Prioresses." *Thomas Merton Annual* 14 (2000): 81–95.

Thurston, Bonnie Bowman, and Mary Swain, eds. *Hidden in the Same Mystery: Thomas Merton and Loretto.* Louisville, KY: Fons Vitae, 2010.

Van Lierde, Emmanuel. "'Verschil Scherp Stellen om Eigenheid te Bewaren': Jezuïet Vincent Ferrant over Interlevensbeschouwelijk Samenwerken in Ziekenhuizen." In *Ontsluitende Zorg: De Toekomst van het Pastorale Beroep,* edited by Dominiek Lootens, 60–67. Antwerpen: Halewijn /UCSIA, 2011.

❧ 8 ☙

THE IMPACT OF INDIGENOUS AFRICAN THOUGHT ON PASTORAL COUNSELING

MAZVITA MACHINGA

SPIRITUALITY AND COSMOLOGY shape how the African people understand life and cope with challenges. Deeply embedded in indigenous African thought is a worldview grounded in relationality, community, wholeness, and spirituality. This mindset has been transmitted orally from generation to generation and permeates all aspects of life. Indigenous African thought also entails a transpersonal ethic and mindset that acknowledges broader human realities extending beyond the usual ego boundaries. The purpose of this chapter is to discuss the impact of indigenous African thought on pastoral counseling interventions with Shona Zimbabweans (Africans). I will describe the various features of indigenous African thought and how these influence the "religious locations" of Shona Zimbabweans.[1] Relations, connectedness, and interdependence of all things, or ubuntu, are central to the lives of Shona Zimbabweans. Thus, pastoral care practices and pastoral counseling interventions that embrace the spirit of ubuntu by promoting connectedness and cultivating meaning and hope will yield better fruits. The chapter draws upon three case studies to illustrate the importance of honoring the religious locations of Shona Zimbabweans by using a relational and transpersonal approach to counseling.

---

1 Kathleen J. Greider, "Religious Location and Counseling: Engaging Diversity and Difference in Views of Religion," in *Understanding Pastoral Counseling*, ed. Elizabeth A. Maynard and Jill L. Snodgrass, 235–56 (New York: Springer, 2015).

Indigenous African Thought

Centuries before the African continent was occupied by adherents of the Christian and Islamic religious traditions, native Africans had their own beliefs, thoughts, practices, and worldviews. Indigenous African thought was handed down from one generation to another and actively influenced individuals' and communities' responses to societal issues. Zimbabweans, like any Africans, had their own spirituality, which consisted of attitudes, beliefs, practices, and rituals that enabled them to cope with day to day realities. They had their own spiritually-informed approaches, perspectives, and structures when dealing with difficult circumstances. For instance, the approaches encompass an acknowledgement of the presence and power of God, nature, the spirits, and the invisible forces in the universe.[2] For Africans, as proclaimed by Mbiti, "The concept of God is no stranger to African people. God is the origin and sustenance of all things. God is outside and beyond creation. God is transcendent and immanent."[3] For Zimbabweans, God is creator (*Mwari* or *Musikawanhu* in Shona). Mwari means "in God all things exist." Hence, God is the ultimate source of nature and advises humanity on what course of action to be followed in times of crisis. This means that Africans have always had a notion of the God who cares. Mwari is the final authority above and beyond the ancestors and nature, and as such Mwari must be approached indirectly through mediums. "This African knowledge of God is up to now expressed in proverbs, songs, stories and religious ceremonies."[4] These continue to be part of the rich African cosmology and way of life.

Regardless of exposure to Western perspectives and worldviews, indigenous African thought directly influences the "religious locations" of Shona Zimbabweans and other Africans.[5] As asserted by Greider, "Whether we are religious or not, all persons inhabit a particular location and identity relative

---

2   Patrick A. Kalilombe, "Spirituality in the African Perspective," in *Paths of African Theology*, ed. Rosino Gibellini, 115–35 (Maryknoll, NY: Orbis Books, 1994).

3   John S. Mbiti, *African Religions and Philosophy*, 2nd ed. (London: Heinemann, 1990), 29.

4   Mbiti, *African Religions*, 29.

5   Greider, "Religious Location and Counseling."

to religion."[6] Pastoral counselors operating in a particular location need to respect and honor the location, i.e., the identity, attitudes, and positions of a people. For pastoral counselors operating in Zimbabwe, although a client may be Christian, the client's religious location, as well as how the client experiences and lives the Christian faith, is deeply informed by indigenous African thought.

While discussion in this chapter focuses on indigenous African thought from a Zimbabwean perspective, most of the concepts are applicable throughout the continent of Africa. Africa is a continent with over fifty countries and hundreds of tribes and languages. As stated by Mbiti, "While the religious expressions in Africa are diverse, concrete and observable, one cannot claim the same thing about the thinking behind them. The philosophy underlying the various religious and cultural expressions of the African people is the same."[7] This indicates cultural diversity and heterogeneity, yet a simultaneous homogeneity in epistemology and philosophy. Thus, the diverse tribes and identities need to be valued and respected. It is improper to view Africa as monolithic; rather, it should be viewed as collectivistic and having a faith factor that is active and powerful. The religious locations of all Africans are influenced, to some extent, by indigenous African thought.

What Is Indigenous African Thought?

Indigenous African thought and worldview are characterized by the basic relational ontology of ubuntu, transpersonal realities, collectivism, and the belief in the Supreme God—*Musikawanhu*. This God is All-powerful or the Almighty. Furthermore, behind everything in African thinking, a mystical power is present, whether one encounters a good or bad experience. Everything is interdependent; hence, traditional African ontology, epistemology, axiology, and cosmology are all relational. These terms describe a value framework and the nature of daily African realities. The value system of most African societies is built around respect of oneself as it relates to others and to the whole. The following is a discussion of the important African values that all those who offer pastoral counseling need to be aware of.

---

6   Greider, "Religious Location and Counseling," 235.

7   Mbiti, *African Religions*, 5.

Ubuntu: A Relational Ontology

The African philosophy of ubuntu accurately expresses the relational ontology that undergirds indigenous African thinking. Relational ontology views relationships as central to how Africans formulate things, expressions, and understanding. The African worldview of *umuntu ngumuntu ngabantu* (a person is a person through other persons) is the pillar of day to day interpretation of life.[8] Du Toit summarized the concept of ubuntu in African thought when he wrote,

> *In Africa, a person is identified by his or her interrelationships and not primarily by individualistic properties. The community identifies the person and not the person the community. The identity of the person is his or her place in the community. In Africa it is a matter of "I participate, therefore I am." Ubuntu is the principle of "I am only because we are, and since we are, therefore I am."*[9]

This means that African thinking is family- and community-oriented more than individualistic. In addition, according to Couture, "ubuntu concept corresponds closely to the idea of human worth and dignity."[10] For Africans, only in community and with the participation of all can life be built. According to Magesa, for Africans, "Relationships receive the most attention in the adjudication of what is good or bad, what is desirable and undesirable in life."[11] The life of the individual can only be grasped as it is

---

8   Dion A. Forster, "African Relational Ontology, Individual Identity, and Christian Theology: An African Theological Contribution Towards an Integrated Relational Ontological Identity," *Theology* 113, no. 874 (2010): 243–53, https://doi.org/10.1177/0040571 X1011300402.

9   Cornel W. du Toit, "Technoscience and the Integrity of Personhood in Africa and the West: Facing Our Technoscientific Environment," in *The Integrity of the Human Person in an African Context: Perspectives from Science and Religion*, ed. Cornel W. du Toit (Pretoria: Research Institute for Theology and Religion, University of South Africa, 2004), 33.

10   Pamela Couture, "Human Dignity, Injustice and *Ubuntu*: Living the Metaphor of *Bwino/Bumuntu*/White Lime in the Democratic Republic of Congo," in *Practicing Ubuntu: Practical Theological Perspectives on Injustice, Personhood and Human Dignity*, ed. Jaco S. Dreyer, Yolanda Dreyer, Edward Foley, and Malan Nel (Berlin: LIT Verlag, 2017), 15.

11   Laurenti Magesa, *African Religion: The Moral Traditions of Abundant Life* (Nairobi: Paulines Publications Africa, 1997), 65.

shared. As asserted by Mulago, for an African, "The member of the tribe, the clan, the family, knows that he does not live to him/herself, but within the community. He knows that apart from the community he would no longer have the means of existence."[12] In addition, indigenous Zimbabweans adhere to rituals which bind together all members of the group, the living and the dead, nature and Almighty God. All this demonstrates clearly the place and role of relations within indigenous African thought.

African Cosmology

African cosmology is based on three worlds: the human world, the spiritual world, and the natural world.[13] These are closely related as the visible (presented by the living) and the invisible (presented by the spiritual world) are integrated. Africans believe that human beings exist in relationships: relationship with the other, with God the creator, with the spirits, and with nature.[14] Every misfortune that Africans encounter is viewed as a diminution of vital force from any of the three worlds. However, outside or beyond personal agents contain a great life force that impacts the living—the Almighty God. From an African perspective, some experiences have spiritual roots and therefore need spiritual/transpersonal remedies. Thus, attention to the embedded nature of one's relationship to the three worlds is central to a relational approach in counseling. In my work with care seekers, I have explored with them their experiences with the three worlds and how that guides them in their day-to-day living. Thus, a pastoral counselor in this setting needs to be aware of the existence of these three worlds. In this way one will be able to contextualize interventions.

Transpersonal Realities

Another key factor in indigenous African thought is the acknowledgement of transpersonal realities when offering counseling. This refers to "across or

---

12   Magesa, *African Religion*, 66.

13   Munyaradzi Mawere, *African Belief and Knowledge Systems: A Critical Perspective* (Mankon, Bamenda: Langaa Research & Publications, 2011).

14   Paul L. Watchel, *Relational Theory and the Practice of Psychotherapy* (New York: Guilford, 2008).

beyond the personal or psyche."[15] The transpersonal reality moves across the personal realm, acknowledging and exploring all aspects of self and placing the self in a larger framework.[16] Each care seeker as they present themselves for counseling is more than what is seen. The care seeker is surrounded by forces that either positively or negatively influence life. Hence, "the importance of looking into an extension of consciousness beyond the limitations of time and space and related to ultimate human capabilities and potentialities."[17] According to Salamone, rituals are symbolic acts that have a religious connotation because they are related to spirits and the supernatural world. Connecting with transpersonal realities may call for use of rituals.[18] Rituals become key when it comes to interpreting and coping with situations. They have a sociocultural and religious symbolism and meaning. In addition, rituals involve power and a way of connecting the three worlds mentioned above.

Belief in the Supreme God

Transcendence and the sacred are major features in indigenous African thought.[19] In indigenous African thought, the ordinary human experience is mimetic of the transcendent and the sacred. There is strong belief in Supreme Deity and at the same time a belief in the connection of the dead to human life. At the top of everything is the Divine force which is the ultimate life-giving power. Belief in God, spiritual forces, values, and indigenous thoughts touch on every facet of individual, family, and community life for Shona Zimbabweans.

This brief explanation of important aspects of indigenous African thought serves as a foundation for understanding how pastoral counselors

---

15   Brant Cortright, *Psychotherapy and Spirit* (New York: State University of New York Press, 1997), 8.

16   Cortright, *Psychotherapy and Spirit.*

17   Raymond J. Corsini, "Transpersonal Psychology," in *The Corsini Encyclopedia of Psychology*, 2nd ed., vol. 3, ed. Irving B. Weiner and W. Edward Craighead (New York: John Wiley & Sons, 1994), 547.

18   Frank A. Salamone, ed., *The Routledge Encyclopedia of Religious Rites, Rituals, and Festivals* (New York: Routledge, 2010).

19   Jacob K. Olupona, ed., *African Traditional Religions in Contemporary Society* (St. Paul: Paragon House, 1991).

should offer their services to Shona Zimbabwean clients. The three case studies presented below, which all employ pseudonyms, provide evidence on how indigenous African though influences clients' hermeneutic of their lived experiences. The cases are utilized to demonstrate how knowledge of indigenous African thought can inform pastoral counseling practices with Shona Zimbabwean clients.

Case Studies

Case One: Jesiwe and the Strong Wind

Jesiwe's parents were seeking help for their daughter, who was now back at home after having disappeared for four days. Jesiwe, a seventeen-year-old female, had gone to a nearby river with her friends. She did not return home when her colleagues did. Upon questioning, Jesiwe's friends reported that when they were at the river fetching some water for the garden, a strong wind came and suddenly they did not see Jesiwe. Seeing what had happened, and clouded with fear and confusion, the friends left the river without Jesiwe. All they knew was that they were together talking and laughing with Jesiwe minutes before she disappeared. The disappearance was reported to Jesiwe's parents and the village leadership. Immediately a search for Jesiwe began.

This search went on for four days without any success. It was only after the fourth day that Jesiwe's parents were advised to visit a religious diviner who also ended up visiting Jesiwe's home. After hearing what had happened, the diviner rallied the whole village to the place where Jesiwe was well kept. While at the river, a series of rituals was conducted. These included chanting, singing, and dancing. During all this, a strong wind suddenly passed by, and to the disbelief of the crowd, a person was noticed sitting on a rock which was at the riverbank. The person was Jesiwe. People started praying more and clapping hands. Others stood there in awe, not understanding what was going on. The spiritualist and other elderly people went to engage this person at the rock. She was taken home to be with her family. Upon being asked what had happened, Jesiwe narrated how a mermaid had taken her in the waters, and she recounted what had happened to her during the four days. Rituals were done to integrate her back to the family. Now months after this event, Jesiwe presented in counseling, seeking help with various physiological, emotional, and psychological symptoms which manifested in unusual behaviors.

Case Two: Masiwa and Her Family

Masiwa, a thirty-one-year-old registered general nurse (RGN), reported for counseling after being referred by her nurse manager. For the first time in her career, Masiwa had not been performing well at work. She showed lack of concentration, slowness in activity in her day-to-day duties, and anhedonia. She had a feeling of general discontent and cried whenever her ward supervisors confronted her. Upon engaging Masiwa, she revealed having marital conflict. The other issue was that of their five-year-old child, who was sick. According to Masiwa, their five-year-old was having convulsions and had not been going to preschool as she should. Apart from seeking medical care for the child, the extended family was now involved. They forced Masiwa and her husband to consult traditional or religious healers since they were not understanding the child's sickness. What was worrying Masiwa was how her husband's relatives were now condemning and blaming her for the sickness of their child. Her husband's family was not supportive at all. Instead, they spent time blaming her. When she came for counseling, Masiwa felt hopeless and helpless. She did not know what to do as she was in emotional and physical pain. All she wanted was to feel better, but every time she tried to feel better, the situation seemed to get worse. She felt isolated and as though her life was tarnished. Masiwa was suicidal, and she reported being tired of suffering and staying in such an environment.

Case Three: The Elephants and the Gerera Community

In another intriguing case, the Gerera community in Zimbabwe was in mayhem when elephants were located roaming around a township. The elephants were beginning to attack people, and this was frightening to adults and children. The presence of the elephants was evoking fear and apprehension. Children and adults were having stress reactions, and some even became afraid of moving outside to do their day-to-day business. When people and the government heard about this incident, I heard some saying, "This community must do something; they certainly angered the spiritual worlds." At first, I thought, *What do these people mean?*, and then later I realized that this was a context where beliefs in the interconnectedness of the living, the natural, and the spiritual world were strong. Even though the Gerera community sent messages to the National Parks asking them to attend to this challenge, they believed the appearance of the elephants in their communities was an indication of some wrongs that the community needed to address. Interestingly, instead of going into the community to address the situation, the National Parks and Wildlife advised the community to engage in rituals that were intended to calm the situation and let the elephants stop appearing in the township. Leaders and community members in the area concurred with the National Parks' proposal. For them, this was more than just elephants appearing; this was a communication to the community to put some things right. Whenever the experiences of humankind realize and identify a dimension that transcends a visual reality, then that experience calls for the evoking of the spiritual world's guidance. This means that the chiefs, the elders, and the spiritual leaders were supposed to guide them as to what to do besides the National Parks and Wildlife's intervention. This also indicated that there was "religious suprahuman" causality such as God and spirits to this happening. Hence, it was echoed that until these community sages intervened, the appearance of these elephants would continue. Thus, days were set aside for the rituals and the ceremonies.

In all the cases above, the African worldview regarding the human world, the spiritual world, and the natural world influenced how the difficulties were to be resolved. When dealing with such cases, effective intervention requires drawing upon existing spiritual and social constructs which encompass patterns of belief, feelings, and knowledge to which the care seekers subscribe. These constructs guide the process and the understanding of wellness and normalcy.[20] Thus, when addressing the cases above, pastoral counselors must employ an approach that realizes the importance of relations, the African cosmology, and transpersonal realities. Realizing the fact that Shona Zimbabweans bring a larger social, cultural, and religious context to psychotherapy helps pastoral counselors to assist care seekers in dealing with their situations. Pastoral counselors need to look for strategies that recognize

---

20   Elias Rantlhane Makwe, *Western and Indigenous Psychiatric Help-Seeking in an Urban African Population*, MA thesis (University of the Witwatersrand, 1985).

"above and beyond" experiences and use them in enabling care seekers to process their experiences.

For the Shona Zimbabweans, who are influenced by indigenous African thinking, effective therapeutic interventions need to be open to the range of experiences that go beyond the personal if they are to yield positive results. As asserted by Cortright, "It is all about developing a self while also honoring the urge to go beyond the self – transpersonal. In moving beyond the confines of the self, consciousness is seen to open up into ranges of experiences which go far beyond."[21] This means that counseling interventions with Shona Zimbabweans are enriched by paying attention to both personal and transpersonal dimensions. Therapeutic modalities that acknowledge the transpersonal must integrate both the spiritual and the psychological. This is what works with Shona Zimbabweans. So, when addressing the cases above, from an indigenous African context, a question comes to mind: How can pastoral counselors utilize existing therapeutic models and integrate the rich, collectivistic, relational aspects of indigenous African thought in a manner that helps Shona Zimbabwean clients to embrace their African identities and religious locations? There are no easy answers to such a question, but as previously mentioned, the adoption of relational, transpersonal, and collectivistic approaches to counseling will yield positive results. The section below explores how to counsel Shona Zimbabweans given that their religious locations are influenced by indigenous African thought.

Integrating Indigenous African Thought into Pastoral Counseling

Having discussed the African context and the various characteristics of indigenous African thought above, it is important to state that what people believe, their basic nature, beliefs, and make-up, is the foundation upon which psychotherapeutic approaches are grounded. Thus, any counseling process that fails to integrate the theological anthropology inherent to indigenous African thought will be woefully inadequate.

In the three cases mentioned above, the problems were not simply psychological or social but also spiritual, and hence required a spiritual remedy.

---

21   Cortright, *Psychotherapy and Spirit,* 9.

In all three cases, engaging the personal as well as the transpersonal realities will be a more viable approach to counseling. The various aspects of indigenous African thought discussed above—namely, the basic relational ontology, transpersonal perspective, holistic approach, collectivism, and the belief in the Supreme God—influence how to conceptualize and intervene in the above cases. Indigenous African thinking also influences the way the care seekers and the communities cope with challenges in order to reach their full potential.

The concept of God as the creator and protector and as a supreme power is expressed in various ways and calls for a relational and transpersonal approach to counseling. The notion that the living are surrounded by hosts of spirit-beings, some good and some evil, influences the actions to be taken by the care seeker and the counselor. Depending upon one's belief, spirit beings could be either ancestors or Jesus Christ/Mohammed, whose influences could not be overlooked if wellness was to be attained.

In the cases above, relational ontology and transpersonal realities informed the way Jesiwe, Masiwa, and the Gerera community responded to their challenges. The counselor's first step in each case should be to help care seekers gain insight into what is happening to them, the origins and development of their difficulties, which will lead to an increased capacity to take rational control over feelings and actions. The second step should be to assist care seekers to alter any disturbed or maladjusted behavior by engaging in liberative, redemptive, and empowerment rituals. The third step is to equip care seekers with coping strategies that can enable them to move in the direction of fulfilling their potential or to achieve an integration of conflicting elements within themselves and their transpersonal realities. Lastly, care seekers need to gain skills, awareness, and knowledge that will enable them to confront emerging shortcomings without expecting themselves to be perfect. In the coming section, I outline the various features of indigenous thought that will impact this counseling process and need not to be disregarded.

Honoring Relationality

Within indigenous African thought, healthy relations are key to one's well-being. People need to fulfill and maintain satisfying relations with the three important worlds—the human world, the spiritual world, and the natural world—in order to function well.[22] Relational therapy originates from relational-cultural theory and the work of Jean Baker Miller in the 1970s and 1980s.[23] In counseling Shona Zimbabweans, one must have a relational ontological approach from which to base one's intervention. In a relational approach, human relations are the center of life. These relations may not be observable to the empiricists, but they are poignantly experienced by African people who truly feel they belong to a loving community and experience meaningful relationships.[24] The cases above call for a relational ontology to counseling where natural and supernatural worlds are intimately related to one another. An equilibrium in between the three is needed for holistic experiences of life to happen.

The basic contention of this relational feature is simply that the relations between entities are ontologically more fundamental than the entities themselves. "For the African it is the lived experience, and reality, of being in relationship that forms his or her identity. Relationship as identity is an active engagement in the development of the concept of 'self.'"[25] This is why Masiwa was struggling. She had no sense of belonging and thereby wished to die. Just because her relationship with her in-laws and husband was not right, her identity was lost. So, in offering counseling to Masiwa, the counselor is encouraged to move away from just exploring her inner personal experiences to exploring a greater understanding of the impact of her relations with others. As indicated in the ubuntu philosophy, "I am only because we are, and since we are, therefore I am." The counselor should explore with Masiwa what she needs to do to remedy her relational dissonance.

As in the elephant case above, while to strangers the elephants may just be animals visiting neighborhoods, to this community, relational issues between the spiritual and the natural worlds needed to be resolved. The only way the relational issues can be addressed is by engaging the three worlds

---

22   Mawere, *African Belief and Knowledge Systems.*

23   Jean Baker Miller, *Toward a New Psychology of Women*, 2nd ed. (Boston: Beacon, 1986).

24   Brent D. Slife, Jeffrey S. Reber, and Frank C. Richardson, *Critical Thinking about Psychology: Hidden Assumptions and Plausible Alternatives* (Washington, DC: American Psychological Association, 2005).

25   Forster, "African Relational Ontology," 245.

through rituals. According to Ring et al., rituals are a primary means of social communication and cohesion. The word *ritual* refers to symbolic action, which focuses a certain kind of power using natural signs and symbols.[26] For the community in Gerera, reconnecting the worlds in harmony is important in order to stop the elephants' recurrent appearance. Rituals also enable healing for those individuals who were showing continuous signs of disturbance as a result of the elephants' appearances.

Relational interconnection is needed in the case of Jesiwe. In the three cases, rituals would enable those involved not to become stuck in emotions and dysfunctional behaviors but to move on, heal, reclaim their identity, and be liberated. The three cases demonstrate how focusing on relationality to the other, nature, and the spiritual world would lead to restoration and reclaiming of an important African value of ubuntu. The community had to come together, *umuntu ngumuntu ngabantu* (a person is a person through other persons), to find a way forward.[27] This ubuntu philosophy calls for a radical relational approach in therapy and influences the therapist's response to care seekers in a way that is transformative and promotes healing. Ubuntu is lived out when people sit together either in circles, under a tree, around the fire, or in other settings to solve issues, support each other, connect, and educate each other. Talking to Jesiwe's family showed that they were grateful for the community support they got. They were grateful for the gift of the ubuntu spirit among their community. A relational counseling approach calls for humility toward care seekers, not the arrogance of an "expert" mentality. I have seen this as an important attitude when counseling Shona Zimbabweans or any indigenous Africans. In each of the three cases above, the fear of rejection, the fear that one does not belong or is not accepted, or the absence of meaningful relationships was the greatest fear and anxiety, hence the importance of a relational approach.

For Africans, relational frameworks imply that we are already in community and community is an important component of what happens to us. Counseling is a learning-oriented process that occurs in an interactive

---

26   Nancy C. Ring et al., *Introduction to the Study of Religion* (Maryknoll, NY: Orbis Books, 1998).

27   Forster, "African Relational Ontology."

relationship with the aim of helping a person to learn more about herself and the other, and to become an effective member of society. From a relational standpoint, important questions during therapy may be: 1) What is your understanding of disconnection in this situation and how could you reconnect?; 2) What styles of interpersonal interaction, if any, have been pushing others away?; 3) How would you reconnect with your significant others?; and 4) When connection is absent, mental and emotional concerns can result. What relations are absent and how is this affecting your day-to-day functioning? These and others are key questions for an indigenous African to explore during a counseling session. Change begins to occur when the counselor and individual build new relational images, which can be done through rituals and other practices. Another important aspect of indigenous African thinking is the transpersonal component.

Honoring the Transpersonal Dimension

"Mainstream psychotherapeutic systems have largely ignored human spiritual and religious experience, except as sources for psychosocial support. In contrast, one of the hallmarks of the transpersonal approaches is the directness with which spiritual experience is addressed as part of the therapeutic process."[28] The overall goal of a transpersonal approach to counseling is to enable care seekers to transcend, or go beyond, the physical realm. So, instead of focusing solely on the body and mind, which is typical of most psychotherapeutic approaches, a transpersonal approach places significant emphasis on spirituality or "transcendent dimensions." A transpersonal approach acknowledges aspects of an individual that are beyond the person or physical realm. Therefore, this aspect fits well the African epistemology and cosmology. This notion of "transpersonal" as an idea was first introduced by William James more than ninety years ago, and ever since, it has evolved in various ways.[29] A transpersonal approach moves one across the personal

---

28   Mark C. Kasprow and Bruce W. Scotton, "A Review of Transpersonal Theory and its Application to the Practice of Psychotherapy," *The Journal of Psychotherapy Practice and Research* 8, no. 1 (1999): 13.

29   Miles A. Vich, "Some Historical Sources for the Term 'Transpersonal,'" *Journal of Transpersonal Psychology* 20, no. 2 (1988), 107–10.

realm, acknowledging and exploring all aspects of self and placing the self in a larger framework.[30] This approach stems from transpersonal theory, which, according to Kasprow and Scotton, "proposes that there are developmental stages beyond the adult ego, which involve experiences of connectedness with phenomena considered outside the boundaries of the ego. In healthy individuals, these developmental stages can engender the highest human qualities, including altruism, creativity, and intuitive wisdom."[31]

Care seekers, when they present themselves for counseling, do not check their spirituality at the door.[32] They are more than the person we see. They are surrounded by forces that either positively or negatively influence their lives and are thus transpersonal. They may have experiences of connectedness with phenomena outside the person, and these need to be explored in the counseling process. So, as a counselor my role is to help care seekers acknowledge the transpersonal experience and draw on spiritual relations. Assurance of support from the supernatural can strengthen a care seeker's coping as in the case of Masiwa. She needed to know that regardless of her husband's family's actions, there was a reason for her to keep living. Helping her to draw on spiritual coping methods tailored to her own understanding and experience of the sacred was key. Masiwa came to therapy struggling and emotionally overwhelmed, and she needed a safe vessel to take refuge and sustenance. For Jesiwe, all she needed was reincorporation and revitalization by the experience of community. This would signal the passage to a new status or to normal social life after her experience in the river. Rituals may be employed, like wearing an insignia such as the rosary or reading the Bible every day. Jesiwe also needed that sense of a sacred communion which will make her ongoing social life possible. This will enable her to discriminate between reality and wishful thinking. To help Jesiwe, relational ontology needed to be operationalized in imagination-forming ritual practices that will help her overcome the negative impact of the river experience. Transpersonal therapy would enable Jesiwe

---

30   Cortright, *Psychotherapy and Spirit.*

31   Kasprow and Scotton, "A Review of Transpersonal Theory," 12.

32   Kenneth Pargament, *Spiritually Integrated Psychotherapy: Understanding and Addressing the Sacred* (New York: Guilford, 2007).

and Masiwa to find deeper meaning and a greater sense of purpose in life. An important aspect was to help them become more deeply connected to their transpersonal side, increase their self-awareness, and broaden the way they look at the world.

Pastoral counselors need to respect and integrate indigenous African thought when offering counseling to Africans. Counseling interventions will be more helpful if they honor the care seekers' experiences and religious location. As indicated by Doehring, "In order to offer care that respects and does not erase the otherness of a care-seeker's religious faith, pastoral counselors need to use a phenomenological approach that pays attention to the differences between the unique religious, spiritual, and existential meaning systems and practices that each person constructs out of her or his various relational matrices."[33]

Conclusion

Counseling with Shona Zimbabweans calls for a relational approach that acknowledges transpersonal realities, emphasizes a holistic approach, and uses spiritual resources as a means for acknowledging and working with clients' religious locations. A transpersonal approach is appropriate in that it honors the entire spectrum of human experience, including various non-ordinary states of consciousness. In indigenous African thought, care seekers must be understood "thickly," i.e., in connection to their relational, situational, and moral contexts. A transpersonal approach offers a broadened view of what it means to be human and promotes relational connection of the three worlds in day-to-day life.

My experience in offering counseling to Shona Zimbabweans indicates that indigenous African thought and Western scientific psychology are distinct but complementary. Instead of being sidelined, indigenous African thought needs to be engaged as it has a unique contribution to offer to the

---

33   Carrie Doehring, "The Practice of Relational-Ethical Pastoral Care: An Intercultural Approach," in *"After You!" Dialogical Ethics and the Pastoral Counseling Process*, ed. Axel Liégeous, Roger Burggraeve, Marina Reimslagh, and Jozef Corveleyn (Leuven: Uitgeverij Peeters, 2013), 162.

universal human quest for healing and wholeness. With the therapist's guidance, and by using relational and transpersonal approaches, care seekers can identify, build, and expand their inner strengths and resources to create a more balanced life and a healthier state of mind. Relationships are central to the formation, expression, and understanding of who an individual person is. Africans believe that people cannot be truly human, truly themselves, until they are in relationship with other persons. Pastoral counselors who honor this will be of great service and successful in their ministries.

Bibliography

Corsini, Raymond J. "Transpersonal Psychology." In *The Corsini Encyclopedia of Psychology*. 2nd ed. Vol. 3. Edited by Irving B. Weiner and W. Edward Craighead. New York: John Wiley & Sons, 1994.

Cortright, Brant. *Psychotherapy and Spirit.* New York: State University of New York Press, 1997.

Couture, Pamela. "Human Dignity, Injustice and *Ubuntu*: Living the Metaphor of *Bwino/Bumuntu*/White Lime in the Democratic Republic of Congo." In *Practicing Ubuntu: Practical Theological Perspectives on Injustice, Personhood and Human Dignity*, edited by Jaco S. Dreyer, Yolanda Dreyer, Edward Foley, and Malan Nel, 9–21. Berlin: LIT Verlag, 2017.

Doehring, Carrie. "The Practice of Relational-Ethical Pastoral Care: An Intercultural Approach." In *"After You!" Dialogical Ethics and the Pastoral Counseling Process*, edited by Axel Liégeous, Roger Burggraeve, Marina Reimslagh, and Jozef Corveleyn, 159–81. Leuven: Uitgeverij Peeters, 2013.

du Toit, Cornel W. "Technoscience and the Integrity of Personhood in Africa and the West: Facing Our Technoscientific Environment." In *The Integrity of the Human Person in an African Context: Perspectives from Science and Religion*, edited by Cornel W. du Toit, 1–46. Pretoria: Research Institute for Theology and Religion, University of South Africa, 2004.

Forster, Dion A. "African Relational Ontology, Individual Identity, and Christian Theology: An African Theological Contribution Towards an Integrated Relational Ontological Identity." *Theology* 113, no. 874 (2010): 243–53. https://doi.org/10.1177/0040571X1011300402.

Greider, Kathleen J. "Religious Location and Counseling: Engaging Diversity and Difference in Views of Religion." In *Understanding Pastoral*

Counseling, edited by Elizabeth A. Maynard and Jill L. Snodgrass, 235–56. New York: Springer, 2015.

Kalilombe, Patrick A. "Spirituality in the African Perspective." In *Paths of African Theology,* edited by Rosino Gibellini, 115–35. Maryknoll, NY: Orbis Books, 1994.

Kasprow, Mark C., and Bruce W. Scotton. "A Review of Transpersonal Theory and its Application to the Practice of Psychotherapy." *The Journal of Psychotherapy Practice and Research* 8, no. 1 (1999): 12–23.

Magesa, Laurenti. *African Religion: The Moral Traditions of Abundant Life.* Nairobi: Paulines Publications Africa, 1997.

Makwe, Elias Rantlhane. *Western and Indigenous Psychiatric Help-Seeking in an Urban African Population.* MA thesis. University of the Witwatersrand, 1985.

Mawere, Munyaradzi. *African Belief and Knowledge Systems: A Critical Perspective.* Mankon, Bamenda: Langaa Research & Publications, 2011.

Mbiti, John S. *African Religions and Philosophy.* 2nd ed. London: Heinemann, 1990.

Miller, Jean Baker. *Toward a New Psychology of Women.* 2nd ed. Boston: Beacon, 1986.

Olupona, Jacob K., ed. *African Traditional Religions in Contemporary Society.* St. Paul: Paragon House, 1991.

Pargament, Kenneth. *Spiritually Integrated Psychotherapy: Understanding and Addressing the Sacred.* New York: Guilford, 2007.

Ring, Nancy C., Kathleen S. Nash, Mary N. MacDonald, Fred Glennon, and Jennifer A. Glancy. *Introduction to the Study of Religion.* Maryknoll, NY: Orbis Books, 1998.

Salamone, Frank A., ed. *The Routledge Encyclopedia of Religious Rites, Rituals, and Festivals.* New York: Routledge, 2010.

Slife, Brent D., Jeffrey S. Reber, and Frank C. Richardson. *Critical Thinking about Psychology: Hidden Assumptions and Plausible Alternatives.* Washington, DC: American Psychological Association, 2005.

Vich, Miles A. "Some Historical Sources for the Term 'Transpersonal.'" *Journal of Transpersonal Psychology* 20, no. 2 (1988), 107–10.

Watchel, Paul L. *Relational Theory and the Practice of Psychotherapy.* New York: Guilford, 2008.

⚜ **9** ⚜

JEWISH VULNERABILITY
AND PROGRESSIVE POLITICS
IN SPIRITUAL CARE

ROCHELLE ROBINS

ANTI-JEWISH DISCRIMINATION IS on the rise in America today.[1] Oppressive rhetoric and acts are perpetrated by anti-Jewish organizations, including white nationalists and neo-Nazi movements, but also by politically progressive individuals and organizations committed to the fight for equity and social justice. Most often such discrimination results from a failure to recognize how Jews' intersectionality places them at the margins religiously, ethnically, and, for Jews of color, racially. This chapter outlines how spiritual care providers and educators can forcefully resist increasingly accepted, sometimes subtle though still powerful, prejudices and assumptions toward Jews and Israel that are too often espoused by political progressives. The chapter begins by presenting two examples, or case studies, wherein Jews, specifically Jewish women, were discriminated against in politically progressive contexts. The chapter then evidences how such discrimination results from a failure to embrace the complex intersectionality of Jewish identity and the ways in which "naming" can both heal and harm. The chapter then concludes by positing five competencies for spiritual care providers and educators to eradicate anti-Jewish discrimination.

Silence among the like-minded can creep up and crash down on society like a thunderous destructive force. German Lutheran Pastor Rev. Martin Neimöller referred to this silence in his well-known poem about the

---

1   ADL, "ADL Audit Finds Antisemitic Incidents in United States Reached All-Time High in 2021," April 25, 2022, https://www.adl.org/resources/press-release/adl-audit-finds-antisemitic-incidents-united-states-reached-all-time-high.

advance of Nazism: "First they came for the socialists, and I did not speak out—because I was not a socialist. Then they came for the trade unionists, and I did not speak out—because I was not a trade unionist. Then they came for the Jews, and I did not speak out—because I was not a Jew. Then they came for me—and there was no one left to speak for me."[2] In spiritual care we cannot tolerate this silence. At the same time there is an imperative to balance the multifaceted nature of our roles.

Anti-Jewish Discrimination in Politically Progressive Contexts

The following section provides two case illustrations wherein Jews, specifically Jewish women, were discriminated against in politically progressive contexts.

Case One: The Lesbians of Color Conference

There is often a question of where advocacy, social justice, and social action intersect with spiritual care. One student of chaplaincy recently asked, "If I am so busy being actively present with care seekers who are in pain, where is there room for me to actively confront social issues in this work? Is there room for advocacy in mainstream spiritual care work?" Where there are places of pain regarding social issues, we are often left bereft of language and connection with others. Rachel Adler wrote in her *Theology of Lament*, "To be present when the sufferer re-achieves relational speech is to be present at the rebirth of redemption."[3] Being present to suffering under any circumstance is advocacy—social, political, and personal.

One of my first and most instructive teachers in demonstrating the power of what it means to be present when the sufferer or sufferers achieve or re-achieve relational speech was a woman whose name I never knew. I was twenty-one years old, had recently come out as a lesbian, and attended the Lesbians of Color Conference in San Francisco in 1988. The Jewish women, both

---

2   Wolfgang Gerlach, *And the Witnesses Were Silent: The Confessing Church and the Jews* (Lincoln: University of Nebraska Press, 2000), 47.

3   Rachel Adler, "For These I Weep: A Theology of Lament," *The Chronicle* 68 (2006): 16.

light-skinned[4] and dark-skinned, experienced a divide within the conference as a whole and among ourselves. One small group argued that the Jewish women should be there to support women of color only as allies. Considering that Jews in the United States are predominantly light-skinned, it is appropriate and essential to honor light-skinned privilege as compared to the overt and sometimes constant oppression that people experience as the result of living with darker skin color. Light-skinned people of all backgrounds are responsible to acknowledge this privilege.

A larger group argued that the conference required a more expansive theoretical framework about the plight and vulnerability of Jewish women. The third, more silent members of the group appeared to be confused and absorbing the arguments—arguments that were new to many of us in a public forum. A number of people, given our young age and lack of exposure to heated public discourse and other historical backdrops of Jewish identity for each person, appeared to be experiencing surprise, mild shock, disorientation, and a lack of ability or readiness to articulate a response.

While the majority of Jews in the United States are light-skinned, with light-skinned privilege, a woman at the 1988 Lesbians of Color Conference said, "I am an Ashkenazi Jew and live and am treated as a woman of color in the United States, but my skin is only dark because of my Jewish heritage. My family is dark only because we are Jewish, not for any other reason! I want to be included as someone relevant to this conference and not only as an ally!" She then described the myriad times she was rejected from participating in activities as a woman of color because she is a Jew. She has no other heritage that meets the "requirements" for a person of color. Another woman in turn said, "And I am a light-skinned Jew and know that I live with this privilege, but this leaves me feeling no less vulnerable to racism and anti-Semitism. My life privileges leave me with no illusion about the realities and even growing dangers of identifying with my culture and community." Another woman, wearing a kiffiyeh to show her solidarity with the Palestinian liberation movement, said, "As Jews it is our obligation to support others

---

4   The term *white* is often used to communicate ethnicity when it communicates skin color. Light skin determines large degrees of privilege in many societies, but it does not categorically determine or define ethnic, cultural, or regional heritage.

who are living under the pressures of oppression. We should only pay attention to others who need our help at this conference and in our society right now!" My memory of the complexities, emotions, confusions, and passions present in the room is vivid.

Hearing about the alienation of the Jewish women within the larger conference and even among Jewish attendees, the conference organizers invited a facilitator to join us. They intentionally asked a middle-aged African-American non-Jewish woman (presumably for reasons of non-partiality about the specific Jewish discourse) to join us. There was also a suspicion that the conference organizers plucked the Jewish women out of the conference to eliminate our arguing about the issues within the conference at large. It was both understandable that those in leadership wished to preserve the integrity of the original conference mission and agenda and also chillingly indicative of the suppression of the Jewish voice that led to the confrontations in the first place.

I strongly recall the pain and emotion in the room and a few robust egos with clear-cut opinions attempting to manage the rest of us into something tidy, but Jewish history and experience is anything but tidy. The facilitator, who I think of as my first chaplain, knowing nothing of her training or of chaplaincy, "facilitated" our discussion by expressing noticeable and remarkable compassion for all of us who spoke through her facial and verbal responses. She showed her compassion, no matter what perspectives, agendas, or words were shared. The impact of her interactions was such that thirty years later I am still learning from her and attempting to emulate her care for others. Looking back, I see her skills and kindness as an example of good spiritual care during a social crisis and relational upheaval between human beings. Ironically, the conference constructed on the theme of intersectionality denied the Jewish contingent their experience as an intersectional people. Did the women of color see their prejudice? Thirty years later, the issues are still prevalent and require attention. The work of advocacy and awareness for Jewish people today, just like all of the shared advocacy in the progressive world, is a perpetual work in progress.

There is advocacy and social justice in meeting others in their concern, social isolation, and pain. The sufferer often faces an indescribable and ineffable experience. There can be a lack of words to describe the Jewish experience of prejudice, especially when Jews may appear, and at times are, a part of a privileged light-skinned class. My spiritual care plea here is that clinicians and educators strive to understand the ways in which people committed to social justice, like the conference organizers and attendees, continue to victimize Jews.

Case Two: Intersectionality and Jews in the Women's Marches

Intersectionality is a theoretical structure, originally developed by Kimberlé Crenshaw, a professor of law, to examine the discrimination of Black women.[5] Crenshaw analyzed the ways in which Black women were affected by both race and gender discrimination. Over time, mainly feminist theorists used Crenshaw's groundbreaking work to explore numerous intersecting identities that include any and all social classifications including, but not limited to, gender, ethnicity, economic status, sexual orientation, religious affiliation, and all stratifications that are subject to discrimination.

Jewish culture, life, and practice are inherently intersectional. There is no monolithic Jewish identity as Jewish identities are complex and intersectional. In order to fully serve the Jewish population with awareness and compassion, spiritual care providers and educators are invited to remember and hold the Jewish story of survival. For well over two thousand years we have survived in an exilic and diasporic circumstance. While all peoples are unique, the Jewish experience is characterized by oppression and survival. While there is also thriving in Jewish cycles of history, the cycle of targeting is recurrent. We have lived as a nation within many nations for centuries. While we are light-skinned and dark-skinned, from both western and eastern civilizations, we have generally remained connected to one another as an ethnic, cultural, and religious group. We are Ashkenazi, of Central or Eastern European descent. We are Sephardi, originally from Spain, Portugal, and the Iberian Peninsula. We are from Africa, India, and other parts of Asia.

---

5   Kimberlé W. Crenshaw, "Demarginalizing the Intersection of Race and Sex: A Black Feminist Critique of Antidiscrimination Doctrine, Feminist Theory, and Antiracist Politics," *The University of Chicago Legal Forum* 140 (1989): 139–67, http://chicagounbound .uchicago.edu/uclf/vol1989/iss1/8.

We are from the Middle East and the Fertile Crescent, the place of our origin before the second and most permanent diasporic condition began in the year 70 of the Common Era. There is hardly a place in the world where Jews have not traversed as part of our escape, survival, coping, and resilience with the world around us.

Any reductionist view of Jewish identity undermines the complexity of its development and intersectional nature, including and especially use of skin color as a barometer. While it is important not to dismiss light-skinned privilege, the measuring stick of skin color is an insufficient gauge in the examination of Jewish identity, experience, exposure to prejudice, and violence. Sociologist Judith Gerson wrote,

> *Attempts to clarify and specify what we mean by Jewishness can easily be distorted by reifying Jewish identity, either through essentializing it or reducing it to its biological origins. In much the same way that biological sex has no meaning apart from the social and cultural dynamics of gender, biologically based definitions of Jewishness have no meaning without understanding the social and cultural forces that generate and sustain them.*[6]

In turn, one might question whether the social and cultural forces of Jewishness have meaning without an equal understanding and examination of the ethnic and biological heritage for those who were born into it.[7] The Jewish people cannot be reduced to the categories that others proscribe for us in social, religious, or political circles. Every marginal group claims the same right to self-definition and determination. Is this in itself a threat to others who want tidy definitions of social stratification and the human condition? We must continue, in compassion, to confront and build relationships with

---

6   Judith M. Gerson, "Gender Theory, Intersectionality, and New Understandings of Jewishness," *Journal of Jewish Identities* 11, no. 1 (2018): 13, https://muse.jhu.edu/article /689638.

7   Converts to Judaism are fully recognized by the community though entrée into it did not take place through birth. This may be similar to being fully recognized as a citizen by a country to which one immigrated. Cultural affiliations in these cases are often strong even when ethnic ties did not occur from birth.

progressive activists and thinkers who fight against rigidly constructed social locations but continue to put "the Jews" in a box. While white supremacists are the most concerning threat to Jews around the world, the prejudices held by political progressives are equally concerning and offensive.

The diversity of Jewish people seems to be perplexing to both Jews and non-Jews. Controversies about the Jewish standing in the Women's Marches across the country are indicative of the way in which Jews are often both privileged and oppressed perhaps in part due to the intrinsic and nuanced intersectionality of our community. The Women's March, which started in 2017 following the election of Donald J. Trump, can serve as a case study for examining how Jewish people are oppressed by progressives who claim to be committed to social justice. From its inception, the Women's March has been criticized as being anti-Jewish.[8] Tamika Mallory, Co-President of the Women's March and National Chair of the New York City Women's March in 2019, is a staunch supporter of Louis Farrakhan, leader of the Nation of Islam, who is widely criticized for being anti-Jewish and homophobic. In her appearance on the television show *The View* in January 2019, Mallory never convincingly denied her alliance with the virulent anti-Semitic views of Louis Farrakhan.

Jewish women around the United States, both light- and dark-skinned for a variety of intersectional reasons and heritages, are grappling with the most effective and authentic ways to support the values and mission of the Women's Marches "to harness the political power of diverse women and their communities to create transformative social change" given the outspoken leadership of both Tamika Mallory and Linda Sarsour.[9] These two leaders have portrayed themselves as the antitheses of understanding and compassion towards the Jewish community and the rich history of intersectionality in Jewish culture and life. However, Rabbi Sharon Kleinbaum engaged in a conversation with both Mallory and Sarsour, and she was convinced of their willingness to engage in deeper conversations of reconciliation and

---

8 Farah Stockman, "Women's March Roiled by Accusations of Anti-Semitism," *New York Times*, December 23, 2018, https://www.nytimes.com/2018/12/23/us/womens -march-anti-semitism.html.

9 Women's March, *Our Vision*, accessed July 14, 2023, https://www.womensmarch .com/about-us.

collaboration. Kleinbaum announced on Facebook that we should not allow our current Presidential office and White House to experience a perverse pleasure of us "spending so much time trashing each other."[10] Kleinbaum offered a message of hope and collaboration to heal and expand the Jewish standing in left-wing communities working toward social change. "Jewish women of color and other intersectional Jewish women have experienced particular turmoil around [the] controversy [of the Women's Marches]. It has felt at times, like Jewish women of Color are being asked to choose between different aspects of their identity and to prioritize either their commitment to fighting racism or their commitment to fighting [prejudice and hatred towards Jews]. Rejecting this false choice, many Jewish Women of Color have been organizing."[11] The question in the end is not whether Jews should march and work toward transformative change with others or if they should fight against anti-Jewish bigotry by not marching. Rather, the social justice work on our own behalf is to articulate more to others about who we are and hope that they will listen, receive, and respond.

The premise that anti-Jewish discrimination is somehow different from racism is problematic, inaccurate, and dangerous. Dismissing concerns about anti-Jewish discrimination has proven historically not to benefit anyone who lives on the margins or at the center of societal threat.[12] In 2013, Brandeis University's Steinhardt Social Research Institute issued a statistical report that claimed that 11.2 percent of the Jewish population in the United States is non-white.[13] The Jewish community ought to be both knowledgeable and inclusive of this reality. This statistic also reinforces the importance of serving everyone within and across the Jewish population and confronting the racism within us. This statistic also informs the non-Jewish world about

---

10   Sharon Kleinbaum, Facebook, January 16, 2019, https://www.facebook.com/sharon.kleinbaum/posts/pfbid031d9rRmhkbS7wNnqpeWLzi7kXbLHXQ8P3xWwT1fvn-QficQfSbb9TGTMwdrQGi5LsZl.

11   Moving Traditions, *The Women's March, Antisemitism & Intersectional Jewish Women,* January 11, 2019, https://www.movingtraditions.org/antisemitism-the-womens-march/.

12   bell hooks, *Feminist Theory: From Margin to Center* (Boston: South End, 1984).

13   Ilana Kaufman, "After Pittsburgh, Is Anyone Considering Jews of Color?" *The Jewish News of Northern California,* November 5, 2018, https://www.jweekly.com/2018/ 11 /05/after-pittsburgh-is-anyone-considering-jews-of-color/.

the diversity within our community. At the same time, the central point here is that skin color is just one of many intersecting identities for Jews and for all people.

Jewish vulnerability is real in progressive politics, and those who dedicate themselves to social justice should reflect this reality and work to eradicate anti-Jewish discrimination. Yet anti-Jewish attacks and violence are on the rise. The ADL, a Jewish organization that tracks Jewish and other hate crimes around the world, stated,

> *Our most recent report on anti-Semitic incidents in the United States showed a significant year-to-year increase: In 2017, anti-Semitic incidents surged nearly 60 percent, according to the 2017 ADL Audit of Anti-Semitic Incidents. This was the largest single-year increase on record and the second highest number reported since [the] ADL started tracking such data in 1979. The sharp rise was due in part to a significant increase in incidents in schools and on college campuses, which nearly doubled for a second year in a row.*[14]

The same report also stated that "a majority of Americans are concerned about violence directed against American Jews. And more than eight in 10 Americans believe it is important for the government to play a role in combating anti-Semitism, up from 70 percent in 2014."[15] Despite the alarming statistic on the rise of violence and hate crimes toward Jews in the United States, Jewish voices and concerns often go unheard in social justice movements and academic think tanks alike.

Naming and Names: Liberation or a Dragging Parachute

The names "Jews" and "Israel" are often laden with negative associations, and we never know when or where we might confront these. Acknowledging

---

14   ADL, "Anti-Semitic Incidents Surged Nearly 60% in 2017, According to New ADL Report," February 27, 2018, https://www.adl.org/resources/press-release/anti-semitic -incidents-surged-nearly-60-2017-according-new-adl-report.

15   ADL, "Anti-Semitic Incidents Surged."

intersectionality dissuades the bifurcation of human experience and identity; all aspects of social location and inner-being interact with all other aspects of who we are. Furthermore, all aspects of oppression and injustice are also interlocked, and becoming aware of them creates opportunity for social, political, personal, and spiritual transformation.[16] Identity politics is a theoretical framework and movement originally based on the foundation of the noble struggle to accept and strengthen diversity.

Being given a name possesses liberating potentials, especially when someone senses our strengths or wants to bestow important qualities upon us. Claiming a name or category ideally has the potential for the same effect of positive affirmation. However, identity politics, shaping our views or assuming the views of others based on identity and social stratification, creates social polarizations within and amongst diverse populations. What frees us also holds us captive. Identity politics and social stratifications save and liberate us. Yet if we are not careful, they can act as what poet Rachel Kann referred to in conversation as a parachute that we keep dragging around for days, years, or lifetimes. After we've dropped from a great height and landed on the ground, we often confine ourselves to the level of freedom gained through the original mechanism—a lifesaving device that brought us home. The metaphorical parachute that once freed us may no longer suit our quest. Freedom is the ability to name and keep naming ourselves. Naming identities within safe frameworks offers liberation and helps us find deeper connections within ourselves and with others.

We name ourselves to claim and embrace our existence. In *Bereishit* 2:19–20, the book of Genesis, Adam, the primordial human being at the initial stage of human development in the *Torah*, is tasked with naming all of the creatures, thus creating named categories of existence. Categories of existence create order and understanding of the essence of a creature. In several rabbinical texts, the rabbis extrapolated on this naming. They wrote that Adam observed the essence of each creature and named it according to a core spirit or heart that emanated from it.

---

16   Patricia Hill Collins, "Intersectionality's Definitional Dilemmas," *Annual Review of Sociology* 41 (2015): 1–20, https://doi.org/10.1146/annurev-soc-073014-112142.

In one commentary on *Bereishit* 2:19, Rabbeinu Bachya wrote that God provided Adam the opportunity to name Godself. Adam chose the word *Adonai*, and when God asked Adam why Adam chose that name, Adam's response was, "Because You are the overlord of all creatures."[17] Adam named God and God's essence as Adam saw it, therefore intimating that when human beings name others, these names are constructs that point toward, but do not capture, one's essence. Thus, Adam, the primordial human being, was given immense power in the world to name the creatures. Kathleen Greider eloquently commented on the power Adam exercised in this biblical narrative when she wrote, "Though the existence of power is judged good, power becomes immediately and profoundly ambiguous in the living out of it. However essential and positive power is as an aspect of human nature, it becomes a confounding mixture of bane and blessing as soon as it is exercised in the context of relationship."[18] Power as a mixture of bane and blessing exists in the act of naming itself. Yet even in the naming of God, a certain form of idolatry is in jeopardy when processes of discovery and the evolution of naming become static. As the result of newfound information and revelation, the renaming of ourselves can even change the name of God.

By naming, what was once unarticulated becomes defined, creating a language with which to share, connect, and empower. Yet we also limit and reduce a more capacious and broader essence of ourselves and others when we name. Categories make identities both seen and unseen. When we live without them, we cannot expand stratifications for the sake of inclusivity. When a being or group of beings cannot share in the process of choosing a name or renaming and expanding an identification based on their own growing and evolving as they see it, the opportunity of relationship diminishes.

The Jewish people are difficult to name not because there is no name but because there are many. This diversity and versatility are central to Jewish

---

17   Bachya ben Asher, *Torah Commentary; Rabbeinu Bahya; Bereshit, Chapter 2:19*, trans. Eliyahu Munk, 1998, https://www.sefaria.org/Rabbeinu_Bahya?lang=bi&p2=Rabbeinu_Bahya%2C_Bereshit.2.19.2&lang2=en.

18   Kathleen J. Greider, *Reckoning with Aggression: Theology, Violence, and Vitality* (Louisville, KY: Westminster John Knox, 1997), 58.

survival. At the same time, for a world wound up in concrete, unmovable definitions, it has been a catalyst for fear, hatred, displacement, and violence. It has also led Jews to cultivate skills of survival, some of which are deeply resented by others.

Jewish Intersectionality, Our Many Names, and Anti-Jewish Discrimination

Throughout my life, people have asked me from where anti-Jewish hatred comes and how the Jews have survived through it all. At the age of twenty-one I served as the director of my small liberal arts college's Jewish student union, and this question arose on a fairly regular basis. Usually the question was posed from the standpoint of authentic curiosity. There were other times that I suspected that it came from a place of ambivalence toward or suspicion of the Jewish people, even from Jews themselves. Initially the question surprised me. As I grew to understand this college environment's intricate relationship with Jewish culture, practice, and Jews, I saw an opportunity to respond in a manner that engaged with others, though never without a degree of trepidation of what felt like responsibility beyond my years.

My studies in twentieth-century political philosophy, and delving into the writings of Hannah Arendt in particular, gifted me with a response that described the Jewish identity and experience as one without rigid boundaries and definitions. For example, Judaism contains a religious framework, but many Jews do not characterize their Jewish identity through the experience of religion or spirituality; the Jewish people are part of a singular culture that includes innumerable cultures; the Jews are a nation whose diasporic people live within many nations; the Jewish religion is not creedal, and connection to it need not be characterized by faith; and while many traditions and philosophies bind us together, multiplicity of thought and practice is a valued aspect of mainstream Jewish discourse. Without determining any exact reason for Jewish hatred, during my college years it seemed reasonable to suspect that the complexity of Jewish intersectionality, and Jews' evolving, somewhat uncontained identity, roused hatred in others. This uncontained identity continues to make Jews an easy target for propaganda during difficult sociopolitical times specifically, and at any time generally.

In 1882, physician, Jewish activist, and Zionist Leader Leon Pinsker was one of many to write about Judeophobia: "To the living the Jew is a corpse, to the native a foreigner, to the homesteader a vagrant, to the proprietary a beggar, to the poor an exploiter and a millionaire, to the patriot a man [*sic*] without a country, for all a hated rival."[19] Although the language is not contemporary, the ideas are still echoed today. While flipping through television channels one night, I heard a white supremacist exclaim, "Jewish people are the host body for all of the other parasites, and every societal problem starts with them," rhetoric that is repeated in all types of white supremacist/Neo-Nazi propaganda. Pinsker's commentary still holds more than a kernel of truth about the reality of the Jew as an alienated scapegoat in the United States, Europe, and around the world.

For those of us who are informed about the mentality and rhetoric of white supremacy, there is no new information here. What may be more of a challenge is examining what we in academia and in politically progressive circles can do to help diminish and even prevent subtler yet just as damaging notions in our own spheres—notions and ideas that we, your Jewish friends, live with daily. Accepting this challenge entails learning from those who experience anti-Jewish discrimination perpetrated by the politically progressive as well as the politically conservative. For example, Rabbi Susan Silverman in January 2019 wrote,

> *Oh yes, yes, the anti-Semitism on the left DOES hurt and scare*
> *me more. Not that it's worse. Just in terms of how I feel able to*
> *function in the world, it is much more impactful. Trump-types'*
> *hatred of me means there are people I do not identify with who*
> *don't want me. But when the people who are my refuge [those who*
> *hold similar values for social justice], who I want to make a home*
> *with me (meaning a home in the world), who I long to celebrate*
> *for and with when they succeed and build, see me, Israel, Jews*
> *(except their approved Jews, maybe, relishing this potential division*
> *from each other?) as uniquely evil and worthy of being pointed out*

---

19   Leon Pinsker, *Auto-Emancipation: An Appeal to His People* [originally published anonymously], October 17, 1882, accessed July 14, 2023, https://www.jewishvirtuallibrary .org/quot-auto-emancipation-quot-leon-pinsker.

Haman-style, whether we are relevant or not to the issue at hand, I fear that I have no home in the world at large.[20]

Or in Yehudah Mirsky's words following the massacre of Jews in the synagogue in Pittsburgh: "Anti-Semitism of the Left and the Right has each seized on one piece of the equation. Right/Trumpist anti-Semitism despises universalism, loves nationalism. Left/Corbyn anti-Semitism despises nationalism, loves universalism. The Jews stand to get it in the neck from both directions."[21]

Mirsky also presented a poignant opinion that in Jewish life, culture, and history, there is no real difference between universalism and particularism by saying, "Passionate love [for peoplehood] and universal reason can go hand-in-hand, in nations as in families. But it takes a lot of work and the road getting there isn't easy."[22] People are afraid of what they don't understand and haven't experienced. The Jewish people continue to represent not just difference in the world, but what the world sees as distasteful at any given moment in history.

Anti-Jewish violence is directly correlated to our inherent intersectionality. The lines of intersection and identity are intricate and varied for all individuals and groups everywhere in the world. Yet it is the elaborate maze and variety of Jewish life, practice, spirituality, culture, nationhood(s), class, gender, politics, viewpoints, etc., that lead to a historically consistent hostility toward Jews from all sides. The supposition presented here is that Jewish oppression mainly occurs because of inherent intersectionality itself and not because individual Jews, groups of Jews, or Israel provoke it. One must wonder why Israel is more of a world provocation among political progressives as compared to the atrocities and oppression that are happening in Syria, Yemen, Sudan, Somalia, Libya, and other places including the United States.

---

20   Susan Silverman, "Why Anti-Semitism on the Left Hurts Me More," *Lilith*, January 24, 2019, https://lilith.org/2019/01/why-anti-semitism-on-the-left-hurts-me-more/.

21   Yehudah Mirsky, "After Pittsburgh: The New Jewish Question and the New Jew Hatred," *The American Interest*, October 28, 2018, https://www.the-american-interest.com/2018/10/28/the-new-jewish-question-and-the-new-jew-hatred/.

22   Mirsky, "After Pittsburgh."

Jewish and non-Jewish religious/spiritual leaders and activists alike need to acknowledge that Jewish intersectionality is a shared concern. Spiritual care providers need to educate themselves in order to understand this complex identity more deeply and to help students to do the same. Non-Jewish allies are essential to the overturning of both the subtle and overt demonstrations of anti-Jewish hostility in homes, congregations, clinical environments, seminaries, and society.

Anti-Jewish Discrimination and Spiritual Care

Often the experience of Jewish oppression by Jews, especially when it is not overtly violent, is difficult to identify and articulate. In my own Clinical Pastoral Education (CPE) residency in 1995 at the Hospital of the University of Pennsylvania, as one of two Jews in an interfaith setting with little to no instruction from other Jews, it was my Christian educators, supervisors, and peers who invited me and helped me achieve relational speech and find my voice to articulate the nuances of my Jewish experience in the then (and still) primarily non-Jewish world of spiritual care training. My Christian pastoral educators were my "rabbis" on this journey. Rabbis Bonita Taylor and David Zucker, in their groundbreaking article, "Nearly Everything We Wish Our Non-Jewish Supervisors Had Known About Us As Jewish Supervisees," posited what remains difficult for many Jews to express and share about their clinical pastoral education processes within predominantly Christian environments, theological frameworks, and andragogical approaches.[23] Taylor and Zucker described eight Jewish beliefs and perspectives that challenge Jewish students of chaplaincy in adjusting to the hegemonic Christian theology central to CPE.[24] The article addresses theological assumptions,

---

23   Bonita E. Taylor and David J. Zucker, "Nearly Everything We Wish Our Non-Jewish Supervisors Had Known About Us As Jewish Supervisees," *Journal of Pastoral Care & Counseling* 56, no. 4 (2002): 327–38, https://doi.org/10.1177/154230500205600403.

24   The eight categories are 1) In Judaism, we partner with God. 2) Judaism is a theology of deeds. 3) In Judaism, deeds take precedence over creeds. 4) Talking about God is newer to many Jews than working with God. 5) God, God's presence, and Lord are synonymous appellations for Jews. 6) Only the unified, indivisible, unseeable God is Divine. 7) Vicarious Suffering/Atonement are not part of mainstream Jewish thinking. And (8) In Judaism, Forgiveness and Repentance are personally achieved.

premises, and language to which Jews were demanded to adjust in order to make it through their educational processes in a meaningful way. Taylor and Zucker made it possible to address both intentional and unconscious anti-Jewish structures in the inherently Christian theological and cultural constructs of CPE. For the non-Jewish educators who were open to the content, this article began a conversation and built an understanding that significantly reduced the suffering of Jewish students and chaplains in their training processes. In turn, the reduction of suffering enhanced and enriched the educational process for the Jewish students and their peers of all religious locations.

Competencies for increased understanding of, and a heartfelt relationship to, the complex identities of the Jewish people are imperative for the future health of the field of spiritual care. Yet the subtle or veiled anti-Jewish discrimination perpetrated by political progressives is more arduous to confront than overt anti-Jewish sentiment and hatred because it is too often minimized in relation to our common plight for a peaceful and compassionate world. Politically progressive individuals and organizations are more likely to learn from and embrace the following competencies; however, anti-Jewish discrimination will continue until all spiritual care providers and educators work to eradicate it.

Competencies for Eradicating Anti-Jewish Discrimination

The following five competencies address the awareness, understanding, and skill that are required for spiritual care providers and educators to offset and confront subtle and overt anti-Jewish discrimination in both caregiving and training.

1. *Rather than stating an opinion or political stance in conversations with Jews about Israel, demonstrate awareness of and sensitivity to the historical and current trauma experienced by Jewish people.*

All too often Jews are exposed to viewpoints against Israel in favor of Palestine that show a lack of awareness and compassion for the intricacy of the situation and of intergenerational trauma on both (all) sides. It is imperative for spiritual care providers and educators to stray away from conversations about policy and politics. Instead, inquire about the experiences and feelings of the person being served or the colleague/student with whom one is working if and only if that person addresses the topic as a point of concern. Each individual may have opinions in their personal and spiritual communities and work for social justice as appropriate to them. Yet in the role of spiritual care provider or educator, compassion about respective and collective trauma and care, and each person's response to it from a political or religious agenda, is vital. The spiritual care educator is also responsible for addressing perspectives that show a lack of awareness or sensitivity even if the person exhibiting it is directly connected to a conflict with Israel or Jews. It is more effective for the educator to have a direct rather than a non-transparent approach in relation to the trauma of peoples.

Several years ago, I attended a powerful spiritual care conference in Belgium. I was the only Jewish person present among clergy and chaplains from all over the world but predominantly from western and central European countries. I felt at home with the warmth, intelligence, philosophical dialogue, and engagement with the other attendees. The Israeli/Palestinian conflict became a focal point of discussion and was led by Christian-European leftist activists who were criticizing Israel and Israeli policy. I sat quietly and listened to the conversation. When I arose from my seat to take a break, the only Palestinian attendee of the conference, a Christian pastor who lives in Palestine, was standing in the back of the room. He looked at me as I was exiting the room for a short break and said, "They're talking about us, aren't they?" His words came forth as both a question and a statement. I responded, "They sure are, and thank you for letting me know that you noticed!" We then smiled at each other. His comment was a compassionate one, perhaps toward both of us. He understood that I most likely felt uncomfortable, and he may have as well for a variety of reasons.

There are numerous levels of possible exploration to this story and interaction. The one that is prevalent in my mind is that the most vocal participants in the conversation came from countries that are greatly responsible for modern Israel's existence and the trauma that holds it and its people captive. Their presentation showed no awareness of this link or their responsibility in the healing process. It was about policy and opinion, and there was nothing pastoral or relational about it toward me or the Palestinian in the room. This experience continues to be an informative one. My ability to articulate what it means continues to reveal itself over time. The nature of it and the pain took place at a pre-verbal, ineffable level, and I felt alienated from the full experience of the conference from that point on.

Spiritual Care Competency: As chaplains and educators, with this topic and others, especially when we feel emotionally and politically invested, we are left with the task of better educating ourselves and our communities about the effects of intergenerational trauma. How we present and discuss these issues has the power to add fury to the conflict or compassion and healing to a world in much need of them. Rather than talking about policies and politics, listen for the feelings of others and of self with compassionate understanding.

2. *Do not ask Jewish colleagues and students to explain their position on the Israeli/Palestinian conflict in a professional environment or ever.*

Concern about the pressure Jewish clergy and students experience to speak out against Israel has become more prevalent in recent times. In 2018 alone, a number of my students were approached by progressive Christian, Buddhist, and other spiritual leaders, teachers, and mentors in a manner that inherently linked their Jewish identities to the Israeli/Palestinian conflict as if this were the sole issue that defines Jewish life. Authentic dialogue is important; however, confronting an individual Jewish person does not promote true interchange due to a power disparity between the non-Jewish mentor and the Jewish student.

The assumptions that all Jews should be either unfalteringly or unquestioningly supportive or unsupportive of Israel diminishes a complex array of emotions, historical associations, traumas, philosophies, and opinions into an either/or simplistic reduction. In addition, some individuals have little to no knowledge about the topic. Just as Jewish people are complex with intersectional identities, so is the State of Israel. Israel and the Israeli/Palestinian conflict are far more complex than archetypes of colonialism, racism, and oppressive regimes. These issues and real archetypes/topics are relevant to all of the places inhabited on the earth, though the establishment of modern-day Israel occurred more recently than some other nations. People do not question the right for other peoples and nations to exist as they do Israel.

Spiritual Care Competency: Humanize the topic of Israel and the Jews who live there. Mitigate suffering and further traumatic responses of defense and open up avenues of authentic exchange and compassion. From a spiritual care perspective, help people learn to refrain from engaging in issues about policy and politics. Prioritize heartfelt discussion about the land of Israel and the diversity of its people, both Jewish and non-Jewish. Part of humanizing the land and its people is refraining from holding it to a double standard that is expected of no other nation in the world. There are numerous organizations and groups for people to individually align themselves to explore policy, issues of social justice, civil rights, and activism. However, guard the safety of your Jewish populations and place the emphasis on tending to the care and deserved compassion of everyone despite anyone's (the educator's included) political leanings.

3. *Acknowledge that Jewish culture is both Eastern and Western, theistic and non-theistic.*

As explored earlier, the Jewish people are infused with different cultural, geographic, religious, and spiritual influences. In mainstream Jewish life, mysticism and faith live conjointly with science and reason. Taylor and Zucker stated that "Judaism is a theology of deeds" and that "in Judaism, deeds take precedence over creeds."[25] One of the challenges that contemporary Jews face is the assumptions that are made about culture and belief. For instance, in my work as an educator, non-theistic chaplains and scholars lump Jewish views into categories called Judeo-Christian or Abrahamic. Both indicate levels of expectation and assumption about collective and individual Jewish belief systems and cultural affiliations. The term *Judeo-Christian* is not readily adopted by scholars of Judaism who are Jewish, as there is a Protestantization or Christianizing of Judaism in this term and many assumptions are embedded within it.

---

25   Taylor and Zucker, "Nearly Everything We Wish," 330.

While there is great pride and gratitude connected to the interfaith coalitions and commonalities shared with our Christian and Muslim friends, in addition to a true context to explore authentic Abrahamic connections between us, when our non-theistic friends describe Jews or any of us as "Abrahamic God people," in an assumptive way, this undervalues the multi-dimensional and intersectional nature of Jewish identity and belief. While I cannot speak for Muslim and Christian traditions with confidence, I assume there is multiplicity here too. Yet specifically in the case of Jews, relegating Judaism to faith or religion alone undermines the richness of the civilization and the multiplicity of thought, belief, and voice contained within it. Judaism is structured within philosophical and religious texts and frameworks. There is no systematic or other theology that defines it with absolute precision. The foundational traditions, practices, and ideas are the cornerstone, but from that cornerstone there are thousands of branches that have grown and evolved.

Spiritual Care Competency: Allow room for the full Jewish experience of ideas—theistic, non-theistic, philosophical, prophetic, and cultural—of the Jewish people you are teaching and serving. When educating non-Jews about the full range of Jewish experiences, practices, and belief systems, incorporate a number of Jewish voices/guests to share their perspectives. In regard to exploring Muslim, Jewish, and Christian commonalities, avoid clichés and assumptions. Create opportunities to learn from those who are members of those communities and involved in interfaith cross-cultural coalitions and dialogues. There are rich opportunities, conversations, and relationships to share in this realm.

4. *Acknowledge that critiques of Israel and Israeli policies need not be anti-Jewish, but often are.*

Many Jews in the United States, around the world, and in Israel itself question Israel's policies and militant action against the Palestinian people. Though it is with certainty that non-Jewish questioning of Israel's right to exist, the lambasting of Zionism as a general category (there are many different Zionistic perspectives), and viewing Israel only in terms of this conflict quickly becomes anti-Jewish. While critique of Israeli policy or the BDS movement need not be anti-Jewish, it oftentimes serves as a smokescreen for palpable prejudice and hatred against Israel and the Jewish people. There is no other nation in the world that is questioned by political progressives with such passion and vehemence for its right to exist as Israel. This in itself triggers traumatic responses that can be prevented through the awareness and sensitivity of others.

Spiritual Care Competency: Listen to individuals who express Zionist perspectives and explore the value and the multiplicity of voices therein. Remain vigilant about confronting ideas that do not support the safety and survival of Israel and the Jewish people around the world.

5. *Practice a healing presence and compassionate voice.*

My Palestinian colleague at the conference in Belgium appeared to understand a shared experience despite our assumed differences. While it was not his responsibility to be my caretaker, his acknowledgment of me and of us as somehow being united during that conversation was ten seconds of powerful spiritual care and relationship. Perhaps my presence comforted him as well. At the very least, our shared presence elicited something compassionate inside of both of us toward one another, and he, the one who lives directly in the conflict, invited me into this relational moment.

My great teacher who held presence and compassion for those of us at the Lesbians of Color Conference who were ignited in pain and struggle demonstrated expressions of sympathy, empathy, and care in the middle of a torrent. Her expression of kindness and honor for each one of us is a gift that I still attempt to emulate. I don't know the exact views of the Palestinian pastor in Belgium, yet I know through his stories that he and his community suffer greatly as the result of Israel and the conflict. Nor do I know the views of the African American, non-Jewish woman who was asked to witness and support thirty younger Jewish women in our intra- and interpersonal struggles. Yet these are the healing presences and compassionate voices that bring healing to the world.

Spiritual Care Competency: Practice empathy and compassion when controversial topics arise with students, colleagues, and care seekers. Offer a comforting countenance and soothing voice while providing care to those in personal and/or political pain. The spiritual care provider should seek and receive professional consultation when one reaches a limit in the feeling and ability to provide empathic care across the spectrum of beliefs and opinions.

Conclusion

This chapter posits a call to acknowledge and embrace the complex intersectionality of Jewish peoples in an effort to address and reduce anti-Jewish discrimination and the suffering that results. Increased awareness of complex Jewish intersectionality is necessary for the psycho-social-spiritual health of the world. Each individual's and group's suffering is both particular and universal. Spiritual care providers and educators are responsible to hold both. Names are not given to us in heaven or by God. It is human beings who name ourselves, one another, all creatures, and even God. In Jewish tradition, the Divine name itself is ineffable, perhaps a message of true divinity that is beyond name. Naming is a pathway toward deeper understanding and relationship but not an end in itself, lest it become a dragging parachute.

In response to anti-Jewish and anti-Israel remarks made by Congresswoman Ilhan Omar, Rabbi Sharon Kleinbaum wrote the following on Facebook:

> *We Jews are so traumatized from the hatred we have endured that it sometimes reminds me of someone who has been profoundly sexually and physically abused as a child and never received deep help and like many adults who were abused as adults end up abusing others. We are so afraid of the very real threat of anti-Semitism that we can't think clearly and the only thing that makes sense to us as Jews is to condemn anything that triggers our very real fears. How to distinguish among the threats in the world? How to act in ways that will protect us and prevent another genocide? These are real and understandable fears.*[26]

---

26   Sharon Kleinbaum, Facebook, February 11, 2019, https://www.facebook.com/sharon.kleinbaum/posts/pfbid0ycxLbMZiF2YmxMWTdgSa75DiGsmB6ZfD3hX-ZQqqSAZBLB13nSzd6jHzQ3QbqLXvJl.

Acknowledging the complex intersectionality of Jewish peoples can help to serve as a roadmap for healing trauma within ourselves and in relationship with others. The future of our world relies on it. When one person is in pain, another is too. When one community bears pain and oppression, it is inevitable that others do too. Spiritual care providers and educators are uniquely positioned to open doorways of healing on a larger scale through emphasizing the study of complex intersectionality in our curricula. Jewish vulnerability serves as a template to understand contexts of "otherness" that go beyond the mainstream definitions of distinctiveness or oppression through marginality. The Jew is an example of the human being who remains vulnerable within and across all sides of the social and political spectrum, sometimes even when we assume safety and like-mindedness. The field of spiritual care offers a compassionate path of safety for those who were born out of the complex intersectionality of many names, identities, and experiences.

Bibliography

ADL. "ADL Audit Finds Antisemitic Incidents in United States Reached All-Time High in 2021." April 25, 2022. https://www.adl.org/resources/press-release/adl-audit-finds-antisemitic-incidents-united-states-reached-all-time-high.

ADL. "Anti-Semitic Incidents Surged Nearly 60% in 2017, According to New ADL Report." February 27, 2018. https://www.adl.org/resources/press-release/anti-semitic-incidents-surged-nearly-60-2017-according-new-adl-report.

Adler, Rachel. "For These I Weep: A Theology of Lament." *The Chronicle* 68 (2006): 16–21.

Bachya ben Asher. *Torah Commentary; Rabbeinu Bahya; Bereshit, Chapter 2:19.* Translated by Eliyahu Munk. 1998. https://www.sefaria.org/Rabbeinu_Bahya?lang=bi&p2=Rabbeinu_Bahya%2C_Bereshit.2.19.2&lang2=en.

Collins, Patricia Hill. "Intersectionality's Definitional Dilemmas." *Annual Review of Sociology* 41 (2015): 1–20. https://doi.org/10.1146/annurev-soc-073014-112142.

Crenshaw, Kimberlé W. "Demarginalizing the Intersection of Race and Sex: A Black Feminist Critique of Antidiscrimination Doctrine, Feminist Theory, and Antiracist Politics." *The University of Chicago Legal Forum*

140 (1989): 139–67. http://chicagounbound.uchicago.edu/uclf /vol1989/iss1/8.

Gerlach, Wolfgang. *And the Witnesses Were Silent: The Confessing Church and the Jews.* Lincoln: University of Nebraska Press, 2000.

Gerson, Judith M. "Gender Theory, Intersectionality, and New Understandings of Jewishness." *Journal of Jewish Identities* 11, no. 1 (2018): 5–16. https://muse.jhu.edu/article/689638.

Greider, Kathleen J. *Reckoning with Aggression: Theology, Violence, and Vitality.* Louisville, KY: Westminster John Knox, 1997.

hooks, bell. *Feminist Theory: From Margin to Center.* Boston: South End, 1984.

Kaufman, Ilana. "After Pittsburgh, Is Anyone Considering Jews of Color?" *The Jewish News of Northern California.* November 5, 2018. https:// www.jweekly.com/2018/11/05/after-pittsburgh-is-anyone-considering -jews-of-color/.

Mirsky, Yehudah. "After Pittsburgh: The New Jewish Question and the New Jew Hatred." *The American Interest.* October 28, 2018. https://www.the -american-interest.com/2018/10/28/the-new-jewish-question-and-the -new-jew-hatred/.

Moving Traditions. *The Women's March, Antisemitism & Intersectional Jewish Women.* January 11, 2019. https://www.movingtraditions.org /antisemitism-the-womens-march/.

Pinsker, Leon. *Auto-Emancipation: An Appeal to His People* [originally published anonymously]. October 17, 1882. Accessed July 14, 2023. https://www.jewishvirtuallibrary.org/quot-auto-emancipation -quot-leon-pinsker.

Silverman, Susan. "Why Anti-Semitism on the Left Hurts Me More." *Lilith.* January 24, 2019. https://lilith.org/2019/01/why-anti-semitism -on-the-left-hurts-me-more/.

Stockman, Farah. "Women's March Roiled by Accusations of Anti-Semitism." *The New York Times,* December 23, 2018. https://www.nytimes .com/2018/12/23/us/womens-march-anti-semitism.html.

Taylor, Bonita E., and David J. Zucker. "Nearly Everything We Wish Our Non-Jewish Supervisors Had Known About Us As Jewish Supervisees." *Journal of Pastoral Care & Counseling* 56, no. 4 (2002): 327–38. https://doi.org/10.1177/154230500205600403.

Women's March. *Our Vision.* Accessed July 14, 2023. https://www.womens march.com/about-us.

❧ **10** ☙

SECRET ATHEIST

*Internal and External Tensions Affecting Buddhists
as Interreligious Caregiving Professionals*

MONICA SANFORD

BUDDHIST TRADITIONS CAN be described as non-theocentric, that is, traditions in which God, gods, or divine forces are not usually central to religious practice and certainly nowhere near as essential as in other world religions. As such, Buddhists have often been uneasy conversationalists in interreligious dialogue. This continues into the present day with growing numbers of Buddhists joining various caregiving professions as therapists, chaplains, counselors, and, in my case, religious life directors at large, secular American universities. This chapter draws from my personal experiences as a white Buddhist in a predominantly Christian country as well as a qualitative research study I conducted in 2017 with other Buddhist chaplains in the United States and Canada.[1]

Part confessional and part scholarly, this chapter serves to highlight the internal and external tensions derived from our religious locations as Buddhists in a predominantly theistic society. Tensions often arise from assumptions, whether our own or those of others, and unconscious or unresolved normativity. What should a Buddhist look like? Who should a Buddhist worship? How should a Buddhist bring their wisdom to the caregiving

---

1   Monica Sanford, "The Practice of Dharma Reflection Among Buddhist Chaplains: A Qualitative Study of 'Theological' Activity Among Nontheocentric Spiritual Caregivers," PhD diss. (Claremont School of Theology, 2018).

relationship (or not)? Although it is rich with vignettes and thick description, the purpose of this work is not to resolve the tensions that often accompany Buddhist religious locations. Rather, the chapter serves both to educate those unfamiliar with these forces and as a call to Buddhists (and other non-theists and atheists in professional care work) that they are neither alone nor unrecognized in their struggles.

Given the number of vignettes drawn from my personal experience, I feel it necessary to foreground this chapter in who I am in order to provide the reader with an appreciation of my point of view and potential biases. I am a white, heterosexual, cisgender, able-bodied woman raised in Nebraska and originally educated in the fields of architecture and community planning. I was raised United Methodist and left the church at the age of fifteen due to a lack of faith in God. I began studying Buddhism on my own at the age of twenty-two, took refuge (became Buddhist) at the age of twenty-six, and moved to California to study Buddhism full time at the age of thirty. I am a Buddhist chaplain. In 2013, I obtained my MDiv in Buddhist Chaplaincy from University of West, one of only four accredited universities in North America that was training Buddhist chaplains at that time. I completed four units of Clinical Pastoral Education (CPE) via a super-extended (nine months per unit) out-placement program (via the Academy for Jewish Religion, California) under the supervision of a Reform Rabbi while serving as campus chaplain at University of the West between 2013 and 2018, where I was also employed full time. I completed my doctoral education at Claremont School of Theology, earning a PhD in Practical Theology, with an emphasis in spiritual care and counseling, in 2018. My doctoral research focused on the experiences of Buddhist chaplains working in interreligious contexts. I was ordained a Buddhist lay minister in a Chan tradition originating in mainland China in 2015, though I do not consider myself exclusively Chan in my Buddhist orientation. This is largely due to my early background as an autodidactic Buddhist and my eclectic graduate education among members of many Buddhist traditions. I now serve as the Assistant Director for Spirituality and Religious Life at Rochester Institute of Technology, a large, private, STEM-focused university in upstate New York, where I live with my partner, dog, and cat. I am not formally affiliated with a sangha in Rochester, though I have visited several in the area since moving here in 2018.

The As-If Space

I believe in the possibility of God. I do not believe in God. As a result, I often operate in an "as-if" space, going about my daily work as-if God existed because so many of those I serve believe in Him (or him, H/her, T/them, or I/it, as one prefers; I have no dog in this particular race). All of that may sound ridiculously contradictory or paradoxical and you may wonder, Who in the world would be inclined to live in such a way? Atheists, mostly. Also, agnostics, humanists, pagans, and, in my case, Buddhists. For us, it is a relatively common way to get along in a predominantly Christian and largely theistic society.

The as-if space is familiar to most members of minority groups trying to get by in a majority-dominated context. African Americans will adopt predominantly white speech patterns and mannerisms often quite contrary to how they speak and behave among other Black people. This is now commonly understood by sociologists and linguists as "code switching." When I was a young woman working at a male-dominated construction company, I often dressed and spoke in more characteristically masculine ways in order to improve communication and elicit credibility among my senior male colleagues. Likewise, atheists in predominantly theistic societies often participate in conversation and communal life as-if God existed, celebrating religious holidays they no longer believe in with their devout family members, returning strangers' wishes for a Merry Christmas or Eid Mubarak, and thanking well-meaning coworkers for offering to pray for their sick dog.

According to the Religious Landscape Study, 88 percent of American adults say they believe in God and 63 percent are "absolutely certain" in their belief.[2] Theistic belief is strongest among Jehovah's Witnesses, Historically Black Protestants, and Evangelical Protestants (99 percent report belief in God). Among non-Christian religions, such as Muslims (99 percent), Hindus (88 percent), and Jews (78 percent), theism predominates. Only 29 percent of Buddhists in the survey (admittedly a tiny sample size of n = 264) reported they were absolutely certain in their belief in God, followed by 29

---

2   Pew Research Center, *Religious Landscape Study: Belief in God*, accessed July 15, 2023, https://www.pewforum.org/religious-landscape-study/belief-in-god/.

percent who were fairly certain, 10 percent who were not too/at all certain, 27 percent who reported they did not believe in God, and 5 percent who simply do not know. Only one group, the unaffiliated or religious "nones" (with a lovely sample size of n = 7,556), reported less theistic belief, with 27 percent maintaining absolute belief in God, 33 percent reporting they do not believe in God, and the remainder falling somewhere in the middle or admitting to ignorance (6 percent). Although some criticized the survey methodology, from selection criteria to question verbiage, the data clearly substantiates that the United States is a predominantly theistic society.[3]

The Pew Research Center also conducted a survey with 3,217 American adults and asked them to rate various religious groups on a "feeling thermometer" wherein 0 = "cooler, more negative" perceptions and 100 = "warmer, more positive" perceptions.[4] When Americans were asked how they feel about members of religious groups other than their own, atheists and Muslims were often viewed negatively, whereas Jews, Catholics, and Evangelicals were often regarded positively, and Buddhists fell somewhere in the middle. Furthermore, members of theistic traditions tended to regard atheists more negatively than any other group. For example, "Atheists receive a neutral rating of 50, on average, from people who say they personally know an atheist, but they receive a cold rating of 29 from those who do not know an atheist."[5] Participants who reported knowing a Buddhist felt moderately warm toward Buddhists, a feeling of 70. But among those who had never met a Buddhist (77 percent of Americans), Buddhists received a cooler response of 48. This was 19 points higher than atheists were rated (29) by Americans who admitted to never having met an atheist. In fact, Americans who had never met a Buddhist nevertheless liked them about equally (48) to those who personally knew an atheist (50). In all cases,

---

3   Christian communities have seen worship attendance fall in recent years and often perceive Christianity or religion as in decline. I do not dispute these trends, only point out that theistic belief still predominates and remains practically synonymous with religion in the minds of most Americans.

4   Pew Research Center, *How Americans Feel About Religious Groups*, July 16, 2014, http://www.pewforum.org/2014/07/16/how-americans-feel-about-religious -groups/.

5   Pew Research Center, *How Americans Feel.*

those who knew someone of a particular group generally had more positive perceptions of that group.

All this data illustrates that atheists' tendency to go along to get along is well founded. Buddhists' ability to similarly "pass" within theistic society may actually be enhanced by popular ignorance. Buddhists are, at least, "religious" people, and religion is popularly associated with belief in God. Moreover, as the Pew Research Center survey illustrated, a majority of Buddhists (62 percent) report some belief in God or gods.[6] Therefore, Buddhists may feel at greater ease among theistic conversations and have less urge to correct peers' assumptions.

In my lived religious experience in the United States, one primary assumption is that God has the same level of importance across religious groups. Another is that when one speaks of God, one always means capital-G God of the Bible, Torah, or Quran rather than little-g god or gods of pagan or non-Abrahamic religions. This assumption is evidenced by the Pew Research Center survey that failed to ask how important G/god(s) or belief in G/god(s) is to respondents.[7] If they had asked, they might have found that among Buddhists, G/god(s) is not always a central feature of religious practice or the spiritual path to enlightenment.

In 2017, I interviewed and collected written reflections from thirten practicing Buddhist chaplains working in interreligious settings. During these conversations we explored how the participants thought about God/divinity and worked with theistic care seekers. Within this data, the concept of God/divinity appeared thirty-four separate times in three hundred pages of transcriptions and text. Although participants often personally struggled with the God-concept, this did not necessarily affect their conversations with care seekers. With care seekers, they dwelled in the "as-if" space. Participant 012 explained,

> *When I'm working with people, it really isn't Buddhist theology that's important. It's really helping them clarify their own theology and their own way of looking at the world and their own way of making meaning. So, for most of my patients that means some sort of relationship with God. That doesn't bother me. Yeah, I'm pretty*

---

6   Pew Research Center, *Religious Landscape Study.*

7   Pew Research Center, *Religious Landscape Study.*

> *open to that, you know? So I'm constantly talking to Christians*
> *about Christianity—you know, how do I make meaning?*[8]

This chaplain relied on their interreligious education about Christianity and empowered care seekers to lead the conversation while providing appropriate spiritual care. The Buddhist chaplains in this study were generally knowledgeable about Christianity and other theistic religions. When they lacked knowledge, their own spiritual practice helped them remain open and accepting to what they did not know. As Participant 005 explained,

> *I do have a very deeply embodied and kind of, um, my supervisor*
> *now calls it "mystical orientation." And that means some of the*
> *experiences that flow through me in these hospital rooms are bigger*
> *than Buddhism and don't necessarily fit into that paradigm,*
> *especially because I'm praying with people and talking to them*
> *about their understanding of God or Allah or Brahma or whoever.*

Several participants were comfortable with the idea that what they might experience as, for example, *bodhicitta* (awakened mind) might be the same thing that a care seeker experiences as God. For others, they tended to believe the experiences were distinct, but that their Buddhist experiences did not preclude care seekers from having experiences of God/divinity that were equally genuine, if different. These mental orientations allowed them to have enriching conversations with care seekers across religious difference in fulfilling and effective ways.

This is not to say that participants never experienced tension when working with theistic care seekers. The question of authenticity came up often. Participant 006 reflected,

> *Sometimes I feel conflicted. I still do, and this is something that a*
> *lot of Buddhist chaplains are grappling with. How do we come to*
> *patients who are Christian who are requesting a prayer, but also still*
> *feel authentic for myself as well as for the patient? Because this is*

---

8   Interview excerpts were lightly edited for readability. For example, monosyllables and verbal pauses were removed.

something that's not just—obviously, this is not something that I do.
This is not something that I take seriously. Like, I don't pray on a daily
basis. I don't believe in God. So, the question is: how could I pray with
a patient in a way that's authentic to them and authentic to me?

This was a question that myself and my classmates carefully discussed during our graduate education. How could we pray authentically to deities we did not believe in? Some felt it was hypocritical or disingenuous. As someone who was raised Christian, but left the United Methodist Church as a teenager, I was familiar with the prayers, though I had always found them hollow. Could I say the hollow words and mean them if someone asked me to?

I found my answer while I was pursuing a Master of Divinity in Buddhist Chaplaincy, when I went to visit a beloved professor in the ICU. This person had helped found the Buddhist chaplaincy program at my university, though he was himself an Episcopal theologian. His wife and mother were with him in the ICU. He was semi-conscious, but could not speak, and clearly in some pain or discomfort. His wife graciously asked me to take his hand and say a prayer. The words, "Our Father, who art in heaven, hallowed be His name," came from a place of deep authenticity inside me. In that moment, if anything I said could be of comfort to him and his family, I would say it. And, if God existed in the way Christians believe God does, I knew God would understand. I don't know if God heard me, but I know my professor did. He stilled and rested through the remainder of the Lord's Prayer and for several minutes thereafter. His wife and mother thanked me. I left with a heavy heart, but knowing that if called on to pray with Christians or Jews or Hindus, I would do so authentically, with a sincere wish that God, if God should be, would hear my prayer and act in whatever way possible to alleviate suffering. Other Buddhist chaplains find their own paths to authenticity, often with the aid of teachers, supervisors, and peers.

Lin Jensen, a Buddhist chaplain and contributor to *The Arts of Contemplative Care*, one of the few books about Buddhist chaplaincy, explored this dilemma and came to a different conclusion.[9] In her chapter entitled

---

9   Lin Jensen, "Wrong Speech: Knowing When It's Best to Lie," in *The Arts of Contemplative Care: Pioneering Voices in Buddhist Chaplaincy and Pastoral Work*, ed. Cheryl A. Giles and Willa B. Miller, 291–300 (Somerville, MA: Wisdom, 2012).

"Wrong Speech: Knowing When It's Best to Lie," Jensen defined "lying" as saying something that does not align with one's personal beliefs. She posited that sometimes "lying" is skillful in the context of interreligious spiritual care. Thus, for Jensen, praying for someone to go to heaven when Jensen does not believe in heaven is a "lie." While she believes this behavior is condemned by the Buddha as wrong speech, she also believes it is permissible to lie when one's heart "consents" for the emotional and spiritual well-being of the care seeker.[10] I do not find this line of reasoning personally or logically satisfactory because it conflates one's personal belief with ontological truth. Neither Jensen nor I can prove or disprove the existence of God or heaven; we just have opinions about it. When I pray for someone, "May you find peace in Jesus Christ," I truly hope they find that peace exactly according to their beliefs. This is not a lie and it is not wrong speech. I doubt that the historical man called Jesus Christ was the son of God, but I nevertheless hope, for the care seeker's sake, that he is listening and capable of granting lasting peace.

The shape of the as-if space in which I dwell is possible because of the particular Buddhist magic of "not-knowing."[11] Sometimes this is also called "beginner's mind," and is particularly emphasized in the Zen schools of Buddhism. In Case 20 of *The Book of Equanimity*, it is said that "not-knowing is the most intimate,"[12] for it is only through not-knowing that we can overcome our preconceived notions, biases, and assumptions and become "intimate" with reality as it is, even perceive truth beyond the ability to conceptualize with language. Several participants in the research study referenced the importance of remembering what they do not know and cannot know. Participant 008 stated,

> *I really try before I go into the room to kind of center myself and take some breaths. It's like, it's not-knowing—I mean, there's so much not-knowing in this practice of chaplaincy. You don't know*

---

10   Jensen, "Wrong Speech," 294–95.

11   Gil Fronsdal, "Not-Knowing," Insight Meditation Center, February 20, 2004, https://www.insightmeditationcenter.org/books-articles/not-knowing/.

12   Gerry Shishin Wick, *The Book of Equanimity: Illuminating Classic Zen Koans* (Somerville, MA: Wisdom, 2005), 63.

*what's behind the door. You really have no idea even if you've
read the chart . . . reading the chart and knowing from the team
what's going on with this family, but then you're going into a fresh
moment.*

In this sense, not-knowing is a very practical skill, not just in relation
to the God-question, but in getting from moment to moment. Several
chaplains also discussed not-knowing or openness as a sign of spiritual
maturity instilled through repeated reflection on their work. Participant
005 shared, "I'm much more comfortable sort of not knowing and leaving
things open than I might've been had I strictly been into Theravada [tra-
dition of Buddhism] the whole time." Participant 007 described how in
earlier self-reflections they might have tried to come to definitive conclusions about the quality of their work with care seekers, whereas now they
are simultaneously more self-critical yet more open regarding outcomes,
replacing thoughts such as "I think I did right" with "I think I am, but,
maybe, did I really though?" While the questions were tougher, comfort
with not-knowing also helped this chaplain remain open to inconclu-
siveness and ambiguity. Participant 007 expressed that this self-directed
not-knowing also helped limit assumptions and preconceived notions
about care seekers and thus remain more open to their experiences. In
this sense, the mundane Buddhist magic of not-knowing helped many of
the chaplains I interviewed remain open to all sorts of ideas and beliefs,
including concepts of divinity, ideas about others, and their own self-
conceptions, which also helped them grow into themselves as authentic
Buddhist chaplains.

Let me illustrate this as-if space with a more personal experience. As the
head of religious life, I co-chair the Spiritual Wellness Team, a group of staff
and faculty concerned with promoting spiritual well-being and resilience
throughout campus. Several months ago, a colleague on the team stated, "I
don't think I've ever met an atheist," despite over 60 percent of our incoming
students reporting no religious affiliation and about one-third reporting that
they are atheist or agnostic. I raised my hand and responded, "You have now.
Or, more accurately, a 'nontheocentrist,' but that's a longer conversation."
We continued on with our meeting, but a month later, my colleague recalled
my passing comment and requested clarification, thankfully from a place of

genuine curiosity rather than shocked judgement. "So who is Buddha?" she asked. "Who do you worship?"

Mind you, this is a well-educated woman who was at my hiring interview several months prior. I give the institution a great deal of credit (and gratitude) for even interviewing a Buddhist candidate, let alone hiring one (myself) to lead religious life. Yet it has become clear in the months since that very few of my colleagues knew what implications that might have for my relationship, as a Buddhist, with G/god(s). Another colleague recently remarked how fortunate I am (and I am!) to have one of the few offices in the building with windows, but he supposed, gesturing to the sky, that it was important to my job to have a direct line to God. I laughed and did not correct him, as we were in the presence of a brand-new staff person I had never met before. Despite the Buddhist ordination certificate hanging on the wall next to my diplomas, I often fall back into my habit of "passing" when among strangers. I regularly question if this is Right Speech.

Passing and Disclosure

Passing is another concept familiar to members of minority and marginalized groups. The idea of passing builds on various original meanings of the term, such as "to cause or enable (a person or thing) to go or proceed somewhere" or "to go by without paying attention to; to leave unnoticed," to result in the sociological definition "to be accepted as or believed to be, or to represent oneself successfully as, a member of an ethnic or religious group other than one's own, esp. one having higher social status."[13] In my case, I generally "pass" as Christian.

Passing is easy partly because I'm white, have a straightforward Midwestern American accent, and wear no obvious signs of my religious affiliation. Christian seems the most likely assumption. The other day, I confessed in a conspiratorial whisper to the new conductor of the school orchestra, that I, as a Buddhist chaplain, had no idea what the "Lessons and Carols" program was about or what biblical scriptures were appropriate to it (though I would find out). The orchestra conductor, herself Taiwanese, was surprised.

---

13   *Oxford English Dictionary*, 2nd ed. (Oxford: Oxford University Press, 2004), s.v. "pass."

I quickly learned that she was Christian, though certain older family members were Buddhist. This is a common response from Asian and Asian-American Christians, who are quick to claim familiarity with Buddhists, while also illustrating that it is somehow an "old-fashioned" thing to be.

I don't mind "passing" in most low-stakes circumstances, but I still struggle with the notion when providing pastoral care. Nor am I alone in my concern, which is shared among Buddhist chaplains, particularly those who are non-monastics and of non-Asian ancestry. The study participants I interviewed were seven white (with one also reporting Hispanic heritage) and six Asian or Asian-American Buddhist chaplains. They reported struggling with if, when, and how to disclose to their patients, soldiers, and students that they were a Buddhist chaplain. For the two military chaplains I interviewed, their religious tradition is disclosed on their uniform, where the Dharma wheel takes the place of a Christian cross or other religious symbol. Anecdotally, my military colleagues have shared that this does not always mean soldiers know what the wheel represents or how a Buddhist chaplain would differ from any other. One participant was a monastic who wore their robes during hospital rounds, but most dressed in Western business attire for their work. Because Buddhists are a minority religious group and Buddhist chaplains even more rare, passing is relatively easy, unless one presents with some obvious outward sign of difference. Thus, the challenge faced is not about being passively identified, but about active disclosure.

Disclosing one's Buddhist identity can quickly derail or even end a conversation. Participant 008 described the dilemma this way:

*I think one of my first struggles with chaplaincy as a Buddhist,
especially in the Bible Belt, was kind of my introductions because,
you know, people just assume you're a Christian pastor. They might
say, "Well, what's your denomination?" or something like that, and
I didn't know how much to disclose. That was, like, a big struggle,
because I'm a person that really values integrity, and honesty, and
openness. And at the same time, we have like skillful-means, and
so, you know, how skillful is it for me to share? If I share one thing
it's like, "Oh, Buddhist! What is that?" you know? I mean, how to
skillfully introduce myself in a way that is most beneficial. So that
was a big kind of learning point for me, and I think that kind*

> *of came through in some of the verbatims [shared reflections with*
> *colleagues] as well.*

Curiosity that can derail a conversation is one risk. Outright rejection is also a risk. Participant 006 shared that during their residency "one patient complained. She thought that I was not Christian enough." This is not unusual for chaplains, whom care seekers reject for all sorts of reasons, even when they are of the same religious tradition. Rejection is often a heightened concern among chaplains of minority traditions, who are rarely of the same background as those they serve.

I mused on this same question in a blog post from February 18, 2018: "As the first week of my new position in Rochester drew to a close, I pondered when and why I choose to disclose to others that I am a Buddhist. Why did I tell the Jewish student-leaders and the Hindu gentleman who visited us, but I did not tell the Catholic bishop or the Campus Crusade for Christ students? What is Right Speech in this instance?"[14] Commenters who challenged me about this pushed me to clarify my position, both to them and to myself. I responded:

> *The biggest reason to not disclose is that the conversation is not*
> *about me. The event is not about me. Being Buddhist frequently*
> *does not meaningfully change what is happening or have any*
> *bearing on the discussion. Disclosure can derail a conversation*
> *from topics meaningful to the other party. This is often the case*
> *with minority identities, especially if one can otherwise "pass."*
> *In addition to not derailing the conversation, it can also help to*
> *wait to disclose until a certain level of comfort and trust has been*
> *built. People do carry assumptions, but that's not always bad. . . .*
> *Assumptions are just mental models that help us navigate in a*
> *world in which we always have incomplete information. If I*
> *disclose too early, someone could mistakenly assume that I am not*
> *a good dialogue partner and stop talking to me. Whereas, if I wait*
> *until some trust is built, then it won't matter because they're already*

---

14   Monica Sanford, "Incognito Buddhist," *Dharma Cowgirl* (blog), February 18, 2018, https://dharmacowgirl.wordpress.com/2018/02/18/incognito-buddhist/.

> *learned from experience that I am a good person to talk to and it*
> *doesn't matter much what I believe. It matters what they believe.*
> *Again, it's not about me.*[15]

This glosses over the very real threat of active discrimination and even physical violence faced by members of minority groups. Thankfully, I have never been subject to the latter, largely because of the context of my work.

The downside of this dilemma is that it can leave others feeling deceived by my omission or embarrassed by their assumptions. Kathleen Greider eloquently depicted this in her vignette about a married couple, Jared and Dinah, who were in conflict with their teenaged son, Elijah, and sought help from a family counselor, Aliyah. The couple was Christian, and the conflict centered around their son's rejection of the Christian faith. After developing a sense of comfort with Aliyah, "the therapeutic alliance is rocked by the emergence of religious difference" when Aliyah discloses she is Muslim, not Christian as Jared and Dinah had assumed.[16] Greider supplied a snapshot of the dialogue: "'You are Muslim?' they ask. 'Not Christian? Why didn't you tell us?' As Aliyah tries in the few remaining minutes to figure out why her Muslim identity seems to be troubling the parents."[17] Suddenly, the session becomes about one's own religious identity, rather than what is happening with the care seeker. Worse, negative feelings can damage the relationship between chaplain and care seeker. This vignette was all too familiar to me and, I suspect, many other Buddhist chaplains.

The question is rarely whether or not to disclose one's Buddhist identity, but when and how to disclose in a way that is appropriate and beneficial to those we serve. Deception, even deception by omission or actively hiding one's identity, could rarely be considered Right Speech. As I mused in the blog post, "Why *had* I told the Jewish students and Hindu gentleman?" I realized that I disclosed to them to create a sense of solidarity and to demonstrate that I understood the struggles they expressed as members of minority

---

15 Sanford, "Incognito Buddhist."

16 Kathleen J. Greider, "Religious Location and Counseling: Engaging Diversity and Difference in Views of Religion," in *Understanding Pastoral Counseling*, ed. Elizabeth A. Maynard and Jill L. Snodgrass (New York: Springer, 2015), 240.

17 Greider, "Religious Location and Counseling," 240.

religious traditions. In both cases, my disclosure was a simple aside in a larger conversation. There was no great pause to explain what that meant, so the conversation was not derailed. Members of minority religious traditions are also much more accustomed to working across lines of religious difference, so the notion that I was a different religion from them (which may already have been assumed, though in a different fashion) was little cause for concern. My disclosure was greeted positively and served to enhance the sense of comfort and trust among the dialogue partners. In one case, it also allowed them to skip the lengthy explanation of the issue they had been about to go into due to my reassurance that, as a member of a non-Christian religious tradition, I understood the context of their concern. We got to the point quicker and spent more time on the main issue they wanted to discuss.[18]

From these vignettes and research among other Buddhist chaplains, we can see that when, how, and whether or not to disclose one's religious tradition to care seekers is highly contextual, a judgment call that must be made by each individual in the moment. Koshin Paley Ellison wrote that during his work supervising spiritual care interns, "I can discern times when it is right to disclose these facets of myself" as a gay man and a Jewish Buddhist "because the act of disclosure models the possibility for others who might be struggling to bring their shadows to the light of consciousness."[19] In other words, Ellison discloses his religious identity when it is helpful to the other person.

Buddhist prison chaplain Richard Torres stated that he often sidesteps the question of religious affiliation, saying instead, "I serve people of all faiths and no faith at all."[20] People "fixate" too much on their assumptions about Buddhists and chaplains, in his opinion, and he does not meet most of

---

18   For members of minority identities, simply educating others about the issues they face can often be exhausting. This can also influence choices to disclose or not disclose. Sometimes one just doesn't have the time or energy to get into it right now.

19   Koshin Paley Ellison, "The Jeweled Net: What Dogen and the Avatamsaka Sutra Can Offer Us As Spiritual Caregivers," in Giles and Miller, *The Arts of Contemplative Care*, 96.

20   Richard Torres, "All My Relations," in Giles and Miller, *The Arts of Contemplative Care*, 145.

those, being neither an Asian in robes (i.e., "Buddhist") nor an older white man with a Bible (i.e., "chaplain"). Instead, he feels authentic de-emphasizing his role or title and being known to the inmates he serves simply as "Torres" because he genuinely values what he has learned from many different religious traditions and "no religion, no person holds the truth exclusively."[21] Torres wrote that although "I don't talk much about Buddhism" with the inmates, "I feel that the most sincere offering I can make is my practice,"[22] which includes treating each person with courtesy and respect and hoping for that same respect in return.

Each situation is contextual, with no one right answer to when one should pass and when one should disclose. Depending on the situation, I may take the same strategy as Torres.[23] When my Buddhist identity seems like a distraction, I wait to build trust and respect in the relationship, to the point where any differences in our respective religious traditions become less important. In other situations, I may disclose early to establish solidarity. Yet in others, I may follow a strategy similar to Ellison and disclose an aspect of my identity or personal history to model or illustrate a particular meaning-making process.[24] Managing this aspect of the caring relationship is something Buddhists and other members of minority religious traditions do on a daily basis. Usually, we must figure it out through trial and error as little educational material explores this issue (thank Buddha for this book!) or provides guidance. Nevertheless, Buddhist chaplains manage, and, according to the study participants, navigating religious differences with care seekers is often less fraught than dealing with their own non-Buddhist professional colleagues and supervisors.

Pressure and Tension

Many chaplains who participated in the study shared that the support they received from supervisors and peers during the Clinical Pastoral Education

---

21   Torres, "All My Relations," 146.

22   Torres, "All My Relations," 147.

23   Torres, "All My Relations."

24   Ellison, "The Jeweled Net."

(CPE) process helped them to become more authentic as Buddhists and to develop their own approaches to navigating their identity that were mutually satisfying for both chaplain and care seeker.[25] Others, while feeling that the CPE process was beneficial overall, struggled with the emphasis supervisors and peers placed on the concept of God/divinity. They could live in the as-if space with care seekers and for care seekers' sake. Yet tensions arose when asked to remain in this space for the sake of coworkers and peers—especially when simultaneously tasked with presenting genuine reflections on their own work and spiritual development.

While the Buddhist chaplains I know and study have, for the most part, found effective ways to navigate religious differences with care seekers, we experience an unexpected source of pressure from the very people who have likewise been trained to respect religious differences: theistic peers and supervisors. Buddhist chaplains also experience tension within our workplaces among multidisciplinary colleagues and teammates. I offered vignettes in the first section on the "as-if" space to illustrate some common assumptions and briefly described the associated tensions; I shall give that tension more shape below. In this section, I explore the pressures and tensions Buddhist chaplains experience, first as we enter the workforce via the CPE process, and later in our professional work. Though this was not the focus of the research study, it was a common and necessary topic of conversation when interviewing the 13 study participants. I will also draw on my own experience and anecdotal accounts from others who have written about their experiences and from Buddhist colleagues and classmates I have remained in touch with over the years. In some cases, the pressure to continually operate in the as-if space of theistic normativity has contributed to Buddhist chaplains leaving the field of spiritual care.

CPE is an invaluable experience for chaplains of all traditions, and the study participants and classmates alike affirmed it as a formative and largely positive experience. My own four units of CPE were certainly critical and beneficial to my development as a chaplain, in relation to both my own spiritual formation and my clinical skills. Nevertheless, CPE is not a universally positive experience, and some Buddhist chaplains report that theistic

---

25   Sanford, "The Practice of Dharma Reflection."

normativity, particularly Christian normativity, shaped their experiences in negative ways. While a difficult experience can also be a critical learning experience, in many cases, they saw no benefit or saw direct harm resulting from the pressure to conform to theistic normativity and the tension that results when they cannot or will not.

Chaplains in this study often struggled when asked (or required) to integrate God/divinity into their own personal reflections on spiritual care or in their process of spiritual formation. Participant 010 explained,

> *I really struggled in CPE, particularly in my residency because there was such an institutional structure I felt pressuring me to think about my spiritual life in relationship to my work in a particular way. Like the pressure was, "What is your definition of God and how does this impact your human relationships?"*

While some of the study participants found the God-concept interesting and remained open to the idea, none of them discussed it as central to their spiritual formation or personal understanding of their work as spiritual caregivers. The interview continued:

> **Participant 010:** *I was constantly like, "How does that translate to what I'm doing, or thinking, or how I'm engaging with the work?" Like, there was just incredible attention around that, how to translate my assigned reflection with my actual reflections. Um, so I think that's given me a lot of insecurity, maybe, at the beginning of my career. . . .*
>
> **Researcher:** *So, you said there was an opportunity related to this pressure to reflect in a certain way, particularly about God. Before you started your CPE, like when you graduated, but before you'd started CPE, did you have a sense of that insecurity or was that new to you in CPE?*
>
> **Participant 010:** *Um, well, I definitely have had insecurity. I can't blame that on CPE, but I think I actually did leave [graduate school] with a sense of confidence and self-worth in my ability to reflect and maybe develop some coherence around how my religious life applies to my work life. I thought that was very*

possible, and I felt kind of galvanized to do that work. And then I think I was hurt and disappointed in CPE that there wasn't a space for that kind of activity, and in fact it was discouraged because I had to do these other things; like I had to develop essentially Christian theology for chaplaincy in order to just function in that environment. And then I had to do so much translating internally for myself. I think it really did thwart—yeah, it really did thwart me. Yeah.

Researcher: I'm sorry to hear that. At the beginning, you articulated the relationship between Buddhism and your chaplaincy, I thought very beautifully, and with a robust narrative structure. Did that come after? Because I remember you talking about that [earlier].

Participant 010: Yeah.

Researcher: That that was not accepted when you got to CPE?

Participant 010: It's more that there was just no space for it. Um, it's like the best metaphor is like my anatomy just wasn't acknowledged or relevant, you know? It was, like, just unseen. And so, I think you're right that I actually do have a, you could say, a theology of spiritual care that is just functional. Like, I've learned to develop it through doing, just organically, but maybe I lack some confidence around how to talk about that professionally.

We can see from this transcript the particular harm done when a CPE program fails to acknowledge, make space for, support, or, in this participant's words, *see* that adherents of traditions like Buddhism are capable of reflecting on their work in a religiously meaningful way without resorting to a theistic paradigm. CPE programs, at their best, train future spiritual caregivers to be deeply present with suffering care seekers, to hear and see them on a profound level. The metaphor of the witness or the practice of witnessing has been invoked in pastoral care literature to describe the work of the caregiver.[26] Yet this chaplain felt unseen and unaccepted by the very people

---

26   James E. Dittes, "The Ascetic Witness," in *Images of Pastoral Care: Classic Readings*, ed. Robert C. Dykstra, 137–49 (St. Louis: Chalice Press, 2005).

who are training in this skill, by the very supervisors who are modeling (or not) this ability. Moreover, this chaplain felt the setback in their ability to explore their own "theology" (for lack of a better word) in a meaningful way and develop the professional language and competencies that would be central to their ability to advance in their field, as judged by those who interpret the standards of professional practice.[27] This chaplain is still gainfully employed in the profession as of this writing, and of great benefit to the care seekers they serve, in my professional opinion.

Another chaplain related an experience in which a CPE peer explicitly asked them not to discuss their differences. It was not clear from the interview how the CPE supervisor responded to the situation, but the Buddhist chaplain was taken aback by their peer's lack of welcome:

> **Participant 005:** *I'll just be blunt and say, the last IPR [InterPersonal Reflection], one of the things that came up with me very strongly, I was having a grief response to one of the things that had come up mid-unit, and, uh, one of my peers in IPR said he was concerned about me talking about my theology because he was afraid it would fragment the group.*
>
> **Researcher:** *Oh, no.*
>
> **Participant 005:** *And that he didn't want us to be different, to speak about difference, because it might change what has so far been a very cohesive and very cooperative group. And my response to that was I do not want to be silenced, and I already feel I'm on the outer fringes of something. There's a way the other three [Christians] bond that I don't because our theologies are very different. And so, it's not only depth but it's also—I'm not gonna say quite social; we all get along—but there's a way in which they're in one tribe and I'm very much not in that tribe and all of us know it.*
>
> **Researcher:** *And there's just four of you in that unit.*
>
> **Participant 005:** *Yeah. It's a tiny cohort.*

---

27   Association of Professional Chaplains, "Standards of Practice for Professional Chaplains," accessed July 15, 2023, https://www.apchaplains.org/standards/standards -of-practice-for-professional-chaplains/.

> **Researcher:** *Little cohort. Okay, well, that's an intense experience in that IPR.*
>
> **Participant 005:** *Yeah, it was fine, but it gave me a visceral sense of what it is like to be a minority. You know, it's not okay we make these things general enough to sound Christian to you. I'm sorry, it's not okay.*

This chaplain was bold enough and brave enough tell their peers that it was not acceptable to expect them to be silent or to "water down" their reflections to sound Christian. Other chaplains adapted to CPE by learning to perform what their supervisors and peers expected to hear, although they confided in me that it was not a practice they found useful or continued for themselves after CPE concluded.

Even in the most welcoming CPE units, chaplains lamented a perceived lack of personal spiritual formation. Their understanding of the Dharma had not developed as they had hoped because reflection with their peers remained at a necessarily surface level and they were rarely challenged about their understanding or interpretations. Participant 007 explained, "It would have taken entirely too long to try and explain things. So, in some cases, yes, I did have to keep it on a surface level." While Buddhist chaplains in North America quickly gain fluency with Christian religions, Christian chaplains rarely gain similar fluency with Buddhism before or during CPE. Mark Power wrote the following about his own CPE experience at a Catholic hospital in California: "I found that very few of the people I met had any understanding of the Buddhist spiritual tradition."[28] Disclosure of his Buddhist identity elicited a range of responses in others and led Power to occasionally pass as a Protestant rather than spend time explaining or risk disrupting the caregiving relationship. He wrote, "In the presence of pervasive misunderstanding and sometimes strong judgement, I often wondered what I was getting myself into."[29] While Power was wary of bias, he was fortunate to find welcoming and supportive supervisors

---

28   Mark Power, "Buddhist Chaplaincy in a Christian Context: A Personal Journey," in Giles and Miller, *The Arts of Contemplative Care*, 63.

29   Power, "Buddhist Chaplaincy," 64.

and peers, who nevertheless needed to be educated regarding his Buddhist worldview. Often, time that should be dedicated to developing one's reflections and spiritual formation is instead dedicated to providing a primer on Buddhism to one's peers. Participant 014 shared their expectations: "I expected to see a growth in my . . . being as a [monastic]. I thought I'll be more compassionate, but I wasn't experiencing it." This chaplain reported that the fast pace and the strict rules of health care chaplaincy simply did not allow for the kind of reflection they felt would really help develop their compassion. While Buddhist chaplains continued to find ways to reflect on their work, to learn, and to grow, sometimes doing so in ways that felt authentic and explicitly Buddhist, this often occurred outside of or despite the training environment.

The examples above are the most explicit data available to me on the harm that can be done by theistic normativity in the education and training of Buddhist chaplains, but such experiences are not outliers. Nor are they examples of "the worst" that can happen, as I am aware of other Buddhists who have had harsher experiences or even left the profession altogether in response to pressure to conform to theistic normativity and the unwelcome climate that perpetuates within their work environments. However, these other examples are not as thoroughly documented as the ones above. Many study participants shared milder examples of the same type of experience while also affirming the important contributions CPE training made to their development as professional spiritual caregivers.

Inside, Outside, Equal

When it comes to how others deal with us as Buddhist chaplains, they tend to follow the three basic approaches to religious diversity according to an inclusive, exclusive, or pluralist worldview. Or, as I colloquially describe it, we are either inside, outside, or equal to them. People who see in us something that reminds them of their home tradition and feel that affinity is sufficient to include us within their worldview consider us "inside," or one of "us," despite any seemingly minor differences. For example, Robert Chodo Campbell recounted a story of a conversation with a nurse who said, "I think your Buddha must have been one of God's children."[30] Campbell joked back, "Perhaps Jesus was a Buddha," and the nurse laughed.[31] Campbell shared this exchange after recounting a story about visiting a dying Christian pastor being cared for by his wife and a nurse in "one of the most exquisite instances of caregiving I have ever witnessed."[32] Such instances come to many of us in our work when we experience the beauty of human beings caring for one another and opening their hearts in a way that allows all the imaginary distinctions between self and other to wash away, if only for a moment. In such instances, everyone is inside. No one is outside. I would call this a moment of *prajñā*, or experiential wisdom beyond concepts or words. A Christian might call it grace. I share this so as not to diminish the power of such inclusive moments and to demonstrate that we, as Buddhists, are just as prone to them as any other. Such moments are real and true, but also rare and not really what I refer to when I speak of "inside," which is a sense of affinity based on false assumptions. These assumptions, when prolonged or pervasive, can, at best, lead to frustration and, at worst, some of the harm described in the prior section.

When I was in second grade, I was sent to sit in the hall as punishment for "rolling my eyes" at the teacher. I sat in the hall very confused, moving my eyeballs this way and that, scowling at the floor, and feeling that this was most unfair. It was not that I hadn't rolled my eyes at the teacher (knowing my seven-year-old personality, I'm quite sure I had). It's just that I'd never heard the expression before and didn't know what it referred to. Since then, I have become much more adroit as suppressing the impulse to roll my eyes. I have attended dozens of gatherings of religious people and been told, "We are all people of faith / believers / God's children / shepherds / etc." The first time one hears this, it can be taken kindly in the spirit it is meant. I have joked from time to time that if I was even remotely a "person of faith," I would still be a Methodist. The best I can say now is that I'm a person of "benefit of the doubt until proven otherwise," and that includes

---

30   Robert Chodo Campbell, "The Turning of the Dharma Wheel in It's Many Forms," in Giles and Miller, *The Arts of Contemplative Care*, 76.

31   Campbell, "The Turning of the Dharma Wheel," 76.

32   Campbell, "The Turning of the Dharma Wheel," 75.

the Buddha and his Dharma. Likewise, my religion rests on my practice, not my beliefs, and I shan't bother to get into the question of God again. The first, second, or third time one hears such things, one can excuse them. The thirty-seventh time, one remembers one's second grade teacher's indignation and strives mightily not to evoke the same response in one's fellow, quite well meaning, religious colleagues. Yet it illustrates that most of the time, being inside means "I can fit you into my preexisting frame of reference, but only by ignoring or erasing distinctive features of your identity or tradition." The assumptions illustrated in the first two sections are case in point. Thus, being "inside" is peculiar in that it feels good and bad at precisely the same time. It feels good to be included and welcomed and bad to be so consistently overlooked. Sometimes it's easier to be outside, because at least that's clear.

People who see in us something antithetical to their own tradition in a way that just feels wrong place us "outside" as not one of "us," but rather one of "them." Despite the pressures and tensions explored in the prior section, explicit exclusion is more likely to come from care seekers and families. Chris Berlin shared a story of meeting an Evangelical Christian woman who, upon learning he was Buddhist, "felt adamant that I was destined for hell and expressed the importance of me embracing Christ."[33] Berlin had an option to step away self-protectively or to step into that relationship with an open heart (which, counter-intuitively, involves dissolving our sense of threat in a way that is also "protective"). Berlin chose the latter and was able to have a meaningful conversation with the woman about her "deep faith in Christ" and "genuine concern for others and her reliance on Christ during difficult times."[34] In unluckier cases, care seekers may either reject religion and chaplains altogether or reject Buddhist chaplains (and others) because they prefer to receive spiritual care from someone of the same religion as themselves. In such cases, chaplains respect the wishes of the care seeker and, when possible, make referrals to colleagues. Cheryl Giles advised chaplains not to take rejection personally. "Indeed, it may be our own fear of failing

---

33   Chris Berlin, "Widening the Circle: Engaged *Bodhicitta* in Hospital Chaplaincy," in Giles and Miller, *The Arts of Contemplative Care*, 81.

34   Berlin, "Widening the Circle," 83.

that tells us we cannot help the person who rejects us when, in fact, she may be too frightened herself to allow us to connect with her."[35] Buddhism teaches us to care about whether others are suffering or happy and to try to help them, but it does not say we are responsible for their happiness.

It may seem like there is no third option. We are either inside or outside, us or them. But many people do hold open a third option, which I call "equal." When we are inside, we are equal because we are inside, one of "us." When we are outside, we are not equal because we are outside, one of "them." But there are those who can and do recognize that we are different, not inside, not one of "us" precisely, but neither one of "them," and still equal regardless of our differences. This is an approach that affirms diversity as natural and good and also responds to it from a place of acknowledgment. Ignorance allows for easier inclusion within a preexisting frame of reference, as with my coworker who believed she had never met an atheist, despite working with several every day. Knowledge of each person's and group's distinctiveness makes that kind of inclusion more difficult, but it also makes easier the recognition of their existence as complex, nuanced people, just as complex as oneself.

Acknowledgement also includes a fundamental recognition of how much we do not know, combined with a willingness to learn and allow others to guide. This is not unlike how chaplains approach spiritual care in general. Thus, I believe that as a discipline we are already well equipped with the skills we need to welcome those of other religious and spiritual traditions (including secular folks) as both care seekers and caregivers and to help guide our professional organizations and institutional employers to do likewise. We have seen recent examples of this in the removal of the ordination from the requirements for becoming a board-certified chaplain, a decision that has enabled many Buddhists, Muslims, Quakers, Humanists, and others to pursue board certification. Ongoing dialogue with other chaplains in the field and professional organizations is productive and crucial to advancing the discipline of spiritual care and reducing

---

35   Cheryl A. Giles, "Beyond the Color Line: Cultivating Fearlessness in Contemplative Care," in Giles and Miller, *The Arts of Contemplative Care*, 49.

the frequency and severity of instances of harm done to Buddhist (and other) chaplains and trainees as illustrated earlier. More importantly, acknowledgment and dialogue will also welcome more gifted caregivers to the field, for the benefit of an also ever diversifying population of care seekers, and model the type of pluralist practice necessary for our work in the twenty-first century.

Conclusion

The title of this chapter, "Secret Atheist," is not entirely an accurate description of my beliefs about God, which tend more toward agnosticism and indifference.[36] Rather, it is a description of the feeling I sometimes have while walking around in the world as a professional religious person under the weight of other people's assumptions. As I step onto the stage in front of several hundred students, faculty, and staff to bless the commemoration of Martin Luther King Jr. Day, wearing my long blue robes with a high collar and golden stole, I feel those assumptions. As I share the words of St. Bernard of Clairvaux and Rumi and Thich Nhat Hanh, as I hold my hands palm to palm and recite "Namo Avalokitesvara," I *feel* like a "secret atheist" despite the Dharma wheel and Chinese characters on the front of that stole. I worry that people will feel deceived, though not because I have deceived them. I worry that people will not accept me or that I will be unable to be the person they need and want in that moment. And I suppose that theistic people, Christians, Jews, Hindus, and Muslims, all have similar fears. There is even a name for it: "imposter syndrome." The imposter syndrome is a feeling of self-doubt or fraud that discounts one's achievements or the status one has earned, and the anxiety associated with feeling that others may discover one to be "undeserving" or not competent in their role.

The title of the chapter simply gives a more nuanced name to a particular kind of imposter syndrome, the kind facing non-theocentric spiritual

---

36   The question of God is not a pressing one to me, though I recognize its importance to others. If God exists, and is of the character theistic folks claim, I think he/she/they/it and I will have no quarrel.

caregivers in a theocentric society. This chapter serves to name and outline the shape of this experience so that those who work in this field can find skillful ways to address it. Inasmuch as imposter syndrome is pervasive among new professionals, I do not think this experience will disappear anytime soon. Though I do hope that by naming and describing it, spiritual caregivers can find effective ways to overcome this particular version of the syndrome. Theistic faculty, supervisors, and peers do much to support Buddhist and other non-theist chaplains through this experience. Buddhist and other non-theist chaplains can carefully consider how this feeling may affect their spiritual formation and the work they do and develop their own approach to dealing with it skillfully.

I do not claim that this experience is universal. After all, the Pew Research Center study found that 58 percent of Buddhists reported some or certain belief in God (or some sense of divinity not fully defined by the good people at Pew).[37] Some Buddhists may not struggle with this at all or may handle it in ways not explored in this chapter. However, inasmuch as the chaplains I interviewed and the writing of other Buddhist caregivers illustrate, we may all, from time to time, feel the weight of assumptions about our religious lives that do not conform to our self-understanding. (I am certain this phenomenon is not unique to Buddhists; I just have a particular investment in the shape it takes among Buddhists.) We may even field these assumptions from our fellow Buddhists, for Buddhism is by no means a singular or unified religion. I may have done a disservice to readers by not taking the opportunity to explore the diversity and distinctiveness of Buddhist traditions here, but there are other resources that do a better job of this than I could have (see Suggested Reading list below). To those whose experiences I may have mischaracterized or omitted, I offer humble apology. I encourage you to take every opportunity to share your own experiences through blogs, articles, and books. The field of spiritual care sorely needs your voices.

I dedicate the merit of this chapter to alleviate the suffering of all beings; may they be happy and well, free from sorrow and danger, and may they find liberation, peace in heaven, or final rest on earth, as their hearts call them.

---

37   Pew Research Center, *Religious Landscape Study.*

Appendix

Study Methods

The study referenced throughout was a constructivist grounded theory study comprised of eighteen semi-structured interviews and eleven written reflections from thirteen Buddhist chaplains and chaplains-in-training working in interreligious contexts, including hospitals, hospices, palliative care, universities and colleges, prisons, and the military. Data was collected between June 1 and October 12, 2017, and resulted in 165,215 words of text, which were continuously analyzed through "theoretical sampling" and iterative analytical coding.[38] That is, interviews were collected in sets (usually two or three), coded, analyzed, and insights gleaned used to drive further interviews and refine interview questions to hone in on important themes that emerged. A theoretical framework, the goal of grounded theory methods,[39] emerged from the data following the tenth interview (and written reflections) and was tested, validated, and refined during five follow-up interviews and via a second literature review. The theoretical framework (named the "Three *Prajñās* Framework for Reflection in Spiritual Care") was fully explicated during my doctoral dissertation, though it is not the focus of this chapter.[40] The goal of the original research was to explore how Buddhist chaplains conduct "theological" reflection, a standard for professional practice per the Association of Professional Chaplains, from the non-theocentric worldview explored in this chapter. Thus, the data was well suited to this chapter, even though the Three *Prajñās* Framework was of limited importance here. In many cases, the participants' quotes used may also be found in my dissertation, though some have been pulled from the raw data purely for the purposes of this chapter. To my knowledge, this is the first grounded theory study to focus on the experiences of Buddhist chaplains, though not the first to explore Buddhist topics or experiences. I find constructivist grounded theory, in particular, to be extremely compatible with Buddhism, as the Buddha continuously advised his followers to test the teachings and see for themselves (*Kalama*

---

38   Kathy Charmaz, *Constructing Grounded Theory*, 2nd ed. (London: SAGE, 2014), 192–97.

39   Charmaz, *Constructing Grounded Theory*, 93.

40   Sanford, "The Practice of Dharma Reflection."

Sutta, AN 65) and because both are based on an understanding that knowledge is constructed of ever-changing concepts, even at the level of selfhood.

Suggested Reading

Fields, Rick. *How the Swans Came to the Lake: A Narrative History of Buddhism in America.* Boston: Shambala, 1992. This book provides a good historical overview of Buddhism in the United States.

Gleig, Ann. *American Dharma: Buddhism Beyond Modernity.* New Haven: Yale University Press, 2019. This book provides what may be the most current overview of Buddhism in the United States.

McMahan, David L. *The Making of Buddhist Modernism.* New York: Oxford University Press, 2008. This book illustratively explains how Buddhism has changed through its encounter with modern Western culture.

Bibliography

Association of Professional Chaplains. "Standards of Practice for Professional Chaplains." Accessed July 15, 2023. https://www.apchaplains .org/standards/standards-of-practice-for-professional-chaplains/.

Berlin, Chris. "Widening the Circle: Engaged *Bodhicitta* in Hospital Chaplaincy." In Giles and Miller, *The Arts of Contemplative Care*, 81–92.

Campbell, Robert Chodo. "The Turning of the Dharma Wheel in It's Many Forms." In Giles and Miller, *The Arts of Contemplative Care*, 73–80.

Charmaz, Kathy. *Constructing Grounded Theory.* 2nd ed. London: SAGE, 2014.

Dittes, James E. "The Ascetic Witness." In *Images of Pastoral Care: Classic Readings,* edited by Robert C. Dykstra, 137–49. St. Louis: Chalice Press, 2005.

Ellison, Koshin Paley. "The Jeweled Net: What Dogen and the Avatamsaka Sutra Can Offer Us As Spiritual Caregivers." In Giles and Miller, *The Arts of Contemplative Care*, 93–104.

Fronsdal, Gil. "Not-Knowing." Insight Meditation Center. February 20, 2004. https://www.insightmeditationcenter.org/books-articles/not-knowing/.

Giles, Cheryl A. "Beyond the Color Line: Cultivating Fearlessness in Contemplative Care." In Giles and Miller, *The Arts of Contemplative Care*, 41–54.

Giles, Cheryl A., and Willa B. Miller, eds. *The Arts of Contemplative Care: Pioneering Voices in Buddhist Chaplaincy and Pastoral Work.* Somerville, MA: Wisdom, 2012.

Greider, Kathleen J. "Religious Location and Counseling: Engaging Diversity and Difference in Views of Religion." In *Understanding Pastoral Counseling,* edited by Elizabeth A. Maynard and Jill L. Snodgrass, 235–56. New York: Springer, 2015.

Jensen, Lin. "Wrong Speech: Knowing When It's Best to Lie." In Giles and Miller, *The Arts of Contemplative Care,* 291–300.

Pew Research Center. *How Americans Feel About Religious Groups.* July 16, 2014. http://www.pewforum.org/2014/07/16/how-americans-feel-about-religious-groups/.

———. *Religious Landscape Study: Belief in God.* Accessed July 15, 2023. https://www.pewforum.org/religious-landscape-study/belief-in-god/.

Power, Mark. "Buddhist Chaplaincy in a Christian Context: A Personal Journey." In Giles and Miller, *The Arts of Contemplative Care,* 63–72.

Sanford, Monica. "Incognito Buddhist." *Dharma Cowgirl* (blog). February 18, 2018. https://dharmacowgirl.wordpress.com/2018/02/18/incognito-buddhist/.

———. "The Practice of Dharma Reflection Among Buddhist Chaplains: A Qualitative Study of 'Theological' Activity Among Nontheocentric Spiritual Caregivers." Ph.D. diss. Claremont School of Theology, 2018.

Thera, Soma, trans. "Kalama Sutta: The Buddha's Charter of Free Inquiry." *Access to Insight (BCBS Edition).* Last modified November 30, 2013. http://www.accesstoinsight.org/lib/authors/soma/wheel008.html.

Torres, Richard. "All My Relations." In Giles and Miller, *The Arts of Contemplative Care,* 141–48.

Wick, Gerry Shishin. *The Book of Equanimity: Illuminating Classic Zen Koans.* Somerville, MA: Wisdom, 2005.

❦ **11** ❧

A HMONG METAPHYSIC OF SICKNESS AND HEALING WITH IMPLICATIONS FOR INTERRELIGIOUS CARE

SIROJ SORAJJAKOOL

IN THE EARLY part of my career in ministry, I made numerous trips to remote Hmong villages in Northern Thailand with a distinctive vision to better the lives of ethnic minorities. My underlying assumption was clear, and it was a pretty common assumption, and still is, among many of my acquaintances: we, the "more civilized," have to reach out to the less fortunate individuals. I saw local pastors in remote villages wear a coat and tie to churches where the majority of the members were ethnic minorities whose sole exposure to the Western dress code was through the local church pastors. I recall numerous missions trips to build toilets for villagers without first seeking to find out what it was that we could do to assist. The plans were in my head and translated into strategies that were funded by my organization. We all thought they were great plans, and we applauded ourselves for the wonderful toilets that we built for these villagers until halfway through one of the projects. A villager came complaining that the exact location of the toilet would only bring negativity to his life since it would block the flow of positive energy and replace it with negative energy and could imply disrespect for the local spirits. That made me pause momentarily but never stopped me from completing the project with just a slight shift in angle which was not in compliance with the villager's perspective. In hindsight I believe this was strongly influenced by my social and religious locations. I was a Christian pastor teaching theology in a conservative seminary in central Thailand who had been exposed to Hmong people but had little knowledge of their beliefs and practices.

I was born and raised in a Christian home in Bangkok, and my entire educational experience was limited to Christian institutions. Diversity—religious, cultural, or otherwise—was hardly a part of the curriculum. While I took courses in Hindu and Buddhist philosophies during my graduate program, ethnic minorities and their belief systems were never a part of the training.

I experienced a slow and gradual shift in my thinking while taking an intercultural pastoral counseling course from Kathleen Greider at Claremont School of Theology. I began to understand the importance of honoring people as they are, respecting their beliefs, and restraining from transgressing their boundaries—religious, social, or otherwise. Not long after, I was asked to teach a course entitled "Anthropology of Mission" at Loma Linda University. This gave me further opportunity to reflect on the "other" more respectfully. I recall inviting Pastor Jeffrey Thomas, who served as the senior pastor for the homeless in Skid Row, Los Angeles, to speak to my class. His message was clear. The best help we can give is to listen and share in solidarity. The shift in my thinking about mission and solidarity for and with the other led me to return to the Hmong people with a revised ethic of care. I went on a journey to find out about, to listen to, and to honor the beliefs of the Hmong people.

The metaphysics of the Hmong people inform their health care beliefs and practices, which often conflict with the assumptions and practices of Western medicine. Western medicine has no room for shamanism or the religious practices of the Hmong. The conflict between these perspectives often leads to increased risk of illness and related complications when Hmong people refuse treatments that go against their religious beliefs. Increasing accessibility to health care among this population requires understanding the healing traditions of the Hmong people. I engaged in a qualitative research study intended to understand the health beliefs and practices, and the role of shamans, among this population in Chiangmai, Northern Thailand. I used a grounded theory method and conducted in-depth interviews to develop a theory of health and healing that reflects Hmong metaphysics. The theory evidences the importance of interreligious and intercultural care within the context of ministry in Northern Thailand.

Health and Healing in Hmong Cultures

The Hmong people originated in Southern China and migrated to Laos, Northern Vietnam, and Northern Thailand.[1] They share a long history of wars and migrations throughout Asia. Hmong were viewed by the Chinese as fearless, uncouth, and recalcitrant for refusing to assimilate to the dominant culture. They preferred to remain in their own enclaves, speak their own language, wear their own tribal outfits, and practice their own religion.[2] They are not intimidated even though they are outnumbered, and they are not easily persuaded to the customs of others.[3] These traits that have made them so resistant to change remain prominent in their culture today and are evident among the Hmong living in the United States. Many Hmong immigrated to California's Central Valley, bringing with them their unique culture and traditional religious practices.

One distinctive component of Hmong cultural and religious practices is shamanic healing. According to Breuilly, O'Brien, and Palmer, shamanism is an ancient religion practiced by indigenous people around the world.[4] These practices spread from Siberia, south to China and beyond with each region's practices differing slightly. Shamans of the Hmong culture (*tut xiv neeb*, pronounced "too tse neng") are traditional healers.[5] "To them, there is considered to be no equivalent health professional in Western biomedicine, and the scope of the shaman as a healer extends beyond the capacities and

---

1   Helda Pinzon-Perez, Neng Moua, and Miguel A. Perez, "Understanding Satisfaction with Shamanic Practices Among the Hmong in Rural California," *The International Electronic Journal of Health Education* 8 (2005): 18, http://www.iejhe.com/archives/2005 /4061-13874-1-CE.pdf.

2   Anne Fadiman, *The Spirit Catches You and You Fall Down: A Hmong Child, Her American Doctors, and the Collision of Two Cultures* (New York: Farrar, Straus & Giroux, 1997), 14.

3   Fadiman, *The Spirit Catches You,* 17.

4   Elizabeth Breuilly, Joanne O'Brien, and Martin Palmer, *Religions of the World: The Illustrated Guide to Origins, Beliefs, Traditions & Festivals,* 2nd ed. (New York: Facts on File, 2005).

5   Robert Cooper, *The Hmong: A Guide to Traditional Life* (Singapore: Marshall Cavendish, 2008), 123.

expertise of physicians."[6] Shamanic practices include the use of herbs, oils, and drums. Slaughtering of livestock such as chicken, cows, goats, and pigs as sacrifices is a common practice. The rituals often include the wearing of a hood covering the eyes, planting a sword at the altar site, ringing a bell to summon the spirits, and entering into a trance if necessary. The shaman and the spirits communicate during this period and return to the physical world, where the spirits will convey to the shaman what they need.[7] Satisfying this need will return the soul to the body and bring back good health. In the Hmong culture, healing is, and always was, the main work of the shaman.[8] Shamans serve as the connection between the physical and the spiritual world and are believed to enter another world to communicate and negotiate with demons or evil spirits that cause people to be ill, and they often offer animals in order to appease angry spirits.[9]

> *Shamanic healing is often at odds with modern medicine. Modern medicine is quick on pills and surgery, when many times the ancestors just want or need something to be taken care of. Most sickness is due to [an] unhealthy spirit or being around an ancestor who may be lost. . . . Shamans do not like foreign objects in bodies as it causes complications and may hurt their chances of going into the after life and reincarnation.[10]*

There is a cultural conflict between the healing practices of Western health care and traditional shamanic practices that can negatively affect treatment outcomes among Hmong patients. "Adaptation and adjustment to western culture, especially western medical culture, have been difficult for Hmong refugees. They have great difficulty accessing the healthcare delivery

---

6   Gregory A. Plotnikoff et al., "Hmong Shamanism: Animist Spiritual Healing in Minnesota," *Minnesota Medicine* 85, no. 6 (2002): 29.

7   Cooper, *The Hmong*, 123.

8   Pinzon-Perez, Moua, and Perez, "Understanding Satisfaction with Shamanic Practices," 19.

9   Pinzon-Perez, Moua, and Perez, "Understanding Satisfaction with Shamanic Practices," 18.

10   T. Saechao, "Questions: Conflicting Beliefs Between Shamanism Practices and Modern Medicine," interview by A. Foronda, April 22, 2012.

system because of linguistic and cultural barriers."[11] Hmong people are suspicious about Western medicine and lack trust in health care providers.[12] Many Hmong people consider Western biomedicine as "alternative" therapy.[13] Many shamans in the United States feel resentment, disrespect, and frustration toward Western medicine.

Conversely, health educators receive little training in understanding the shamanic practices of the Hmong people.[14] Doctors trained in Western medicine often experience difficulties with the shamanic practices of the Hmong because they do not understand the concept of "lost soul" and thus their treatments are not culturally relevant. They are often unable to explain and reconcile pathophysiology and shamanism and are unable to retrieve the lost souls of Hmong patients. Confused and fearful Hmong patients are often caught in the middle of the struggle between shamans and biomedical providers.[15]

Empirical research investigating the intersection of Western medicine and shamanism among Hmong living in non-Western countries, including Thailand, is limited. However, two studies conducted in the United States offer helpful insights. Pinzon-Perez, Moua, and Perez administered a questionnaire among 115 Hmong residents in central California that asked various questions regarding perceptions of Western medical practices and traditional shamanic practices when dealing with illness.[16] Forty-nine percent of the respondents indicated that they first consulted their primary care physician, yet 54 percent of participants consulted a shaman, herbalist, or earth doctor. Fifty-four percent of participants stated that they were very

---

11   Miriam E. Warner and Marilyn Mochel, "The Hmong and Health Care in Merced, California," *Hmong Studies Journal* 2, no. 2 (1998): 9.

12   Warner and Mochel, "The Hmong and Health Care."

13   Plotnikoff et al., "Hmong Shamanism," 29.

14   Pinzon-Perez, Moua, and Perez, "Understanding Satisfaction with Shamanic Practices," 19.

15   Deborah G. Helsel, Marilyn Mochel, and Robert Bauer, "Shamans in a Hmong American Community," *The Journal of Alternative and Complementary Medicine* 10, no. 6 (2004): 933, https://doi.org/10.1089/acm.2004.10.933.

16   Pinzon-Perez, Moua, and Perez, "Understanding Satisfaction with Shamanic Practices."

satisfied with the services they received from their shamans.[17] In the United States, many Hmong rely heavily on shamanic practices to heal illness but are also beginning to consider the benefits of Western medicine. Helsel, Mochel, and Bauer conducted a study of 934 patients who were served by 36 shamans over an eighteen-month period in order to gain a better understanding of shamanic care.[18] Data was collected on patient treatment, outcomes, and complaints. Results evidenced the need for spiritual healing provided by the shamans as rituals affirmed and strengthened patients' connection to family, culture, and community.[19]

A Grounded Theory Investigation

In an effort to understand the beliefs and practices pertaining to health and healing among a Hmong population in Chiangmai, Thailand, I conducted semi-structured interviews with ten Hmong adults, between thirty and eighty-three years old, living in Hmong villages and knowledgeable about traditional Hmong practices of health and healing. To recruit participants, I visited a number of Hmong villages in order to identify villagers who were familiar with traditional healing methods. The ten participants were from six villages in Chiangmai Province, Thailand. Participants consisted of one female and nine males, and five of the participants were shamans. Among non-shamans, one was married to a shaman and two were sons of shamans.

Interviews were semi-structured, conducted in Thai, and guided by the following open-ended questions:

1. What causes sickness?
2. What is the diagnostic process?
3. What are the methods for healing?
4. Can you describe some healing rituals?

Grounded theory was used to analyze data and develop a Hmong theory of health and healing. The interview transcripts were coded. As

---

17   Pinzon-Perez, Moua, and Perez, "Understanding Satisfaction with Shamanic Practices," 20.

18   Helsel, Mochel, and Bauer, "Shamans in a Hmong American Community."

19   Helsel, Mochel, and Bauer, "Shamans in a Hmong American Community," 933.

various themes developed, I went back to the interviews to see if the analysis explained each case. Once themes were identified, I shared the emerging themes with Hmong people for further confirmation. In instances where analysis did not offer sufficient explanation, the analysis was revised. Revisions involved renaming themes, developing new themes, and identifying alternative paths or processes.

A Hmong Theory of Health and Healing

Hmong villages in northern Thailand are located among the hills at high altitudes with population density anywhere from fifty to one hundred families. They are agricultural communities. Most of the roads leading to these villages are dirt roads, and participants' homes are made of bamboo and thatched roofs, mostly in a rectangular shape. The size of the homes differs based on the level of wealth. Like most villages influenced by modernization, there are homes made from block cement or teak woods. Most homes still have dirt floors with two stoves, a central pillar, one main entrance, an altar, and a sleeping area on a raised platform made of either wood or bamboo. Shamans' homes also have a distinct shrine against the wall with numerous incense sticks, candles, bowls of water, and saucers.

A Hmong Theory of Health and Healing

Analysis of the interviews conducted with the ten Hmong participants in Chiangmai Province, Thailand, resulted in the following themes: the shamans, causes of sickness, methods of diagnosis, and healing rituals. Together these themes provide a theoretical understanding of the causes of sickness and the role shamans play in diagnosis and treatment.

The Shamans

Two Thai words were commonly used by participants to describe healers in their communities: *Mor Pi*, which is literally translated as "spirit doctor," and *Mor Song*, which is "spirit-possessed doctor." Of the five shamans interviewed, one was a *Mor Song*. However, the terms *Mor Pi* and *Mor Song* are used interchangeably with one distinctive function: a *Mor Song* shaman goes into a trance to enter the world of spirits in order to seek help from the spirit world and identify the location of lost souls. A *Mor Pi* shaman does not go into a trance but has acquired knowledge of the spirit world through intergenerational transmission and thus is able to diagnose and prescribe through healing rituals. According to participants, when illnesses become severe, it normally requires the work of a *Mor Song*. A *Mor Song* is better able to diagnose, and a *Mor Song* possesses access, that a *Mor Pi* does not, to powerful spirits to assist in the healing process.

One of the participants was married to a *Mor Song* and told the story of how his wife was called to the role of *Mor Song* at a later age. Due to prolonged sickness and pain which she could not recover from, she was informed that this was a calling by the spirit for her to become a *Mor Song*. She finally agreed to the calling and was relieved from her pain. Similar stories were repeated during the interviews regarding how *Mor Song*, through personal sickness, received a calling to take on this special role of healing within the community.

Both *Mor Song* and *Mor Pi* receive some form of compensation through their healing practices, but their livelihood does not depend primarily on this role they serve. Most have a career of some kind, many in agriculture. However, their schedules are practically filled during special functions and festivals such as the New Year celebration, where religious functions by either *Mor Song* or *Mor Pi* are essential for ushering in the new year.

Causes of Sickness

Participants' responses regarding the causes of sickness are organized into three broad categories: 1) natural causes that have nothing to do with spirit world, 2) sickness caused by offending spirits, and 3) sickness that results from soul loss.

Natural Causes

Natural causes refer to sicknesses that happen because a person is exposed to diseases, germs, cold weather, etc. Diseases caused naturally are treated through natural means such as herbs and other alternative measures. Hmong shamans do not prohibit use of modern medicine. Often utilization of modern medicine, where accessible, is encouraged. A person may go to see the shaman for diagnosis, and the shaman may recognize the cause as completely natural and prescribe herbs or encourage the use of modern medicine.

However, when a patient seeks modern medical treatment for a simple, obvious medical issue and sickness persists, the cause may be identified as coming from the spirit world. Or during a diagnosis the shaman may recognize the cause as metaphysical in nature and hence recommend spiritual interventions as means for treatment.

Offending Spirits

According to one participant, who is a practicing shaman and head of the village, there are internal and external spirits. Internal spirits refer to spirits of the family. There are five spirits that reside in homes located in five sacred sites. These sites are ancestral spirit (*dab xwm kab*) attached to the side wall of the home, main pillar (*dab ncej cuab*) that stands right in the center of the house, big stove (*dab qhov cub*) used for ceremonial purpose, small stove (*dab qhov txos*) for daily use, and the main entrance (*dab txhij meej*) to the house, where the spirit guards everything that enters the home in order to provide protection and ensure happiness. Sickness may be caused by deliberate disrespect toward these spirits or unintended actions that provoke the displeasure of the spirits. The examples given were cursing and swearing at the spirits, spitting on one of these sacred sites, or accidentally stumbling upon one of these sacred objects.

External spirits refer to spirits outside one's home, which mostly reside in the forest or river. A person may be attacked by external spirits for various reasons. Offending the spirits is not the only explanation for sickness. There are spirits that are out to get a person because the spirits fancy that person's soul. Or the spirit may be hungry, and attacking is a way of getting attention in order to make sure that people will bring food to quench the hunger. According to a participant from Khun Chung Kien, the spirit of a dead person may cause sickness in an attempt to get attention and be fed. Another participant from Buak Tuey reported coming home from farming and becoming seriously ill. The local doctor tried every possible treatment, but nothing worked. Finally the participant consulted the shaman and through the process of diagnosis learned that he was being attacked by *Pi Tai Hong* (spirit of a person who died a tragic death) who was out to cause harm. Once the healing ritual was performed to placate the spirit, he became well.

Soul Loss

In accordance with a Hmong cosmology, when a child is born, the child does not come with a soul. The shaman plays a role in determining the right name for the child because the right name represents the soul of the child. According to the Hmong people, it is not unusual for them to change their names if things are not going well. When bad things happen, it may be because the soul was given the wrong name. It is believed that finding the right name may get rid of misfortune in one's life. However, the soul may also leave the body, and once the soul leaves the body, a person becomes ill. Symptoms of soul loss include fatigue, lack of appetite, bad dreams, inability to get up, turning pale, insomnia, hallucinating, or pain that does not respond to conventional medical treatments. There are a number of ways soul loss can occur. Most participants mentioned two primary ways a soul is lost. One is when a person is startled by an incident such as a tree branch dropping, falling from a motor vehicle, falling into a river, and falling from the staircase. These are some examples cited, and the term *startle* was mentioned in relation to soul loss by all the participants. Another cause of soul loss is when a person is attacked by the spirit. It may be because the spirit is out to attack a person, the spirit is hungry and needing to attract the attention of the passerby in order to feed his hunger, or the spirit would like to claim the soul of the person.

One participant shared the following story of his chronic illness. He experienced pain, fever, and fatigue. He did not have any appetite and had nightmares every night. All these symptoms started when he fell into a pond while riding his motorcycle, which he described as being "startled." After the accident, he experienced chronic illness until he sought help from a shaman. Another participant told the story of being in a forest when all of a sudden, a big heavy branch dropped right in front of him. He was startled by the incident, after which he started experiencing dizziness and fatigue.

The soul plays a very crucial role in the well-being of the Hmong people, and soul loss may result in symptoms that are both psychological and physiological. The soul is fluid. It has to be invited to become a part of a person, and if the wrong soul inhabits the person, this could result in various types of misfortune. The soul can also be lost or dropped or taken away by other spirits. This concept of the lost soul and wandering soul is affirmed by Plotniko et al.[20] For this reason, many Hmong people seek help from shamans to restore balance. The Hmong believe souls, like errant children, are capable of wandering off or being captured by malevolent spirits, causing illness.[21] *Ua neeb kho* is the shamanic ritual performed for the soul of a sick person.[22] They believe doctors can fix some illnesses but most can only be resolved spiritually, and a shaman is requested to perform rituals before and after visiting a physician.

Diagnosis

When a person is sick, it is important to first find out if the cause of sickness is natural or if the cause is within the realm of the world of spirits and beyond. Physical causes require physical remedies, and spiritual causes require spiritual interventions. According to participants, there are three methods of diagnosis. The most common form of diagnosis is the use of divination horns. This consists of two halves of a single buffalo horn split into two; hence, each horn has a round and flat side. After clicking the horns together, they are then thrown to the ground. The direction of the horns on the ground indicates an answer to the question raised by shamans. There are a number of possible combinations which offer various answers, such as both showing the round sides or flat sides or one side showing the flat side while the other shows the round side. It can also be the combination of where the tips of the horns are pointing. They may be pointing out or pointing toward each other or crossing over each other. The answers may be yes, no, or maybe. The answers may also reveal the type of spirits affecting the patient or if the treatment will be successful.

Besides divination horns, there is also the use of counting. Two of the participants interviewed indicated the use of counting. Here the shaman counts the exact day and time of the sickness, the season, the length of sickness, and whether it took place during a full moon or a new moon. By

---

20   Plotnikoff et al., "Hmong Shamanism."

21   Patricia Leigh Brown, "A Doctor for Disease, a Shaman for the Soul," *The New York Times*, September 20, 2009, https://www.nytimes.com/2009/09/20/us/20shaman.html.

22   Fadiman, *The Spirit Catches You.*

counting, the shaman is able to determine the type of animal represented by the number. And the type of animal will offer a clue as to the cause of sickness and an insight into what might be the outcome.

Trance is another method of diagnosis. It is used when other types of diagnosis have not been successful in determining the cause. When the shaman enters into a trance, he or she is able to enter into the world of spirits and navigate himself or herself in ways that will assist the diagnostic process by locating the whereabouts of the lost soul in the realm of the beyond. Identifying the location of the lost soul will enable him or her to determine the cause of sickness and the necessary steps needed to retrieve the lost soul.

The participant who fell into a pond during his motorcycle accident, through shamanic diagnosis, learned that his soul was trapped in the pond. Within this pond his soul was not able to swim nor move around. And although his soul was screaming for help, no one was there to rescue his soul.

Healing Rituals

Healing rituals are designed to provide remedies for sicknesses originating in the spirit world or the realm of the beyond. They require a thorough understanding of rules, norms, and needs of the world of spirits and processes whereby healing can take place through negotiations with the spiritual dimension. There are various types of healing rituals representing varieties of illnesses and their causes. There are levels of severity as well corresponding with the spirit world. Some spirits are easier to negotiate with while others may be more difficult. With the levels of difficulty come levels of shamanic skills and ceremonial practices. Some spirits are easier to negotiate with, and simple rituals may suffice. Some spirits are much stronger and harder to please, and hence the shamans may enter into the spiritual realm calling for help from among spirits in order to retrieve lost souls. The ritual may ask for forgiveness for offenses made, feed the hungry spirits, or negotiate with and trick the spirit to release the soul. The most common form mentioned by the participants consists of chanting (evoking the spirits), burning of incense, sacrificing chicken, and burning ghost money.

For the participant who fell into a pond, the shaman burned seven incenses and a pack of ghost money at the scene. He also made wooden steps against the side of the pond, making a way for the soul to be able to climb out. He sacrificed a chicken and chanted a request to the local spirit to help rescue the lost soul out of the pond. He then started digging in the dirt, and and the first insect found represented the lost soul. The insect was wrapped and brought back to the house. For the participant who startled when a big branch dropped in front of him, the shaman went to the location where the soul was, dropped burning incense and ghost money, and sacrificed a chicken. The diagnosis indicated that while the participant was wandering through the forest, the spirit fancied the soul of this participant and hence broke the branch. When the soul dropped out from the body, the spirit captured his soul. Through sacrifices and burnt offerings, the shaman negotiated with the spirit, asking the spirit to take this gift offering in exchange for the soul of the participant. The chicken bones were brought back to the house, and the structure of the bones, through shamanic reading, allowed the shaman to figure out if the ritual was a success and whether health would return to the participant. Not long after the healing ritual, this participant started recovering from his sickness.

Another related ritual pertaining to sickness as indicated by participants is a pre-treatment ritual. When a person is going in for some serious treatment, whether by local shamans or conventional medical treatment, a shaman may be called upon to pray to ancestral spirits for protection and a positive outcome. After the request is made, a vow has to be offered to the spirits. This vow may consist of the promise to offer a chicken, a pig, or wine in exchange for protection and recovery. Chicken bones are often used to determine what outcome may be expected and, based on this prediction, what further rituals may be needed.

Talinh Saechao, a practicing shaman for over forty years, explained,

[Illness] is mostly inflicted by ancestors or spirits. Spirits touching a person usually makes a person sick. It is our ancestors' way of contacting us and letting us know they need something. Most things can be cured by ceremonies if you know exactly what is wrong and do the right ceremony. Most of the time shamans will do a ceremony before and after the sick goes to the hospital to make sure the right thing was done and ancestors are at peace. Hmong do not

like surgeries or anything leaving scars as they believe it will not be welcomed in after life.[23]

Implications for Interreligious Care

Interreligious spiritual care in the context of health care requires suspending assumptions when navigating religious difference. Within the context of the Hmong people, metaphysics plays an essential role in the healing process. The Hmong perspective on health and healing, as outlined above, shows close integration between physical, psychological, and spiritual dimensions of a person. Taking into consideration the tendency toward somatization among Asian populations, this view of health takes on even more significant meaning since physical symptoms are usually associated with interventions from the spirit world. Hmong people believe there is the world of daily functioning and there is the world of the spirits. And there is a close interconnection between both worlds, and hence the physical realm can affect the realm beyond and vice versa. The unseen world manifests itself in phenomena that cannot be explained through natural explanation. Diagnosis and healing come with insights and mastery of skills of the unseen world of spirits and the power to negotiate.

In her article on shamanism, Linda Gerdner cited a story of a man who suddenly was not able to speak.[24] When he went to visit a Western doctor, he was diagnosed with a stroke and was told that nothing much could be done. Unsatisfied with the answer, he consulted a shaman. After performing a *ua neeb saib* (diagnostic ceremony), he learned of the displeasure of the spirit because he had neglected to take proper care of the altar. The loss of speech was the direct result of the lack of care of the altar. After performing *ua neeb kho* (healing ceremony), the man took corrective measures to maintain the altar. His speech returned, and he was convinced that the physician had misdiagnosed his illness.[25] Another example recounted by Gerdner was the story

---

23   T. Saechao, "Questions: Conflicting Beliefs Between Shamanism Practices and Modern Medicine," interview by A. Foronda, April 22, 2012.

24   Linda A. Gerdner, "Shamanism: Indications and Use By Older Hmong Americans with Chronic Illness," *Hmong Studies Journal* 13, no. 1 (2012): 1–22, https://www.hmongstudiesjournal.org/uploads/4/5/8/7/4587788/gerdnerhsj13.pdf.

25   Gerdner, "Shamanism."

of a daughter who cared for her eighty-one-year-old father. Hospitalization did not improve her father's condition, and after he was discharged, his condition continued to worsen. "The daughter tearfully explained, 'we thought we were going to lose him, and I honestly believe the reason he is still alive is because my brother and I contacted a shaman who performed a healing ceremony.' She concluded, 'we were able to preserve his soul.'"[26]

For health care providers and chaplains, it is important to recognize the impact a belief system has on Hmong patients. In their metaphysical reality, there is a place where the essential self is located, and this location is beyond the material self. The soul as essence belongs to another realm, and yet in belonging to another realm, it determines the quality and wellness of a person in every aspect. Hence, while Western diagnosis and treatment plans focus on the material self, the realm of the beyond has to be negotiated by those who understand the operation of the unseen in order to bring about recovery of the aspect of a self that transcends the physical world. Problems with the essential self will continue to impact every dimension of a person, rendering Western medicine's healing of the physical self insufficient. In reflecting on the health beliefs among the Hmong population, it seems it is the beliefs that determine the state of the mind and the body. Fixing of the body alone cannot sufficiently restore the essence of the self. When an internal conflict causes stress and subsequent somatization, one has to address the primary factor since physical symptoms are only external manifestations of the internal struggle. Fixing the latter fixes only the peripheral. Hence, the ability of health care providers to suspend their assumptions and enter into solidarity with patients may be the most essential part of the recovery process.

Bibliography

Breuilly, Elizabeth, Joanne O'Brien, and Martin Palmer. *Religions of the World: The Illustrated Guide to Origins, Beliefs, Traditions & Festivals.* 2nd ed. New York: Facts on File, 2005.

Brown, Patricia Leigh. "A Doctor for Disease, a Shaman for the Soul." *The New York Times,* September 20, 2009. https://www.nytimes.com/2009/09/20/us/20shaman.html.

---

26   Gerdner, "Shamanism," 14.

Cooper, Robert. *The Hmong: A Guide to Traditional Life*. Singapore: Marshall Cavendish, 2008.

Fadiman, Anne. *The Spirit Catches You and You Fall Down: A Hmong Child, Her American Doctors, and the Collison of Two Cultures*. New York: Farrar, Straus & Giroux, 1997.

Gerdner, Linda A. "Shamanism: Indications and Use By Older Hmong Americans with Chronic Illness." *Hmong Studies Journal* 13, no. 1 (2012): 1–22. https://www.hmongstudiesjournal.org/uploads/4/5/8/7/4587788/gerdnerhsj13.pdf.

Helsel, Deborah G., Marilyn Mochel, and Robert Bauer. "Shamans in a Hmong American Community." *The Journal of Alternative and Complementary Medicine* 10, no. 6 (2004): 933–38. https://doi.org/10.1089/acm.2004.10.933.

Pinzon-Perez, Helda, Neng Moua, and Miguel A. Perez. "Understanding Satisfaction with Shamanic Practices Among the Hmong in Rural California." *The International Electronic Journal of Health Education* 8 (2005): 18–23. http://www.iejhe.com/archives/2005/4061-13874-1-CE.pdf.

Plotnikoff, Gregory A., Charles Numrich, Chu Wu, Deu Yang, and Phua Xiong. "Hmong Shamanism: Animist Spiritual Healing in Minnesota." *Minnesota Medicine* 85, no. 6 (2002): 29–34.

Warner, Miriam E., and Marilyn Mochel. "The Hmong and Health Care in Merced, California." *Hmong Studies Journal* 2, no. 2 (1998): 1–30.

⚜ **12** ⚜

I KNOW I'VE BEEN CHANGED

*Black Womanist Buddhist and Christian Spiritual Formation
and Spiritual Care for a Homicidal White Male Buddhist*

PAMELA AYO YETUNDE

AS A PASTORAL counselor who is a relatively new professor in the field of academic writing, I am aware that many academics demand empirical scholarship. I understand we are trained and formed to accept evidence-based conclusions and taught to view with suspicion scholarship that is based on one person's experience, opinion, and speculation. This chapter is about the pastoral counseling experience of one Black female Buddhist pastoral counselor and a white male Buddhist homicidal client. I know instinctively there is little to no research on the subject because there is scant Black Buddhist presence in the pastoral counseling field, academy, and literature. The purpose of this chapter is to demonstrate how my early spiritual and vocational formation as a Christian and subsequently as a Buddhist chaplain impacted my clinical work, and how my recent reflections on Jesus's encounter with the Canaanite woman helped me transform my own aggression toward my client. This chapter is offered with the intention to be inspirational, not empirical.

The Case of David

I worked as a chaplain and pastoral counselor for a mental health care organization that offered in-patient and out-patient care. My colleagues knew I practiced Buddhism. One of our new clients expressed to his primary counselor that I practiced Buddhism, and he asked his counselor if he could meet with me. They agreed. I met with David.[1] I vividly remember meeting

---

1   I employed pseudonyms for all clients, colleagues, and friends to protect their confidentiality.

David because he reminded me of a younger version of my old friend James, who I had known for about twenty years. David looked like James when I met him, and our interaction was friendly and affectionate from the start. I agreed that a meeting would probably be beneficial.

In our beautiful facility, counselors did not have private offices, so like other counselors seeking privacy, I had to find a vacant room. There were no vacancies at the time I scheduled my meeting with David, so rather than reschedule our meeting, we agreed to meet outside because we thought the climate was conducive to a pleasant outdoor experience. We found two reclined chairs and sat across from each other on a patch of green grass as the breeze enveloped the outdoor counseling room we created for ourselves. I could tell he was relieved to find a counselor who practiced Buddhism and I was happy to be with a client who appreciated the fact that I could support his Buddhist practice.

After we settled into the comfort of our chairs, David began to tell me that his Buddhism was in the Theravada-Insight tradition. I am familiar with this tradition because of my early chaplaincy education through Sati Center for Buddhist Studies, my written commentaries on Buddhist pastoral care in the Pali Canon,[2] and my lay leadership training through Spirit Rock Meditation Center's Community Dharma Leaders (CDL) program. The conditions were near perfect for joining my client. David reminded me of James, so the countertransference was positive. I understood David's spiritual path, so his transference was initially positive. We were outdoors on a beautiful day in reclined chairs, and I could tell he was relaxed, as was I. David began to tell me about his life, and as I listened, he suddenly stopped and slumped to the side with his eyes fixated on my chest. It was not a lustful stare, so I did not feel threatened or aroused. I was confused and curious. I stared at him staring at me. I paused to see how long he would hold the posture. After several uncomfortable seconds I said, "David, you are staring at my chest." David replied, "I know. I just want to kill you." I was unprepared to actually hear what David said. "What?" I asked. He said, "I just want to kill you."

---

2   Pamela Ayo Yetunde, "Dharma Care: Pastoral Care and Counseling from Buddhist Perspectives," *Dharma Care* (blog), accessed May 5, 2019, https://www.dharmacare.com/default.html.

I heard it clearly the second time. I tried to bring all my powers of mindful observation to bear to determine if he was serious, if he had the intention, if he had the means, if he would do it in broad daylight. While bringing my powers of observation to bear, through mindfulness of the breath, body, feelings, mind, and mind objects (David and James), known in Buddhism as the Four Foundations of Mindfulness, along with knowledge of our Buddhist practices, I was able to appear relaxed with his desire to kill me. However, my experience of his desire to kill me transformed that initial friendliness that temporarily transcended cultural, gender, and racial differences into David becoming a violent white male bent on destroying my Black female body. We became players in the sordid racial history of slavery in the United States whereby white men could say and do whatever they wanted to Black women. I was able to notice a rise in aggression toward David without showing it or acting upon it. After David made his admission, I affirmed, as a "good" Buddhist would to another "good" Buddhist, that at least he was aware of the fact of how he felt, and this power of awareness would help him in his recovery. I was able to sit with David and simply listen to him for another twenty minutes, the time remaining in our session, attempting to remain in a joining capacity with a white man who talked about wanting to kill me, a Black woman, and what it felt like to want to kill. Why did I let him go on without interruption, knowing he was engaged in "wrong speech"? I was David's pastoral counselor, but in retrospect, I believe as a Buddhist pastoral counselor I should have asked him to consider practicing "Right Speech" by refraining from talking about committing violence.

Right Speech, an element in the Noble Eightfold Path in Theravada and Insight Buddhisms, entails criteria for deciding what is and is not worth stating. In the Abhaya Sutta, the Buddha taught Prince Abhaya the following six criteria for determining Right Speech:

1. *In the case of words that the Tathagata (the Buddha) knows to be unfactual, untrue, unbeneficial (not connected with the goal), unendearing and disagreeable to others, he does not say them.*

2. *In the case of words that the Tathagata knows to be factual, true, unbeneficial, unendearing and disagreeable to others, he does not say them.*

3. *In the case of words that the Tathagata knows to be factual, true, beneficial, but unendearing and disagreeable to others, he has a sense of the proper time for saying them.*

4. *In the case of words that the Tathagata knows to be unfactual, untrue, unbeneficial, but endearing and agreeable to others, he does not say them.*

5. *In the case of words that the Tathagata knows to be factual, true, unbeneficial, but endearing and agreeable to others, he does not say them.*

6. *In the case of words that the Tathagata knows to be factual, true, beneficial, and endearing and agreeable to others, he has a sense of the proper time for saying them. Why is that? Because the Tathagata has sympathy for living beings.*[3]

Right Speech means refraining from speech that is untruthful, untimely, said with ill intent, of no benefit, and distasteful. Some Buddhist practitioners refrain from speech if they think anyone will be upset. For example, I, along with one of my Filipino American dharma brothers, wanted to talk about the possibility of creating a people-of-color (POC) sangha in the Community of Mindful Living. The hosts of the sangha, two white people, were adamant that talking about creating a POC sangha would be upsetting, and therefore prohibited the conversation. Did David, as a white male counselee in mental health treatment, think he did not have to practice Right Speech with me because his counselor was a Black woman in an authoritative position? Did I think it was not my role to remind him of our practice because I was not his "Buddhist teacher"? Did our social locations and intersubjectivity result in our Buddhisms becoming different in praxis? Did our initial fantasies of meeting as Buddhists fade in the face of racial, gender, and perceived power differences? Was it simply a case of potential murder? One thing is clear—David, as a Buddhist practitioner, did not practice Right Speech, and I, as a Buddhist lay leader and pastoral counselor, did not remind him to do so. We both engaged in praxis failures.

---

3   Bhikkhu Thanissaro, trans., *Abhaya Sutta: To Prince Abhaya (On Right Speech)*, last modified 1997, https://www.accesstoinsight.org/tipitaka/mn/mn.058.than.html.

In-Office Decomposure

The "good" Buddhist in me who practiced the Four Foundations of Mindfulness in my session with David learned, humbly, that my mindful composure was not sustainable. When I walked calmly back to the office that I shared with two counselors, one was there. I asked Susan, who had been at the mental health care organization for three years, if any client had ever told her that they wanted to kill her. Upon hearing my question, her body became erect, as if a marionette was manipulating a string from the top of her head, jerking her body off the seat of the chair. Her arms flailed momentarily, and I knew before she opened her mouth that treating homicidal patients was not the work we were accustomed to doing. Susan said she had not counseled anyone who wanted to kill her, nor was she aware that any of our colleagues had similar experiences. The Four Foundations of Mindfulness, as a doctrine and an experience, began to crumble as I made an attempt to remain cool and calm. For some reason it was important for me to remain cool. I had momentarily convinced myself that David had not really gotten to me. I told Susan that I was hungry and was going to get lunch. I walked calmly to the cafeteria. I had normal conversation with folks in line as well as the chef and the food servers. I walked calmly back to the office, sat my tray of food (which was always delicious) on the table, sat down, and proceeded to stare at my plate. My arms did not move to handle my silverware. I was not practicing mindful eating. I had completely lost my appetite. I remember that I had a moment of dissociation from my food. When I returned to awareness, I felt unease which intensified to fear and near terror upon the realization that I worked in a place that had no security and that I, along with others, could be killed and that no one could save us. My mind traveled in many directions with fantasies and imaginations of many kinds. How would David kill me? What if he couldn't find me? Would he kill others? Should I tell someone other than Susan about David, and if so, who should I tell, what should I tell them, and what should we do about the fact that we had a potential murderer in our midst? These questions arose in my mind, but my body remained calm.

I decided to tell my supervisor what happened, and my supervisor did not respond with the panic I reasonably expected, the panic that Susan displayed when I told her. I said that I needed to go home and that I did not know if or when I would be back. I sensed understanding and compassion, but because there was no attempt to tell me that I would be safe, that the organization would protect me, nor that the organization knew exactly what to do, I did not feel physically safe. My decision to go home was supported. For three or four days after David said he wanted to kill me, and before returning to work, I contemplated the Angulimala Sutta.

Reflecting on Our Encounter Via the Angulimala Sutta

In the Angulimala Sutta,[4] a story I was first introduced to in the early 2000s during my chaplaincy course at the Sati Center for Buddhist Studies, I learned that a man named after his garland of human fingers, Angulimala, was attempting to murder the Buddha to add one of the Buddha's fingers to his garland. Angulimala spotted the Buddha in the forest and called out his intentions to kill the Buddha. The Buddha heard this threat and continued to walk slowly even as Angulimala ran faster toward the Buddha. Unable to catch up to the Buddha, he called on the Buddha to stop so that he could catch up to him, but the Buddha replied that he had stopped and that Angulimala should also stop. Anguimala stopped because he did not understand what the Buddha meant. The Buddha explained that he stopped being like Angulimala—full of unwholesome desire, craving, clinging, wrong views, etc. Upon hearing this, Angulimala became one of the Buddha's adherents, and the Buddha invited Angulimala to come live with him and other monks in their monastery.

When the Buddha and Angulimala, whose reputation had preceded him, entered the monastery, the monks were aghast that the Buddha would bring a mass murderer into the monastery. The fact that Angulimala had become a monk did not protect him from the retribution he received for killing loved ones in the village. He wanted to know how to deal with this kind of suffering, and the Buddha told him that it was his karma and he was to accept it. Angulimala accepted his karma and eventually went to heaven.

For nearly fifteen years, this sutta was lodged in my unconscious mind. Why? Because when I first read it, it sounded ridiculous to me. Placing

---

4   Bhikkhu Ñānamoli and Bhikkhu Bodhi, *The Middle Length Discourses of the Buddha: A New Translation of the Majjhima Nikāya* (Boston: Wisdom, 1995).

myself in the position of someone about to be killed by a mass murderer, would I engage that killer as a person able to be transformed into a peace-loving person? Can a mass murderer be trusted? Would I bring a mass murderer into my religious community? Ridiculous and unwise! Why would our chaplaincy teachers have us read and contemplate this sutta? Perhaps so that it might take hold and bear fruit fifteen years later?

In the days following my encounter with David, I asked myself, What did the Angulimala Sutta mean to me now that I had actually faced someone who wanted to kill me, counseled him, told our manager about him, and then left him in the presence of other patients, colleagues, and administrators? What did the sutta mean in relation to the knowledge that if I returned, I would return to someone who wanted to kill me? What, in my preparation, education, supervised residencies, chaplaincy studies, etc., prepared me for working with a client who wanted to kill me? How could I return to work knowing that this white male had told this Black female that he wanted to kill me and it did not matter that we both practiced Buddhism? How was I to return to someone and to a setting where I had been taught as a pre-teen, starting with reading *The Autobiography of Malcolm X*,[5] that white people could not be trusted and that if someone places their hands on you, you are obligated to ensure that they do not do that to someone else? I contemplated quitting my job, work that I loved in a place I loved, over this one situation. I learned that I was clinging to my own life and that it was futile to do so, no matter the fact that I resented being a part of a population that has to live with racism, sexism, and the disregard and disrespect of Black bodies. I had become a Black woman who practices Buddhism because it has helped me experience equanimity, and now that I felt that my life was on the line and that a white man could be the one to end me, my obligation as a Black Buddhist woman was to determine who could best help David.

After I reset my intentions to determine how to best support David, I had another revelation—I realized that though David is a white man, I, as his Black Buddhist female counselor, was in a power position over him as it related to his treatment! I was a potential victim and in a power position

---

5   Malcolm X and Alex Haley, *The Autobiography of Malcolm X* (New York: Grove Press, 1965).

simultaneously, nondualistically. So was the Buddha in his relationship with Angulimala. Now what?

Back at Work

I decided to return to work with fear. Fear is one of the emotions I detest the most because of its paralyzing effects. I like to think of myself as active, a person of agency, and possessing the power to discern. Fear is only my friend in that it "inspires" me to grow, but first it annoys me, frustrates me, and causes me to be irritable and perhaps irritating. I returned to work fearful that we had nothing in place to keep ourselves safe, and I requested, then demanded, that we do something to keep ourselves safe. I was assured that there would be no change in security, but there would be a training offered in how to care for someone who is homicidal. Before the training took place, a change had taken place in me. I was willing to learn, and it did not matter that David wanted to kill me. I became ready to serve his well-being but without the delusion that my engaging him in conventional pastoral counseling would ease his homicidal desire. I decided not to meet with him again until his homicidal desire disappeared. What would be the point? I'm not the Buddha, I do not possess magical powers, and David was not actually trying to kill me. However, upon reflecting on the Angulimala Sutta, I kept returning to the koan in the story—that the Buddha, while in motion, said he had stopped, which made Angulimala stop. Stopping was the strategy and koan would be the means.

Koan Contemplations and Practices

Koan is not a word I have heard used much in the Insight sanghas and Community of Mindful Living sanghas I have sat with. I do not remember when I first heard the word *koan*; perhaps it was when I was sitting with a Soto Zen community, but I learned that a koan is a statement, phrase, or short story that offers an unanswerable question with the purpose of causing the thinker to stop thinking and experience a moment of "enlightenment." In 2013 I purchased *The Book of Equanimity: Illuminating Classic Zen Koans* by Gerry Shishin Wick.[6] In 2014 or 2015 I lent it to David without having

---

6   Gerry Shishin Wick, *The Book of Equanimity: Illuminating Classic Zen Koans* (Boston: Wisdom, 2005).

read it myself. I wanted *The Book of Equanimity* to represent a few things: 1) I wanted the book to be a transitional object, something to represent my intentions for David even though I did not think it was wise that I continue counseling him; 2) I wanted the title to become an aspiration for him, for him to come to a sense of peace as he was working on freeing himself from homicidal ideation; and 3) I wanted him to have a method of stopping his thoughts and the possible behaviors that could follow from his thoughts. For myself, I wanted to remain connected, and I did not want him to kill anyone.

Reflecting on Our Encounter Via the Canaanite Woman's Koan

I mentioned above that when I went home to determine if I would return to work, I realized that I was in a position of power over David as it related to our counseling relationship. It still strikes me as confusing that I would have power in a relationship with someone who had the desire to kill me where I had no desire and no plan to make it impossible for him to do so. But there was a time when I wanted him removed from our care and sought to do just that. Since this encounter, I have reflected more on Jesus's encounter with the Canaanite woman. I am a Buddhist practitioner who grew up in the United Methodist Church. I still believe in much of what I was taught in church about how people should be treated, and Jesus's love is still a guiding example for me. Although I was not present to witness it, the interrelational dynamics that I imagine occurred between the Canaanite woman and Jesus are truly inspirational. The woman offered Jesus a koan, and he stopped and was transformed.

As I understand the story in the book of Joshua, Jesus, as a Jewish person, was commanded, as all Jewish law-abiding people were, to participate in the genocide of the Canaanites because the Canaanites were polytheistic and the Jews were monotheistic. Jesus and his disciples were in Canaanite territory to spread their message. A Canaanite woman saw Jesus and reached out to him, apparently having heard that he could heal people, and asked that he heal her daughter. Jesus's disciples implored him to ignore her, and Jesus told her that he was there to speak to his people, not hers. He said that her people were no better than dogs. He was caught in hatred. Hatred of her, her people, and her daughter would not lead to healing. The woman replied that even dogs eat the scraps from their masters' table. Jesus noted what the woman said and offered her not just healing for her daughter, but anything she wanted. Who was in the position of power? They were both vulnerable and powerful. The Buddha and Angulimala were both vulnerable and powerful. David and I were both vulnerable and powerful. How can the recognition of our power and vulnerability and our clients' power and vulnerability and the use of koans serve to heal an "us against them" mentality?

Our Incremental Healing

David gladly received the offer of my book. I do not remember exactly what I said to him except something like, "I believe this will get your mind off of killing." Though I was no longer meeting with David one-on-one, I saw him in the halls with *The Book of Equanimity* under his arm.[7] He participated in my spirituality groups. He kept my book for two weeks before I asked for it, and he asked if he could keep it longer because "I read a koan every day." I agreed that he could keep it another week. Several days passed, and I asked for my book, and he pleaded to keep it longer and promised he would get his own copy and return my book when his book arrived. He returned the book within a week. It is important to note that after our first of two one-on-one meetings, he never again told me that he wanted to kill me (though he told others he wanted to kill them, sending ripples of anxiety throughout our health care community). His interactions were "normal." He'd acknowledge my presence, smile, greet me with friendliness, and continue on to his next meeting. Even when he told me he wanted to kill me, in retrospect, he did not say it in anger. It was said in a flat, matter-of-fact tone with a hint of sadness, but I was unable to interpret his vocal tone and emotionality at the time.

David remained in treatment, including individual counseling with his primary counselor, meetings with the psychiatrist, medication, group therapy and classes, and recreational therapy, for several weeks or a few months until he decided to discharge himself. Before he left treatment, David requested a second meeting with me. David requested to meet with me to ask me if I thought his post-discharge plan was a good one. I was shocked

---

7   Wick, *The Book of Equanimity.*

that he wanted to talk with me again, shocked that he wanted my opinion, and shocked that he trusted my opinion. He did not tell me that he wanted to kill me. We laughed and imagined a positive future through the continuation of Buddhist practice, and the possibility of improved relationships for him. I knew he had been changed, and I knew I had been changed.

Discussion: Black Womanist Pastoral Buddhology

Black Buddhist practitioner, novelist, poet, playwright, and activist Alice Walker coined the term *womanist* in 1979 and defined it in 1983 as

> *A woman (of color) who loves other women, sexually and/or nonsexually. Appreciates and prefers women's culture, women's emotional flexibility (values tears as natural counterbalance of laughter), and women's strength. Sometimes loves individual men, sexually and/or nonsexually. Committed to survival and wholeness of entire people, male and female. Not a separatist, except periodically, for health. Traditionally universalist, as in "Mama, why are we brown, pink, and yellow, and our cousins are white, beige, and black?" Answer: "Well, you know the colored race is just like a flower garden, with every color flower represented." Traditionally capable, as in "Mama, I'm walking to Canada and I'm taking you and a bunch of other slaves with me." Reply: "It wouldn't be the first time."*[8]

Before meeting David, I had already considered whether I identified as a womanist. I love people. Our particular gender identity and expression does not make me love someone more or less. I do not love my daughter any more or any less because she is cisgender and heterosexual. I appreciate emotional flexibility and have found some men to be emotionally flexible despite the US culture that portrays "real" men as stoic. Though some of my political ideas came from Malcolm X, I am not a separatist. I believe we are all related, and I believe we all should be free. Is the universal love and

---

8   Alice Walker, "Womanist," in *The Womanist Reader: The First Quarter Century of Womanist Thought*, ed. Layli Phillips (New York: Routledge, 2006), 19.

relatedness of all, with an appreciation for emotional flexibility, enough to care for a white man who wants to kill a Black woman?

In 2015, as part of my dissertation where I combined, in womanist theological methodology, the art of Walker's 1979 short story *Coming Apart* with her 1983 definition of womanism from *In Search of Our Mother's Gardens*, I created the following definition of womanism:

> *Womanism is the willingness on the part of women of all sexualities, to seek out wisdom from African American lesbians on how to create a safe space for themselves, in the midst of threats to their emotional, mental, physical, and spiritual health,* and take the risk of sharing that wisdom with their oppressor(s) in a way that does not intentionally harm the oppressor(s), with the potential for helping the oppressor(s) awaken from ignorance and violence, *and to be advocates for African American lesbians in the African American community.*[9]

Even in the counseling encounter, I argue that a womanist-inspired pastoral counselor needs to consider taking the risk of sharing her wisdom with the one or ones attempting to or actually in the act of oppressing her in a way that does not intentionally harm the oppressor, with the potential for helping the oppressor awaken from ignorance and violence. This is a Buddhist womanist posture toward others. This was the Buddha's posture toward Angulimala, with the use of a koan, and this became Jesus's posture toward the Canaanite woman after she educated him through the use of her koan.

Meditation became central to my life and practice long before I met David. I have meditated almost every day since October 8, 2001. I have been on meditation retreats lasting days at a time. I have engaged in day-long mindfulness practices, and even after more than eighteen years of doing so, the twenty minutes of mindfulness I practiced during my first meeting with David gave way to terror when I was about to eat lunch. Why didn't it last longer? This may be a subject for someone else's research, but the fact that the mindfulness

---

9   Pamela Ayo Yetunde, *A New Spelling of Our Names: An Exploration of the Psycho-Spiritual Experiences of African-American Buddhist Lesbians*, ThD diss. (Columbia Theological Seminary, 2016), 33.

did not last is not a reason to discontinue the practices. Since saying goodbye to David, I have continued my daily practice because it has positively transformed my relationships with self and others. For example, more than ever, I take the risk of sharing wisdom with oppressive people in a way that does not intentionally harm them, with the belief that every person has the potential to awaken from ignorance and violence. I consider this attitude the metaphorical equivalent of Jesus's command to turn the other cheek, and Malik El-Shabazz's (Malcom X's) dictum to do one's level best to ensure the oppressor does not oppress anyone else. Doing this helps us to avoid becoming the oppressor and to live out our aspiration to cultivate wholeness for all people, which is central to Walker's womanism.[10] There is reason to believe the Canaanite woman thought Jesus and his disciples had the potential to kill her, but rather than run and hide from them, she appealed to the part of Jesus that had healing potential. In this way, the Canaanite woman was to Jesus as the Buddha was to Angulimala. Am I equating Jesus with Angulimala? If I did, would it be sacrilege? No matter what we think of ourselves, no matter whether we put others on a pedestal, like all other human beings, we have the capacity to diminish others as the Buddha initially did regarding women entering the monastic life, as Angulimala did by being a mass murderer, as the Buddhist monks did by committing acts of violence against Angulimala, as Jesus's disciples did by telling Jesus to ignore her, and as Jesus did by likening her people, the polytheistic Canaanites, to dogs. Who was I to David and who was he to me? When we are in the counseling room, the impulse to harm others does not automatically disappear, but it can be temporarily managed through mindfulness. If temporary mindfulness and a Buddhist womanist ethic are enough to motivate me to risk sharing wisdom with oppressors in a way that does not intentionally harm them, in a way that honors Right Speech, and is grounded in the belief that everyone has the potential to awaken from ignorance and violence, then mindfulness and other womanist practices are worth our time.

Conclusion

According to news reports, homicide and public mass shootings seem to be on the rise in the United States (although statistics both support and dispute

---

10   Walker, "Womanist."

this perception).[11] The public face of these killers tends to be young white men. Their victims include innocent young school children, high school students, African Americans in church, Jewish people in synagogues, gamblers at casinos, gay people in bars, and crowds of people gathered in public places. I do not know how likely it is that pastoral counselors will encounter homicidal clients. However, I trust that many counselors would react as I did, with fear, if they were the target of a client's homicidal ideation. I suspect the counselor's fear would be even greater if the client represented a population that is seen by the counselor as "the oppressor," as I saw David, a white man, telling me, a Black woman, that he wanted to kill me. How might we as pastoral counselors cultivate our spiritual selves to be in the service of a client's well-being when we are the target of their homicidal intent?

From a Buddhist perspective, everything is impermanent. From a Zen Buddhist perspective, one might argue that it makes no meaningful sense to place a positive or negative value on how our lives will end, be it illness, murder, an accident, or a natural disaster. From the Noble Eightfold Path, we have teachings on Right Speech and Right View. Right View, put simply, means understanding things just the way they are, holding no opinion tightly, and transcendentally, having no view at all and not confusing the body with a self. To put it another way, just because someone says they want to kill you doesn't mean they will, and even if they do, Consciousness continues. From my experience as an African-descended person living in the United States, born in 1961, and having grown up in Indianapolis, I have never felt that I would live a long life. This is why #BlackLivesMatters resonates so strongly with me and perhaps many others. Practicing mindfulness of the body and remembering that our lives are impermanent can be supported by reflecting on the Five Remembrances from the Pali canon:

1. *I am sure to become old; I cannot avoid aging.*
2. *I am sure to become ill; I cannot avoid illness.*

---

11   Mark Follman, Gavin Aronsen, and Deanna Pan, "US Mass Shootings, 1982–2023; Data from Mother Jones' Investigation," *Mother Jones*, last updated August 27, 2023, https://www.motherjones.com/politics/2012/12/mass-shootings-mother-jones-full-data/; Alan Reynolds, "Are Mass Shootings Becoming More Frequent?," *Cato at Liberty* (blog), Cato Institute, February 15, 2018, https://www.cato.org/blog/are-mass-shootings-becoming -more-frequent.

3. *I am sure to die; I cannot avoid death.*
4. *I must be separated and parted from all that is dear and beloved to me.*
5. *I am the owner of my actions, heir of my actions, actions are the womb (from which I have sprung), actions are my relations, actions are my protection. Whatever actions I do, good or bad, of these I shall become the heir.*[12]

I am sure to die. How? I do not know at this moment. Does it matter how? If I die a violent death in the service of my clients, is that a more noble death than dying serving only myself? Sometimes, often times, pastoral counseling is risky business, a risky profession, and a risky vocation. We submit ourselves regularly to the suffering of others, and often suffer ourselves as a consequence. If we are wise, we will know how much to take on, how to relieve our suffering, and actually work toward its alleviation. From my womanist perspective, if I care about the wholeness of entire people and believe non-Black people are my cousins, then even as a Black Buddhist womanist pastoral counselor I am called to create safe spaces for myself and my cousins, including white people with homicidal ideation. Creating a safe space for a man who wanted to kill me, but had no intention to do so, required the deepest empathy I could muster as well as a non-clinging attitude towards my own life—something I did not have when I first met David. With practices in mindfulness, an understanding of our nondual nature, and regular reflection on our impermanence, I believe, like the Buddha believed about Angulimala, that the homicidally-afflicted person can also be the life-giving person. And just as the Canaanite woman believed Jesus could move past the cultural conditioning of his affinity group to see beyond "us" and "them," we can also be generous toward those we have deemed as the dogs of the world. Believing in the positive potential of others, especially the ones we label dangerous, is our great offering in this world of dualism and negative self-delusion. Thank you, David. I know I have been changed.

---

12   Bodhipaksa, "Five remembrances for deep peace (Day 90)," *Wildmind's meditation blog*, Wildmind Meditation, July 11, 2013, https://www.wildmind.org/blogs/on-practice/five-remembrances-for-equanimity.

Bibliography

Bodhipaksa. "Five remembrances for deep peace (Day 90)." *Wildmind's meditation blog.* Wildmind Meditation. July 11, 2013. https://www .wildmind.org/blogs/on-practice/five-remembrances-for-equanimity.

Follman, Mark, Gavin Aronsen, and Deanna Pan. "US Mass Shootings, 1982–2023; Data from Mother Jones' Investigation." *Mother Jones,* last updated August 27, 2023. https://www.motherjones.com /politics/2012/12/mass-shootings-mother-jones-full-data/.

Ñānamoli, Bhikkhu, and Bhikkhu Bodhi. *The Middle Length Discourses of the Buddha: A New Translation of the Majjhima Nikāya.* Boston: Wisdom, 1995.

Reynolds, Alan. "Are Mass Shootings Becoming More Frequent?" *Cato at Liberty* (blog). Cato Institute, February 15, 2018. https://www.cato .org/blog/are-mass-shootings-becoming-more-frequent.

Thanissaro, Bhikkhu, trans. *Abhaya Sutta: To Prince Abhaya (On Right Speech).* Last modified 1997. https://www.accesstoinsight.org/tipitaka /mn/mn.058.than.html.

Thera, Nyanaponika, and Bhikkhu Bodhi. *Numerical Discourses of the Buddha: An Anthology of Suttas from the Anguttara Nikay.* Walnut Creek: AltaMira, 1999.

Thich Nhat Hanh. "Please Call Me By My True Names." *Plum Village,* June 3, 2020. https://plumvillage.org/articles/please-call-me-by-my-true -names-song-poem.

———. *Transformation and Healing: Sutra on the Four Establishments of Mindfulness.* Berkeley, CA: Parallax, 1990.

Walker, Alice. "Womanist." In *The Womanist Reader: The First Quarter Century of Womanist Thought,* edited by Layli Phillips, 19. New York: Routledge, 2006.

Wick, Gerry Shishin. *The Book of Equanimity: Illuminating Classic Zen Koans.* Boston: Wisdom, 2005.

X, Malcolm, and Alex Haley. *The Autobiography of Malcolm X.* New York: Grove Press, 1965.

Yetunde, Pamela Ayo. "Dharma Care: Pastoral Care and Counseling from Buddhist Perspectives."*Dharma Care* (blog). Accessed May 5, 2019. https://www.dharmacare.com/default.html.

———. *A New Spelling of Our Names: An Exploration of the Psycho-Spiritual Experiences of African-American Buddhist Lesbians.* ThD diss. Columbia Theological Seminary, 2016.

❦ **13** ❧

THE RELIGIOUS LOCATIONS OF LGBTQ+ SURVIVORS OF CHRISTIAN NONSEXUAL SPIRITUAL ABUSE

JENNIFER YATES AND JILL L. SNODGRASS

ACCORDING TO KATHLEEN GREIDER, *"whether or not we are religious, all persons inhabit a particular location relative to religion."*[1] Individuals' religious locations are influenced by myriad factors, including religious tradition, theological/spiritual beliefs, and their lived, subjective experience of religion. The religious locations of LGBTQ+ individuals in the United States are both directly and indirectly influenced by Christian perspectives on sexual orientation and gender identity.[2] Christianity has condemned and rejected sexual and gender minorities, causing significant psychospiritual harm.[3] Academic literature has variously described the harm to include spiritual/religious

---

1   Kathleen J. Greider, "Religious Location and Counseling: Engaging Diversity and Difference in Views of Religion," in *Understanding Pastoral Counseling*, ed. Elizabeth A. Maynard and Jill L. Snodgrass (New York: Springer, 2015), 235.

2   It is far beyond the scope of this chapter to summarize the diversity of Christian perspectives on sexual orientation and gender identity. The reader who seeks a greater understanding of this phenomena is referred to William Stacy Johnson, *A Time to Embrace: Same-Sex Relationships in Religion, Law, and Politics*, 2nd ed. (Grand Rapids, MI: Eerdmans, 2012).

3   Brenda L. Beagan and Brenda Hattie, "Religion, Spirituality, and LGBTQ Identity Integration," *Journal of LGBT Issues in Counseling* 9, no. 2 (2015): 92–117, https://doi.org/10.1080/15538605.2015.1029204; Ski Hunter, *Effects of Conservative Religion on Lesbian and Gay Clients and Practitioners: Practice Implications* (Washington, DC: National Association of Social Workers, 2010); Andrew William Wood and Abigail Holland Conley, "Loss of Religious or Spiritual Identities Among the LGBT Population," *Counseling and Values* 59, no. 1 (2014): 95–111, https://doi.org/10.1002/j.2161-007X.2014.00044.x.

abuse,[4] loss of religious or spiritual identity or conflict with religious or spiritual identity,[5] and a variety of mental health issues,[6] including higher risk for self-harm,[7] mood disorders, negative self-worth, and suicidal ideation.[8] Although some progressive Christian traditions affirm the sexual orientations and gender identities of LGBTQ+ individuals, the official stance of the three largest denominations in the United States—the Catholic Church, the Southern Baptist Convention, and the United Methodist Church—is non-affirming.[9]

---

4   Bernadette Barton, "'Abomination:' Life as a Bible Belt Gay," *Journal of Homosexuality* 57, no. 4 (2010): 465–84, https://doi.org/10.1080/00918361003608558; John T. Super and Lamerial Jacobson, "Religious Abuse: Implications for Counseling Lesbian, Gay, Bisexual, and Transgender Individuals," *Journal of LGBT Issues in Counseling* 5, no. 3–4 (2011): 180–96, https://doi.org/10.1080/15538605.2011.632739; Wood and Conley, "Loss of Religious or Spiritual Identities."

5   Beagan and Hattie, "Religion, Spirituality, and LGBTQ"; Eric M. Rodriguez, "At the Intersection of Church and Gay: A Review of the Psychological Research on Gay and Lesbian Christians," *Journal of Homosexuality* 57, no. 1 (2010): 5–38, https://doi.org/10.1080/00918360903445806; Wood and Conley, "Loss of Religious or Spiritual Identities."

6   Stephan Kappler, Kristin A. Hancock, and Thomas G. Plante, "Roman Catholic Gay Priests: Internalized Homophobia, Sexual Identity, and Psychological Well-Being," *Pastoral Psychology* 62, no. 6 (2013): 805–26, https://doi.org/10.1007/s11089-012-0505-5.

7   Joseph Longo, N. Eugene Walls, and Hope Wisneski, "Religion and Religiosity: Protective or Harmful Factors for Sexual Minority Youth?" *Mental Health, Religion & Culture* 16, no. 3 (2013): 273–90, https://doi.org/10.1080/13674676.2012.659240.

8   Jeanna Jacobsen and Rachel Wright, "Mental Health Implications in Mormon Women's Experiences with Same-Sex Attraction: A Qualitative Study," *The Counseling Psychologist* 42, no. 5 (2014): 664–96, https://doi.org/10.1177/0011000014533204.

9   Human Rights Campaign, *Stances of Faiths on LGBTQ Issues: The United Methodist Church*, accessed July 20, 2023, https://www.hrc.org/resources/stances-of-faiths-on-lgbt-issues-united-methodist-church; Human Rights Campaign, *Stances of Faiths on LGBTQ Issues: Roman Catholic Church*, accessed July 20, 2023, https://www.hrc.org/resources/stances-of-faiths-on-lgbt-issues-roman-catholic-church; Human Rights Campaign, *Stances of Faiths on LGBTQ Issues: Southern Baptist Convention*, accessed July 20, 2023, https://www.hrc.org/resources/stances-of-faiths-on-lgbt-issues-southern-baptist-convention; National Council of Churches, *2012 Yearbook of American and Canadian Churches* (New York: National Council of Churches, 2012).

This chapter examines how nonsexual spiritual abuse (NSA), perpetrated by Christians/Christianity in the United States, impacts the religious locations of LGBTQ+ survivors. The harm that results from NSA is compounded by the way LGBTQ+ clients' intersecting social locations result in multiple oppressions and experiences of marginalization in America's heteronormative, Christian-dominated culture.[10] Understanding the deleterious impact of NSA will help therapists to provide relational-ethical counsel amid religious difference.[11]

The chapter begins by detailing the authors' social and religious locations and offers insight into Jenny's own experience of NSA and complex trauma. The second section defines NSA and complex trauma and presents an overview of how, when perpetrated by Christians/Christianity, NSA influences the religious locations of LGBTQ+ survivors. A case illustration is used to evidence the complex relational and therapeutic dynamics such religious difference can engender. Three competencies for relational-ethical counseling with LGBTQ+ survivors of NSA are offered and are then demonstrated using the case illustration.

Foremost, it is important to say a word about language and our attempt to practice language care.[12] The chapter employs the acronym LGBTQ+ for individuals who identify as lesbian, gay, bisexual, transgender, queer, or questioning. This acronym is fluid and changes as the experiences and voices of gender and sexual minorities are acknowledged and included. The chapter

---

10   Kimberlé Crenshaw, "Mapping the Margins: Intersectionality, Identity Politics, and Violence Against Women of Color," *Stanford Law Review* 43, no. 6 (1991): 1241–79, https://doi.org/10.2307/1229039; Nancy J. Ramsay, "Intersectionality: A Model for Addressing the Complexity of Oppression and Privilege," *Pastoral Psychology* 63, no. 4 (2014): 453–69, https://doi.org/10.1007/s11089-013-0570-4.

11   Carrie Doehring, "The Practice of Relational-Ethical Pastoral Care: An Intercultural Approach," in *"After You!" Dialogical Ethics and the Pastoral Counseling Process*, ed. Axel Liégeous, Roger Burggraeve, Marina Reimslagh, and Jozef Corveleyn, 159–81 (Leuven: Uitgeverij Peeters, 2013).

12   Leah Dawn Bueckert and Daniel S. Schipani, "Interfaith Spiritual Caregiving: The Case for Language Care," in *Spiritual Caregiving in the Hospital: Windows to Chaplaincy Ministry*, ed. Leah Dawn Bueckert and Daniel S. Schipani, 245–63 (Kitchener: Pandora, in association with the Institute of Mennonite Studies, 2006); Greider, "Religious Location and Counseling."

refers to LGBTQ+ individuals as gender or sexual minorities given that heterosexuals are the majority population in the United States, which is a heteronormative context wherein particular identities and social locations are privileged over others. The chapter also employs the term *queer communities* to acknowledge the diversity of communities in which LGBTQ+ individuals gather and belong, and how members' intersecting social locations render privilege and subjugation that both unify and fracture queer communities.

The Authors' Social and Religious Locations

Jenny (first author) and Jill (second author) met at Claremont School of Theology in 2007 while doctoral students under the tutelage of Rev. Kathleen J. Greider, PhD. Jenny is a white, middle-class, former evangelical, queer, cisgender woman. For the past eighteen years she has worked as a school psychologist in a large, culturally-diverse, urban school district. Jill is a white, middle-class, heterosexual, cisgender woman, ordained in the United Church of Christ as a clergywoman. For the past eight years she has taught pastoral counseling at Loyola University Maryland.

As editor of this book, Jill asked Jenny to contribute a chapter drawing upon her doctoral dissertation in which she used qualitative and quantitative research methods to uncover whether nonsexual spiritual abuse can result in post-traumatic stress disorder. Jenny readily agreed to contribute, but the writing process resulted in a retraumatization of the NSA and complex trauma that Jenny has worked to overcome for the past twenty years. Jenny and Jill agreed to coauthor this chapter based upon the mutual conviction that therapists have a prophetic role to play in accompanying LGBTQ+ survivors of NSA, but we are not equipped to do so unless we understand how such experiences impact religious location. Jenny and Jill also agreed that the reader needs to understand, in a rudimentary way, how NSA impacted Jenny as her experiences afford her both wisdom and bias.

Jenny was raised in a fundamental, evangelical, charismatic Christian tradition. She was taught that homosexuality is a sin that occurs when one allows a "foothold for Satan." Jenny played soccer at a Christian college. She watched as her same-sex attracted teammates were made to go to counseling intended to change their sexual orientation or risk expulsion. She recalls fervently praying with teammates who were attempting to change their sexual orientation and participated in rituals aimed at casting out one of her teammate's "demons." As Jenny became more aware of her own sexuality, she made a covenant with God that she would kill herself, a less egregious sin, rather than live each day as a lesbian.

Jenny's parents asked her if she was homosexual. When she said yes, they kicked her out of the house. Jenny was told that she could return home if she participated in an ex-gay ministry, but because she refused, she was homeless. She lost her best friends, all of whom were Christian. She lost her community. She lost her church. She lost her personal relationship with Jesus. All of her closest attachments, whether secure, ambivalent, or disorganized, seemed to be obliterated as the result of her sexual orientation.

Jenny was motivated to understand the church's teachings on same-sex relationships. She enrolled as a seminary student at Boston University. She intellectualized her experience and tried to make sense of it cognitively because the relational betrayal was too traumatic to name or begin to understand. But Jenny's experience of nonsexual spiritual abuse continued. Some of her student colleagues circulated a petition to get her kicked out of the dorms because she was gay.

In the throes of complex trauma, faith served as Jenny's reason to live. She lived her faith defiantly, clung to her Christian identity as an act of resistance, and sustained hope by maintaining a relationship with what seemed to be an absent God. She fought to keep from internalizing the violence and abuse inflicted on her in Jesus's name.

Jenny's story is inextricably woven within this chapter. Jenny feels called to educate spiritual care professionals and therapists about NSA and to raise awareness regarding the unique ways this experience influences LGBTQ+ survivors' religious locations. I (Jill) am thrilled that Jenny has trusted me to collaborate in the writing of this chapter and to stand in solidarity with her as she fulfills her call.

Nonsexual Spiritual Abuse and Complex Trauma

This section defines nonsexual spiritual abuse and complex trauma as a foundation for understanding how these phenomena influence the religious locations of LGBTQ+ individuals.

Nonsexual Spiritual Abuse

The disciplines of pastoral theology, counseling, and care, as well as practical theology, have extensively engaged issues of trauma, abuse, and challenges associated with gender minorities in faith communities.[13] Yet these disciplines have, with few exceptions, failed to adequately define spiritual abuse as a psychospiritual construct and to explore the experience and its effects.[14] The absence of attention to NSA within the fields of practical and pastoral theology, coupled with its frequency, substantiates this chapter's relevance and import.

Secular psychological research offers far more insight into the phenomena of spiritual abuse.[15] Oakley and Kinmond defined spiritual abuse as

> *coercion and control of one individual by another in a spiritual context. The target experiences spiritual abuse as a deeply emotional personal attack. This abuse may include: manipulation and exploitation, enforced accountability, censorship and decision making, requirements for secrecy and silence, pressure to conform,*

---

13   Pamela Cooper-White, *The Cry of Tamar: Violence Against Women and the Church's Response*, 2nd ed. (Minneapolis: Fortress, 2012); Carrie Doehring, "Posttraumatic Stress Disorder: Coping and Meaning Making," in *Transforming Wisdom: Pastoral Psychotherapy in Theologial Perspective*, ed. Felicity Kelcourse and K. Brynolf Lyon, 150–67 (Eugene, OR: Cascade Books, 2015); Horace L. Griffin, *Their Own Receive Them Not: African American Lesbians and Gays in Black Churches* (Cleveland: Pilgrim, 2006); Storm Swain, *Trauma and Transformation at Ground Zero* (Minneapolis: Fortress, 2011); Leanne McCall Tigert, *Coming Out Through Fire: Surviving the Trauma of Homophobia* (Eugene, OR: Wipf & Stock, 1999); Deborah van Deusen-Hunsinger, *Bearing the Unbearable: Trauma, Gospel and Pastoral Care* (Grand Rapids, MI: Eerdmans, 2015).

14   Karen Lebacqz and Joseph D. Driskill, *Ethics and Spiritual Care: A Guide for Pastors, Chaplains, and Spiritual Directors* (Nashville: Abingdon, 2000).

15   Julie J. Exline, "Religious and Spiritual Struggles," in *APA Handbook of Psychology, Religion, and Spirituality (Vol. 1): Context, Theory, and Research*, ed. Kenneth I. Pargament, Julie J. Exline, and James W. Jones, 459–75 (Washington, DC: American Psychological Association, 2013); James Griffith, *Religion That Heals, Religion That Harms: A Guide for Clinical Practice* (New York: Guilford, 2010); Lisa R. Oakley and Kathryn Kinmond, *Breaking the Silence on Spiritual Abuse* (New York: Palgrave Macmillan, 2013); David J. Ward, "The Lived Experience of Spiritual Abuse," *Mental Health, Religion & Culture* 14, no. 9 (2011): 899–915, https://doi.org/10.1080/13674676.2010.536206.

*misuse of scripture or the pulpit to control behavior, requirement
of obedience to the abuser, the suggestion that the abuser has a
"divine" position and isolation from others, especially those external
to the abusive context.*[16]

For the purposes of this chapter, this mistreatment excludes sexual abuse so as not to conflate the damaging impact of spiritual abuse that is sexual in nature. Nonsexual spiritual abuse (NSA) is both an abuse of power and a unique form of abuse in its own right.[17] As an abuse of power, spiritual abuse is characterized and maintained by a system of coercion and control that is often upheld in myriad ways, including by discourse. Discourse is a system of thoughts containing ideas, images, narratives, and metaphors that collectively construct particular meaning for a group of events, which informs one's understanding of the world.[18] The institution of the Christian church, therefore, holds particular discourses of meaning through which spiritual power is exercised. Although using the Bible as a guide for behavior is not abusive in itself, it can become abusive when biblical tenets are reconstructed into abusive discourses that emphasize the agendas of certain individuals or institutions. Nonconformity, or an unwillingness to submit to coercion and control, results in various forms of rejection and isolation, including public shaming for rule breaking. Leaving the abusive context may be considered tantamount to "disobeying God," which may be particularly harmful for those who hold devout conservative beliefs. The "spiritual consequences of leaving can become a psychological trap for the individual, rendering them incapable of leaving."[19]

NSA is "multifaceted" as it most often impacts survivors' biological, psychological, social, and spiritual well-being.[20] NSA leaves few areas of survivors' lives untouched. NSA is uniquely damaging in that those who

---

16   Oakley and Kinmond, *Breaking the Silence*, 21–22.

17   Oakley and Kinmond, *Breaking the Silence*.

18   Michel Foucault, *The Archaeology of Knowledge: And the Discourse on Language*, trans. A. M. Sheridan Smith (New York: Pantheon Books, 1972); Oakley and Kinmond, *Breaking the Silence*.

19   Oakley and Kinmond, *Breaking the Silence*, 24.

20   Ward, "The Lived Experience of Spiritual Abuse," 912.

perpetrate the harm are often understood as holding a "divine position."[21] NSA can occur in the process of insisting that individuals live up to a "spiritual standard" without regard for the individual's well-being.[22]

Complex Trauma

Definitions of trauma are currently a matter of discussion and debate within the mental health community. Trauma literature differentiates between two primary types of trauma exposure, each possessing distinct sequelae—post-traumatic stress disorder (PTSD) and complex trauma (CPTSD). While PTSD is often associated with more violent and unexpected events, CPTSD refers to the experience of those who have endured more long-term and chronic exposure to interpersonal forms of abuse that threaten one's self-integrity, developmental capacity, or ability to interact with others in an emotionally healthy manner. Therefore, complex traumatic stressors may include "abandonment, neglect, lack of protection, and emotional, verbal (including bullying), sexual, and physical abuse by primary caregivers or others of significance or loss of these primary attachment figures through illness, death, deployment, or displacement of some sort."[23] The symptom sequelae of complex trauma mimics the intrusion, avoidance, arousal, and negative changes in mood and cognition associated with PTSD; however, it also includes difficulties with affect regulation, impulsivity, dissociation, and sustaining a sense of self-integrity, as well as altered perceptions of self and changes in sustaining beliefs.[24]

---

21   Oakley and Kinmond, *Breaking the Silence*; Ward, "The Lived Experience of Spiritual Abuse."

22   David Johnson and Jeff VanVonderen, *The Subtle Power of Spiritual Abuse* (Minneapolis: Bethany House, 1991), 21.

23   Christine A. Courtois and Julian D. Ford, *Treating Complex Traumatic Stress Disorders in Children and Adolescents: Scientific Foundations and Therapeutic Models* (New York: Guilford, 2013), 10.

24   Alan Scoboria et al., "Exploratory and Confirmatory Factor Analyses of the Structured Interview for Disorders of Extreme Stress," *Assessment* 15, no. 4 (2008): 404–25, https://doi.org/10.1177/1073191108319005; Bessel A. van der Kolk, Alexander C. McFarlane, and Lars Weisaeth, eds., *Traumatic Stress: The Effects of Overwhelming Experience on Mind, Body, and Society* (New York: Guilford, 1996).

Within this chapter, "abuse" is understood as the harm inflicted upon an individual, while "trauma" is the impact of the abuse. All NSA results in trauma, but not all NSA results in complex trauma. Therefore, in the remainder of the chapter, the term *NSA* refers not only to experiences of abuse but also to the trauma that results. When NSA results in complex trauma, it is defined in this chapter as "complex trauma in response to NSA."

The Impact of NSA on LGBTQ+ Survivors' Religious Locations

According to Greider, "Whether we call ourselves religious or not, are appreciative of religions or skeptical or ambivalent, we embody attitudes and positions toward religion."[25] Our religious location is one of many intersecting social locations that comprise our cultural identities, including race, age, economic status, and more, all of which afford power and privilege in some contexts and powerlessness and oppression in others.[26] No two individuals occupy the same religious location even if born into the same religious tradition and the same family. This is because every individual's lived experience of religion differs and is uniquely influenced by social and cultural locations. Moreover, our religious locations "are alive, synergistically evolving. As with other aspects of identity, through our lifetimes, we inhabit more than one religious location. We become more, less, or differently religious."[27] How NSA influences LGBTQ+ survivors' religious locations is unique to each individual and will change and evolve. However, this chapter posits three ways in which NSA commonly impacts LGBTQ+ survivors' religious locations—all of which carry potentially traumatic dimensions. NSA may result in the shattering of assumptions about the safety of the world, pose a threat to psychospiritual existence, and impact affective and neurobiological experiences of religion.

First, NSA can disrupt and even shatter one's assumptive worldview.[28] Human beings carry a tacit set of assumptions about themselves and how

---

25   Greider, "Religious Location and Counseling," 235.

26   Crenshaw, "Mapping the Margins"; Greider, "Religious Location and Counseling"; Ramsay, "Intersectionality."

27   Greider, "Religious Location and Counseling," 237–38.

28   Ronnie Janoff-Bulman, *Shattered Assumptions: Towards a New Psychology of Trauma* (New York: Free Press, 1992).

the world works. Basic assumptions entail beliefs about "the benevolence of the world," "the meaningfulness of the world," and "the worthiness of self."[29] This set of assumptions is deeply held, informs cognitive schema, and can both inform and be informed by our religious beliefs.

> *There are times when one's guiding "paradigms"—one's fundamental assumptions—are seriously challenged and an intense psychological crisis is induced. These are times of trauma. . . . These traumatic events do not produce the psychological equivalent of superficial scratches that heal readily, but deep bodily wounds that require far more in the way of restorative efforts. The injury is to the victim's inner world. Core assumptions are shattered by the traumatic experience.*[30]

This experience is particularly challenging when the sense of existential security gained from religion/spirituality is disrupted or when deeply held assumptions of the fundamental goodness and existence of God are upset.

LGBTQ+ survivors of NSA may struggle to assimilate their abuse and trauma with their assumptive worldview and cognitive schema. Assimilating the trauma necessitates modifying one's assumptive worldview in a way that accommodates and makes meaning of the traumatic experience. Generally speaking, many Christians turn to religion and religious resources to inform their beliefs about how the world works and why their lives have meaning. LGBTQ+ survivors of NSA, however, often cannot look to churches, pastors, or other Christian resources to help modify their schema as these are the very people and institutions that caused the abuse and trauma. Survivors of NSA are then likely to experience insecure attachment to relationships associated with Christianity, including relationships with family members, faith communities, the sacred, and/or God; this experience then directly impacts their religious locations. Some LGBTQ+ survivors of NSA do find Christian people and churches who affirm their sexual orientation

---

29   Ronnie Janoff-Bulman, "Assumptive Worlds and the Stress of Traumatic Events: Applications of the Schema Construct," *Social Cognition* 7, no. 2 (1989): 117–18, https://doi.org/10.1521/soco.1989.7.2.113.

30   Janoff-Bulman, *Shattered Assumptions*, 51.

and/or gender identity and who help them to modify their disrupted world assumptions in a way that assimilates and makes meaning of the abuse. However, the attachment to relationships associated with Christianity, the sacred, and/or God may never be secure in the way it was prior to the experience of NSA.

Second, for some LGBTQ+ survivors of NSA the condemnation and rejection perpetrated by Christianity/Christians are experienced as a threat to existence. NSA can disrupt the intersection of world assumptions and self-worth to the extent that one lives in a chronic state of fear, self-blame, and hopelessness. Many conservative LGBTQ+ Christians try to deny or overcome their sexual orientation or gender identity without success, which can then result in perceived threats to existence (i.e., being sent to hell). Jenny's dissertation entailed a qualitative component wherein she sought to uncover participants' lived experiences of NSA. One participant described sitting through a sermon series in which scripture was used to demonstrate that the attacks of September 11 were God's wrath upon queer communities. The participant recounted,

> *Week after week Romans 1:18–28 was used to maintain 9/11*
> *occurred as God's judgment against the gays. I was 14 years old*
> *and experienced ongoing anxiety attacks and depression resulting*
> *in an eventual suicide attempt. I grew up sincerely believing I was*
> *perverse against nature, an abomination, and that God hated me;*
> *this intrinsic part of me I couldn't pray away or change.*

Participants described their experiences of NSA in concrete terms that reflected very literal beliefs about heaven and hell. As such, some participants experienced their sexuality and participation in their faith community as having a life and death dimension characteristic of trauma. Oakley and Kinmond described this aspect of trauma—particularly when one resists spiritual authority that is understood to represent God—as akin to "spiritual suicide."[31] LGBTQ+ survivors of NSA who believe that their sexual orientation or gender identity is a death sentence—that it is the cause for

---

31   Oakley and Kinmond, *Breaking the Silence*, 44.

national or natural disasters or that by God's judgment they will be sent to hell—must modify or abandon their beliefs.

Third, as evidenced above, LGBTQ+ survivors of NSA often struggle cognitively to assimilate their experience of abuse, which influences their religious location. Too often emphasis is disproportionately placed upon cognitive dimensions of religious location (beliefs, worldviews, theologies), when affective and neurobiological dimensions of religious experience also play a significant role in informing one's religious location. Describing the impact of NSA on LGBTQ+ survivors' affect and emotion is extensive and merits far greater attention than this chapter allows. NSA can disrupt psychological attachment with family, friends, and religious community. Equally destructive is the insecure attachment with God that can result from the lived experience of divine betrayal. In the qualitative aspect of Jenny's dissertation, participants wrote at length about the ways they felt betrayed by God. Participants depicted God as rejecting, arbitrary, unreasonable, uncaring, mean-spirited, and sometimes hateful. Participants reported experiencing God as one who demanded self-damaging behaviors to demonstrate devotion, denied the full humanity of the participants, found the participants to be detestable and abominations, and required them to be punished for eternity in hell. These God images were mediated by the participants' faith communities, family, friends, and professors and were reified by the participants' own belief systems. For example, one participant reported,

> *They [the church] taught me that I was irreparably broken and sick. I was raised in the church and I believed them when they said god didn't want "the gays." It took me years to get over the idea that this part of me is wrong.*

Another participant explained, "As an intersex individual, I was told that God only created man and woman. Since I was neither, I was not created by God, and as such, was not human." For most participants, God was viewed as complicit in the spiritual abuse perpetrated by family, friends, and the faith community. Furthermore, many participants experienced a double-bind relationship with God wherein one attains devotion to God by demonstrating self-denial and self-hate. As one participant shared,

> *I believe the most abusive experiences were within an ex-gay
> ministry where many different emotionally abusive tactics were
> used to get me to change my sexual orientation—brainwashing
> techniques, mind control, or mind manipulation, activities that
> would basically generate devotion to God, but the underlying effect
> was a generating of more and more self-hate, which was viewed sort
> of as success of achieving straightness.*

The experience of divine betrayal both explicitly and implicitly influences one's lived religious experience and informs the religious locations of LGBTQ+ survivors of NSA.

For some but not all LGBTQ+ survivors, the experience of NSA is so traumatizing that it incites a neurobiological response. Survivors who experience neurobiological responses may suffer from complex trauma in response to NSA. This can impact the endocrine system, including the production of the stress hormone cortisol, and can influence the neurochemical regulation of dopamine, norepinephrine, serotonin, and other neurotransmitters that, via brain circuits, regulate stress and fear responses.[32] In this way, the lived religious experience of LGBTQ+ survivors of NSA may be such that particular triggers, such as a terrorizing scriptural passage or the sign of the cross, may produce a flood of neurochemicals wherein the fight-or-flight response is activated. For example, a participant in Jenny's dissertation study described how she continues to experience

> *symptoms of PTSD including living in a chronic state of arousal
> and holding negative beliefs about being created as "invisible" to
> people of faith. I live in a constant state of fear around God and
> my sexuality. I am unable to walk into a church without having
> a panic attack. I have spent the last 22 years in secular therapy
> as a result of this incident and many others having to do with my
> sexuality and spirituality. After decades of trying to find a faith
> community, I can no longer enter a church without panic attacks*

---

32   Jonathan E. Sherin and Charles B. Nemeroff, "Post-Traumatic Stress Disorder: The Neurobiological Impact of Psychological Trauma," *Dialogues in Clinical Neuroscience* 13, no. 3 (2011): 263–78, https://doi.org/10.31887/DCNS.2011.13.2/jsherin.

and I now believe I was created to be invisible to those of faith, while living in fear that the wrong person will realize I am not straight.

For individuals like this participant whose experience of NSA was traumatizing to the extent that it resulted in symptoms or a diagnosis of PTSD, their religious location is influenced by the neurobiologically toxic and destructive responses that result from triggers associated with Christianity/Christians.

A Case Illustration

Mark is a thirty-five-year-old, white, middle-class, gay, cisgender man. Mark was born and raised in the Midwest and has two younger brothers. His parents and brothers live in the same small town where he was raised, but Mark moved away after college when he took a job on the West Coast with an engineering firm. Mark is successful in his career and has a large social circle, but for the past seven months he's been feeling anxious and on edge.

Mark's agitation started after he traveled to the Midwest for Christmas. He had not seen his family in six years, but his grandmother's health was declining quickly. He felt guilty and thought he should spend time with her as she was always less judgmental than the rest of Mark's family. Mark's parents, brothers, and extended family are all evangelical Christian. When he was in high school, Mark was severely teased and bullied and accused of being gay. Mark wondered sometimes if he was gay, but because he knew he could not be gay and a Christian, he worked hard to repress any thoughts about his sexuality. Mark's parents, due to their own fears about his sexual orientation, were zealous in quoting scripture to remind Mark that homosexuality is against God's natural law. When Mark was seventeen, his parents and his pastor agreed that he needed individual counseling with the pastor to understand fully that homosexual acts are detestable and abominations. Mark met one-on-one with the pastor for three months. He memorized every biblical passage his parents and his pastor so frequently cited, and he made a vow to never defile the sacred life God gave him and to never, ever succumb to impure and sinful thoughts or actions that were a direct affront to God's goodness and creation.

Mark received a scholarship to study engineering at a large state university about eight hours from where he grew up. Mark was a good student. He joined the intramural lacrosse team. And he went to church faithfully every Sunday. During his senior year, Mark met Mario while volunteering with the lacrosse team at a service day event. Mark knew that the way he felt toward Mario made him an abomination. He knew that he could never tell his family he was gay. He knew that he was sinning against God and was a perversion of God's good creation. Mark tried to deny his attraction to Mario. He felt ashamed and blamed himself for following Satan's lure. But as Mark and Mario started spending more time together, Mark stopped going to church, and he worked hard to repress any thoughts about God, the Bible, or Jesus.

When Mario announced he was moving to the West Coast following graduation, Mark pursued every engineering job he could find that would allow him to follow. Mario knew at the time that moving west would separate Mark from his family and his faith, but in many ways he welcomed the geographic and relational distance. Mario broke up with Mark two years after graduation, but Mark remained living and working in the West.

Over the years, Mark returned to the Midwest a couple of times, but he only ever stayed for two or three days, and he always avoided being there on Sundays or Christian holidays. Being with his family on Christmas awoke in Mark the deep-seated anti-gay prejudice that he had internalized but suppressed for the past thirteen years. On Christmas Eve, Mark entered the evangelical church of his childhood and escorted his grandmother to her pew. He immediately experienced shortness of breath, tightness in his chest, and a racing heartbeat. Mark's stomach cramped up, and he realized he must be coming down with the flu. Mark told his family he would meet them back at the house. Mark stayed in bed on Christmas Day and flew back west early the following morning. Mark was grateful that the flu bug seemed to be short-lived.

Mark never thought much about his time in the Midwest or his experience on Christmas Eve. But over the next seven months, despite the fact that his work was going well, Mark felt a constant sense of apprehension. At times he would find himself distracted at work and then realize that condemning Bible passages seemed to be playing in his mind on repeat.

He would be engrossed in a project one minute, and the next he would be drenched in sweat thinking about his childhood pastor or the kids at his high school. Mark wasn't sleeping well like he normally did, and he found it hard to concentrate. After seeing his general physician twice and completing routine lab work, Mark's doctor suggested that he speak with a therapist about his anxiety.

Implications for Spiritually-Integrated Psychotherapy

Therapists can equip themselves to provide competent care for the intersection of religious location and mental health in the lives of LGBTQ+ survivors of NSA. Survivors of religiously-motivated abuse and violence frequently feel reluctant to discuss their spiritual/religious experiences with "secular" therapists yet are simultaneously unlikely to seek the counsel of religiously-affiliated mental health professionals.[33] Therapists can take care in how they market themselves if they wish to attract and welcome LGBTQ+ survivors of NSA. This section presents three competencies for relational-ethical counseling with LGBTQ+ survivors of NSA and posits implications for spiritually-integrated psychotherapy with Mark.

Competency 1: The Importance of Self-Reflexivity

Self-reflexivity entails "disciplined, accountable practices to decrease our unconsciousness and increase in depth our understanding of our life narrative, sense of self, participation in relationships, and social-historical location,"[34] as well as our religious location. Therapists cannot effectively engage in self-reflexivity related to their religious location unless they first acknowledge their own experiences of NSA. Self-reflexivity on religious location can be retraumatizing if a therapist's NSA experience is overlooked or repressed. An in-depth assessment of NSA is, for some, an important precursor to self-reflexivity. Guidance on assessing for NSA is the focus of the second competency below.

---

33   Oakley and Kinmond, *Breaking the Silence*.

34   Greider, "Religious Location and Counseling," 248.

Therapists without histories of NSA should engage in self-reflexivity regarding 1) their own religious location and 2) "the effect of [their] religious location on clients and clinical situations."[35] Relational-ethical counseling with LGBTQ+ survivors of Christian NSA requires self-reflexivity and acknowledgement of the therapist's values related to Christianity, NSA, and spiritual trauma. The following section suggests how to engage in this self-reflexive process.

First, as Greider argued, self-reflexivity is both a private and a communal practice.[36] Therapists are encouraged to spend quiet, solitary time reflecting on their values related to Christianity, NSA, and spiritual trauma. However, the insights gained can then be tested, corrected, or confirmed by engaging in "*relational* self-reflexivity."[37] Through supervision or through conversations with colleagues, spiritual companions, trusted friends, and others, therapists will understand how their values influence their religious location better by engaging with others in critical dialogue.

Whether in isolation or in dialogue, therapists are encouraged to reflect upon the personal, familial, historical, sociopolitical, and economic values that influence their religious location.[38] Greider identified tools that can generally assist in this process, including spiritual genograms, spiritual life maps, and spiritual ecomaps and ecograms. In addition, the following list of questions can help to guide the therapist in reflecting on these issues:

> *What value do I place on Christianity in comparison to other religions? How is my perspective on Christianity influenced by historical and familial events? Does being Christian require communal religious participation? How is my belief on religious participation influenced by family, community, and culture? How do I understand harm inflicted on individuals and communities in the name of Christ? What is the role of reparations in atoning for such harm, and whose responsibility is that? How does God view abusive acts committed by Christians and Christian leaders? What*

---

35   Greider, "Religious Location and Counseling," 248.

36   Greider, "Religious Location and Counseling."

37   Greider, "Religious Location and Counseling," 249.

38   Greider, "Religious Location and Counseling."

> *is God's role or responsibility in causing or preventing NSA and
> spiritual trauma?*

These and many other questions can help to guide therapists in reflecting on their values related to Christianity, NSA, and spiritual trauma.

Therapists are also encouraged to reflect upon the effect of their religious location on clients who are LGBTQ+ survivors of NSA and the clinical relationship. In therapeutic relationship, the therapist's and the client's religious locations contribute to intersubjective dynamics that can include transference and countertransference, resistance, positive and negative projections, and helpful and unhelpful power differentials. Moreover, the therapist's religious location can directly and indirectly inform clinical judgment. The following list of questions can help to guide therapists in reflecting on the effect of their religious location on clients and the clinical relationship:

> *What from my own experience may prevent me from empathetically
> responding to LGBTQ+ survivors of NSA? Am I prone to
> minimize, pathologize, or catastrophize the impact of NSA on
> LGBTQ+ survivors based on my values and religious location? Do
> my values motivate me to encourage LGBTQ+ survivors of NSA
> to either seek out or avoid religious or spiritual community? How
> important is it that LGBTQ+ survivors speak out about the abuse
> they endure(d) and confront Christianity/Christians for the harm
> perpetrated in the name of Christ? What are my values related to
> forgiveness, specifically the forgiveness of self, others, and God by
> NSA survivors? Do my values encourage or discourage healing and
> restoration between LGBTQ+ survivors of NSA and the church?*

Self-reflexivity can serve to increase insight into religious location and to raise awareness of values and beliefs about Christianity, NSA, and spiritual trauma.

Implications for Therapy with Mark

At the suggestion of his doctor, Mark decided he needed to speak with a therapist about his anxiety. Mark had never been to therapy before, and he was skeptical about whether it would help. Mark looked on his insurance company's website and found the names of four therapists with offices close to his work. Mark called Anna first because the website indicated that she specializes in anxiety and trauma.

Anna's clinical training emphasized the importance of multicultural competence in therapy, including attention to religious difference. Therefore, Anna was taught the importance of both individual and communal self-reflexivity, which included attending to her religious location. A second-generation Vietnamese American, Anna was born and raised in the Roman Catholic Church. Anna has very strong feelings about the clergy sexual abuse crisis and its impact on survivors, perpetrators, and the global Church. She ardently believes that religion can both harm and heal. Although Anna goes to mass most Sundays with her cousin, three years ago she began practicing Vipassana meditation. She became interested in Vipassana after learning to incorporate elements of mindfulness in her therapeutic practice.

Anna is intentional about asking her clients about their religious and spiritual beliefs and practices. She participates in a monthly peer supervision group in which one of the five members is an Episcopal priest, trained as a spiritually-integrated psychotherapist. The small group experience helps to facilitate Anna's ongoing self-reflexivity regarding her religious location, whether in relation to her own or a colleague's clinical experience.

Competency 2: Assessing for NSA and Complex Trauma in Response to NSA

Therapists need to be adept at assessing for both NSA and complex trauma in response to NSA, which require distinctive methods of assessment. Competence in this is particularly important because NSA is seldom recognized as abuse.[39] LGBTQ+ survivors of NSA rarely refer to the discrimination and even violence they experienced as abusive, and even well-intentioned therapists who regularly assess for physical, sexual, childhood, and other abuses are unlikely to assess for NSA. When a client has experienced NSA and the therapist fails to adequately assess for and identify it, the therapist runs the risk of misdiagnosis in a way that negatively pathologizes and can even retraumatize the client.

---

39   Oakley and Kinmond, *Breaking the Silence.*

Assessing for NSA

Foremost, the therapist is discouraged from asking about NSA during the initial appointment and thereafter until sufficient rapport is established. The therapist should ask about the client's spiritual and religious beliefs and practices, and may consider acknowledging that some beliefs and practices can be life-giving while others can be life-limiting. This signals an openness to explore issues related to spiritual abuse and its effects. As with assessing for any form of abuse, the therapist can listen for abusive dynamics in the client's story and observe the client's body responses (i.e., tensing up, rapid breathing, dissociating) when discussing topics related to religion or spirituality.

Once sufficient rapport is established, the therapist may consider utilizing Keller's twenty-item Spiritual Abuse Questionnaire (SAQ; see Appendix).[40] Most therapists will prefer to ask select questions verbally to the client rather than giving the client a printed copy of the questionnaire to complete. Further guidance on using the SAQ is offered below in the case of Mark.

Assessing for Complex Trauma in Response to NSA

In addition to assessing for NSA, therapists need to know how to asses for complex trauma in response to NSA. Therapists are encouraged to assess for complex trauma in response to NSA when the client 1) acknowledges experiencing NSA, past or present, and 2) reports experiencing disruption or impairment related to attachment, affect regulation, behavioral control, cognition, or self-concept in a manner consistent with complex trauma. What follows is an adapted version of the Primary Care PTSD Screen for DSM-5 designed to assess for complex trauma in response NSA.[41] Again, therapists may prefer to pose these questions verbally to clients rather than asking them to complete the screening measure on paper.

---

40   Kathryn Hope Keller, "Development of a Spiritual Abuse Questionnaire," PhD diss. (Texas Woman's University, 2017).

41   Annabel Prins et al., "The Primary Care PTSD Screen for DSM-5 (PC-PTSD-5): Development and Evaluation Within a Veteran Primary Care Sample," *Journal of General Internal Medicine* 31, no. 10 (2016): 1206–11, https://doi.org/10.1007/s11606-016 -3703-5.

*At any point in your life have you had spiritual or religious
experiences that were so frightening, horrible, or upsetting that in
the past month you:*

1. *Had nightmares about the event(s) or thought about the event(s)
   when you did not want to? YES/NO*
2. *Tried hard not to think about the event(s) or went out of your way to
   avoid situations that remind you of the event(s)? YES/NO*
3. *Been constantly on guard, watchful, or easily startled? YES/NO*
4. *Felt numb or detached from others, activities, or your surroundings?
   YES/NO*
5. *Felt guilty or unable to stop blaming yourself or others for
   the event(s) or any problems the event(s) may have caused?
   YES/NO.*[42]

Finally, in assessing for any type of NSA or complex trauma in response
to NSA, it is important for the therapist to explore how the client makes
meaning of the events. Labeling their experience as NSA or complex trauma
in response to NSA can be viewed as validating and empowering by some
clients and limiting or pathologizing by others.

Implications for Therapy with Mark

At the initial appointment, Anna asked Mark to complete intake paperwork
that included questions about his religious location. Mark indicated that he
did not have a religious affiliation; that spirituality/religion were of "little"
importance to him; that he was raised Christian; and that he was "unsure"
if he wanted to address spirituality/religion in counseling. During the initial
appointment, Anna sought to understand some about Mark's background
and to explore his current experiences of anxiety. Anna and Mark did not
discuss his religious location during the initial appointment.

After two additional sessions, Anna began to intuit that Mark's anxiety
was influenced by his family and their views on his sexual orientation. She
understood more about his childhood and the circumstances that caused
him to distance himself, physically and relationally, from his family. Anna

---

42   Adapted from Prins et al., "The Primary Care PTSD Screen," 1208.

then thought back to the intake paperwork and Mark's response that he was "unsure" if he wanted to address spirituality/religion in counseling. Anna tested the waters and said, "Mark, it seems to me that your upbringing as an evangelical Christian and the way that influences your family's beliefs about same-sex relationships is important for us to discuss. Is that something you're open to exploring?" Anna observed Mark as his body stiffened, his shoulders rose, and his breathing quickened. Before Mark could respond, Anna asked him, "Does that make you anxious?" Mark thought for a bit and responded, "Yeah. I guess it does make me somewhat anxious. I don't know if it's really worth talking about." Based on Mark's somatic response, Anna realized the importance of pacing their conversation about religion, Mark's family, and his sexual orientation.

Over the next three sessions, Anna and Mark periodically returned to the discussion about Mark's religious upbringing, his family, and his sexual orientation. Anna asked Mark if he felt that his family viewed his sexual orientation as "ungodly" (SAQ #20). Mark spoke at length about the ways he was judged and punished by his family, his pastor, and his church based on their suspicion and fear related to his sexual orientation, and how that caused him to feel isolated and misunderstood (SAQ #10, 19, 20). Anna asked Mark if he ever questioned whether or not he could live "God's way" when "God's way," at least as his parents and pastor taught him, had caused him so much pain (SAQ #2). Mark's body stiffened, his breathing became rapid, and he shut his eyes. Mark stayed that way for nearly two minutes and did not say a word. Once Mark's posture relaxed and his breathing slowed, Anna said, "Mark, what you experienced growing up is spiritual abuse. No one should be abused. You did not deserve to be abused." Anna gave Mark a second to process this, then continued, "I think the spiritual abuse you experienced growing up directly relates to some of the anxiety you're experiencing now." Based on Mark's somatic responses, Anna wondered if he might be experiencing complex trauma in response to NSA. She wanted to understand more about the ways Mark may experience impairment related to attachment, affect regulation, cognition, and self-concept, but she knew the importance of pacing that type of assessment so as to avoid disrupting the relational safety between herself and Mark in a way that could result in retraumatization.

Competency 3: Facilitating Relational Safety and Avoiding Retraumatization

The therapeutic context and relationship are both directly and indirectly influenced by NSA. For LGBTQ+ survivors of NSA, the therapeutic context and relationship can be retraumatizing. Though intended to serve as a place of refuge—a safe container to heal disrupted attachments—because many LGBTQ+ survivors of NSA experienced trauma in what were previously safe contexts, like family of origin, peer group, or church, the therapeutic context may also be triggering or feel dangerous to the client. According to Courtois and Ford,

> *When primary relationships are sources of profound disillusionment, betrayal and emotional pain, any subsequent relationship with an authority figure who offers an emotional bond or other assistance might be met with a range of emotions, such as fear, suspicion, anger, or hopelessness on the negative end of the continuum and idealization, hope, overdependence, and entitlement on the positive.*[43]

The development of a safe and attuned therapeutic relationship is critical, particularly when working with clients struggling with symptoms of complex trauma in response to NSA, because the therapeutic relationship addresses fears associated with relational abuses and betrayal.

What follows are three strategies therapists can use to create relational safety with LGBTQ+ survivors of NSA and avoid retraumatization in the therapeutic context. First, because NSA is often characterized by betrayal, abandonment, and abuses of power by attachment figures, these issues may interfere with the development of a secure therapeutic relationship. Therapists are encouraged to address fear of betrayal by communicating that the client's development of trust in the therapeutic relationship is not automatic, may take time, and is something that is within the control of the client to decide when and whether a therapist can be trusted. Along these lines, it may be also important for the

---

43   Courtois and Ford, *Treatment of Complex Trauma*, 134.

therapist to emphasize that she or he will likely make mistakes and communicate the importance of being able to openly discuss the therapist's mistakes in the eventuality of therapeutic misunderstandings.[44] Distrust and suspicion of authority figures is not uncommon among LGBTQ+ survivors of NSA, which makes the above strategies to empower the client, and thus to share power, important to the therapeutic relationship. Power sharing shifts the position of "expert" to the client, who becomes the teacher of the therapist.[45]

Second, creating a relationally safe environment for LGBTQ+ survivors of NSA may also entail engaging survivors' potential fear of abandonment. This may be addressed by expressing an understanding of how rejection and abandonment associated with NSA can understandably impact close relationships, including therapeutic ones. Providing the client with a standing invitation to inquire about perceptions of relational disruption, including abandonment, without the threat of retaliation may assist in creating a safer therapeutic environment. Embedded in this invitation may be an acknowledgment of humility, and inevitable imperfections, on the part of the therapist. This is particularly important given that many LGBTQ+ survivors of NSA experienced an abuse of power, and therapy entails an inherent power differential.

Third, the power differential in the therapeutic relationship may elicit a sense of discomfort in LGBTQ+ survivors of NSA. The client may fear the therapist could misuse relational power, "authority and expertise to intimidate, coerce, belittle, or otherwise usurp or violate the client."[46] Paying attention to a client's attachment styles and needs may facilitate relational safety and assist in avoiding retraumatization. Therapeutic relational styles characterized by an objective, detached, or quietly authoritative presence on one end of the continuum, or characterized by a style that is overly attentive and exceedingly available on the other end, may heighten a client's expectation of an abuse of power. Care must be taken to understand the client's attachment needs and adjust one's style to better meet those needs. For example, a client

---

44   Courtois and Ford, *Treatment of Complex Trauma.*
45   Greider, "Religious Location and Counseling."
46   Courtois and Ford, *Treatment of Complex Trauma,* 136.

with an anxious attachment style may benefit from a therapeutic presence that is more engaged, while a client with an avoidant style may feel more comfortable with a more distant approach.[47]

Failure to accurately conceptualize a client's complex trauma in response to NSA may result from lack of awareness or training in this area; however, it may also result from countertransference that can harm and risk retraumatization for the client. The intense and theoretically uncharted nature of complex trauma in response to NSA brings with it risks of traumatic transference and countertransference. Clients with complex trauma may enter therapy with relational patterns, cognitions, and beliefs about themselves and others learned from chronic experiences of complex trauma.[48] Clients may experience "traumatic transference" and "invite their therapists (with conscious intention or not) into complimentary or contrasting countertransference positions and into enactments."[49] Working with clients experiencing traumatic responses may be overwhelming and destabilizing for the therapist, particularly as there is little research on the topic of NSA and its relationship to complex trauma. Therefore, therapists may be ill-prepared to identify spiritual trauma or may be caught off guard by their own stress reactions to clients presenting with complex trauma in response to NSA. Therapists may even experience vicarious traumatization. If therapists' vicarious trauma is not acknowledged and attended to, it may have a deleterious impact on the therapist's mental health, relationships, and judgment.[50] In these instances, therapists may move to one extreme by minimizing, avoiding, or misunderstanding the impact of NSA or to the other extreme by overpathologizing the client and the client's experience.

Finally, it is important to note that LGBTQ+ survivors of NSA may have experience with so-called "ex-gay ministries," "reparative therapy," or other sexual orientation change efforts (SOCE). Their perceptions of self and therapy may negatively impact the development of relational safety. The APA Taskforce on Appropriate Therapeutic Response to Sexual Orientation

---

47   Courtois and Ford, *Treatment of Complex Trauma*, 136.

48   Courtois and Ford, *Treatment of Complex Trauma*.

49   Courtois and Ford, *Treatment of Complex Trauma*, 272.

50   Courtois and Ford, *Treatment of Complex Trauma*.

found that SOCE may present iatrogenic risks.[51] The report stated that some who have undergone SOCE have reported emotional harm including "anger, anxiety, confusion, depression, guilt, grief, hopelessness, deteriorated relationships with family, loss of social support, loss of faith, poor self-image, social isolation, intimacy difficulties, intrusive imagery, suicidal ideation, self-hatred and sexual dysfunction."[52] An important component of creating a safe environment may entail providing an accepting space wherein clients can express internalized homonegative perceptions about self and others. It may also involve assuring the client that therapy does not necessitate the client embrace a pro-gay perspective and that confusion and ambivalence regarding one's same-sex attraction is a safe and valued topic to engage.[53]

Implications for Therapy with Mark

Anna and Mark had now met six times, and Mark still did not seem very willing to trust Anna and the therapeutic process. As Anna learned more about Mark's childhood experiences of NSA and the way it disrupted his relationships with attachment figures, Anna knew she needed to be more explicit about their relational dynamics. Therefore, at the beginning of the seventh session, Anna said, "Mark, I was reflecting on everything we've talked about since we first met, and I want to acknowledge how hard it can be, especially given what you experienced in the past, to risk vulnerability and to trust someone else with your story. Especially because your parents and pastor, people you wanted to trust, hurt you so much. I was also thinking about how trusting others takes time, and only you can decide how much or how little to trust me and to trust our work together. And I may mess up! I may

---

51   American Psychological Association, *Report of the American Psychological Association's Task Force on Appropriate Therapeutic Responses to Sexual Orientation*, 2009, http://www.apa.org/pi/lgbt/resources/therapeutic-response.pdf.

52   American Psychological Association, *Report of the American Psychological Association's Task Force*, 42.

53   Ariel Shildo and John C. Gonsiorek, "Psychotherapy With Clients Who Have Been Through Sexual Orientation Change Interventions or Request to Change Their Sexual Orientation," in *Handbook of Sexual Orientation and Gender Diversity in Counseling and Psychotherapy*, ed. Kurt A. DeBord, Ann R. Fischer, Kathleen J. Bieschke, and Ruperto M. Perez, 291–311 (Washington, DC: American Psychological Association, 2017).

say things you don't agree with or view things differently than you do. When that happens, I want you to tell me so we can talk about it and understand each other better." Mark simply said, "Okay," and spent the remainder of the session talking about a lacrosse tournament he played in over the weekend.

Although Anna was deeply committed to working with Mark, she noticed she was becoming annoyed by Mark's difficulties with trust; as a result, she experienced impulses to dismiss Mark's distress. Although she did her own therapeutic work related to clergy-perpetrated sexual abuse (CPSA), she began feeling overwhelmed and disoriented and began to wonder if Mark's challenges were primarily associated with something other than NSA. After all, she reasoned, he was not sexually abused by someone in spiritual authority. Why were his relational attachments and his sense of existential insecurity fraught with a complexity reminiscent of CPSA survivors? Anna decided to explore her confusing countertransference reactions with her monthly peer supervision group. Through that process, she came to acknowledge that her strong feelings about CPSA were activated by hearing Mark's description of NSA. The acknowledgment that the devastating impact of spiritual abuse was not relegated to survivors of CPSA suggested a potential ubiquity of the phenomenon with which she had not fully reckoned. This awareness, combined with the intensity of Mark's distress, had an overwhelming impact: Anna had lost her bearings. Though it did not happen overnight, through the support of her supervision group, Anna was empowered to learn more about NSA, and she recommitted to the therapeutic journey with Mark.

Anna and Mark worked together for three years. The first year and a half of therapy centered on developing trust and a safe therapeutic relationship. During that time, Anna continued to learn about Mark's anxiety, and Mark learned cognitive-behavioral strategies to facilitate coping. It took a year and a half before the level of trust in the relationship enabled Anna to conduct an explicit assessment for complex trauma in response to NSA. Slowly Mark was able to acknowledge that what happened to him on Christmas Eve four years before was a panic attack and the reawakening of his trauma. He was able to see how hard he had worked since college to avoid his family, to avoid the church, and to avoid God. He realized why condemning Bible passages sometimes played in his mind on repeat. He realized how the thoughts he had about his childhood pastor and the congregation were intrusive and disturbing. He began to see that even though he'd always had many friends, he held himself at a distance and had not experienced emotional intimacy in the fourteen years since his relationship with Mario ended. Anna helped Mark to address the complex trauma he experienced in response to NSA and to begin recovery.

Conclusion

NSA perpetrated by Christians/Christianity in the United States both directly and indirectly impacts the religious locations of LGBTQ+ survivors. NSA is too often overlooked, misdiagnosed, or mistreated in therapy. Therapists, particularly those who specialize in spiritually-integrated psychotherapy, are uniquely equipped to honor how NSA impacts the religious locations of LGBTQ+ survivors and to provide relational-ethical counsel amid religious difference. As evidenced in the case of Mark, by engaging in self-reflexivity, conducting a therapeutically-appropriate assessment for NSA and complex trauma in response to NSA, and developing a relationally safe therapeutic environment, Anna was able to help Mark to begin recovering from the trauma perpetrated against him in the name of Christ.

APPENDIX

20-Item Spiritual Abuse Questionnaire[54]

Instructions:

Please consider your current or previous involvement in a Christian or Bible-based church or group (ex: a church, student organization, missions organization, etc.). Respond by checking the box that most closely matches your experiences in that group. **If you have been involved in more than one church or group, please answer according to the church/group that stands out to you the most.**

If the church/group that stands out to you the most is one in which you are currently involved, please answer the items as if they are written in the present (felt→feel, etc).

Strongly disagree → Disagree → Agree → Strongly Agree

1. It was acceptable to express my true emotions in my church/group
2. At times I asked myself, "How can I live 'God's way' when 'God's way' was itself a source of so much pain?"
3. Leaders in my group acknowledged harm they caused to others
4. I know some religious leaders shared information about other people (through prayer requests or otherwise) that should have been kept private
5. I believed that God's love and acceptance of me was dependent upon my performance in the church/group
6. I currently have no trouble trusting religious leaders/churches/ groups
7. I no longer trust myself to find a good spiritual community

---

    Keller, "Development of a Spiritual Abuse Questionnaire."

8. I was harshly criticized by religious leaders or church/group members
9. I felt like a spiritual failure and I depended on my leader/church group to "get it right"
10. I believed God would punish me if I didn't do what my church/group encouraged me to do
11. I discerned an inner conflict between the narrow teachings of group and my own understanding of God
12. I now feel cynical about church/religious groups
13. I felt freedom to ask questions or express concerns in my church/group
14. I felt dependent on the church/group
15. My religious leaders used fear to control people
16. I know that I or others were asked to serve as the "eyes and ears" for our leader to get information about our members
17. At times, I was scolded by my leader and made to feel ashamed and helpless
18. I believed I could be totally surrendered to God if I did everything perfectly according to the church/group's instructions
19. I now feel lonely and misunderstood because of my church/group experiences
20. Others were judged as inferior or ungodly for not conforming with my church's/group's norms

Bibliography

American Psychological Association. *Report of the American Psychological Association's Task Force on Appropriate Therapeutic Responses to Sexual Orientation.* 2009. http://www.apa.org/pi/lgbt/resources/therapeutic -response.pdf.

Barton, Bernadette. "'Abomination:' Life as a Bible Belt Gay." *Journal of Homosexuality* 57, no. 4 (2010): 465–84. https://doi.org/10.1080 /00918361003608558.

Beagan, Brenda L., and Brenda Hattie. "Religion, Spirituality, and LGBTQ Identity Integration." *Journal of LGBT Issues in Counseling* 9, no. 2 (2015): 92–117. https://doi.org/10.1080/15538605.2015.1029204.

Bueckert, Leah Dawn, and Daniel S. Schipani. "Interfaith Spiritual Caregiving: The Case for Language Care." In *Spiritual Caregiving in the*

Hospital: Windows to Chaplaincy Ministry, edited by Leah Dawn Bueckert and Daniel S. Schipani, 245–63. Kitchener: Pandora, in association with the Institute of Mennonite Studies, 2006.

Cooper-White, Pamela. *The Cry of Tamar: Violence Against Women and the Church's Response.* 2nd ed. Minneapolis: Fortress, 2012.

Courtois, Christine A., and Julian D. Ford. *Treatment of Complex Trauma: A Sequenced, Relationship-Based Approach.* New York: Guilford, 2013.

Crenshaw, Kimberlé. "Mapping the Margins: Intersectionality, Identity Politics, and Violence Against Women of Color." *Stanford Law Review* 43, no. 6 (1991): 1241–79. https://doi.org/10.2307/1229039.

Doehring, Carrie. "Posttraumatic Stress Disorder: Coping and Meaning Making." In *Transforming Wisdom: Pastoral Psychotherapy in Theologial Perspective,* edited by Felicity Kelcourse and K. Brynolf Lyon, 150–67. Eugene, OR: Cascade Books, 2015.

———. "The Practice of Relational-Ethical Pastoral Care: An Intercultural Approach." In *"After You!" Dialogical Ethics and the Pastoral Counseling Process,* edited by Axel Liégeous, Roger Burggraeve, Marina Reimslagh, and Jozef Corveleyn, 159–181. Leuven: Uitgeverij Peeters, 2013.

Exline, Julie J. "Religious and Spiritual Struggles." In *APA Handbook of Psychology, Religion, and Spirituality (Vol. 1): Context, Theory, and Research,* edited by Kenneth I. Pargament, Julie J. Exline, and James W. Jones, 459–75. Washington, DC: American Psychological Association, 2013.

Focus on the Family. *Transgenderism – Our Position.* February 1, 2018. https://www.focusonthefamily.com/socialissues/sexuality/transgenderism/transgenderism-our-position.

Foucault, Michel. *The Archaeology of Knowledge: And the Discourse on Language.* Translated by A. M. Sheridan Smith. New York: Pantheon Books, 1972.

Greider, Kathleen J. "Religious Location and Counseling: Engaging Diversity and Difference in Views of Religion." In *Understanding Pastoral Counseling,* edited by Elizabeth A. Maynard and Jill L. Snodgrass, 235–56. New York: Springer, 2015.

Griffin, Horace L. *Their Own Receive Them Not: African American Lesbians and Gays in Black Churches.* Cleveland: Pilgrim, 2006.

Griffith, James. *Religion That Heals, Teligion That Harms: A Guide for Clinical Practice.* New York: Guilford, 2010.

Human Rights Campaign. *Stances of Faiths on LGBTQ Issues: Roman Catholic Church.* Accessed July 20, 2023. https://www.hrc.org/resources/stances-of-faiths-on-lgbt-issues-roman-catholic-church.

———. *Stances of Faiths on LGBTQ issues: Southern Baptist Convention.* Accessed July 20, 2023. https://www.hrc.org/resources/stances-of-faiths-on-lgbt-issues-southern-baptist-convention.

————. *Stances of Faiths on LGBTQ issues: The United Methodist Church.* Accessed July 20, 2023. https://www.hrc.org/resources/stances-of-faiths -on-lgbt-issues-united-methodist-church.

Hunter, Ski. *Effects of Conservative Religion on Lesbian and Gay Clients and Practitioners: Practice Implications.* Washington, DC: National Association of Social Workers, 2010.

Jacobsen, Jeanna, and Rachel Wright. "Mental Health Implications in Mormon Women's Experiences with Same-Sex Attraction: A Qualitative Study." *The Counseling Psychologist,* 42, no. 5 (2014): 664–96. https://doi.org/10.1177/0011000014533204.

Janoff-Bulman, Ronnie. "Assumptive Worlds and the Stress of Traumatic Events: Applications of the Schema Construct." *Social Cognition* 7, no. 2 (1989): 113–36. https://doi.org/10.1521/soco.1989.7.2.113.

————. *Shattered Assumptions: Towards a New Psychology of Trauma.* New York: Free Press, 1992.

Johnson, David, and Jeff VanVonderen. *The Subtle Power of Spiritual Abuse.* Minneapolis: Bethany House, 1991.

Johnson, William Stacy. *A Time to Embrace: Same-Sex Relationships in Religion, Law, and Politics.* 2nd ed. Grand Rapids, MI: Eerdmans, 2012.

Kappler, Stephan, Kristin A. Hancock, and Thomas G. Plante. "Roman Catholic Gay Priests: Internalized Homophobia, Sexual Identity, and Psychological Well-Being." *Pastoral Psychology* 62, no. 6 (2013): 805–26. https://doi.org/10.1007/s11089-012-0505-5.

Keller, Kathryn Hope. "Development of a Spiritual Abuse Questionnaire." Ph.D. diss. Texas Woman's University, 2017.

Lebacqz, Karen, and Joseph D. Driskill. *Ethics and Spiritual Care: A Guide for Pastors, Chaplains, and Spiritual Directors.* Nashville: Abingdon, 2000.

Longo, Joseph, N. Eugene Walls, and Hope Wisneski. "Religion and Religiosity: Protective or Harmful Factors for Sexual Minority Youth?" *Mental Health, Religion & Culture* 16, no. 3 (2013): 273–90. https://doi.org/10.1080/13674676.2012.659240.

National Council of Churches. *2012 Yearbook of American and Canadian Churches.* New York: National Council of Churches, 2012.

NetCE. "Understanding and treating spiritual abuse." Accessed July 20, 2023. https://www.netce.com/studypoints.php?courseid=1676&printable =yes& showans=1.

Oakley, Lisa R., and Kathryn Kinmond. *Breaking the Silence on Spiritual Abuse.* New York: Palgrave Macmillan, 2013.

Pew Research Center. "Views About Homosexuality." Accessed July 20, 2023. https://www.pewforum.org/religious-landscape-study/views-about -homosexuality/.

Prins, Annabel, Michelle J. Bovin, Derek J. Smolenski, Brian P. Marx, Rachel Kimerling, Michael A. Jenkins-Guarnieri, Danny G. Kaloupek, Paula P. Schnurr, Anica Pless Kaiser, Yani E. Leyva, and Quyen Q. Tiet. "The Primary Care PTSD Screen for DSM-5 (PC-PTSD-5): Development and Evaluation Within a Veteran Primary Care Sample." *Journal of General Internal Medicine* 31, no. 10 (2016): 1206–11. https://doi .org/10.1007/s11606-016-3703-5.

Ramsay, Nancy J. "Intersectionality: A Model for Addressing the Complexity of Oppression and Privilege." *Pastoral Psychology* 63, no. 4 (2014): 453–69. https://doi.org/10.1007/s11089-013-0570-4.

Rodriguez, Eric M. "At the Intersection of Church and Gay: A Review of the Psychological Research on Gay and Lesbian Christians." *Journal of Homosexuality* 57, no. 1 (2010): 5–38. https://doi.org /10.1080/00918360903445806.

Schlosser, Lewis Z. "Christian Privilege: Breaking a Sacred Taboo." *Journal of Multicultural Counseling and Development* 31, no. 1 (2003): 44–51. https://doi.org/10.1002/j.2161-1912.2003.tb00530.x.

Scoboria, Alan, Julian Ford, Hsiu-ju Lin, and Linda Frisman. "Exploratory and Confirmatory Factor Analyses of the Structured Interview for Disorders of Extreme Stress." *Assessment* 15, no. 4 (2008): 404–25. https://doi.org/10.1177/1073191108319005.

Sherin, Jonathan E., and Charles B. Nemeroff. "Post-Traumatic Stress Disorder: The Neurobiological Impact of Psychological Trauma." *Dialogues in Clinical Neuroscience* 13, no. 3 (2011): 263–78. https://doi .org/10.31887/DCNS.2011.13.2/jsherin.

Shildo, Ariel, and John C. Gonsiorek. "Psychotherapy With Clients Who Have Been Through Sexual Orientation Change Interventions or Request to Change Their Sexual Orientation." In *Handbook of Sexual Orientation and Gender Diversity in Counseling and Psychotherapy*, edited by Kurt A. DeBord, Ann R. Fischer, Kathleen J. Bieschke, and Ruperto M. Perez, 291–311. Washington, DC: American Psychological Association, 2017.

Super, John T., and Lamerial Jacobson. "Religious Abuse: Implications for Counseling Lesbian, Gay, Bisexual, and Transgender Individuals." *Journal of LGBT Issues in Counseling* 5, no. 3–4 (2011): 180–96. https://doi.org/10.1080/15538605.2011.632739.

Swain, Storm. *Trauma and Transformation at Ground Zero.* Minneapolis: Fortress, 2011.

Tigert, Leanne McCall. *Coming Out Through Fire: Surviving the Trauma of Homophobia.* Eugene, OR: Wipf & Stock, 1999.

van der Kolk, Bessel A., Alexander C. McFarlane, and Lars Weisaeth, eds. *Traumatic Stress: The Effects of Overwhelming Experience on Mind, Body, and Society.* New York: Guilford, 1996.

van Deusen-Hunsinger, Deborah. *Bearing the Unbearable: Trauma, Gospel and Pastoral Care.* Grand Rapids, MI: Eerdmans, 2015.

Ward, David J. "The Lived Experience of Spiritual Abuse." *Mental Health, Religion & Culture* 14, no. 9 (2011): 899–915. https://doi.org/10.1080/13674676.2010.536206.

Wood, Andrew William, and Abigail Holland Conley. "Loss of Religious or Spiritual Identities Among the LGBT Population." *Counseling and Values* 59, no. 1 (2014): 95–111. https://doi.org/10.1002/j.2161-007X.2014.00044.x.

CONTRIBUTORS

Duane R. Bidwell teaches at the Center for Health Professions Education, Uniformed Services University of the Health Sciences, in Bethesda, Maryland. His most recent book is *After the Worst Day Ever: What Sick Kids Know About Sustaining Hope in Chronic Illness* (Beacon, 2024). Duane serves as a volunteer fire lookout for the US Forest Service and Southern California Mountains Foundation.

Carrie Doehring is the Clifford Baldridge Professor of Pastoral Care and Counseling at Iliff School of Theology and also teaches in the Joint PhD Program in the Study of Religion at Denver University. She is ordained in the Presbyterian Church USA and licensed as a psychologist in Colorado. Her book *The Practice of Pastoral Care* is widely used as a textbook for ministers and chaplains.

Victor Gabriel is an Assistant Professor in the Department of Buddhist Chaplaincy at the University of the West. He was chair from 2014–2018 and 2022 to the present. Victor has been the program director for the Master of Divinity in Buddhist Chaplaincy since 2014. His research areas include applied Buddhist "theology"; feminist and queer theory; conceptualizations of the body as seen in Buddhist art; and ritual studies and the inculturation of American Buddhism. He was a psychotherapist and a Buddhist congregational minister.

Kathleen J. Greider completed twenty-four years of service to Claremont School of Theology in 2015 as the Edna and Lowell Craig Professor of Practical Theology, Spiritual Care, and Counseling. She remains on the faculty as Research Professor, working with PhD students completing their programs. Since her first publication on the subject in 2009, her writing has focused on the effects of religious pluralism in spiritual care. Throughout her career, Kathleen's teaching, research, and writing interests have centered on the interplay of social and personal change, justice and interculturality, and depth psychological contributions to psychospiritual, relational, and communal life. Committed to international partnerships, she has taught and consulted in France, Germany, Ghana, Great Britain, Israel, Palestine, South Africa, South Korea, and Poland.

Nazila Isgandarova is an Assistant Professor at Emmanuel College of Victoria University in the University of Toronto, teaching mental health, psychopathology, and psychotherapy courses. She has a PhD from the University of Toronto and a Doctor of Ministry degree in pastoral counseling and marriage and family studies from Wilfred Laurier University. She is a Registered Psychotherapist. Nazila is the recipient of the prestigious Forum for Theological Exploration research award for her study on domestic violence against Muslim women, the Canadian Association for Spiritual Care Senior Research Award, and the Society for Pastoral Counselling Research Award. Nazila is the author of *Muslim Women, Domestic Violence, and Psychotherapy: Theological and Clinical Issues* (Routledge, 2018) and *Islamic Spiritual Care* (Pandora, 2019).

Insook Lee is a retired Professor and the former Director of the Master of Arts in Pastoral Care and Counseling at New York Theological Seminary (NYTS). Insook continues to contribute to academia as an adjunct professor at both NYTS and the Blanton Peale Counseling Center in Manhattan. She is a Marriage and Family Therapist who specializes in working with traumatized couples, offering therapeutic interventions that address the complex dynamics of their relationships.

Dominiek Lootens is Head of The Center For Dialogue at Campus Riedberg in Frankfurt am Main, Germany. He holds a Master's degree in Philosophy and a PhD in Practical Theology. For twenty years he worked as a pastoral educator and supervisor at Caritas Flanders. He is guest-lecturer at Goethe University (Frankfurt am Main), president of SIPCC (Frankfurt am Main), and international advisor of ITMS (Louisville, KY). Through the years he introduced health care chaplains, pastoral supervisors, and theology students to the life and work of Thomas Merton. He is the author of *Open to the Full Dimension: Thomas Merton, Practical Theology, and Pastoral Practice* (Eugene, OR: Wipf & Stock, 2022). He currently lives in Schmitten im Taunus, Germany, together with his wife Nina and their dog Bonnie.

Mazvita Machinga is a psychotherapist and practitioner in charge of the Pastoral Care and Counseling Services in Mutare, Zimbabwe. She is the founding director of a registered mental health service provider and pastoral care center in Mutare, Zimbabwe. She has twenty-three years of experience in care and psychotherapy practices at local hospitals and communities. She offers trauma therapy and is trained in EMDR. Mazvita's goal is to work with others in promoting sound mental health for individuals, families, and communities and to reduce the stigma surrounding mental illness in Zimbabwe. She recently established a substance rehabilitation center. She has authored numerous articles in the areas of pastoral care, trauma care, and transpersonal psychology.

Rochelle Robins serves as Vice President and Dean of the Chaplaincy School at the Academy for Jewish Religion, California. Rochelle is also an ACPE Certified Educator and directs the Academy's Clinical Pastoral Education program. She earned her smicha/ordination at the Hebrew Union College – Jewish Institute of Religion, New York. Rochelle is also a Board Certified Chaplain through the National Association of Jewish Chaplains and currently serves as a board member.

Monica Sanford serves as the Assistant Dean for Multireligious Ministry at Harvard Divinity School, where she supports the needs of students from historically un-/underserved religious and spiritual traditions (including those of no tradition) to pursue a graduate-level education in ministry, theology, or religion. Monica received her PhD in Practical Theology from Claremont School of Theology, and an MDiv in Buddhist Chaplaincy from University of the West. She is the author of *Kalyāṇamitra: A Buddhist Model for Spiritual Care* (Sumeru, 2021) and numerous chapters on Buddhist chaplaincy and practical theology.

Daniel S. Schipani is Professor Emeritus of Pastoral Care & Counseling at Anabaptist Mennonite Biblical Seminary, and Affiliate Professor of Pastoral and Spiritual Care at McCormick Theological Seminary and San Francisco Theological Seminary. He serves as a volunteer pastoral counselor at a church-based counseling ministry and lectures widely in Latin America and the Caribbean. Daniel is the author or editor of thirty books in the areas of practical theology, education, and care and counseling.

Jill L. Snodgrass is Professor of Theology at Loyola University Maryland. Her research focuses on spiritual care and counseling with traditionally marginalized populations. She is the coauthor of *Moral Injury After Abortion: Exploring the Psychospiritual Impact on Catholic Women,* the author of *Women Leaving Prison: Justice-Seeking Spiritual Support for Female Returning Citizens,* the coeditor of *Understanding Pastoral Counseling,* and the author of numerous peer-reviewed articles. Jill is an ordained minister in the United Church of Christ.

Siroj Sorajjakool received a PhD from Claremont School of Theology in the field of personality and theology. For two decades he served as professor of religion, psychology, and counseling for the school of religion, and subsequently professor in the department of counseling and family sciences for the school of behavioral health, at Loma Linda University. He earned his second PhD in policy, management, and educational leadership from Chulalongkorn University, Thailand. After returning to Thailand, he served as president of Asian-Pacific International University. He is currently professor of religion and theology at Asian-Pacific International University. His research interest focuses on exploring the issue of mental health within the Asian context and among ethnic minorities in Northern Thailand.

Jennifer Yates is a school psychologist in the Long Beach Unified School District in Southern California. She is a graduate of the Ph.D. program in practical theology/spiritual care and counseling at Claremont School of Theology. Her areas of research include exploring the nature of spiritual abuse and its relationship to trauma, spiritual resilience, and post-traumatic growth.

Pamela Ayo Yetunde is a pastoral counselor. She is the author of *Casting Indra's Net: Fostering Spiritual Kingship and Community,* the coeditor of *Black and Buddhist: What Buddhism Can Teach Us About Race, Resilience, Transformation, and Freedom,* and the author of Buddhist womanist books *Buddhist-Christian Dialogue, U.S. Law, and Womanist Theology for Transgender Spiritual Care* and *Object Relations, Buddhism, and Relationality in Womanist Practical Theology.* Ayo is also the author of numerous articles in *Religions, Feminist Theology, Journal of Buddhist-Christian Studies, Buddhadharma,* and *Lion's Roar.*

AUTHOR INDEX

SUBJECT INDEX